"A well-known writer of New Testament commentaries tackles a well-known New Testament book. The result is an instructive reading of this often-discussed text. Read Osborne's commentary on Revelation and learn."

—**Darrell L. Bock**, Senior Research Professor of New Testament Studies, Dallas Theological Seminary

"Somehow and seemingly at every turn in this most unusual of New Testament books, Grant Osborne has studiously avoided the cliché as well as the trendy. Instead, he has kept a steady eye on the big ideas of Revelation: the Christ of this book is the Lion, the Lamb and the Lord; the victory over evil most assuredly comes from a cosmic battle waged by the Father of the Lord Jesus against evil and all its dominions; and our means to that victory is a Spirit-generated faithful obedience through suffering."

—**Scot McKnight**, Julius R. Mantey Professor in New Testament, Northern Seminary

"Many people avoid the book of Revelation because it seems strange and its interpretation is controversial. Grant Osborne brings his many years of intense and intelligent study of Revelation to bear in this compelling reading of this book's powerful vision of Christ's second coming. I recommend it to all readers and especially pastors."

—**Tremper Longman III**, Robert H. Gundry Professor of Biblical Studies, Westmont College

"Grant Osborne has spent his entire professional career teaching and writing about good principles for the interpretation of Scripture and then modeling them in his own scholarship, not least in commentaries on numerous New Testament books. The Osborne New Testament Commentaries, therefore, are a welcome new series by a veteran New Testament scholar determined to spend as much time as God gives him in his retirement years distilling the conclusions of the finest of scholarship without bogging down the reader in the detailed interaction with all the various perspectives that have been suggested. If all the volumes are as good as this inaugural work on Revelation, the series will become a most welcome resource for the busy pastor or teacher."

—**Craig L. Blomberg**, Distinguished Professor of New Testament, Denver Seminary

"Grant Osborne has produced a marvelously written volume on the book of Revelation that will be immensely helpful for pastors and church leaders, including both students and teachers of Scripture. Carefully designed and thoughtfully structured, this commentary will enable readers to understand both the historical and textual meaning of this challenging book, as well as to grasp its theological and contemporary significance. It is genuine joy to recommend this fine volume. I pray it will receive the wide readership it deserves."

—**David S. Dockery**, President, Trinity International University

"The book of Revelation provides plenty of passages for challenging exegesis and interpretation. In this verse by verse commentary, Grant Osborne does not back away from the often controversial issues, but distills reams of previous material into useful insights and potential, effective teaching points. I am sure that pastors and other lay teachers will benefit greatly from this commentary on Revelation."

—**Stanley E. Porter**, President, Dean, and Professor of New Testament, Roy A. Hope Chair in Christian Worldview, McMaster Divinity College, Hamilton, Ontario, Canada

"Revelation is well known for its historical quagmires and hermeneutical imponderables, and is sometimes characterized by idiosyncratic and even perhaps eccentric interpretations. Grant Osborne's thoughtful approach, being fiercely biblical in nature, attempts to strip away what may be modern and superficial in thinking and seeks to unveil the book's central message by placing it into its ancient historical setting."

—**Barry J. Beitzel**, Professor of Old Testament and Semitic Languages, Trinity Evangelical Divinity School

"One of our premiere evangelical scholars on the New Testament, Grant Osborne has applied years of his life to the text of the New Testament's most challenging book. Yet his commentary on Revelation is no ivory-tower tome. The rich, deep-rooted research on display here weaves its way through a down-to-earth prose that is at once wonderfully accessible and devotional, sure to stretch the minds and warm the hearts of Christian leaders and laypeople alike."

—**George H. Guthrie**, Benjamin W. Perry Professor of Bible, Union University

"Revelation is the most confusing and the least taught, read, or studied book in the Bible. It also has the most radically different interpretations by pastors and scholars. FINALLY, Dr. Osborne has provided a most effective, easy to comprehend, and qualitative orthodox interpretation of the book of Revelation. Dr. Osborne is conservatively trained and prophetically insightful and sensitive—a rare and valuable combination. How do you eat an elephant? One bite at a time. How can you effectively understand the book of Revelation? One verse at a time. Dr. Osborne's verse-by-verse interpretation is a must-read and must-study for pastors, scholars, and the laity, each of whom will solve the confusion by reading this commentary."

—**Raleigh B. Washington**, President and CEO, Promise Keepers

REVELATION

Verse by Verse

OSBORNE
NEW TESTAMENT
COMMENTARIES
O

REVELATION

Verse by Verse

GRANT R. OSBORNE

Revelation: Verse by Verse
Osborne New Testament Commentaries

Lexham Press, 1313 Commercial St., Bellingham, WA 98225
LexhamPress.com

Unless otherwise noted, Scripture quotations from the book of Revelation are the author's own translation.

Print ISBN 9781577997344
Digital ISBN 9781577997351

Lexham Editorial Team: Elliot Ritzema, Lynnea Smoyer
Cover Design: Christine Gerhart
Back Cover Design: Brittany Schrock
Typesetting: ProjectLuz.com

CONTENTS

Series Preface		xi
Introduction to Revelation		1
1:1–11	The Work of the Triune Godhead	19
1:12–20	The Glory and Power of Christ	35
2:1–7, 12–29	Letters to the Seven Churches, Part 1	44
2:8–11; 3:7–13	Letters to the Seven Churches, Part 2	69
3:1–6, 14–22	Letters to the Seven Churches, Part 3	82
4:1–11	The Throne Room Vision, Part 1	97
5:1–14	The Throne Room Vision, Part 2	108
6:1–17	The First Six Seals	120
7:1–17	The Saints on Earth and in Heaven	136
8:1–12	The Seventh Seal and the First Four Trumpets	148
8:13–9:21	The Fifth and Sixth Trumpet Judgments	157
10:1–11	The Little Scroll and John's Commissioning Service	173
11:1–19	The Altar, Witnesses, and Seventh Trumpet	182
12:1–17	The Dragon and the People of God in Conflict	202
12:18–13:18	The Beasts from the Sea and the Land	219
14:1–20	The Destinies of Saints and Sinners Contrasted	237
15:1–8	Angels with the Final Plagues	253
16:1–21	The Seven Last Bowl Judgments	262
17:1–18	The Great Prostitute on the Scarlet Beast	277

18:1–24	The Fall of Babylon the Great	291
19:1–21	The End of the Evil Empire at the Parousia	306
20:1–15	The Thousand-Year Reign and Final Judgment	321
21:1–27	A New Heaven and a New Earth	337
22:1–5	The Final Eden Returns to the Faithful	356
22:6–21	Epilogue to the Book	362
Glossary		374
Bibliography		375
Subject and Author Index		377
Index of Scripture and Other Ancient Literature		394

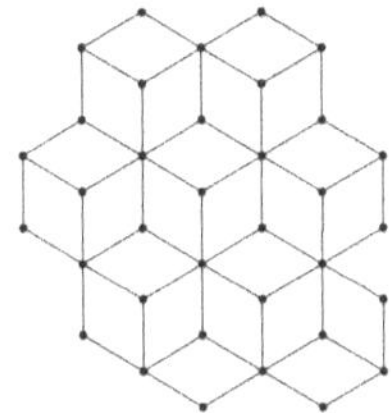

SERIES PREFACE

There are two authors of every biblical book: the human author who penned the words, and the divine Author who revealed and inspired every word. While God did not dictate the words to the biblical writers, he did guide their minds so that they wrote their own words under the influence of the Holy Spirit. If Christians really believed what they said when they called the Bible "the word of God," a lot more would be engaged in serious Bible study. As divine revelation, the Bible deserves, indeed demands, to be studied deeply.

This means that when we study the Bible, we should not be satisfied with a cursory reading in which we insert our own meanings into the text. Instead, we must always ask what God intended to say in every passage. But Bible study should not be a tedious duty we have to perform. It is a sacred privilege and a joy. The deep meaning of any text is a buried treasure; all the riches are waiting under the surface. If we learned there was gold deep under our backyard, nothing would stop us from getting the tools we needed to dig it out. Similarly, in serious Bible study all the treasures and riches of God are waiting to be dug up for our benefit.

This series of commentaries on the New Testament is intended to supply these tools and help the Christian understand more deeply the God-intended meaning of the Bible. Each volume walks the reader verse-by-verse through a book with the goal of opening up for us what God led Matthew or Paul or John to say to their readers. My goal in this series is to make sense of the historical and literary background of these ancient works, to supply the information that will enable the modern reader to understand exactly what the biblical writers were saying to their first-century audience. I want to remove the complexity of most modern commentaries and provide an easy-to-read explanation of the text.

But it is not enough to know what the books of the New Testament meant back then; we need help in determining how each text applies to our lives today. It is one thing to see what Paul was saying his readers in Rome or Philippi, and quite another thing to see the significance of his words for us. So at key points in the commentary, I will attempt to help the reader discover areas in our modern lives that the text is addressing.

I envision three main uses for this series:

1. ***Devotional Scripture reading.*** Many Christians read rapidly through the Bible for devotions in a one-year program. That is extremely helpful to gain a broad overview of the Bible's story. But I strongly encourage another kind of devotional reading—namely, to study deeply a single segment of the biblical text and try to understand it. These commentaries are designed to enable that. The commentary is based on the NIV and explains the meaning of the verses, enabling the modern reader to read a few pages at a time and pray over the message.
2. ***Church Bible studies.*** I have written these commentaries also to serve as guides for group Bible studies. Many Bible studies today consist of people coming together and sharing what they think the text is saying. There are strengths in such an approach, but also weaknesses. The problem is that God inspired these scriptural passages so that the church would understand and obey *what he intended the text to say*. Without some guidance into the meaning of the text, we are prone to commit heresy. At the very least,

the leaders of the Bible study need to have a commentary so they can guide the discussion in the direction God intended. In my own church Bible studies, I have often had the class read a simple exposition of the text so they can all discuss the God-given message, and that is what I hope to provide here.

3. ***Sermon aids.*** These commentaries are also intended to help pastors faithfully exposit the text in a sermon. Busy pastors often have too little time to study complex thousand-page commentaries on biblical passages. As a result, it is easy to spend little time in Bible study and thereby to have a shallow sermon on Sunday. As I write this series, I am drawing on my own experience as a pastor and interim pastor, asking myself what I would want to include in a sermon.

Overall, my goal in these commentaries is simple: I would like them to be interesting and exciting adventures into New Testament texts. My hope is that readers will discover the riches of God that lay behind every passage in his divine word. I hope every reader will fall in love with God's word as I have and begin a similar lifelong fascination with these eternal truths!

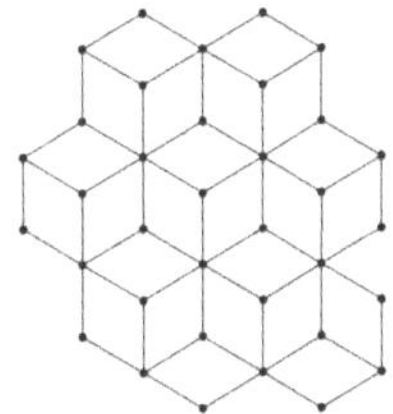

INTRODUCTION TO REVELATION

People are both fascinated and confused by the book of Revelation. The widely divergent ways the book is interpreted in different churches cause many people to be afraid of tackling the work. You can attend one church and hear that every symbol is meant literally, the temple is going to be rebuilt, and Christ will return before the tribulation period. Then you can attend another church three blocks away and hear that every detail is symbolic and that there will be no tribulation period or millennial reign of Christ. You end up so confused that you're afraid to study the book. I want to clear up all the confusion and bring out the exciting message the book has to offer. By the end of this commentary, I hope you will find Revelation both mesmerizing and spiritually stimulating, feeling that it is a must read for every Christian.

Revelation is a fascinating part of the Bible to preach and teach, and it is highly devotional. Its timeless message is that the future of this world is not uncertain, and for the believer there is no doomsday. We can know that Christ will return and put an end to evil. We can know that we will indeed be caught up to heaven, join Christ's army, and celebrate the greatest victory this world will ever know over the powers of evil. Through this book we are guaranteed an eternity with Christ in the new heavens and new earth. Our future and our eternity are secure.

WHAT KIND OF BOOK IS REVELATION?

You may have heard that Revelation is "apocalyptic" literature, which comes from *apokalypsis*, the Greek title for the book. But what does it mean? Apocalyptic designates both a type of literature and a mindset. As a type of literature, it describes a book that presents the revealing of hidden secrets by heavenly beings who communicate through a seer to God's people. Esoteric symbols are at the heart of apocalyptic writings, for they both hide and reveal the truths the work intends to convey. Numerous Jewish writings—such as 4 Ezra, 1 Enoch, the Sibylline Oracles, and the *Testaments of the Twelve Patriarchs*—were written in this genre between 200 BC and AD 100. All of them are built on similar material found in Old Testament books like Isaiah (chs. 24–27), Ezekiel (chs. 1–2, 37–39), Zechariah, and Daniel. The primary intent of such books is to contrast the transcendent nature of God's realm with the temporary, illusory realm of this world. In an apocalyptic work, a reversal takes place: the heavenly mysteries become true reality; and the earthly powers arrayed against the saints become the illusion, because they are soon to be destroyed. Revelation, as a distinctly Christian example of this genre, challenges Christ followers to persevere in light of the promise that God will soon intervene and transform this world for the faithful.

The apocalyptic mindset centers on God's sovereignty. God controls the past, present, and future; he is "the one who is, who was, and who is to come" (Rev 1:4, 8; 4:8; 11:17; 16:5). This is the reason his suffering followers can endure present opposition and suffering: They know that God is sure to vindicate his people. They can overcome the pressure to conform to this world and refuse to live for its pleasures because they know it is fleeting and soon to disappear. It is not the present "Caesar" who matters but rather the "Lord God Almighty" (the primary title for God in Revelation) who is in charge. He alone deserves our allegiance and our worship. The apocalyptic Christian knows that the wicked will be judged and the righteous will be rewarded.

Revelation is also prophetic, and it is probably best to label it "apocalyptic prophecy." Prophecies are primarily oracular (God speaking to the people through the prophet, as in 1:8, 17; 16:15; 22:7, 18–19), while apocalypses are literary (with the visions being presented in a narrative framework). Prophetic works generally have a positive component (if the people repent, judgment will not come), while apocalyptic literature is more pessimistic (judgment is imminent, with little hope for the present). John calls his book "prophecy" (1:3 and 22:7, 10, 18, 19), and he leads a circle of prophets who oppose the false teachers (22:6, 9). At one point, John is commissioned as a prophet and told to "prophesy about/against" the nations.[1]

In addition to being apocalyptic and prophetic in nature, the book takes the form of a letter, with a greeting in 1:4–5 and a benediction in 22:21. The seven letters of chapters 2–3 are addressed to local situations in seven churches respectively, and the material is reflected throughout the visions of the book. There are frequent challenges addressed to the readers, and so this work can also be called a "prophetic letter" sent to these seven churches.

Finally, we should consider the book a narrative with a plot structure—a sequence of actions detailing the story of the battle between good and evil conducted by God on behalf of his people. In this story, they struggle against the animosity of this world and turn to God in worship to gain strength to defeat the world's evil powers, both cosmic and human.

METHODS OF INTERPRETATION

Before we can determine the meaning of the book of Revelation, we must decide what to do with the imagery in it. We may wonder if a relative of Tolkien wrote it—as we feel, at times, as though we're traversing Middle Earth and fighting orcs. Should the imagery be taken as literal or symbolic? Those who take it as

1. See the commentary on 10:11.

completely literal miss the very nature of the apocalyptic genre, yet to take it as entirely symbolic misses the mark as well. In Jewish apocalyptic literature the two aspects are blended and interdependent, and each symbol must guide us as it functions in its context. For example, no one doubts that the seven heads and ten horns of the beast is symbolic, and it is in fact interpreted as such in Revelation 17:9–14. The seal, trumpet, and bowl judgments are not so easily interpreted: The Egyptian plagues on which they are based were literal judgments, so we cannot rule out a literal interpretation. The volcanic eruptions, leveling of mountains, and earthquakes could be literal or symbolic. Likely both dimensions are at work (the turning of the oceans to blood is literal in Exod 7:14–21), and we will have to wait and see.

Although the exact interpretation of some symbols may be unclear, it is important to remember that they all have their background in the common symbols inherited from the Jewish apocalyptic works written from 200 BC to AD 100. Much of the symbolism stems from the historical situation of the church connected to both the Jewish and Roman worlds of the first century. What we will be seeking is "the language of equivalents"—that is, we want to consider the social and religious worlds behind the various images by noting each symbol's use in both its literary and historical contexts. Many of us have grown up with the "newspaper approach," a particular kind of futurist interpretation (see below) that claims all the symbols of Revelation primarily prophesy current events. However, this is somewhat dangerous. That is not the intention of the book, and we will thereby keep misinterpreting things. We must understand Revelation as John wrote it, and he understood all the symbols through his first-century Jewish perspective.

Background knowledge of the first century will unlock the symbols of Revelation, and we will sift through the possible understandings to determine the most likely background. For instance, the 12 jewels that form the foundation of the new Jerusalem in 21:18–21 could be the 12 signs of the zodiac or the jewels on the ephod of the high priest; in light of the priestly imagery in the book and the likelihood that the new Jerusalem symbolizes the holy of holies, the priestly understanding is best.[2]

We must also be aware of the overall schemes of interpretation that have been adopted throughout church history. This is critical, for the meaning of the book changes with each interpretation. There are four main options:

1. The *historicist* approach understands the sections of the book as prophesying the successive periods of world history. For example, many think the seven letters prophesy seven periods of the church age.
2. The *preterist* view believes the book describes the "present" age in which John lived, either the first-century situation of Roman oppression and Christian marginalization or the fall of Jerusalem as divine judgment for Israel's apostasy and rejection of their Messiah, Jesus.
3. The *idealist* school argues that the symbols of the book do not describe historical events but timeless spiritual truths, thereby presenting a general description of the church age between Jesus' first and second comings rather than a specific prediction of future events at the end of days.
4. The *futurist* understanding sees the visions as detailing the events that will take place at the end of history when Christ returns and God ushers in the end of the present age.

These views at first seem incompatible, but many scholars in recent years have taken an eclectic approach that combines the latter three. Few today take the historicist approach because the details of the book have to be forced to fit the shifting sands of world history. However, the other three can be combined by saying that the book addressed the church of John's

2. See the discussion at that point in the commentary.

day (the preterist) and the church in every period of church history (the idealist) by linking them to the church at the end of history (the futurist). For example, the beast of Revelation 13 may refer to false teachers, as well as to the nations and rulers who have opposed God's people throughout history, and also to the final antichrist at the end of history. This interpretation is supported by 1 John 2:18, "As you have heard that the antichrist is coming, even now many antichrists have come." This will be the approach of this commentary, noting all three dimensions in the book.

AUTHOR

Revelation was written by someone who called himself "John" (1:1; 22:8), but even in the early church there was not full agreement on who this John was. Some (such as Dionysius of Alexandria) understood the book to be written by a man named John who was otherwise unknown. Others (such as the fourth-century church historian Eusebius) believed the author was the "elder John" mentioned by Papias in the second century. However, the vast majority of church fathers (e.g., Justin Martyr, Irenaeus, Tertullian, Clement of Alexandria, and Origen) believed the book was written by the apostle John.

In recent times, the predominant view among critical commentators has been that Revelation is pseudonymous (a work "falsely ascribed" to John). This would follow the common practice in Jewish apocalyptic writings; books like 1 Enoch, 4 Ezra, and 2 Baruch were written using the pseudonym of an ancient "hero" of the past. Other issues have also contributed to ascribing the book to someone other than John the apostle. First, the language of the book is different from John's other writings, with Greek that is often clumsy—mixing up pronouns, gender, or cases, and supplying broken sentences. However, this could also be seen as a deliberate ploy: The author is using language to draw the reader into the powerful emotions caused by the ecstatic visions and the imagery they contain. The Greek would then be not so much clumsy as emotionally charged, used for theological emphasis.

Second, there seem to be theological differences between John's Gospel and Revelation. John, the argument goes, is a Gospel of love and seeks the conversion of the world, while Revelation is a book of judgment and condemnation, seeking the destruction of the world. This, however, is a misnomer, for John's Gospel has a great deal of judgment (e.g., John 5:22, 30; 9:39), and Revelation also promotes repentance and conversion (e.g., Rev 9:20–21; 14:6–7; 16:9, 11). It is also said that terms like "lamb" or "word" are used differently in the two books. Yet this does not demand different authors, but can be accounted for by the fact that the books are different genres. John is a Gospel and so centers on one side of the terms "lamb" (Jesus as the paschal sacrifice for sin) and "word" (Jesus as the living revealer of the Father), while Revelation is an apocalypse and so centers on Jesus as the conquering "lamb/ram" in its messianic sense and on the "word" as the voice of God/Christ proclaiming judgment. These are not distinct concepts but interlocking ideas. They point to a deeper unity between the two works, as both contain the twin themes of salvation and judgment—the two pillars of gospel proclamation.

In short, by far the most likely hypothesis is that the author of Revelation is John the apostle and disciple of Jesus.

DATE

In the 19th century and the beginning of the 20th, it was widely believed that Revelation was written late in the reign of the Roman Emperor Nero and near the beginning of the destruction of Palestine, around AD 66–68. The central theme of persecution and martyrdom would indeed fit the events when Nero blamed the burning of Rome on the Christians and instigated a terrible time of persecution and slaughter in the city. However, from the second through the 18th centuries and from the 20th to today the predominant view has been that the book was penned during the reign of Emperor Domitian (AD 81–96).

This latter view seems more likely for several reasons. First, the persecution under Nero was restricted to the environs of Rome itself, while that in Revelation is global. Second, the historical situation as found in the seven letters better fits the later date, as we will see when we discuss chapters 2–3. Third, it is possible that the *Nero redivivus* myth may well lie behind chapters 12–13. This myth, which developed in the 70s and 80s, was the belief among some in the Roman Empire that Nero was going to return with an army of Parthians and destroy Rome. Finally, as we will see in the next section, the background best fits the situation during the time of Domitian. Therefore, I will opt for a date in the latter years of Domitian (around AD 95) as the likely time God sent the visions to John.

HISTORICAL BACKGROUND

Opposition, rejection, and persecution are central to the book of Revelation, but no official Roman persecution is mentioned, and only two letters (Smyrna and Thyatira) emphasize it. Most of the oppression seems to be future (see, e.g., 12:11; 13:7, 10; 16:6), so some think the mentions of persecution in the book are intended to wake up the church from its growing secularity, challenging it to center on Christ and refuse the attraction of the pagan world. It is likely that there was little or no official persecution under Domitian. Overall, he was an able administrator who was greatly loved because he righted much economic exploitation on the part of the wealthy class. But for this reason, he was hated by the elite and denigrated by Roman historians like Tacitus and Suetonius.

This does not mean that persecution was completely absent, only that it was not instigated officially from Rome. The seven churches were in the province of Asia (the western third of modern-day Turkey), which was well-known for its pro-Roman stance. They were governed partly by the "Asiarchs" who oversaw civic and religious life and demanded that the populace participate in emperor worship (see below). No one in that time and place could conduct the affairs of everyday existence, even commerce, without recognizing the gods. When Christians refused to participate, the effects were considerable. Persecution may not have been official, but it was widespread at the local level. Social ostracism, slanderous rumors, and loss of jobs were the natural result. It is likely that the social situation behind this book included both internal pressure from prosperity and secularization as well as external opposition and persecution.

A key ingredient in God's decision to send the visions to John around AD 95 may have been the growing influence and power of the imperial cult in the province of Asia. This refers to the worship of the emperor as a god. For many years before this, Romans had refused to allow their leader to be regarded as a god. They even disliked dictatorships and hereditary rulerships. In the first 700 years of the Roman republic, the nation was led by consuls, who governed a year at a time and were chosen by popular vote. That all changed when Octavius was victorious over Mark Antony, established the Roman Empire, and named himself Augustus. He declared his uncle, Julius Caesar, a god. Most emperors refused to allow themselves to be called gods until after they died (such as Tiberius and Claudius), but this began to be relaxed in the time of Domitian. Also, cities began to compete to be allowed by Rome to build temples to the emperors and be labeled *neokoros*, or a "temple warden" city (the first was erected in Pergamum in AD 29). Of the cities addressed in Revelation, at least Ephesus, Pergamum, and Smyrna had this so-called honor.

This cult intensified under Domitian, who was especially popular in the provinces. The province of Asia in particular was at the epicenter of pro-Roman feelings and therefore was also among the wealthiest of the provinces. Domitian was called "lord and god"; a bath and gymnasium in Ephesus were erected and dedicated to him as "Zeus Olympios." Coins of that period even label Domitian's wife as "mother of the divine Caesar." In addition, frequent banquets held by the guilds (trade associations that controlled the activities of artisans in a city) were always dedicated to the patron gods—to refuse to attend often meant one would be prohibited from working in the city. This led to tremendous pressure on Christians to participate in emperor worship. Every aspect of civic and even private life was affected by the imperial cult, so believers were under severe oppression.

We can see that the book of Revelation is responding to pressures inside and outside the church. As seen especially in the letters to Sardis and Laodicea, the church to some extent participated in the wealth of the province of Asia. These churches were struggling with the very real issue of the impossibility of serving both God and money (Luke 16:13). False teachers like the Nicolaitans (Rev 2:2, 6, 14, 20) convinced many that assimilation to the practices of the pagan world was acceptable, and as a result the church was being acculturated and spiritually endangered. But the battle between good and evil—between serving God and surrendering to the world—calls Christians to reject compromise and avoid complacency.

First-century Christians also experienced external economic and social pressure to participate in Roman life, and those in the church who refused to do so faced the antipathy of the rest of the populace. They were ostracized and persecuted, with punishments including imprisonment and death (2:9, 10; 13:10). In response to these pressures, the book of Revelation presents a vision of reality in which God reigns and rewards the faithful who persevere in the midst of crisis. This is a counter-reality, a transcendent realm in which God's people are faithful to him and live in a Christian counterculture. Moreover, God's children, the saints, are willing to endure suffering, for they realize that that this new realm is actually the real world and the pagan world is simply an illusion doomed for destruction. It is not just an ephemeral hope, but a new citizenship that means believers are "aliens and strangers" in this world (1 Pet 1:1, 17; 2:11; compare Phil 3:20). This calls for endurance and faithfulness to God, leading the faithful to become victors over these pressures.

USE OF THE OLD TESTAMENT

The book of Revelation uses the entire Old Testament as its playground. It has nearly as many allusions to the Old Testament as the rest of the New Testament put together. In order of frequency, John uses material from Isaiah, Daniel, Ezekiel, the Psalms, and finally Genesis, Deuteronomy, Jeremiah, Joel, and Zechariah. Amazingly, there are only two word-for-word quotations (Rev 1:7; 2:28–29) but anywhere from 400 to 700 references, depending on whether one counts them as allusions or echoes. Allusions consist of near equivalence, and echoes are characterized by approximate parallels. Echoes are therefore often questionable, so it is hard to know for certain how many there are. The point is that John fails to quote verses but instead embeds the Old Testament material into his ongoing prose, stringing allusions together apart from their original context and using them in a contemporaneous fashion to add richness to his communication. This makes the interpretive task very difficult.

The major debate over John's use of the Old Testament is the extent of his freedom in using the material. Many believe he ignores the original context and adapts Old Testament concepts to his current purposes, changing their meaning to make his point. But it is more likely that John knows the original context but transforms and extends its meaning as he applies it to the point of his text. Note, as an example, John's use of Zechariah 12:10 in Revelation 1:7. In the original context, Zechariah speaks of the house of David as it mourns for its sins and comes to repentance. John changes the focus from David's house to "all peoples on earth" and may center not on repentance but on mourning for the judgments in the book that will fall on them. I believe there is a double meaning here and that John uses this passage to trace the two paths the nations will take in responding to God's judgments: some will repent and others rejecting God's offer of salvation and experiencing divine condemnation.[3]

In other words, John is fully aware of the original context but adapts it to cover the new apocalyptic situation of the visions. John's unique style of embedding allusions in the narrative does not mean he is being unfaithful to the original context. Rather, he is simply applying the Old Testament stories to new biblical events. Jesus and Paul also point to this kind of promise-fulfillment relationship between the Old Testament event and New Testament reality. Certainly John adapts the Old Testament to the contemporary message of his visions, but that does not mean he lacks consideration for the original meaning. Rather, John expects his readers (probably with help from the leaders of the churches) to understand the movement from Old Testament context to New Testament application. Both dimensions are part of the message.

STRUCTURE OF THE BOOK

There are likely as many suggested outlines for this book as there are commentaries. This is not new; most biblical books face this conundrum. It does not mean the determination of structure is an impossible task, for Revelation is a united whole with a definite plot movement. We simply must be humble about what we come up with. Everyone can agree about the basic movement:

- *prologue and original vision (1:1–20)*
- *the seven letters (2:1–3:21)*
- *the throne room vision (4:1–5:14)*
- *the seal judgments (6:1–8:1)*
- *the trumpet judgments (8:2–11:19)*

---

3. For repentance, see Rev 5:9–10; 11:13; 14:6–7. For condemnation, see 6:15–17; 11:18; 14:8–11.

- *the conflict with the false trinity* (12:1–14:20)
- *the bowl judgments* (15:1–16:21)
- *the destruction of the evil empire* (17:1–19:5)
- *the* ***eschaton*** (19:6–20:15)
- *the new heavens and new earth* (21:1–22:5)
- *the epilogue* (22:6–21)

The problem is how to organize this material, and there are several complications. First, do we see the book organized chronologically (seeing the seals, trumpets, and bowls as 21 successive events) or topically (seeing them as cyclical, describing a progressively intense sequence of judgments)? I will argue for the latter. Second, do we place chapters 4 and 5 with the introduction or with the seals (since chapter 5 centers on the Lamb opening the seals)? I believe they function both ways. Third, there are three interludes (7:1–17; 10:1–11:14, 12:1–14:21) that interrupt the groups of seven judgments and need to be accounted for. I argue that they tell what part the saints play in the narrative and describe the conflict between good and evil. Fourth, how do chapters 17–18 relate to the bowl judgments of chapter 16 and the events of the **eschaton** (the end) that follow? They further describe the destruction of the evil empire that is typified in the bowl judgments and form the prelude to the events of chapters 19–20. The outline that will be followed in this commentary is as follows:

A. Introduction (1:1–5:14)
1. Prologue: The Triune Godhead behind the Book (1:1–11)
2. First Vision (1:12–20)
3. The Seven Churches: Comfort and Warning (2:1–3:22)
4. The Throne Room Vision (4:1–5:14)

B. Central Section: Seals, Trumpets, Bowls (6:1–16:21)
1. First Six Seals (6:1–17)
2. First Interlude: Sealing of the Saints and Multitude in Heaven (7:1–17)
3. Seventh Seal and Introduction to Trumpets (8:1–5)
4. First Six Trumpets (8:6–9:21)

5. Second Interlude: The Angel and Little Scroll, Measuring the Temple, the Two Witnesses (10:1–11:13)
6. Seventh Trumpet (11:14–19)
7. Third Interlude: The Woman, Dragon, and Child, War in Heaven and on Earth, the Two Beasts, the Three Angels (12:1–14:20)
8. Seven Bowls (15:1–16:21)

C. Conclusion (17:1–22:21)
1. Destruction of the Great Prostitute (17:1–18)
2. Destruction of Babylon the Great (18:1–24)
3. Hallelujah Choruses and Return of Christ (19:1–21)
4. Millennial Reign (20:1–10)
5. Great White Throne Judgment (20:11–15)
6. New Heaven and New Earth (21:1–22:5)
7. Epilogue: Warning and Promise (22:6–21)

THEOLOGY OF THE BOOK

The Sovereignty of God

The central theme of Revelation is the absolute sovereignty of God. It seems as if evil is triumphing, as if Satan is in control and the world just keeps getting worse and worse. The visions prove the falsehood of this premise. God is creator, and he sustains this world. As such, he is also Judge, Lord over history, and he is in process of bringing it to a close. He is the omnipotent divine warrior who will triumph over all evil. The throne of God appears 46 times and symbolizes his dominion over this world. The creation theme is also a dominant motif. God's creation has been polluted by sin, so God is about to destroy it and create "a new heaven and a new earth" (21:1).

The Futility of Satan

The flipside of divine sovereignty is the futility and frustrated rage experienced by the Great Usurper(s), Satan and the fallen angels. The book does not portray the dragon as a powerful being. Rather, he is seen as an adversary (the meaning of "satan/devil") who operates solely by deceit (12:9; 20:2, 8, 10). Armageddon is not the final battle that settles the outcome but the last act of defiance by an already defeated foe. Every act of Satan/the red dragon (12:3) is a parody or imitation of what God has already done. Satan may be filled with insane rage, but he is not stupid. He knows that to do anything right he can only imitate the perfect work of God. His futility and frustrated anger are featured throughout the book.

The Doctrine of Christ

In many ways, Christ is the focus of the book. His major title is "lamb," which occurs 29 times and depicts Jesus as the paschal lamb. The great end-time victory over the powers of evil is not Armageddon but the cross. The "wrath of the Lamb" causes the nations to cower in fear because "the great day of their wrath has come" (6:16–17 NIV). God and Christ are also depicted as one essence (compare John 10:30), and Jesus is Yahweh. As is the case with the Gospel of John, the book of Revelation emphasizes the deity of Christ and the unity of the Godhead.

The Holy Spirit

The normal titles for the Spirit of God are missing from the book, and the primary title is "the sevenfold Spirit."[4] The Spirit is presented as a member of the Trinity (see list at 1:4–5) who stands with the Father and Son "before the throne" and is the Spirit of Christ (the "seven eyes") sent into all the world (5:6). Overall, the Spirit is the source of inspiration and prophecy in the book. In short, the Holy Spirit is sent by Father and Son to inspire the witness of the people of God and to reveal the prophetic oracles that form the core of the visions in the book.

---

4. This is literally "seven spirits," and occurs at 1:4; 3:1; 4:5; and 5:6. See discussion at 1:4. This refers to "the perfect Holy Spirit" (from Isa 11:2 in the Septuagint; Zech 4:2, 10).

Cosmic War

Christ replicates the work of God in the Old Testament as the Divine Warrior who defeats the bastions of evil in the cosmic realms as well as in this world. Military imagery abounds throughout the book. The God who makes war in the Old Testament (Exod 15:3; Isa 42:13–16) will soon execute the final war against the world of evil. Christ defeated Satan utterly in his death on the cross, and his followers duplicate that victory in their own suffering and death as witness to Christ.

The Doctrine of Sin

This book is supreme among the biblical books in its detailed portrayal of the total depravity of humanity. The basic definition of the doctrine ("whenever sinful humanity has a choice, it always chooses to reject God and Christ") is seen throughout. The seal, trumpet and bowl judgments have several purposes, and one of them is to prove the depravity of humankind.[5] They replicate the plagues of Egypt, but one added aspect is God's intention to use the judgments as an evangelistic force and through them give the earth-dwellers a final opportunity to repent (9:20–21; 16:9, 11, 21). With every chance to repent, sinful humanity proved anew its basic depraved nature by refusing to repent and preferring the very gods who were torturing and killing them.

Mission and Evangelism

Revelation emphasizes God's deep desire to rescue the lost. Those among the nations who respond to God's call will repent (11:13) and discover Christ's blood has "purchased them for God" (5:9). From the nations a great multitude will stand before the throne in triumph (7:9), worship God (15:4), and bring their glory into the new Jerusalem (21:24, 26). I will argue that in 9:20–21; 16:9, 11 there is a true offer of repentance that is

---

5. See the introduction to 6:1–17.

rejected by sinful humanity. In this sense, the judgments of the trumpets and bowls have an evangelistic purpose to provide a final call to repentance. This is evidenced in 14:6–7 where the angel proclaims the "eternal gospel" to the world and calls them to "fear God and give him glory," the language of repentance in the book (see also 15:4; 16:9). In 11:13, in fact many do repent. The witness of the persecuted saints throughout (1:9; 6:9; 12:17) is part of this call to repentance, and it is clear that Revelation reveals not only God's wrath but also his compassion and mission to a lost world.

THE PERSEVERANCE OF THE SAINTS

All ancient apocalyptic literature exhorted God's people to remain faithful and triumph over temptation to sin. Throughout the New Testament, **eschatology**—the study of the end times—always leads to ethics; future promise demands present faithfulness. Christ as "faithful witness" (1:5; 3:14) provides the model, and his followers participate in him via faithful living and obedience. The Greek *martyria* ("witness") did not connote martyrdom until the second or third century, but in Revelation is clear that "witness" entails martyrdom, and this book was a major factor in that shift of meaning. In Mark 8:34, true followers are extolled to "take up their cross," namely to be willing to die for him, so death is the ultimate act of perseverance and faithfulness to the Lord. Throughout the book, a series of exhortations call the saints to a life of persevering faithfulness.

WORSHIP

Worship takes place in virtually every chapter and becomes the unifying center of the action. It is the natural response to God's absolute sovereignty and Christ's atoning sacrifice. The worship scenes elevate readers into the very presence of God and lift them above events to the Almighty Lord. In fact, there is an antithetical element, for readers are asked to choose between worship of the Triune Godhead and the false trinity. The throne room scene in chapter 4 celebrating the majesty of

God is in direct contrast with the imperial cult and its worship of Caesar as a god. It has often been said that there is a political dimension to many of the hymns—they formed a counter to the imperial cult and to Roman hegemony. We should extend that to worship of God vs. worship of the things of the world.

The well-known challenge says it well—who is on the throne of your life? There is serious idolatry in the Western world today; there is a god-shelf in our homes, and it can contain anything we choose to put above God in our lives—even good things like our checkbook, our possessions, our family, our comfort, or our security. God and the Lamb are alone worthy of worship (4:11; 5:9). In fact, the best way to persevere and be a victor is to live a life of worship.

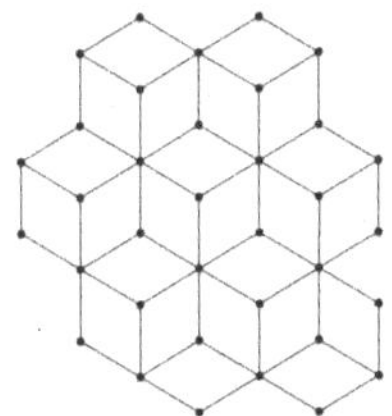

PROLOGUE

THE WORK OF THE TRIUNE GODHEAD

(1:1–11)

John begins his visionary tract with an introduction showing he considers this to be a prophetic letter addressing the situation of the churches in the Roman province of Asia (the western third of modern-day Turkey). The letter greeting occurs in 1:4–5, and is preceded by a highly theological foreword. This foreword contains the most dramatic statement in Scripture on the process of revelation (1:1–2) and the first of seven blessings, or beatitudes, in the book (1:3). The core part of the section has to be 1:4b–5, in which the work of each member of the Trinity is placed at the center of the apocalyptic action to come. The passage continues with the motto of the book (1:7–8), which establishes the perspective that the Lord over history is in control and that readers must repent or face divine judgment. Finally, John specifies his situation as the seer communicating the visions to the churches (1:9–11). He encourages them with the news that even though he is in exile on the island of Patmos, his kingdom ministry to the province's churches continues. Like other prologues in the New Testament (e.g., Mark 1:1–15, John 1:1–18), the purpose of this section is to establish the theological foundation for the book. Through this the readers understand the basic themes, and they will then see these theological themes worked out in the rest of the book.

JOHN DISCLOSES THE FOUR-STAGE PROCESS OF REVELATION (1:1–2)

John uses a highly unusual foreword—there is nothing like it in any of the other New Testament letters—to establish at the outset the divine authority behind the book. God is not silent as the churches face the crisis of persecution but speaks powerfully through apocalyptic visions sent to assure the believers that he is still in control. The title itself is important, as the opening should be rendered "the revelation *from* Jesus Christ." Jesus wants to strengthen their resolve by revealing to them God's "hidden secrets" or mysteries (the meaning of *apokalypsis*) about the end of history and his sovereign control over this world (see also Matt 10:26; Luke 17:30; 1 Cor 1:7, 14:6; Gal 1:12; Eph 3:3, 5). Through the visions sent to John for the church, the formerly hidden truths about the end of this age and the destruction of evil powers are now being uncovered.

This is the only place in all of Scripture where the actual process of revelation is explained. It is a four-stage movement: God gave it to Jesus, who had the angels mediate it to John, who then wrote it down for the churches.[1] This nearly parallels the Gospel of John, where the process is God—Jesus—Holy Spirit—disciples—world (John 7:16–18; 8:26, 28, 38; 14:10). This also begins the theme of oneness in the book, as God and Jesus together show these visions "to their slaves," meaning they unveil the reality and meaning of the divine actions in present and future (as in John 5:20; 10:32). The saints are "slaves," a special term used often in the New Testament for Christians as the "special possession" of God (1 Pet 2:9; see Rom 1:1; Phil 1:1; Titus 1:1; Jas 1:1). The content of the revelation is the imminent events of the end of history ("what must soon take place"). This stems from

1. For the place of the Spirit in this, see the commentary on 1:10.

Daniel 2:28–29, where Daniel interprets Nebuchadnezzar's dream about "things to come." It is found at other key points in this book regarding God's absolute control over future events (Rev 1:19; 4:1; 22:6).

The adverb in the phrase "what must soon take place" can refer to imminence ("soon") or the swiftness with which God will act ("suddenly, without delay"). While "I come quickly" in 2:16; 3:11; 11:14 refers to God's swift actions, the phrase here more likely refers to time. Yet this is also problematic, for it has been nearly 2000 years since these prophecies and little has happened. It is important that "soon" in the New Testament seldom means there is nothing yet to occur. It is **eschatological** (= end times) language intended to draw the reader into a sense of expectation and responsibility in order to recognize God's hand in the events of history. It means that God has initiated the events of the last days, and we must ready ourselves for the end. Remember the twofold clarification in 2 Peter 3:8–9: "With the Lord a day is like a thousand years, and a thousand years are like a day. ... He is patient with you, not wanting anyone to perish, but everyone to come to repentance." We all must be grateful to the Lord for his patience—if we have been Christians for 20 years, we thank God that Christ did not return 21 years ago! Revelation 6:11 recognizes that a period of time will ensue before the **Parousia** (the second coming), so "soon" does not mean "in the next moment." Rather, it means the climactic events have already started, and in God's own time the end will be soon.

The phrase "made it known" contains the idea of revealing via signs or symbols. It likely refers to the symbols used in the visions to depict the imminent events that will lead to the end. So Christ will show John and the churches the symbols that will signify God's actions in present and future and bring world history to its God-intended conclusion. John will receive these visions and witness or testify to the churches regarding their meaning.

John tells his readers that these visions constitute "the word of God" and "the testimony of Jesus." There are two implicit sentences here emphasizing the heavenly origin of the visions—God has spoken his word, and Jesus has testified through these divinely inspired pictures to the churches. Throughout the book, these two phrases frequently emphasize the actual source of everything written down in it (Rev 1:9; 6:9; 17:17; 19:9–10; 20:4). The emphasis is on the trustworthy nature of these God-sent communications. These are not subjective dreams or imaginative stories but visions stemming from God in heaven (see also Rev 1:11, 19; 19:9; 21:5; 22:6–9). They are absolutely true, and the church must carefully study the book's message.

JOHN BLESSES THE READER AND THE HEEDER (1:3)

The seven beatitudes, or blessings, in the book are linked to the ethical purpose of the visions, with some challenging to persevere and live exemplary lives (Rev 1:3; 16:15; 22:7) and others promising future rewards for doing so (Rev 14:13; 19:9; 20:6; 22:14). The meaning of "blessed are" is the same as in the Sermon on the Mount (Matt 5:3–12): "God blesses those who … ." The emphasis is on reading the prophecies in a church setting. The "reader" refers to the official reader in the service. In the second century, this person was a church officer, and in synagogues there were five readers for festivals and seven for the Sabbath. At times a rabbi would read a passage and then preach on it like Jesus did in Luke 4:16–30. The important thing to note is that this book was treated as Scripture from the start. It is sad that in many churches today the reading of Scripture is falling by the wayside. I have even heard it said that we must limit oral reading because Scripture is boring! We are dealing with the only eternal truth we have—the Word of God! We must recover the privilege and excitement of letting God speak in our services by reading his written Word as an act of worship.

The second divine blessing in this verse falls on those who listen and live by the exhortations. This dual injunction to hear and keep occurs often in the New Testament (e.g., John 4:42;

8:38; 12:47; 14:23–24). In this book it is a key formula in the seven letters—"Let the one who has an ear hear what the Spirit says" (2:7, 11, 17, 29; 3:6, 12–13, 21–22)—and occurs frequently elsewhere (3:3; 12:17; 14:12; 16:15; 22:7, 9). We persevere by remaining faithful to God's required lifestyle. These visions are not cute stories or imaginative fictions meant to entertain. This is a prophetic book of comfort (to the saved) and warning (to the unsaved) that calls the saints to accountability. Moreover, it is not enough just to "hear" these truths; until one "keeps" or obeys them, the Christian is disobedient to God and headed for judgment.

The reason for the special seriousness of this injunction is because "the time is near." As in verse 1, the emphasis is on the imminence of the final events of human history. In fact, the book is framed by warnings regarding the imminent **eschaton** (here and in 22:10). The nearness of the Lord's return appears frequently in the New Testament as a call to live responsibly toward God and Christ.[2] Since Christ could appear at any minute, we must live decisively and completely for God.

JOHN GREETS THE CHURCHES AND PRAISES THE TRINITY (1:4–6)

These three verses go far beyond the normal prescript of a letter (with a sender, a recipient, and a greeting). Only 1 Peter 1:1–2 is similar, with its own Trinitarian anchor to the greeting. Here the work of the Trinity in 1:4–5a is followed in 5b–6 with core statements for the book having to do with salvation (1:5b) and the church (1:6).

The normal conventions of ancient letter writing begin this section, with John addressing the recipients, "the seven churches in the province of Asia." It is hard to know why these particular churches were chosen, when many like Hierapolis

2. As in the parables in the Olivet Discourse (Matt 24:42–25:30) or in passages like Rom 13:11–12; Phil 4:5; Heb 10:25; Jas 5:8; 1 Pet 4:7.

or Colossae (a few miles from Laodicea) are omitted. It is possible they were chosen because these cities lay on the major Roman roads through the province, and they were intended to be representative of the rest of the churches. The cities are addressed in the geographical order by which a courier could drop off copies of the book traveling on these Roman roads.[3] Each letter addresses the historical situation and needs of each church in turn. At the same time, they are intended to typify the problems of all churches. The message is plural: "what the Spirit says to the *churches*."

The greeting is common to nearly all New Testament letters, with "grace" the regular Greek greeting and "peace/shalom" the Jewish greeting. This is in effect an **eschatological** promise and offer of God's grace and peace to those who will turn their lives over to Christ. In the world these are a mere unrealized hope, but in Christ these become a reality. This is especially so because John goes on to anchor this promise first in the triune Godhead and then in the salvation that Christ has won by his death for his followers.

Present, Past, and Future (1:4a)

God is given a unique title, "the one who is and was and is to come." This is a paraphrase of the divine name "Yahweh," defined in Exodus 3:14–15 as "I am who I am." It occurs four more times in the book (Rev 1:8; 4:8; 12:17; 16:5), and means that God is sovereign over past, present, and future; he is Lord over history and guides the affairs of mortal humanity according to his will. Here the present aspect is listed first, and this order is significant. The readers know that God controlled the past; the entire Old Testament recalls that truth. They also know he controls the future, for the visions of this book prove that. But they aren't so certain regarding the present. It seems the powers of evil, in particular the Roman Empire, are actually in control.

---

3. See commentary on 1:11.

This title corrects that erroneous conclusion, saying in effect, "The God who controlled the past and is in charge of the future is actually sovereign over the present situation, even though it may not seem like it."

SEVEN SPIRITS (1:4B)

The second anchor for the greeting, "the seven spirits before his throne," is debated (see also 3:1; 4:5; 5:6). Some think the spirits are angels, perhaps the seven archangels mentioned in Jewish apocalyptic literature[4] or the angels to whom the seven letters are written in chapters 2–3. However, the term "spirit" is not used of angels in the book, and the context is more favorable to a Trinitarian emphasis here. The use of "seven" probably stems from Isaiah 11:2 in the **Septuagint** (which adds a seventh virtue, "godliness," to the six in the Hebrew Bible) and Zechariah 4:2, 10 (which has seven lamps as the "eyes of the LORD that range throughout the earth"). In Zechariah 4:6 the "LORD Almighty" says these things take place "not by might nor by power, but by my Spirit." In Revelation 5:6 this "sevenfold Spirit" has "seven eyes, which are the seven Spirits of God sent out into all the earth," a further allusion to Zechariah 4:6. Inlight of this background, it is best to translate, "the sevenfold (or perfect) Holy Spirit." The perfect Spirit is both "of God" (3:11; 4:5) and of the Lamb (5:6); thereby he stands "before the throne," the place of divine sovereign rule over this world. In 4:2 God sits on the throne, and in 5:6 the Lamb is "standing at the center of the throne." Thus the Spirit of God and of Christ stands with the other members of the Godhead "before the throne."

THE ATTRIBUTES OF JESUS (1:5–6)

The third anchor is Jesus Christ, described here with two threefold attributes, first dealing with who he is (1:5a) and second with what he does (1:5b–6). All six of these are themes that will

4. 1 Enoch 20—Uriel, Raphael, Raguel, Michael, Saraqa'el, Gabriel, and Remiel.

continue in the rest of the book. As "faithful witness," Jesus in his earthly life is the model for his followers of one who perseveres in faithfulness to God in the midst of opposition and persecution. The witness theme in the book is closely tied to martyrdom. Jesus' witness (also 3:14) is reproduced in the faithful lives of the saints as they remain true to God in a world that has turned against them (see 1:9; 6:9; 12:11, 17; 17:6; 19:10; 20:4).

Jesus is also "firstborn from the dead," turning to his post-resurrection glory. There are two emphases here: First, he is sovereign over life and death. In Psalm 89:27 in the **Septuagint** David is described as "firstborn, the most exalted of the kings of the earth," and Jesus as Davidic Messiah is supreme over all earthly rule. In Colossians 1:15 Christ is "firstborn over all creation," meaning supreme or sovereign Lord over God's creation. So Christ controls the powers of death and life on behalf of his followers. This is part of the oneness motif in the book: God is sovereign over his creation, and so is his Son. Second, he is the prototype for those who will be raised with him. As in 1 Corinthians 15:20–23, Christ was raised as the "firstfruits" who guaranteed our own future resurrection from the dead. Throughout, Revelation stresses that all the faithful will share in his resurrection and exaltation (see 2:7, 11; 7:15–17; 20:6; 22:2–3, 14, 17).

The emphasis on Jesus' absolute sovereignty continues in "ruler of the kings of the earth." This is another central theme, preparing for Christ as "King of kings and Lord of lords" in 19:16. The same Christ who is Lord over life and death is naturally sovereign over all earthly rulers. This is contra Caesar, thought to be king of kings in his own earthly empire, with the rulers over provinces as client kings of the emperor. In Revelation, kings of this world are enemies (10:11; 17:18), evil rulers (17:2; 18:3), and gather together under the beast for the final war (16:14; 19:19) when they will be utterly defeated (17:18; 18:9; 19:18). Christ will rule them "with a rod of iron" (Psa 2:9 in Rev 2:27; 12:5).

The three attributes with a salvation-oriented thrust occur in a doxology of praise (1:5b–6) that celebrates Jesus' work on behalf of believers. The central event in Revelation is not the **Parousia**; it is the cross. The final defeat of Satan is not the battle of Armageddon. The great victory over the cosmic powers and the basis of our salvation is Christ's atoning sacrifice on the cross, as seen here and in 5:5–6. Armageddon is simply the consummation of Golgotha.

The first aspect worthy of praise is Christ's love. This emphasizes his ongoing love rooted in his past loving sacrifice on the cross, his present love for his followers, and his future love in defeating the cosmic powers on our behalf. This love of Father and Son permeates the book. The result of that love is now spelled out clearly—the atoning blood that has freed us from our sins. In the book two phrases predominate: the slain Lamb as seen in 5:6, 12; 13:8; and the sacrificial blood as seen in 5:9; 7:14; 12:11. The emphasis is on the atoning effects of his death, which has freed us from sin. Sin, as in Romans 6, is an invading army that seeks to enslave us, but the blood of Christ has liberated us. The sins of the nations are bringing the wrath and judgment of God down upon their heads, but God's people have already experienced their Independence Day!

The second result of Christ's love is his inclusion of us in his royal and priestly offices. This is an incredible gift that fulfills one of the central covenant promises of the Old Testament, "You will be for me a kingdom of priests and a holy nation" (Exod 19:6). The verb "make" here likely has the same force it has in Acts 2:36 and Mark 3:14, namely an official commissioning to office. Here and in Revelation 5:10 the emphasis is upon the twofold work of Christ as royal (Davidic) Messiah and high priest, passed on to the church. The people of God are kingdom not only as being part of the realm in which God rules but also of ruling with Christ in it—in other words, we are both kingdom citizens and royalty within it, a frequent emphasis in the book (see 2:26; 3:21; 5:10; 20:4, 6; 22:5).

The priestly work of the church is another important theme. In Isaiah 61:6 (see also Exod 19:5–6), Israel is called "priests of the LORD," and the church as new Israel has inherited that office.

This would include serving God but also sharing God's mission to the world, an important stress in Revelation.[5] Angels are the priests of heaven, and the saints share that joyous task (see 5:10; 7:15; 20:6). Yet this also includes the spiritual lives of believers as they serve "his God and Father" both in their direct access to God (the privilege) and in their lives of sacrificial service (the responsibility). When we serve with Christ as priests, we serve the same God and Father he does. The powers of evil may control this world, but Christ has already freed us from its power (Mark 3:15, 6:7) and made us part of God's kingdom, in which we are both royalty and priesthood. No Jew could ever be both king and priest. The attempt of Simon, a Maccabean ruler in 140 BC, to make himself high priest as well as king led to the revolt of the Essenes and the formation of the Pharisaic movement. Only the Messiah could be such; Jesus alone had the right to combine the royal and high priestly offices. Christ has given us, his joint heirs (Rom 8:17), the incredible privilege of sharing in this with him.

The natural response of his followers to this wondrous list of Christ's loving gifts to them can only be high praise: "to him be glory and power forever." The attribution of glory and power occurs also in 5:13 and 7:12, and centers on Christ's dominion and authority over his created world. This power guarantees his ultimate victory over the evil forces confronting the church. They are not truly "cosmic powers," because they have no power over Christ. Our victory depends entirely on our submission and reliance on him, but in him that triumph is completely certain. Thus Christ alone has the glory because he alone is truly sovereign and majestic over this world. In this there is a further contrast with earthly rulers like Caesar. All their pomp and circumstance is mere pretense, for Christ reigns over them as King of kings. Moreover, their so-called glory is

5. See "Theology of the Book" in the introduction.

earthly and temporary, while Christ's is eternal. And all God's people say, "Amen!"

JOHN PRESENTS THE MOTTO OF THE BOOK (1:7–8)

The book's basic message is now presented in the style of a hymn, with four lines that combine two of the primary messianic passages of the Old Testament: Daniel 7:13 and Zechariah 12:10. These are also combined in Matthew 24:30 and John 19:37, so this combination likely stems from Jesus himself. The Daniel reference speaks of the "one like a son of man" who will "come with the clouds of heaven" (an image for the second coming in Mark 13:26; 14:62; Acts 1:9–10; 1 Thess 4:17) to establish "an everlasting dominion" in "glory and sovereign power" (Dan 7:14—note "glory and power" above in 1:6). Daniel 7 tells of the four beasts and the rise of the "little horn" who will oppose God and his people. The son of man figure will come with "authority, glory, and sovereign power" and spell doom for the little horn. So this passage shows that Christ's return is the central event of the **eschaton** and prophesies the doom awaiting the beast of chapter 13.

The passage then immediately segues into Zechariah 12:10, which foretells what awaits the nations in the visions of the book. The question is whether this quote centers on repentance or judgment. The context here would seem to favor judgment, as in the Daniel quote and the themes of the visions, yet Zechariah itself speaks of repentance. After God has rescued the nation and destroyed its enemies (Zech 12:1–9), the people will weep and mourn for "the one they have pierced," namely Yahweh himself as the Shepherd of Israel (Zech 14:1–14), and they will be "cleansed ... from sin and impurity" (13:1). Therefore, while some scholars believe that the cosmic victory over the earthly powers in Revelation leads the nations to join Israel in repentance, most conclude that the switch in the quote from "the house of David" (Zechariah) to "all peoples on earth" (here) switches the imagery to the judgment of the nations, and they will mourn in consternation over their own defeat by the messianic Shepherd.

I believe it is best to see a deliberate ambiguity in this verse, with John intending the reader to see both a repentance theme from Zechariah and a judgment theme in light of God's wrath against evil in this book. The conversion of the nations and the judgment of the nations develop side by side throughout the visions. It is likely that this verse introduces the two paths the nations will take throughout the book. Many among the nations will turn to Christ and find forgiveness: they will respond to "the eternal gospel" (14:6–7) and repent (11:13), find that they are "purchased for God" (5:9), stand before the throne (7:9) and worship God (15:4), then bring their glory into the holy city (21:26) and walk in its light for eternity (21:24). On the other hand, the majority among the nations who turn against God and his offer of salvation (11:18) are described as those who drink the wine of passion for immorality (14:8, 18:3), worship the false trinity (13:4, 7–8), and persecute and kill the saints (6:10; 12:10; 17:6). Thus they are the objects of divine wrath (11:18; 14:10) and are worthy of double punishment (18:6), indeed both present (the cycles of seven judgments) and eternal punishment (20:11–15). One conclusion seems clear: this does not refer to a "secret rapture." This passage pictures the return of Christ as an event so public that "every eye will see" it, and every person will respond, some in repentance but the majority with complete rejection leading to judgment.

Two concluding exclamations affirm the righteousness of this declaration. Both the Greek (*nai*, "so shall it be") and the Hebrew (*amen*, "may it be so") affirmations stress the rightness of God's decision. This also functions as the church's liturgical affirmation to the action. The "amen" frames the motto in verses 6 and 7 and makes it a virtual prayer, saying, "Yes Lord, may this come to pass."

In 1:8 the Lord God speaks explicitly for one of only two times (with 21:5). His words include three of the important titles in the book; they act as a summary of the themes in the prologue.

God is first described as "the Alpha and Omega." These are the first and last letters of the Greek alphabet and sum up everything in between. God is being depicted as the Lord over history, the one who created this world, will end this world, and is in control of it right now. The title occurs four times, twice at the beginning (1:8, 17) and twice at the end (21:6; 22:13). In each, the first refers to God (1:8; 21:6) and the second to Christ (1:17; 22:13). The unity of Father and Son is again stressed, and the Godhead is sovereign over their created world.

The second title, "the one who is and was and is to come," is repeated from 1:4, and once more adds the nuance of the eternal God who unites past, present, and future in himself. The final title could actually be called two titles, for it combines "I am" with "Lord God ... Almighty." A central theme in the Gospel of John is that Jesus is the "I Am," drawn from the sacred name *yhwh* ("Yahweh") in Exodus 3:14. Here it means the God who speaks is Yahweh, Lord of the universe. The final title, "the Almighty," is combined with "Lord God" nine times in the book, and becomes the major title for God. It often translates the Old Testament title "LORD of hosts" in the **Septuagint** (2 Sam 5:10, Jer 5:14; and so on). In the grammar of the title, it means "God shows he is Lord of all by exercising his mighty power." As a whole, this verse presents God as absolutely sovereign, in control of this world and the next.

JOHN REVEALS HIS OWN SITUATION (1:9-11)

This stand-alone description notes John's part in the action behind the book. "I, John" is found here and in 22:8, framing the book and identifying the author. John identifies himself as "your brother and partner" to demonstrate commonality and shared experience with his readers. They are both a family and a fellowship of fellow-sufferers; John writes as one of them. As they experience opposition, John stands exiled on the Isle of Patmos.

There are three areas in which John and his readers share, and they are interrelated. There is an A-B-A pattern, where suffering in persecution (A) and the endurance it demands (A) are seen as part of the kingdom (B) experience for believers. In Revelation, enduring affliction and opposition means a lot more than just gritting your teeth and getting through it. It means overcoming temptation and remaining faithful and true to God when the world has turned against you. You must wait on God and stand fast against the evil demands of secular society. The basis for doing so is the kingdom, which means God has begun his reign. We are both citizens of heaven (Phil 3:20) and aliens in this world (1 Pet 1:1, 17; 2:11). The believer already participates in Christ's royal reign and lives a life that is antithetical to the demands of the earthly realm. As Paul says in Acts 14:22, it is "through many hardships" that we will "enter the kingdom of God."

John is the perfect example of this life of hardship as kingdom people. He had ministered for many years in the province of Asia and had a successful and powerful ministry as the church grew. That success was bound to conflict with the leaders and the demand for citizens to participate in the imperial cult.[6] John says here his banishment was "because of the word of God and the testimony of Jesus"; the language stems from 1:2. He undoubtedly made quite a stir with many converts, threatening the state religion. So the officials banished John to exile on Patmos, a six-by-ten-mile island about 37 miles southwest of Miletus, a harbor city south of Ephesus. It was not a prison colony, but was fairly cosmopolitan and had two gymnasia and a temple to Artemis. John likely lived a normal life there but could not leave. He was likely only there a year or two, for the early church historian Eusebius says he was exiled in AD 95, and he would have been allowed to go back when the emperor Domitian died in AD 96.

While on the island, John received a commission from God to write down and deliver the visions to the churches. We are told

6. See "Historical Background" in the introduction.

he was "in the Spirit," a phrase that occurs also in 4:2; 17:3; 21:10 for the trancelike state in which the Spirit gave the visions to John. Thus the Spirit must be added to the list in 1:1–2 describing the revelatory process—from God to Christ *to the Spirit* to the angel to John. The emphasis is on the Spirit as the source of the prophetic visions, which is a frequent Old Testament theme (Num 24:2; 1 Kgs 18:12), especially in Ezekiel (3:12, 14; 18:3; 37:1, and so on). Joel 2:28 is very apropos: "Your old men will dream dreams, your young men will see visions" (used in Acts 2:17). John is introducing a Spirit-sent set of visions intended to tell the church that the sovereign God is in process of bringing history to a close.

The Spirit chose "the Lord's day" to begin the process. This is a reference to Sunday, chosen as the day of worship by the early church on the basis of the resurrection of the Lord on the first day of the week (in the Jewish calendar). The earliest Jewish Christians likely worshiped in the synagogue on Saturday and in their house churches on Sunday. Note that the prophetic message is heard before it is seen, as John "hears a loud voice," which is a frequent experience in the book (see 5:2; 7:2; 19:3, and elsewhere). Here it is probably the voice of Christ himself, as in 1:19. His cry resembling a trumpet is significant, for throughout the New Testament a trumpet sounds to signify the day of the Lord (Matt 24:31; 1 Cor 15:52; 1 Thess 4:16) or a manifestation of God (see Heb 12:19). The trumpet blast of the Lord's voice presages the visitation of God himself and initiates the final events that will end the reign of evil as depicted in these visions.

This is the first of 12 commissions to write, preparing for the command to write in the seven letters of chapters 2–3 and four other places (1:19; 14:13; 19:9; 21:5). This reproduces the Old Testament charge to the prophets (Isa 30:8; Jer 36:28) and emphasizes to the readers that these are not just John's dreams—they are God-sent visions that must be followed. The order of the cities here and in chapters 2–3 is geographical, tracing the route of a courier as he moves from the mother church of Ephesus along the major Roman roads of the province in a horseshoe pattern, first north to Smyrna and Pergamum, then turning southeast to Thyatira, south to Sardis, east to Philadelphia and finally southeast to Laodicea. As said above on 1:4–6, these particular cities were likely chosen for their central position on the inner Roman roads and were meant to be representative of the others. Each letter contains "hear what the Spirit says to the *churches*," meaning each message was intended to be applicable to all the churches.

This prologue is critical for everything that follows. Here we learn the kind of book Revelation is (an apocalyptic-prophetic letter) and the source of the information in it (the Triune Godhead). Since God, indeed all of heaven, is the source, we must treat the book all the more seriously; it can't be ignored at will! The Father, Son, and Spirit are on the throne, sovereign over this world even though it seems as if evil is in charge. We see not only who God and Christ are but also who we are as both royalty and priesthood, citizens of heaven who follow Jesus in witness and mission to a lost world that has turned against us. The reality is clear, as 1:7–8 show us. The return of Christ is imminent, and the last days have indeed begun. The nations are the object of both mission and judgment. We have joined God in calling the nations to repentance, but those who refuse to respond will face God's wrath.

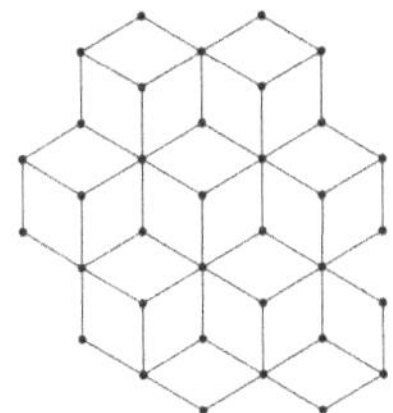

THE FIRST VISION
THE GLORY AND POWER OF CHRIST
(1:12–20)

The opening set of visions covers 1:12–3:22 and centers on the situation of the churches themselves. In fact, the seven letters to the churches are actually part of this inaugural vision and an extension of it. This introductory vision reveals to them that they are "golden lampstands," among whom Christ stands as "one like a son of man." They are not on their own but are watched over and protected by the glorified Christ who is Yahweh himself, the cosmic victor and judge (1:13–16) as well as the Risen One who is sovereign over history (1:17–18). The rich echoes of the Old Testament stem especially from Daniel but also from the priestly imagery of Exodus and the prophetic imagery of Ezekiel.

JOHN SEES A VISION OF THE EXALTED CHRIST (1:12–16)

This opening vision sets the tone for much of what follows, and details from it will be repeated in several of the letters. This becomes the official portrait of the glorified Christ; here he is depicted as the end-time sovereign and judge of the world. The rest of the visions in the book elaborate on these descriptive snapshots.

When John turns after hearing the voice behind him (1:10), he sees seven golden lampstands. This image is built on Exodus 25:31–40, where God commanded Moses to build a gold lampstand with seven branches—the sacred menorah that became a symbol of Judaism. In 1 Kings 7:49, Solomon placed five each on both sides of the altar of incense. In Zechariah 4:2, 10, lampstands signified "the eyes of the LORD that range throughout the earth." Here it is not one sevenfold lampstand but seven separate lampstands, referring to the seven churches. Still, as with the old covenant people of Israel, the new covenant church is depicted as shining lights for God in the midst of a hostile world.

In the middle of the seven lampstands stands Christ in his role as "one like a son of man." This is taken from Daniel 7:13, which describes a messianic deliverer who opposes the four beasts and the little horn and is given sovereign power over the nations.[1] The fact that Christ stands in the midst of the lampstands means he is not aloof from his people. He is deeply involved in their situation, superintending and guiding them. Note the language: He is in the middle of them, holds them in his right hand (1:16), and walks among them (2:1). He is deeply committed and acting on behalf of his followers.

John then expands this point with eight images from the Old Testament that are intended to evoke awe as we contemplate the glorified, exalted Christ. In their Old Testament context, these are descriptions of Yahweh, and here they indicate the deity of Christ, who indeed is Yahweh. The primary background is Daniel 10:5–6, and the order of the images follows a similar path: first the clothing (the linen to the belt), then the hair (the body in Daniel), then the eyes, followed by the feet, the voice, the hand, the mouth, and the face. This is a graphic picture of Christ the Divine Warrior who will go to war against God's enemies.

1. See also 1 Enoch 46:1.

The Long Robe and Golden Sash (1:13)

Most likely this refers generally to the long robe and sash of dignitaries and rulers in the ancient world rather than to the robe of the high priest. The robe down to the feet signifies authority and status, and the golden sash draped diagonally across the chest alludes to Daniel 10:5 and the man "dressed in linen, with a belt of fine gold." This parallels Revelation 15:6, where the seven angels wear golden sashes across their chest. This pictures Christ as an exalted, dignified figure.

White Head and Hair (1:14a)

Daniel 7:9 says that the hair of the Ancient of Days "was white like wool," which in ancient culture represented accumulated wisdom and dignity. Interestingly, white wool was also a major industry in the region of Revelation's original audience, especially of Laodicea (Rev 3:18). The wool and the snow picture dazzling whiteness, as depicted at the transfiguration (Mark 9:3, "His clothes became dazzling white, whiter than anyone in the world could bleach them"). The emphasis here is on Christ's incredible wisdom, purity, and splendor. White symbolizes both moral purity and absolute victory over the forces of evil.

Blazing Eyes (1:14b)

This also stems from Daniel 10:6 ("his eyes like flaming torches") and will recur in Revelation 2:18 and 19:12. At one level, it pictures the divine insight that penetrates to the core of the human situation. At a deeper level, it continues the image of the judge who knows and acts against his enemies. In both 2:18 and 19:12, judgment is the prime thrust. God is the Divine Warrior who knows the deep depravity of the nations and is going to war against them.

Bronze Feet (1:15a)

Feet signify purpose and direction. This image is connected to the blazing eyes in both Daniel 10:6 and Revelation 2:18 (also Ezek 1:7). The idea is that of polished bronze, and the added "refined by fire as in a furnace" pictures the metal in a molten state, glowing in all its purity and glory. This is another military image, with the bronze depicting a fierce warrior about to wreak havoc upon the nations. In 2:18, it portrays judgment upon the cult followers of Jezebel in Thyatira. Glory and strength abound as the Divine Warrior goes to war.

Powerful Voice (1:15b)

This is probably an allusion to Ezekiel 1:24 (the wings of the living creatures "like the roar of rushing waters") and 43:2 (the voice of Yahweh "like the roar of rushing waters"). It could picture a waterfall or cascade, but more likely portrays the roar of the ocean's waters breaking over the shore, as in the Aegean Sea or the Mediterranean. The awesome voice of God (Ezekiel) and Christ (here) is proclaiming judgment upon the nations and salvation for his people.

Stars in His Right Hand (1:16a)

The right hand in Scripture symbolizes power and authority (see Psa 110:1; Matt 26:64). The image of holding the stars signifies both possession and protection. The glorified Christ is in complete control. In this military context, the emphasis likely is more on power than on protection. The seven stars in verse 20 are the angels of the seven churches. Stars are often used in the Old Testament as symbols for angels, and in the ancient world were often identified with the powers that controlled the world.[2]

Sword from His Mouth (1:16b)

The sword was the primary image of Roman might, called the *ius gladii*, "the law of the sword." The message is that Rome is not in control; Christ is. The Old Testament background is Isaiah 11:4 ("he will strike the earth with the rod of his mouth") seen through Isaiah 49:2 ("he made my mouth like a sharpened

2. See further the commentary on 1:20.

sword"). The kind of sword here is the great sword, often used in cavalry charges like a scythe. Here it is the sword of judgment, which destroys the army of the beast in 19:15, 21. The note that it comes out of his mouth stresses the proclamation of judgment, and the sword itself the carrying out of that judgment.

RADIANT FACE (1:16C)

This recalls Moses when he descended Sinai with his face "radiant because he had spoken with the LORD" (Exod 34:29) as well as Jesus at his transfiguration ("his face shone like the sun," Matt 17:2). God is called "a sun and shield" in Psalm 84:11 and "everlasting light" in Isaiah 60:19. Furthermore, there is an aspect of judgment in the apocalyptic use of sun imagery in the Old Testament (Isa 13:10; Ezek 32:7; Joel 2:10). This also shows up in Revelation 6:12; 8:12; 9:2; 16:8; and 19:17. So the twin themes of glory and judgment continue in this image.

CHRIST EXPANDS JOHN'S COMMISSION (1:17–20)

The divine presence, God in Christ, dominates this vision. It further demonstrates Christ's unity with his Father by adding an additional description of him. These verses depict him as the eternal one (1:17–18), strengthen the commission to write from 1:11 (1:19), and add an interpretive key for understanding the vision of 1:12–16 (1:20).

In this opening vision, John has experienced a **theophany** (a manifestation of God). As is typical of visions of heavenly beings, he responds in fear and worship.[3] The sense of apocalyptic presence and power is overwhelming; Christ is indeed present in all his glory! Jesus touches John not only for comfort and reassurance but also for a symbolic investiture; it is a kind of "laying on of hands" to confer prophetic office and authority to write.

3. See, for example, Josh 5:14; Ezek 1:28; Dan 8:17–18; 10:10–18; Matt 14:27; Luke 1:13, 30. John will do this again in Rev 19:10; 22:8.

In Scripture, fear is the usual response when God manifests himself (as in Dan 10:10–18; Matt 14:27; Luke 1:13, 30). Jesus gives reason to not be afraid by describing who he is. He is the "I Am," Yahweh of the burning bush (Exod 3:14), God of very God.[4] There are four "I am" sayings in Revelation, parallel to the seven in John, claiming that Jesus is Yahweh, the "I Am" (compare Rev 1:8, 17; 2:23; 22:16 with John 6:35; 8:12; 10:7, 11; 11:25; 14:6; 15:1). Jesus then clarifies this by calling himself the first and the last, parallel to the "Alpha and Omega" of 1:8. This title derives from Isaiah (41:4; 44:6; 48:12), where it refers to God as Creator and Sovereign over all. The sovereignty and power of God is extended to the second member of the Trinity.

The "first and the last" is further defined as the one who was dead and now "is alive forever and ever." This refers to Jesus' death and resurrection but also adds the idea of his exaltation to reign eternally. This means that "the last" is not only a reference to sovereignty but also to eternality. It is a key characteristic of God in Revelation that he is "the one who lives forever and ever" (2:8; 4:9, 10; 10:6; 11:15; 15:7). The stakes in Revelation far transcend the mundane issues of this earthly life. Eternity is at stake, and there is only one who has the power to grant eternal life: God himself.

The final characteristic of Christ in these verses, his holding the "keys of death and Hades," points to one of the critical aspects of the book—his power over the cosmic forces. The emphatic placement of "the keys" stresses this power. Christ triumphed over death in his resurrection, and now he has complete control over the power of death. Death and Hades are personified in Revelation as demonic forces also at 6:8 and 20:13, 14. This refers to the fallen angels, the evil powers at work in this world. Christ has defeated and subjugated them (Mark 3:27) and given his followers authority over them (Mark 3:15; 6:7). Satan is filled with frustrated rage "because he knows his time is short"

---

4. See commentary on 1:4.

(Rev 12:12). There is likely also a reference here to Sheol or the grave, the place of the dead. Jesus has power over life and death as well as power over the cosmic powers. In Graeco-Roman religion this would be control of the underworld. The Roman gods are powerless. Mainly, however, Jesus is the one who has overcome and gained mastery over the cosmic forces.

The one who controls death and the powers of death now turns his attention to John, the chosen messenger for these apocalyptic truths. He has already commissioned John to write in 1:11. This passage goes further and enumerates the content of the prophetic messages. In light of Jesus' cosmic victory over death and the evil powers, John is now commanded to write down what God is revealing to him. The threefold description of this revelation is difficult to interpret, and there have been three main options. Some think "what you have seen" = the vision of chapter 1, "what is" = the seven letters, and "what will take place later" = the visions of chapters 4–22. Others take the first as referring to the commission to write in 1:11 and the other two (present and future) as the rest of the book. Still others take this phrase as a common apocalyptic formula meaning God is in charge of past, present, and future (similar to the title of 1:4), and define the book as an intertwining of past, present, and future perspectives. In this sense, it may well build on Daniel 2:28–29 and the interpretation of Daniel's dream as a future prophecy. This third view has the most promise. We have in this timeline the **eschatological** perspective for the book.

Jesus explains the lampstands and the stars in 1:20. They are called "mysteries," an important New Testament term used to describe the new truths God reveals to his people. "Apocalyptic" describes the process by which God unveils these hidden truths, and "mystery" is the content of these truths. Both terms relate to the uncovering of those hidden secrets God has decided not to unveil until the present time.

First, the "seven stars" are a reference to the angels of the seven churches in chapters 2–3. The identification of these angels is highly debated, and the solution is tied to the use of these angels as the recipient of each letter:

1. They could be actual angels who serve as guardian angels assigned for each church. An important feature of apocalyptic literature is the frequent presence of angels who mediate the visions and provide interpretive keys to the meaning of critical symbols. The problem with this option is the content of the letters—would actual angels be called upon to repent?
2. They could be personified spirits of the churches—heavenly counterparts, so to speak. This image would typify the spiritual nature of the churches. Yet this seems overly subtle, as the lampstands represent actual churches.
3. This may refer to the tendency in Judaism and parts of the early church to worship angels, so this might be a denunciation of such practices. Yet this does not fit the seven letters, and there is no hint of such a cult in the rest of the book.
4. Many think the angels are really "messengers" (another meaning of *angelos*)—that is, a leader of the church, a bishop or pastor. This is viable, since a "star" in the ancient world referred to sovereigns and major leaders. However, everywhere else in this book, *angelos* refers to heavenly beings, not human messengers.
5. Perhaps this is a messenger in the sense of bearers of this letter/book to the churches. Yet this seems even less likely given the common usage of both "star" and "angel," as noted in number four above.

The best answer is probably a combination of the first two. These are angels God has placed in charge of the churches, and they were also corporately identified with the church each watched over. They are addressed in the seven letters as representatives of the churches, as embodying God's intentions for the churches, and they are asked to intervene in the spiritual needs of the churches. Addressing each letter to the angel God had assigned to superintend the churches in that city tells each church that they are not just an assembly meeting on earth; all of heaven is involved in their life and conduct. Through them God oversees his plan worked out in their midst. Their earthly life and the heavenly reality underlying it are interdependent aspects of the Christian life.

The lampstands, as already noted on 1:12, refer to the seven churches themselves and build on the menorah or seven-branched lampstand of the holy place in the temple. The point here is that Christ is in control of both the angels, "holding" them in 1:16, and the churches; he is "in the midst of" them in 1:12. He is with them, protecting and vindicating them in a world that repudiates and acts against them. Yet he also holds them accountable to live faithful lives that overcome that world.

The vision of 1:12–20 tells us that Jesus is indeed Lord of all and is absolutely sovereign not only over us but also over the world in which we live. This theme will dominate the entire book of Revelation. Jesus is the conquering Messiah, and we can rest secure, knowing that he is watching over us. Not only this, but we also know that his angels are indeed messengers of God and Christ to us, and they too are watching over us. All of heaven is involved in our lives, and we can place our trust in the fact that we are indeed "shielded by God's power" (1 Pet 1:5).

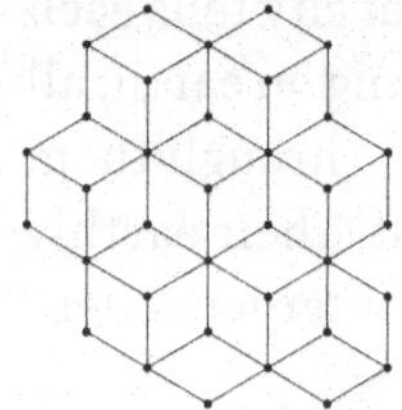

LETTERS TO THE SEVEN CHURCHES, PART 1

A TRULY BIBLICAL CHURCH

(2:1–7, 12–29)

The character of this work, the recipients of this work, and its basic apocalyptic purpose were established in chapter 1. Now Christ turns to a detailed description and challenge addressed to the specific situation of each church. John becomes a stenographer, a secretary. Every word comes from Jesus as dictated to John.

There was a time in my life when I believed these letters were meant to signify the seven periods of church history.[1] One major difficulty with this interpretation is that the details of each letter fit the historical situation of that church. These are letters meant to discuss the actual situation of each church at the end of the first century. At the same time, though, these churches are representative of the others, as all the letters end with "hear what the Spirit says to the churches." The plural

1. This is the historicist scheme mentioned in "Methods of Interpretation" in the introduction. According to this scheme, for example, Ephesus would represent the early church, Smyrna the patristic era with its persecution, and so on. We would then be living in the "Laodicean period."

"church*es*" means that each letter is meant to be applied to every church. Readers then and now are to ask of each letter, "How does this fit my church?" At a secondary level, we also ask how these points fit our own lives.

These letters build on prophetic challenges/letters in the Old Testament (Jer 29:1–23; 2 Chr 21:12–15, and so on) and build on similarities with Israel in the prophetic period. They ask the churches to determine whether they are failing like apostate Israel or persevering like the righteous remnant. They are also form letters; each has seven sections into which the details of each church's situation are inserted:

1. Address ("to the angel of the church … write")
2. Messenger formula ("these are the words of him who …")
3. Strengths ("I know your works …")
4. Weaknesses ("But I have this against you")
5. Solution (commands to "repent," and so on)
6. Call to listen ("Let anyone willing to hear listen to what the Spirit says to the churches")
7. Challenge to overcome ("To the one who is victorious …")

The introduction (the first two) and the conclusion (the last two) frame the body of each letter, which contains the actual situation, the challenge, and the solution for that church's needs. The key section is the one dealing with strengths and weaknesses; this guides us into the way the letters relate to each other. When we focus on this section, we find that three churches have both strengths and weaknesses (Ephesus, Pergamum, Thyatira), two have only strengths with no weaknesses (Smyrna, Philadelphia), and two have only weaknesses with no strengths (Sardis, Laodicea). That is the order in which I will cover them below, and it's also a good order to follow when organizing a sermon or Bible study series.

This first section covers the three churches that have both strengths and weaknesses. When we look carefully at the problems in these churches, we discover they have to do with the two criteria that make up a truly biblical church: faithfulness to the Word of God and a community characterized by love. Ephesus was strong in the first and weak in the second, while Pergamum and Thyatira were weak in the first and strong in the second. The situations of these churches emphasize the need to be both a Bible-centered community characterized by strong teaching and a biblically caring fellowship characterized by strong relationships.

EPHESUS: RESTORE YOUR FIRST LOVE (2:1–7)

THE CITY

Ephesus, the fourth-largest city in the Roman world (after Rome, Alexandria, and Antioch of Syria) had a quarter of a million people and was a harbor city on the west coast of the province of Asia. It had become a center of commerce, one of the most prosperous cities in the ancient world. Three major trade routes met at Ephesus. It also contained one of the seven wonders of the ancient world: the temple of the goddess Artemis (see Acts 19), which at 425 feet by 220 feet was four times larger than the Parthenon in Athens. It had 127 sixty-foot pillars, was the first temple made completely of marble, and was home to a black meteorite believed to be a statue of Artemis. Ephesus also contained three temples to emperors, including one to Domitian, and the imperial cult thrived there.[2] Furthermore, a significant Jewish population who was opposed to Christianity dwelled there (Acts 19:8–9).

The Ephesian church may have been established by Priscilla and Aquila aided by Apollos (Acts 18:18–25). During Paul's third missionary journey, it became the center for evangelizing the cities of the province (Acts 19:10). The church struggled with false teachers, first prophesied by Paul in AD 57 (Acts 20:29–31) and then typifying the problems of the church for the next 30

2. See "Historical Background" in the introduction.

or so years.[3] There is no evidence the church ever defeated the false teachers until after this letter in AD 95!

Jesus Identifies Himself (2:1)

The address in each letter applies the character of Christ—often with details drawn from his description in chapter 1—to the situation of the church. Here Ephesus, the mother church of the region, is reminded that Christ is in charge. Jesus, not they, "holds the seven stars" (1:16), meaning he gave the guardian angels their authority and sent them into the midst of each church. He, not they, "walks among the lampstands" (1:13); he maintains both watchful care and absolute authority over the churches.

Situation and Strengths (2:2–3)

Jesus knows the works of the Ephesian church. These works refer to "good deeds," yet also to the whole spiritual walk of the believers there. The works are defined further as both hard work (expanded in the rest of 2:2) and endurance (expanded in 2:3). The three are found together in 1 Thessalonians 1:3: "your work produced by faith, your labor prompted by love, and your endurance inspired by hope." The successful labor in the church of Ephesus entailed a battle with false teachers. These teachers' basic character is seen as evil, and the faithful are unable to endure these heretics. They were instructed to utterly oppose such evil people.

The form this opposition took is biblical: they tested them and proved them false. In both the Old Testament and New Testament, the people of God are instructed to test, or critically examine, prophets and teachers to see if their ministry is based on truth or falsehood.[4] In Ephesus, these will be identified later as the Nicolaitan cult (2:6, 15), who apparently passed

3. See Eph 4:14 and the letters of 1–2 Timothy (circa AD 64) and 1 John (early 80s).

4. See especially 1 John 4:1–3: "test the spirits" of the false teachers.

themselves off as wandering missionaries and went from house church to house church calling themselves "apostles." In reality, they were savage wolves, rending the flock (Acts 20:29). By labeling themselves apostles, they claimed to be the divinely chosen leaders and teachers of the church. The Ephesians unmasked their deceptions, however, testing and proving that they espoused satanic falsehood, not God's truth.

This is critical for our day as well, but we have to distinguish carefully between theological differences and heresy. The key is that heresy goes against Scripture and denies a cardinal doctrine of the faith. We must make this charge very carefully, for by definition a heretic has denied the faith and become an apostate, a tool of Satan. Disagreements over charismatic gifts or eternal security or the rapture do not come under the category of heresy. On these issues, we should agree to disagree and respect each other. In the early church decisions about what to call heresy were made by the whole church in an official council, like the council of Nicea or the council of Chalcedon. Today there must be widespread discussion by the great minds and leaders of the church before labeling a movement heretical, as seen in recent discussions on the prosperity movement (considered a heresy by most) or the openness of God movement (widely considered dangerous but not heretical).

The endurance mentioned in 3:2 is expanded in the next verse as patient perseverance in the midst of trying circumstances. This is a major theme in the book; it is a comprehensive concept demanding trust and patient steadfastness in hard times.[5] Moreover, these followers have done so for the sake of Christ's name, meaning they have been mistreated because they stood up for Christ and said no to the pagan demands on them. They have refused the lies told them by the false teachers and remained faithful in the midst of serious opposition. To "grow weary" would be to surrender to the demands placed

5. See "Theology of the Book" in the introduction.

upon them, to experience spiritual exhaustion caused by their labor for the Lord and the difficulties of remaining true to him. We all too easily lose heart in the midst of our trials and wallow in despair. Passages like 1 Peter 1:6–7 and James 1:12–14 tell us that when we are God-centered, trials become an opportunity to watch him work in our situations. Rather than being a cause for despair, they actually become a source of joy in him.

Weakness (2:4)

The formula "I have this against you" introduces God's reaction to the spiritual and moral failures of the churches. The divine displeasure in these practices will bring judgment down upon them. The problem of the Ephesian church is that it has abandoned its "first love," which could mean either its primary love or the love it had in the beginning. The latter is more likely, for 2:5 tells them to do the works they did at first. This must refer to the early years of the church.

The love Christ is discussing is not just love for God but love for one another. Of course the two are tied together, as seen in Jesus' summary of the Torah in Mark 12:29–31 and parallels: Love the Lord your God, and your neighbor as yourself. We cannot truly love God without loving the children of God, and vice versa (1 John 2:9–10, 4:16–21). The fight for orthodoxy had robbed the Ephesians of harmony, and they had ceased to be a loving church. In the days when Paul wrote his letter to the Ephesians he spoke of a conflict between Jewish and Gentile members (Eph 2:14–18); by the time of this letter that disharmony had become general, and love had fled from the church.

Solution (2:5–6)

As we will see in the letters to Pergamum and Thyatira, the solution takes the form of a serious warning, a demand for repentance and change. First, Christ calls them to enter the process of remembering, which here is a present-tense verb demanding ongoing reflection. This is an important biblical concept that involves not just recalling the past but acting on the memories and returning to your previous right walk with God (Isa 44:21; 46:8–9; Mic 6:5; Rom 15:15). The Ephesians must specifically bring to mind how far they have fallen, acknowledging the seriousness of their sin. In a sense, since this whole letter is addressed to the angel of the church, this is an accusation that the Ephesians have turned their guardian into a "fallen angel," not literally but for rhetorical effect. This is a very serious situation.

The only proper response is to repent. As they reflect on their serious dilemma, it must convict them of their sin and lead them to repentance and lifestyle change. The form the repentance must take is not a new turn but a return to the past: They must do the works they did at first. With 2:4, these are to be acts of love or good deeds toward one another and thereby toward God. In other words, what is needed is a return to those relationships they had when they were a young church. Their successful battle with the heretics was insufficient when it was not accompanied by love (as in 1 Cor 13:1–2). Right belief without right practice results in a false religion!

To make this point more emphatically, John then states it negatively. If they refuse to repent and return to the loving community they used to be, they will face Jesus as Judge, the God with the blazing eyes and sharp double-edged sword. The warning is stated two ways to stress its seriousness—"if you do not," and "unless you repent." The penalty is incredibly severe: Christ will remove their lampstand. He will come to them in judgment, not just at his second coming but in the near future. So the judgment is "inaugurated," that is, taking place now in anticipation of the future reckoning. The removal of the lampstand could be the loss of their witness, but most likely it is stronger than this. They will be treated as apostates, as Israel was in the prophetic period, and lose their status before God. The church in Ephesus will cease to be listed as among God's people but will join the heretics as Satan's people, joining the Jewish groups in 2:9 and 3:9 that are called a synagogue of Satan. Fortunately, as the church father Ignatius of Antioch tells us in his letter to the Ephesians written early in the second century, the church did heed this warning, repented, and once again became a thriving church.[6]

Jesus ends this section with a word of encouragement. Although they have failed in their moral/spiritual responsibility, their commitment to biblical and doctrinal purity stands in their favor. There is a wordplay on "works" in 2:5–6: "you must return to the *works* you did in the beginning ... but at least you hate the same evil *works* I do." There is also a progression of thought in the letter: In 2:2 they found the teaching to be false, and now they hate the evil works that resulted from the teaching. "Hate" is a strong word that at first glance seems to contradict the law of love, but we must remember that God hates evil (Psa 45:7; Zech 8:17) and those who practice evil (Psa 5:5; Amos 6:8). Hebrews 1:9 says that Christ has "loved righteousness and hated wickedness." Since sin is the ultimate abomination, God must hate sin and will destroy it forever. His people must follow this and also hate evil teaching and practices. The statement here fits the old adage: love the sinner, hate the sin.

We don't know much about the Nicolaitans; they are mentioned only here and in 2:14–15, 20–23. The second-century church fathers Irenaeus and Clement of Alexandria link them with Nicolaus, one of the seven deacons of Acts 6:5, but there is no known evidence for this. Most modern interpreters associate them with an early form of Gnosticism, a second-century movement in which the "knowledge" (Greek *gnosis*) of secret teachings becomes salvation. This is linked also with the heresies opposed in 1–2 Timothy and 1 John. The Nicolaitans' practices apparently centered on idolatry, including participation in temple rites and trade guild banquets ("food sacrificed to idols" in 2:14, 20), and sexual immorality. Broadly speaking, there were two problems. The first was syncretism: having an accommodating attitude toward paganism and allowing Christians to participate in emperor worship. The second was

6. Ignatius, *To the Ephesians* 1:1; 9:1.

libertinism: showing freedom from sin by doing what you want on the premise that it doesn't affect your salvation.

Call to listen and Challenge to Overcome (2:7)

This exhortation, common to all seven letters, is built on Jesus' call, "Let the one who has an ear listen" (Mark 4:23; Matt 11:15; Luke 8:8)—a prophetic warning to open our mind and heart to kingdom truths. God has given us his hidden truths that are now openly revealed. It is up to us to heed them and change accordingly. As in 1:3, hearing must lead to heeding.

The second half of the verse centers on the Spirit and is an all-important reminder that each of us should apply the Ephesian situation to our own churches—note the emphatic plural in the text. The perfect (sevenfold) Spirit (see on 1:4) is the revealer of eternal truth, and he is speaking directly through each of the letters. Moreover, he is making certain that every detail is made available to all *churches*, so I must ascertain the extent to which my church also has the Ephesian problem. Too many of our churches stress right doctrine to such an extent that we become judgmental and unloving. While I want my church to care deeply for doctrinal truth, I also want my people to care just as deeply for each other!

The letter closes with an athletic and military metaphor that pictures victory by vanquishing a foe. In Revelation this term occurs 15 times, often of the **eschatological** war. The beast conquers the two witnesses (11:7) and the saints by taking their lives (13:7), yet in their act of martyrdom the saints conquer (12:11). The powers of evil have a transitory, temporary victory, but ultimate victory belongs to God and his people. Still, the believers are responsible to "overcome" or "be victorious" over temptation, the pressures of the world, and the cosmic powers. The final victory was won on the cross, and our victory comes when we participate in Christ's victory and find strength from him.

The reward for the faithful is that they will participate in the very blessing intended at creation but never realized by Adam and Eve—eating from the tree of life. Because of sin, the two had been expelled from the garden so that they might not have access to this tree. In addition to Genesis, this recalls Proverbs, where the tree of life is a symbol for the life-giving properties of wisdom (Prov 3:18, 11:30), and Ezekiel, where "fruit trees of all kinds" at the river flowing from the temple provide healing and life (Ezek 47:12). In Jewish apocalyptic literature the tree signified the eternal life given by God to his people, and in Revelation 22:2 the curse of the first Eden is lifted and eternal life is extended to the saints. There is also a close connection with the cross, the "tree" on which Christ died and brought life to a dying world. This tree of life is in the "paradise" of God, originally a Persian loan word depicting the royal gardens. All this points to the fact that, in the new heavens and new earth of 21:1–22:5, the original Edenic paradise will be restored and reinstated on behalf of the victors—the people of God.

PERGAMUM: LIVE FAITHFULLY IN SATAN'S REALM (2:12–17)

The City

The strengths and weaknesses of Pergamum and Thyatira were the opposite of the situation in Ephesus—they were strong in love and weak in faithfulness to God's word and truths. Pergamum was the northernmost of the seven cities that received Revelation. It was also the capital of the Roman province of Asia, so it was politically stronger even than the larger Ephesus. Moreover, it was also the leading religious center of Asia, with temples and shrines dedicated to Zeus, Athena, Dionysus (the patron god of the city), and Asclepius (the god of healing). A great 40-foot-high altar to Zeus situated on a terrace at the top of a mountain overlooked the city. Pergamum was the first city allowed to erect a temple to Augustus Caesar in AD 29, and it had three temples, making it the core of the imperial cult. Here, the opposition to Christians who refused to participate in Roman religion was especially intense.

Jesus Identifies Himself (2:12)

This letter has the simplest description of Jesus of any of the letters. As the provincial capital, Pergamum was the residence of the Roman governor. Christ's claim to wield "the sharp double-edged sword" is a reference to a Thracian broadsword often used in cavalry charges. It was the symbol of Roman authority and justice; the phrase for Roman might was *ius gladii*, "the law of the sword." By Christ's opening words, therefore, the city stands corrected: it is not the Roman governor but Christ who actually carries out just judgments. It is Jesus' authority as the true and final wielder of the sword that actually will bring justice to the world.[7] It is the exalted Christ, not a Roman official, who has ultimate power. The *Pax Romana* ("Roman peace") was a façade, because it was actually the Roman sword that ruled the land. Peace can only come through Jesus Christ.

Situation and Strengths (2:13)

The risen Lord emphasizes three things about the church in Pergamum: the pagan world in which they live, their faithful witness in that world, and their endurance under persecution. The pressure comes from the fact that this world is "where Satan has his throne." It is difficult to know for sure what the reference is here. Two options are the altar to Zeus that dominated the city and typified Roman religion, or the cult of Asclepius, symbolized by a serpent that was also the symbol of the city and an image of Satan (see 12:9, 20:2). However, most interpreters agree that the best option is the imperial cult, the major difficulty behind the letter.[8] Emperor worship most directly caused persecution in that place and time.

The major strength of the church in Pergamum was their witness. In all of the pressure, they remained true to Christ's name. The verb "remain true" means to hold firm to Jesus, to

7. See the commentary on 1:16.
8. See "Historical Background" in the introduction.

live up to their responsibility and resist the lure of their pagan environment. In other words, they refused to renounce their faith.[9] The Nicolaitan heresy allowed participation in Roman religious rites, but that was a dangerous lie. You cannot worship Caesar and Christ at the same time. This is nothing but syncretism, a Christo-paganism that is not a combination of the two but a denial of Christ. The same is true today. Those quasi-Christians who attend church services regularly but are more committed to their pleasures than they are to Christ may want to go to heaven, but they seem to want their earthly toys even more. In reality, they are faithless to Christ, and the Lord will say at the final judgment, "I never knew you" (Matt 7:23). Still, this was not true of the Pergamum church as a whole; the majority remained faithful to Jesus.

As 2:13 proceeds, their faithful endurance is embodied in a person: Antipas. We know little about Antipas; he seems to be the only one martyred in Pergamum to this date, perhaps in the whole province. He is called a faithful witness, and the combination of the word for "witness" (*martys*) with "put to death" probably helped pave the way for the development of *martys* to mean "a faithful person who is put to death" in the second century. Antipas certainly was treated as a hero here, and he became a major example for the other Christians of faithfulness in the face of the most severe persecution. The added "where Satan dwells" at the end of the verse frames 2:13 with the reality that Pergamum is the heart of anti-Christian pressure. Pergamum is Satan's hometown, and Satan is the true source of the church's troubles.

Weakness (2:14–15)

Where the Ephesians were weak, the Pergamum Christians were strong (their church life). But where the Ephesians were strong, this church was weak, namely in their tolerance for

9. The Greek of 2:13 literally reads, "did not deny faith in me."

the false teachers. This is a huge issue today: When should we "agree to disagree" and accept our differences, and when should we go to war against pernicious lies? I discussed this in the Ephesian letter, but some points can be added here.

The key to determining whether a theological difference is important enough to fight about is to provide criteria for distinguishing cardinal doctrines from non-cardinal issues. A cardinal doctrine is an essential teaching that defines Christianity. To deny a cardinal doctrine is to deny the Christian faith. A noncardinal issue is a teaching that is important but not essential. Christians can differ on these and still remain faithful to Scripture. The cardinal doctrines have been established in the Bible and church history. The non-cardinal doctrines are not as clear as we often think (by the design and purpose of God), and scholars with the same view of Scripture disagree regarding them. Examples of cardinal doctrines include the Trinity, the deity of Christ, the nature of the Holy Spirit (but not the charismatic debate), salvation by grace alone, the cross as the only basis of salvation, substitutionary atonement (but not predestination or eternal security), the return of Christ (but not the rapture or millennial issues).

By allowing false teachers to flourish, the Pergamum church was endangering every member. Jesus makes the problem clear in 2:14 by likening the false movement to the Old Testament "teaching of Balaam." Balaam was a Gentile prophet whom Balak king of Moab asked to curse the Israelites in Numbers 22–24, but instead he uttered only blessings. His "teaching" refers to his later advice that Balak use Moabite women to seduce the Israelites into immorality and idolatry (Num 25:1–3, 31:16). As Balaam showed the Moabites how to lead Israel into sin, so the false teachers were showing these Christians how to fall into sin. They were throwing a stumbling block into the church that led the people into apostasy.

It is unclear whether the teaching of Balaam in 2:14 and the Nicolaitans in 2:15 are the same or separate movements. The adverb "likewise" seems to suggest a comparison, but it is better to see the parallel not between two similar movements but between a single movement (the Nicolaitans) and the Jewish tradition about Balaam. The Nicolaitans were apparently saying that there was nothing wrong with participating in the imperial cult or the idolatrous trade guild banquets, but such accommodations constituted idolatry. Religious festivals dominated civic life in the Roman world; there were constant festivals celebrating the gods. The same is true with immorality, as evidenced by the pornographic frescoes on the walls of homes in Pompeii. Some think the immorality in the book only refers metaphorically to spiritual adultery—namely idolatry, as in Isaiah 57:3, 8, and Hosea 2:2–13. That is true of passages like Revelation 2:21; 14:8; 17:2, 4; 18:3, 9, but it refers to literal promiscuity in 9:21; 21:8; 22:15 and certainly here. These false teachers were, like Balaam, guiding the people of God into both idolatry and immorality. Syncretism is also common today. People see no problem embracing, for example, biblical doctrines on Christ and salvation and also accepting such things as abortion or homosexuality, even though the Bible is clear on those issues. Or they can be partly Christian and partly secular in their lifestyles. God's Word is adamant against these things.

SOLUTION (2:16)

The church's tolerance of the false teaching resulted in the extreme danger of bringing God's wrath down upon them. While the Ephesians had forgotten how to love, the Pergamum church had neglected to tell the truth. However, the solution is the same: repent, change the dangerous direction the church has been going, and get right with God. To fail to take a strong stance against the heretics would constitute sin and invite divine judgment.

The warning is similar to 2:5. Christ will come—a term connoting imminent ("soon," as in 1:1) judgment both now and at the second coming—and fight against them. The verb for "fight" (*polemeō*) is very strong, meaning to "wage war." The verb occurs five times and the noun nine times in Revelation, often referring to the "war" of the dragon/beast against the saints (11:7; 13:7) or the Lamb (16:14; 17:14). Jesus will conduct his war with the sword from his mouth, drawing the image from the address of this letter (2:12) and meaning a proclamation of judgment that is soon to be carried out. This war will be "against them," meaning the wrath will be directed at the heretics rather than the believers. But it will still be a judgment of the church, for the true followers allowed the cult to remain among them and even more seriously allowed some of them to join it. The war would be directed at their loved ones whom they let defect to the Nicolaitan camp.

Call to Listen and Challenge to Overcome (2:17)

The call to listen carefully centers on the Holy Spirit as the source of the message and on the necessity that every church apply the prophetic material to themselves. We must ask, "Have I tolerated false teaching? How concerned am I for biblical truth?" As I travel to literally hundreds of churches, I am too often chagrined at the lack of a serious teaching ministry among them. Where is the concern for truth? It is at the heart of Scripture but too rarely emphasized today. This is why so many churches have gone astray. Too many average Christians do not have a firm grasp of doctrine or care much about retaining the truths of God's Word. They cannot tell when they are being fed false ideas.

Those who do hear and obey will find victory over sin and falsehood. For them Christ has a double reward, two divine gifts—note the repeated "I will give" before each one. The first is "the hidden manna," referring to the manna in the wilderness by which God fed the Israelites for 40 years, which God called "bread from heaven" (Exod 16:4). Moses then commanded that a jar of the manna be preserved with the tablets of the Ten Commandments "for generations to come" (Exod 16:32–34), and they were stored in the ark of the covenant (Heb 9:4). According to one Jewish tradition, just before the temple was destroyed in 586 BC Jeremiah took the ark and hid it in a cave under Mount

Sinai (2 Maccabees 2:4–7; 2 Baruch 6:7–10). There it would await the **eschaton**, when the Messiah would place it in the new temple. In John 6:35 Jesus said, "I am the bread of life," and so in one sense he is the hidden manna that is given to bring life. In this passage the primary idea is the bread of life that will be ours in the eternal kingdom. This manna, along with the white stone, refers to entrance to the messianic feast when we get to heaven (see Rev 19:6-10).

The second gift is a white stone with a new name on it. There are several possible options for its meaning. It may symbolize or be:

1. the jewels in the breastplate of the high priest;
2. the white and black stones placed in an urn during a trial to vote for guilt/acquittal;
3. the white stones with names on them as a kind of ticket given to guild members or victors at the games for admission to feasts;
4. secret amulets with the names of gods on them; or
5. a token signifying a gladiator was freed from the arena.

Of these, the one that best fits the context is option three, the use of stones as tickets for admittance to a feast. This continues the idea of the messianic feast as reward to the victors in the race of life (compare Heb 12:1–3).

The "new name" could be the name of God/Christ inscribed on the believer. In 19:12, we are told that Christ when he returns will have "the name that no one knows but he himself." But the letter here adds that this name will be unknown except to "the one who receives it," and that would be believers themselves. This means that like Christ, we too will have a new name, an identity linked with our victory over evil in this world. Our final reward will be a new name, a new body, and a new heavens and new earth. Newness will characterize the start of eternity (Rev 21:5).

THYATIRA: PROTECT THE CHURCH (2:18–29)

THE CITY

Thyatira was the least important city of the seven and yet has the longest letter of the group. It was a commercial town on the Lycus River (the same as Laodicea and Colossae) and was well-known for its guilds in trades such as cloth, bronze, leather-working, and pottery. Lydia, the dealer in purple cloth whom Paul encountered in Acts 16:12–15, came from here. Towns in the Roman world tended to be laid out in squares, with each guild controlling its section. These guilds also were at the heart of religious life, with each having a patron god and frequent feasts in honor of their god. Thus Christians experienced pressure to participate, as their livelihood was at stake.

JESUS IDENTIFIES HIMSELF (2:18)

In this address, as with the others, the church is reminded that the angel God has placed over them is affected by their conduct. All of heaven is involved in the life of the church. Here Christ is called "the Son of God," the only place in the book this exact title is used, probably because of both the emperor cult and the centrality of Apollos, son of Zeus, as the patron god of Thyatira. It is Jesus, not Caesar or Apollo, who is the true Son of God. The two images here of Christ's eyes and feet from 1:14–15 (with Dan 10:6 the source) are both military and center on Christ as Judge. In this serious situation, with false religion running rampant, the church in Thyatira must be made aware that the exalted Christ sees all, and judgment is imminent. Apollo may have often been depicted astride a warhorse and wielding a battle-ax, but it is Christ who is the true Divine Warrior.

SITUATION AND STRENGTHS (2:19)

Jesus spells out four good works of the Thyatiran church, perhaps with the first two defining the motivation behind their conduct and the second pair describing the results in their lives. While there is no grammatical evidence for this, it works at a topical level. Unlike Ephesus and like Pergamum, the

Thyatiran church members were strong in love, and certainly this combines love of God and of others. This love is coupled with faith, described in the book as both trust in God and living a life of faithful obedience to him. Love and faith are part of the core three Christian virtues (with hope, 1 Cor 13:13). Here there is also emphasis on an orthodox faith as opposed to the false teachers.

When love and faith characterize a church, the result will always be an excess of service and endurance. The term for "service" used here also means "ministry." It refers to an active life of care and help, to charitable service and ministry to others. We have already repeatedly seen endurance (1:9; 2:2, 3) as a major theme referring to a dynamic perseverance in faith and life in the midst of pressure and hard times.[10] It is a key attribute of the overcomer who remains true in all circumstances.

Probably the major difference between Ephesus and Thyatira, as well as Pergamum, is that Ephesus had "forsaken its first love" and needed to return to the things they had done at first (2:4–5), while the believers in Thyatira not only retained their original love but were now doing more than they did at first. The quality of life in this church was not diminishing but increasing both in quantity and quality.

WEAKNESS (2:20–23A)

Like Pergamum, the believers in Thyatira had grown lax in their theological vigilance, tolerating the very heresy that Ephesus had rejected. For this reason, the risen Lord castigates them for their shallow doctrinal commitment to truth. In the letter to Pergamum, Christ centered on the dangerous teaching; here he centers on the pernicious leader, the self-styled prophetess Jezebel. This is surely not her actual name but a nickname meant to recall her predecessor, the Phoenician wife of the Israelite King Ahab who led the Israelites step-by-step

10. See "Theology of the Book" in the introduction.

into Baal worship and sorcery (1 Kgs 16, 21). The "Jezebel" here claimed her message was directly from God, possibly not in the form of systematic teaching but via oracles and pronouncements. We do not know who she actually was; some link her with the pagan prophetess Sibyl Sambathe, who had a shrine outside Thyatira, but there is not enough evidence to know for certain. Most likely she was prominent in the church and community, with her prophetic utterances making her the leader of the movement.

The early church recognized prophets (1 Cor 12:28; Eph 4:11), and women often prophesied (1 Cor 11:5) and were counted among the prophets (Acts 21:9). At the same time, there were many false prophets, with the Old Testament Jezebel herself using 900 of them (1 Kgs 18:19). This Jezebel would clearly be numbered among the false prophets. She was encouraging compromise, allowing her followers to participate in the licentious behavior of the pagan world and in the guild banquets devoted to the patron gods. A Christian could not practice a trade without connections within the guild, and this meant attending the common meals of guild life with their idolatrous atmospheres. Jezebel would have reasoned that such participation was merely civic duty. Since idols are nothing, the reasoning goes, Christians do not endanger their faith when taking part in such banquets, as Paul said in 1 Corinthians 8:4–8. But Paul was only discussing eating the meat, and later disallowed the banquets themselves as idolatrous (1 Cor 10:18–22). Jezebel conveniently ignored the larger repercussions. Christ is clear here; in reality she deceives those who belong to him. Deception is the major weapon of Satan (Rev 12:9; 20:3, 8, 10) and of the "false prophet" (13:14; 19:20). Clearly Jezebel is a tool of Satan in the community.

There continue to be many "Jezebels" in our day, people who deliberately teach falsehood to gain money and power. These false teachers establish their own cults and prey upon the gullible to win their allegiance and steal their money. People are looking for something to give them stability and hope, and too easily they fall under the influence of these religious hucksters.

Still, even with Jezebel, God is full of mercy and has given her time to repent of her immorality (2:21), probably both spiritual adultery and sexual immorality. She has refused to accept his offer, and the time is almost up. John and other leaders had already warned her of the consequences; they had tested her life and teaching (in the style of 1 Cor 14:29, 32; 1 John 4:1) and proven her serious error. She, and likely her followers, would not repent.

As a result of her refusal, Christ utters a judgment oracle against her (Rev 2:22–23a). There is no warning here like there was with Pergamum.[11] The judgment is simply and devastatingly proclaimed. She threw herself at pagan gods and lay on a bed of debauchery. Christ would now throw her into illness and pain, and she would lie on a sickbed of suffering. She would taste the bitter fruits of her folly. Note the progression of intensity in the punishments—from illness to intense suffering to death. Even here there is an opportunity to escape the punishment, for Christ adds, "unless she (her followers are also implied) repent of her ways." This is always the case with divine justice in Scripture. Even the most intense punishment, like the Babylonian exile, always had as part of its purpose the opportunity to repent and get right with God. Divine judgment in this world is redemptive more than it is punitive; its purpose is to wake people up and bring them back to God.

Three groups are mentioned in 2:22–23: Jezebel, those who commit adultery with her, and her children. There is debate as to whether the second and third are one group or two. Many believe they are simply two different ways of describing her followers—they have joined her in sin and become part of her "family" in the cult. However, the second group still has a chance to get right with God ("unless they repent"), while the

11. See commentary on 2:16.

third does not, and God is about to take their lives. The second group could be church members who have been drawn into her syncretistic teaching but have not yet become full followers, while the third group has completely joined Jezebel in her unwillingness to repent. There are parallels with the children of Ahab in 2 Kings 10:7, judgment on Israel in Ezekiel 33:27, and those in Corinth who desecrated the Lord's Supper in 1 Corinthians 11:30. All this points to the extreme seriousness of doctrinal purity in churches. The lack of concern for truth in so many churches is a very dangerous thing!

Warning to the Churches (2:23b)

Jesus now calls the readers to realize that he is the one "who searches hearts and minds," undoubtedly connected to the "eyes like blazing fire" of 1:14 and especially 2:18, the address of this letter. This is reminiscent of Jeremiah 17:10: "I the Lord search the heart and examine the mind." Christ in his omniscience knows exactly how we feel and what we think. Nothing can be hidden from his scrutiny, so all the churches and the members of those churches had better examine themselves carefully and stop rationalizing their cherished sins![12]

This necessity of self-honesty before God is then anchored in an important biblical principle: God will repay all people according to their deeds. This is positive (reward) or negative (punishment), depending on the righteous or evil nature of the deeds. It is a theme in Scripture, beginning with the Old Testament (Psa 62:12; Prov 24:12; Hos 12:2) and reiterated by Jesus (Matt 16:27), Paul (Rom 14:12; 2 Cor 11:15), and Peter (1 Pet 1:17). In Revelation it is used of God repaying the righteous in 11:18, 22:12, and sinners in 18:6; 20:13. First Peter 1:17 says it well: We have a Father who does not play favorites but judges everyone entirely on the basis of what they have actually done.

12. See 1 Cor 11:28: "everyone ought to examine themselves."

Further Words for the Faithful (2:24–25)

There are faithful members at Thyatira, and Jesus now addresses them in complete contrast to the groups in 2:22–23. They may have tolerated Jezebel's cult, but they have not become followers of it. Moreover, they have never "learned Satan's so-called deep secrets," probably meaning they have not accepted or believed the teachings. Calling these teachings "deep secrets" has an ironic, sarcastic air; the cult's claim to know "the deep things of God" is shown to be in reality "the deep things of Satan." As a false prophet, Jezebel's teachings are satanic at the core, and her followers are steeped in the ideas of the evil one. In addition, she foolishly teaches her followers that they can best triumph over the idolatry and immorality of the guilds and the Roman world by immersing themselves in those practices, that is, experiencing the *depths* of paganism in order to show their mastery over it, like the heretics of 1 John 1:8–10; 3:9. Such rationalization is deadly.

The glorified Christ wants to encourage the saints by telling them he has no other burden to impose on them. This is similar to Acts 15:28–29, when after listing the four stipulations for Gentile Christians, the Jerusalem Council stated it did not wish "to burden you with anything beyond" those requirements. Most likely here it points forward, meaning Jesus demands no further requirement than "to hold on to what you have until I come." This is a further aspect of the demand that believers persevere, this time in their adherence to true doctrine and the Word of God (= "what you have"). To hold on to this means to keep a tenacious hold on truth as well as on the Christian way of life that is the outworking of truth. We are dealing here with right doctrine and right practice. Until the return of Christ, believers must both teach the truths of God and oppose those who fail to do so.

Challenge to Overcome and Call to Listen (2:26–29)

John reverses the normal order of the letters and closes this one with the call to listen, probably due to the seriousness of the situation. This church had better listen carefully or face serious judgment. The overcomer is defined here as the one "who keeps my works to the end." The only way to overcome is to maintain a firm grasp on Jesus' words (2:25) and works (2:26). Once more, orthodoxy is incomplete until it results in orthopraxy; true belief must lead to right living. "The end" could be for the rest of one's life, but in this book it must refer to the **eschaton**, the return of Christ. The church is to reproduce Jesus' works as long as this world lasts.

The risen Lord has two promises for the victor, and they are great indeed. The first is a remarkable paraphrase of Psalm 2:8–9, a passage understood messianically in the first century.[13] This is the only place in the New Testament where it is applied to the saints rather than to the Messiah, which makes it all the more powerful. The psalm begins with "I will make the nations your inheritance." That is replaced here with the idea of a new authority over the nations. This is virtually a thesis statement for the whole book, but first we need to decide whether this is authority to rule the nations or power to destroy them (the term can mean either). Both are viable, as ruling authority is seen in 20:4 ("thrones ... authority to judge ... reigned with Christ a thousand years") and destruction of the nations is mentioned in 17:14 and 19:14. With the details in Psalm 2 of "shepherd with an iron rod" and "dash to pieces," the latter is the primary meaning, but the two are interdependent and likely both intended. Jesus taught that the meek would inherit the earth (Matt 5:5) and that his followers would judge the 12 tribes (Matt 19:28). Paul adds that they would also judge the earth, even the angels (1 Cor 6:2–3).

This strong language continues in the rest of the paraphrase in Revelation 2:27. Many translations have "rule with an iron scepter," but that does not fit the imagery of the psalm. This is not a ruling scepter but a shepherd's club. A literal translation

13. See Psalms of Solomon 17:23–25.

is "shepherd them with a rod of iron." This refers to an iron-tipped club the shepherd used to kill predators that threatened the sheep. The nations, and false teachers, who endanger God's sheep will be destroyed by the Messiah and his army. In 12:5; 19:15 it is Christ the Divine Warrior who wields the iron rod, and it is startling here that the saints will wield the rod as well (17:14; 19:14). The rest of the psalm continues the violent imagery—"dash them to pieces like pottery." Shattered pottery was an ancient image of national victory over enemies. Since pottery was a major industry in Thyatira, this was a poignant image.

In 2:27c Jesus shows the two-stage process by which the victory is won. He has "received this authority from the Father" and then has passed it on to his followers. The war and the resultant cosmic victory involved this triad of participants—the Father, the Son, the saints. This chain of authority and power from Father to Son to conqueror is at the heart of John's Gospel as well as his Apocalypse.

The second promise to the victor is the gift of "the morning star" (2:28). This is another symbol in the visions with multiple proposals for its possible connotation. Some are unlikely, such as a reference to "Lucifer" in Isaiah 14:12 or to the Holy Spirit, or difficult to prove, such as the resurrection/exaltation of the saints from Daniel 12:3. The best option is probably a combination of two: First, an allusion to Numbers 24:17 (Balaam's prophecy, saying "a star will come out of Jacob"), which refers to Christ as the "morning star," preparing for its further use in Revelation 22:16; second, Venus, the morning star in the sky, was carried on the banners of many Roman legions as a symbol of Roman sovereignty. The point would be that true sovereignty and power lay with Christ and his followers, not with Rome and its armies.

In the letters to the churches of Ephesus, Pergamum, and Thyatira, the message is clear. God demands that his communities exemplify two characteristics to be a truly biblical church: a deep, abiding love in the relationships in the church (contra

Ephesus) and a deep commitment to biblical and doctrinal truth (contra Pergamum and Thyatira). Failure to exemplify either one will bring divine displeasure down upon the church. However, when both are at the heart of a church, it is already successful, whatever its size and influence, for then it pleases God deeply. A truly biblical church will be faithful to Christ both in terms of love among the brothers and sisters in the congregation (see 1 Pet 1:22) and in terms of adherence to biblically taught Christian doctrines. For God to be pleased with our churches, they must be equally strong in both areas.

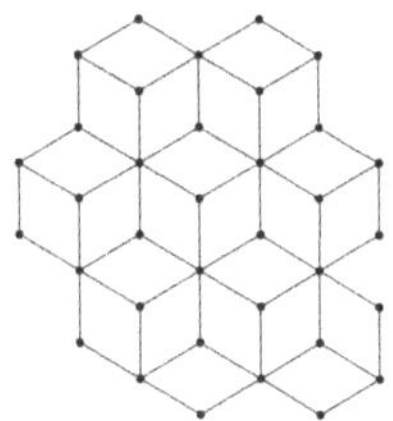

LETTERS TO THE SEVEN CHURCHES, PART 2

VINDICATION IN THE MIDST OF PERSECUTION

(2:8–11; 3:7–13)

What defines a truly successful church? Many of us follow a model in which success is defined by size and budget, but that is not the definition that Christ provides for his churches here. Among the recipients of the letters in Revelation, Smyrna and Philadelphia were the great successes in the eyes of God and Christ, yet they were the smallest of the seven and had the least influence from an earthly perspective. But God does not judge on the basis of the world's statistics. God's criteria are spiritual and Christ-centered, and in this area these two churches were resounding successes!

SMYRNA: SUFFERING IS THE PATH TO GREATNESS (2:8–11)

The City

Smyrna is the only city of the seven still in existence; it is now called Izmir, Turkey. It was a harbor city on the Aegean 35 miles north of Ephesus and was renowned for its beauty, calling itself "the first in Asia." Like many of the other cities, it too was a center of the emperor cult, erecting a temple to Tiberius in AD 26. It was also the first city to build a temple to *Dea Roma* (the goddess Rome). It also had famous temples to Zeus and Cybele connected by a majestic mall. Important for this letter, it also had a large Jewish population who was violently opposed to Christianity. Anti-Jewish sentiment following the destruction of the temple made Jews especially concerned to guard their Rome-given right to practice their religion, and they felt Christianity endangered what little freedom they enjoyed. In AD 155, Polycarp, bishop of Smyrna, was burned alive for refusing to call Caesar "Lord" in a persecution instigated by the Jews of the city.

Jesus Identifies Himself (2:8)

As before, the letter is sent via the guardian angel to remind Smyrna that all of heaven is involved in their church and its situation. The characteristics of Christ are specially chosen to address the needs of the Smyrna churches. Christ is "the first and the last," a paraphrase of God as "Alpha and Omega" in 1:8 and used of Christ also in 1:17; 22:13. Jesus, like his Father, is sovereign over history, in control of the present as well as the future. He is the Eternal One, watching over his people and vindicating them in the midst of their suffering. Smyrna may have called itself "first in Asia," but Jesus is first over all creation.

The second title is even more relevant. He "died and came to life again," a description that would be very meaningful to a church under intense persecution. Smyrna was destroyed in 600 BC and rebuilt in 290 BC to even greater magnificence, but that is earthly and temporary. As 1 Corinthians 15:20 states, Jesus was raised from the dead as the "firstfruits" for his followers, guaranteeing their own eternal life. Their persecutors may take their lives, but their vindication is certain. With the risen Lord, their eternity is absolutely secure. Smyrna can take away their present life, but their future in heaven is certain.

Situation and Strengths (2:9)

In Jesus' eyes, Smyrna and Philadelphia are the only two churches with all strengths and no weaknesses. Yet it is clear that Jesus' barometer of success is radically different than it is in today's church; many seemingly successful churches are a mile wide but only an inch deep! They can be large numerically and wealthy in terms of budget, like the church of Laodicea, but fail to help their members to grow spiritually. Note the triad of strengths here—affliction, poverty, slander. None of these would register positively; for us they would define struggle and troubles. Yet Jesus says that in spite of their poverty, they are actually rich! Rejected and mistreated by the world, these two churches turned to God and experienced the eternal riches of his grace (Eph 1:7–8). Today the Western church has forgotten the importance of the fellowship of Christ's sufferings (Phil 3:10). Suffering for Christ is a privilege, not a sorrow, a participation in Christ at a deeper level. Affliction is the overarching ingredient and refers to persecution, linked with the tribulation of the last days. We must examine our priorities: Do we prefer the temporary riches of this world or the eternal riches of God?

The other two aspects, poverty and slander, describe the particulars of this tribulation and suffering. The poverty of the church in Smyrna is the result of opposition and mistreatment. Those who did not give in to pagan pressure would lose their jobs; mobs would destroy their property and mistreat them, as happened to Paul.[1] In the Old Testament "the poor" became a semi-technical term for the righteous remnant who stayed true to God in an apostate nation (Isa 41:17; 51:21–23; 54:11). It is poignant that the poverty-stricken churches (Smyrna, Philadelphia) please God, while the wealthy churches (Sardis, Laodicea) are failures. Slander was the basic form of persecution, mentioned often in 1 Peter (2:12, 15, 23; 3:16; 4:4, 14). The term for "slander" is *blasphēmian*, used for blasphemy against God, and slandering God's people is one form of blaspheming God. Jewish persecution takes place throughout the New Testament, especially

1. As he describes in 2 Cor 11:25—three times beaten, once stoned.

in the Gospels (mainly the leaders) and Acts (all the people). Smyrna, with the high number of Jews living there, was a center of this opposition, as in the martyrdom of Polycarp noted above.

The rest of the verse sets the record straight—these persecutors are no longer "Jews," for they have turned from God by rejecting his Son.[2] Their claim to be the people of God is obviated by the fact that they are tools of Satan against God's true people, the church. This is exactly the same as John 8:31–47 when Jesus responded to his opponents' claim to be "Abraham's children" by saying, "You belong to your father, the devil" (8:44). So here the exalted Christ is saying that in reality they are "the synagogue of Satan." *Satan* is a Hebrew loanword meaning "adversary," and this fits the fact that the devil and his children, the Jewish persecutors, are the archenemies of Jesus and his people.

We must remember that John here is not speaking of all Jews but only of those persecuting followers of Christ. All too often in history this passage has been used to support anti-Semitism. We must remember that the Jewish people are still especially loved by God and should have some priority in our evangelistic efforts—"first to the Jew, then to the Gentile" (Rom 1:16).

Coming Affliction (2:10)

Jesus' pronouncement is both a prophecy and a word of encouragement: There is no need of fear at all. This is a theme throughout the Bible, as in Psalm 46:1–3, "God is our refuge and strength, an ever-present help in time of trouble. Therefore, we will not fear" (see also Matt 10:28; Heb 10:31; 13:3, 6; 1 Pet 3:14–15; 4:12–14). What they are about to suffer is imminent and unavoidable, but the exalted Christ is assuring them that he will be with them, and their ultimate vindication is certain. There is no promise

2. The name "Jews" stems from the fourth son of Jacob, Judah (*Yehudah*), meaning "praise the Lord" (Gen 29:35).

in Scripture of an easy life, only of divine comfort and blessing in the midst of struggle.

The purpose of their suffering is to test them. "Devil" is the Greek translation of the Hebrew *satan*, and their enemy continues to work overtime to ensure their suffering. There is some question as to whether it is God or Satan who is doing the testing. Likely the answer is similar to the testing/temptation of Jesus in Matthew 4 and parallels. In that instance, God was using Satan's temptation to test his Son. It is the same here; Satan is *tempting* them to apostatize, while God is *testing* their faith—the Greek word *peirazō* here means both. The trial is limited to 10 days; God is ensuring them a manageable time, in accordance with 1 Corinthians 10:13: "God is faithful; he will not let you be tempted beyond what you can bear." The "ten days" is not meant literally but alludes to the 10-day testing of Daniel in Daniel 1:12–14. It refers to a limited period in which the saints will triumph through endurance. It will be a terrible time of severe suffering, but God will get them through it. This is stated well in 1 Peter 1:6: "In all this you greatly rejoice, though now for a little while you may have had to suffer grief in all kinds of trials." Note the two points: Suffering is temporary ("a short time") and under God's control ("if necessary").

The solution is faithful endurance "even to the point of death." Faithfulness is the key to true perseverance. It means to put one's whole trust in the sovereign God and to follow him to the end in the assurance that he will vindicate his people in their suffering. We obey God even when it results in the world's animosity, trusting that he will bring victory out of seeming defeat. When that trial is "to the point of death," the need for trust is all the greater. In the Roman world, imprisonment often meant awaiting trial for a capital crime, so martyrdom was a very real possibility.

The promised reward is "the crown of life." Crowns in Revelation signify honor and authority (4:4; 14:14). Here and in 3:11 when used of believers it is *stephanos*, not the ruler's crown but the victor's crown, an athletic and military metaphor connoting one who has overcome the obstacles of the race or the battle. Here the victor's reward is eternal life. The major theme of this letter is that Christ will bring life out of death. We may have to pay for our faithful walk with Christ with our lives, but in reality that is the path to eternal life.

Call to Listen and Challenge to Overcome (2:11)

As in the other letters, Jesus closes by demanding that the reader listen carefully and respond. Moreover, every church must apply the material to its own situation. All the indications are that the Smyrna Christians did indeed respond and overcome in their struggles. Even though their present lot in life was pain and suffering, this would end soon, for they would "not be hurt at all by the second death." This idea of a death beyond the end of this life is not found in the Old Testament, though it may flow out of ideas of divine judgment in Genesis 19:24; Ezekiel 38:22; and Daniel 12:2 and did appear in Second Temple Judaism.[3] In Revelation 20:6, 14; 21:8 it refers to eternal punishment in the lake of fire. We can be confident that, while martyrdom may end this life, there will be "no more death or mourning or crying or pain" (21:4) for the faithful. We might be hurt by the first death but cannot be destroyed by it. Our destiny is life.

PHILADELPHIA: THE SEEMINGLY INSIGNIFICANT WILL INHERIT THE EARTH (3:7–13)

The City

Philadelphia lay on the main Roman postal route from Pergamum through Sardis to the east. It was strategically located for commerce and called "the gateway to the east." After coming under the influence of Pergamum, it was made the center of **Hellenistic** culture in the region. In spite of its prosperity, it had a fault line under it, and in AD 17 it suffered a devastating earthquake from which it took years to recover. Rome

3. For example, Philo, *On Rewards and Punishment*, 12:70.

removed the required payment of tribute money for five years so it could rebuild, and out of gratitude the city became closely tied to Rome. There was a strong grape and wine economy, and the patron deity was Dionysius, god of wine. There is not a lot of extrabiblical evidence for a large Jewish population, but the problems in the letter indicate that was indeed the case.

JESUS IDENTIFIES HIMSELF (3:7)

As with Smyrna, the names of Christ here are intended to encourage the Philadelphian church in the midst of severe pressure and persecution from their Jewish opponents. The risen Lord wants to reassure them that the Messiah prophesied about in the Jewish Scriptures stands with them and not with "the synagogue of Satan" (3:9). What appears in many English translations as "holy and true" is actually two titles—"the holy one, the true one." They define Christ using terms that in the Old Testament are used for Yahweh. Holiness is the core aspect of God's person; he is "wholly Other," set apart from the things of this world that are abomination to him. Jesus as "true" fits the two aspects of the term—objectively he is the genuine Messiah, and subjectively he is completely faithful to his followers. For these persecuted Christians, Christ is saying that he can truly be counted on to vindicate them in their trials and reward them for all they endure.

As the one "who holds the key of David," Jesus, not their Jewish persecutors, decides who is allowed entrance into the true Israel. In Isaiah 22:20–22 Eliakim the chief steward of Hezekiah's household has "the key to the house of David; what he opens no one can shut, and what he shuts no one can open." In Isaiah this was access to the king and his palace; in this letter it is access to the Davidic Messiah and the kingdom of God. In Matthew 16:18–19 Jesus passes on the authority of the key to his followers, and "the gates of Hades will not overcome" them. The Christians in Philadelphia had probably been excommunicated from the synagogue, but only the exalted Christ has the authority to declare who belongs to God's people. In actuality it is the Jewish persecutors who are excommunicated.

Situation and Strengths (3:8)

As with Smyrna, there is nothing but approval here. There are no weaknesses. In 3:8–9, Jesus uses "behold/look" three times to draw attention to the importance of what is being said. He wants them to know that the dire straits in which they find themselves have not come from any fault of theirs. They are right with God, and their struggle has arisen entirely from those who are not right with God, even though they think they are. The opening statement takes the form of a gift, using the same word that states the reward in the overcomer passages. Their reward for faithful perseverance is an open door. Some take this as an open door for missions and evangelism, and there is a distinct emphasis on the "eternal gospel" (14:6–7, see also 1 Cor 16:9; 2 Cor 2:12) in the book. However, in this context it is better to see this as entrance into the kingdom of God, with Jesus holding the keys that open the gate. He alone can shut the door, not these adversarial Jews.

The Philadelphians' strengths relate to their endurance. Though they were a small church facing many difficulties, they were faithful and persevered. It is possible to take the little strength Jesus refers to as a rebuke, meaning they have "little (spiritual) power." But that is hardly likely, for the entire context is positive. Rather, it means the Philadelphian church lacks authority or influence. Yet through all of their extreme difficulties they have "kept my word and have not denied my name."[4] In 2:26 and 3:3 Jesus commands a life of faithfulness to the Word, and this is modeled by these beleaguered Christians. They were a church that deeply pleased God. The Nicolaitan

4. Note that the same truth is stated positively and then negatively for emphasis.

heretics have indeed "denied the name of Christ," but now the Philadelphians have refused to do so.

REWARD (3:9–11)

Since this church has been so faithful, the section on rewards is especially lengthy. First, the risen Lord centers on their vindication. These verses begin with the same point as 2:9—their Jewish persecutors claim to be "Jews, but they are not." Instead, they are liars because they are "the synagogue of Satan." As Paul says in Romans 2:28–29, the true Jew is one "inwardly ... of the heart." God is authenticating them, not their enemies.

Then comes a wonderful promise regarding the form the vindication would take. These false "Jews" would be forced to acknowledge their error and made to "come and fall down at your feet," an allusion to Isaiah 60:14. In the Old Testament context, the Gentiles will be forced by Yahweh to pay homage to the Jews (Isa 14:2; 49:23; Ezek 36:23). Now this promise is turned on its head. The apostate Jews will pay homage to true Israel, these Christians they are persecuting. In all this, Christ's purpose is the universal recognition that these faithful sufferers are truly loved. Jesus the Divine Warrior will conquer all enemies of his people, place the conqueror's boot on their necks, and force them to acknowledge that his (and the Father's) true love is reserved for those who accept him as Messiah. In Isaiah 43:3, 4 the defeat of the nations is "because I love you." That is the point here. How wonderful to hear, from Christ (and forcefully admitted by our persecutors as well), "I have loved you!"

A justly well-known verse follows (3:10), detailing Christ's protection of believers. It is actually a third promise to the Philadelphians, after the two in 3:9. Since they have kept his command to endure—that is, they have persevered or remained vigilant and obedient to his truths—he would return the favor and "keep" or protect and preserve them in the time of peril to come. The "hour of trial" could refer to all the world's travails (the wars, earthquakes, famines), that would signify the coming end of history as the harbinger of the last days, which Jesus called "the beginning of birth pains" (Mark 13:8). It could also refer to the events of the **eschaton** themselves, the "great tribulation" of Revelation 7:14. Most likely both are intended. This is an example of inaugurated eschatology, the view that present events initiate the events of the end in an "already/not yet" framework. In the present, Jesus watching over the Philadelphia church in the midst of its distress is certainly part of it, but the clarification that this time will "come upon the whole world to test" it makes the future the primary thrust. These will be the events of the end of history.

Will the Philadelphians be protected from the hour of trial, or removed out of it? The Greek preposition *ek* can mean either "from" or "out of," and those who opt for the latter consider this verse major evidence for a pre-tribulation rapture, in which God will remove the saints "out of" this world before the end-times hour of trial occurs. However, there is a close parallel to this verse in John 17:15, "My prayer is not that you take them out of the world but that you *protect them from* (the same Greek as here) the evil one."[5] This view is more likely in this context, meaning that God will protect his people from the judgments to come. In fact, this promise has a literary function in the book that will be acted out in nearly every chapter. God will protect the saints from the judgments that he will pour out upon the nations. The saints are sealed (7:2, 3), and the judgments of the seals, trumpets, and bowls fall on the earth-dwellers and not on the believers (9:4, like the Egyptian plagues). It is important to understand that this does not mean Christians are exempt from suffering. Persecution and martyrdom are major components of this book. The saints are protected spiritually rather than physically; their suffering will be their victory. What they are exempt from are God's judgments. Believers will be protected from the wrath of God against unbelievers, but not from the wrath Satan and his minions direct at them.

5. So also 2 Pet 2:9, "rescue from trials."

The risen Lord now reminds them (3:11) that he is "coming soon." The last days have begun, and the return of Christ is imminent (see 1:1, 3). This is the fourth time his "coming" is stressed in the letters—see 2:5, 16; 3:3—but the others are warnings, while this is promise of vindication and reward. As in 3:10 there is also an inaugurated thrust: Christ is coming *now* in comfort and protection, and *then* at the end of history to end the world of evil and give the Philadelphians their eternal reward. Their responsibility is to persevere, to hold on to what they have—the same command as given to the faithful in Thyatira (2:25). The present tense here demands constant effort to maintain their walk with Christ. What they have is the "open door," namely, their citizenship in the kingdom of God.

There is still an important warning that someone may take their crown. What is happening at Pergamum and Thyatira could happen in Philadelphia. Since the "crown" is an athletic metaphor (see on 2:10), the picture is of another athlete stealing the victory in a race, leading to forfeiting the reward or being disqualified from the race. These faithful believers are winning through to victory, but they must be all the more vigilant so that they can go all the way with Christ.

Challenge to Overcome (3:12–13)

Since the Philadelphia church is already a victorious church, these are promises that become rewards. It is interesting that there are more promises in this letter than in any other. So often those small churches that are considered by some to be the weakest are in reality the strongest and have the greatest rewards. Size is not always a sign of success!

Here there is a new security and a new status for this supersize (spiritually) church. The new security is seen in Christ's building project—the verb "will make" is often used of creation in the New Testament, so they will be part of the new creation in heaven (see Mark 10:6; Acts 4:24; Heb 1:2). As "a pillar in the temple of my God" they will have permanence and security. The background is found in 1 Kings 7:21 and 2 Chronicles 3:15–17, where the two pillars Solomon placed in the temple are named *Jachin* ("he establishes") and *Boaz* ("in him is strength"). This could also be the "king's pillar" in Solomon's temple (2 Kgs 11:14, 23:3), which would emphasize the royalty of God's people. It was a common **Hellenistic** practice to write the names of important people on pillars, so these Christians have not only stability but status. The temple referred to here is undoubtedly the temple in heaven. Theirs is a heavenly reward and an eternal dwelling place. They will "never again leave it," which literally means that they will never again go outside it. Jesus promises they will be absolutely secure in the city of God; nothing will ever dislodge them. Their current lives may be characterized by uncertainty and distress, but that will cease forever. That is a promise we all need!

Not only will they have a permanent home but also a new name written on them. This is a threefold name: First it is "the name of my God," fitting the adoption imagery of Romans 8:15 (by the Spirit we cry "Abba Father!") and signifying that we partake of his essence as his children. There is also probably an echo of Isaiah 62:2, the "new name bestowed" by Yahweh on faithful Israel.

The second name is "the city of my God, the new Jerusalem." This is likely an allusion to Ezekiel 48:35, which comes at the end of Ezekiel's vision of the **eschatological** temple in Ezekiel 40–48 and is the closing verse of the book. There the name of the city is said to be "The Lord is there," meaning the Lord will dwell there permanently. The name of the new Jerusalem on the saints recalls citizenship records in the ancient world. As in Philippians 3:20, the believers are citizens of heaven. Here the idea of the new Jerusalem stresses the consummation of this, for now they are not just citizens in a spiritual sense while they reside on earth but citizens in a final sense, as they will reside in heaven for eternity. There is a close connection with Galatians 4:26 ("the Jerusalem that is above") and Hebrews 12:22 ("the heavenly Jerusalem"), and the idea comes to full expression in Revelation 21:2–4 where the holy city, the new Jerusalem, descends and initiates the new heavens and new earth, where God himself dwells with his people and is their God.

Third, the exalted Christ will write on them "my new name." There is an A-B-A pattern in the three, as the names of God and of Christ frame that of the heavenly city. In 7:3 and 14:1, the name of the Father and of the Lamb are placed on the forehead of the believers, sealing them as belonging to the Triune God. In Philippians 2:9 the exalted Christ is given "the name that is above every name," and in Revelation 19:12 the returning Lord has "a name written on him that no one knows but he himself." That name cannot be Yahweh, for both John and Revelation proclaim that truth. Most likely this is a name hidden until the Lord returns and eternity begins. The amazing thing is that we, the saints, will share that name. We will have a new name (2:17) and have his new name written on us (here).

These two churches are important reminders to us that God prefers faithful churches over big and seemingly successful ones. Many of us may feel insignificant, and our churches may seem small and unimportant. But when we remain centered on Christ and live for him, God greatly honors both us and our churches. We must not allow the world to determine the criteria for success. God will lift us up and open the doors of heaven to us when we endure hardship for him and remain faithful. This is what really matters.

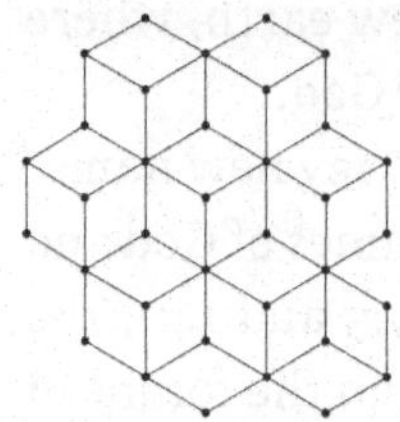

LETTERS TO THE SEVEN CHURCHES, PART 3

THE DANGER OF THE WORLDLY CHURCH

(3:1–6, 14–22)

The next two churches were polar opposites of the previous two. Whereas the churches of Smyrna and Philadelphia could do nothing wrong, the churches of Sardis and Laodicea could do nothing right. In these churches there are no strengths, only weaknesses, and the basic problem illustrates the warning that Paul gives in 1 Timothy 6:9–10, 17: "Those who want to get rich fall into temptation and a trap and into many foolish and harmful desires that plunge people into ruin and destruction. For the love of money is a root of all kinds of evil. … Command those who are rich in this present world not to be arrogant nor to put their hope in wealth." This challenge fits churches as well as individuals, and a materialistic and secular approach to church life was the basic problem in these two churches. They were culture-bound rather than countercultural.

SARDIS: RESIST COMPROMISE (3:1–6)

The City

Sardis was 30 to 40 miles southeast of Thyatira. While it was one of the most glorious of the cities in Asia, by the time Revelation was written, much of its splendor lay in the past. It had been the wealthy capital of the Lydian kingdom and had an acropolis that was also a fortress. The fortress lay on top of a 1,500-foot cliff with a steep approach on the south side that rendered it almost impregnable to attack. Whenever the city was attacked, the populace would go up to the acropolis and wait for the opposing army to tire and leave. Sardis was a military power as a city-state that was feared by all and became even wealthier due to trade and commerce.

One of the famous warrior-kings of Lydia was Croesus, who traveled east to fight against Cyrus of Persia in 546 BC and then returned home for the winter. Cyrus followed him and the people of the city went up to the fortress, prepared for a siege. However, one of Cyrus' troops climbed up a crevice on the "unscalable" cliff at a point where the watchmen were missing and opened the gates to the fortress. Sardis fell 14 days later. For the next 300 years the city had its ups and downs, but in 214 BC Antiochus III (father of Antiochus IV, who precipitated the Jewish revolt of the Maccabees) invaded, and once more the cliff was scaled, the gates were opened, and the city was sacked. This time Sardis never really recovered. Its commercial prosperity continued, but for the most part it lived in the past.

Like Philadelphia, the earthquake of AD 17 destroyed the city, and it rebuilt through the aid of Augustus Caesar. Artemis was the patron goddess of the city, and religious life centered on nature worship, focusing on the fertility cycle and achieving life after death. There was a large wealthy Jewish population, many of whom attained Roman citizenship. In fact, there is evidence that Jewish and **Hellenistic** cultures amalgamated to an extent, and both Jewish and Christian communities adapted to the Roman way of life. This helps to explain the situation addressed in this letter.

Jesus Identifies Himself (3:1a)

The address continues the rhetorical emphasis on the **eschatological** importance of this message, reminding the believers in Sardis that all of heaven is involved in the life of their church.

Also, the characteristics of Christ as the messenger are chosen as a challenge to the Sardis church regarding its situation and needs. There are two aspects of the exalted Jesus emphasized here. First, he "holds the seven spirits of God," which, as mentioned on 1:4, refers to the sevenfold (or perfect) Holy Spirit. Jesus is in control of the Spirit (the Father controls the Son, the Son controls the Spirit) and has sent the Spirit, seen here as "the Spirit of Christ" (see Rom 8:9; Phil 1:19), to this church. As we will see, this church is nearly dead and can only be revived if the Spirit takes over and they heed what the Spirit tells them. In fact, this idea frames the letter, as the challenge is repeated at the end (3:6).

The second emphasis of the address is that Christ also holds "the seven stars," which as 1:20 tells us is "the angels of the seven churches." Through the guardian angels the Lord is sovereign over each church. Note that Jesus controls and has sent both the Spirit and a guardian angel to every church, including modern-day churches. The question is whether the Sardis church will listen and follow the risen Lord's instructions. That will determine whether it has a future. So far it has refused to do so, and as a result it is in danger of losing its place in God's community. If Jesus is in control, the church will answer to him and to him alone. There must be an end to listening to the world and following its terrible path. We must not, as in 1 Peter 4:4, "join them in their reckless, wild living."

So-called Strength (3:1b)

The next section begins like the letters to Ephesus or Thyatira: "I know your deeds." Here it is ironic, for their "strength" is no strength at all. There is no need for a section on weaknesses ("I have this against you"), for their strength *is* their weakness! The deeds of the Sardis church are detailed in a strange way: "you have a reputation," literally, a "name." They claim the Christian name "Life," but actually retain the pagan name "Death." Their past deeds and wealth have given them a good reputation for being alive for Christ, but in reality their present deeds prove they are spiritually dead, part of the world. The people of Sardis were obsessed with the antithesis between life and death, so this was a powerful metaphor for their true spiritual state.

Solution (3:2–3)

There are five commands in this section, all focusing on the need for spiritual vigilance. The rhetorical effect is strong—the church resembles the city. Its former greatness has virtually disappeared because its people were not watchful and allowed their enemies to open the gates. Twice before, the city was destroyed because the watchmen were not on the walls and invaders were able to enter its gates. The church has committed the same egregious error and so is commanded to "wake up," to start being vigilant. They have fallen asleep spiritually and are allowing sin to invade their church. We also see this in Mark 13:35, 37; and Matthew 24:42, 25:13, where it refers to a watchfulness and readiness for the Lord's return.

Connected to this vigilance, the Sardis church must strengthen what little that remains and get into survival mode. This church is dead with only a small amount showing any sign of life. They have been letting it all die, and their only hope is to begin to shore up that small amount, for it too is about to die. In fact, the church has been on the verge of death for some time. The small minority who can turn things around will be addressed in 3:4; they are called to be missionaries to the rest of the church.

The next phrase is best translated literally, "I have not found any of your works to be complete." There is judicial imagery in this. The church has been investigated by the risen Lord and found wanting. Their deeds do not meet God's standards, and the divine Judge has rendered them guilty. Other churches look at their wealth and think of them as healthy and successful, but they are under God's indictment for their inadequacies. The great temple of Artemis in Sardis was unfinished, and

Christ is saying this also describes their church—unfinished and useless.

The three other commands in 3:3 flow out of this sense of inadequacy—remember, hold fast, repent. Their current status is incomplete and almost dead, so drastic action is called for in the short time left. The command to remember is the same as given to the Ephesian church in 2:5, and like them they at one time were walking with the Lord but have fallen away. It is insufficient just to bring to mind the truths they have been taught; they must put them into practice in their church. So when they remember they must keep or hold fast to these truths, which includes obedience. Finally, there is need to repent, which means not just sorrow for sin but also turning their lives around and beginning a life of faithfulness to God contra the world.

The consequences for failing to do this are severe. In the same way that enemy combatants in the past stole over the walls of their city and destroyed it, a thief would enter and destroy their church. Jesus used this image in an apocalyptic parable to warn of a lack of vigilance (Matt 24:43, "if the owner of the house had known at what time of night the thief was coming, he would have kept watch"), and the idea of Christ returning unawares like a thief became a metaphor for readiness in light of the approaching end (see 1 Thess 5:2–4; 2 Pet 3:10; Rev 16:15). The danger is stated in Jesus' added comment, "You will not know at what time I will come to you." Without a renewed vigilance they can never be ready, for the coming will be sudden and unexpected like a thief, and the consequences will be terrible.

As in other letters, there is both a present and future sense to judgment. As at Ephesus in 2:5, there will be a present arrival of Christ, and this may well be the primary meaning here. Yet the final coming at the **eschaton** also has to be part of its meaning. The parables of Matthew 24:42–25:30—the thief, the wicked servant, the ten virgins, the talents—all center on the need for readiness in light of the unexpected return of Christ. The message is that when he returns, Christ will hold his people accountable for the way they are living their lives. Judgment, now and at the end of history, will be the result.

Promise and Challenge to Overcome (3:4–6)

The exalted Christ begins this section with a word of encouragement to the righteous remnant who are the only hope for this terminally ill church. There were only a few who had not "soiled their clothes," a metaphor that builds on one of the major trades at Sardis, the wool industry. In a religious context this pictures a defiled life. The quasi-Christians of Sardis have become unclean, like soiled clothes, by being assimilated into the Roman worldview and becoming Christopagan—part Christian, part pagan. Their only hope lay in these few who could intervene and lift them out of the quicksand into which they had fallen.

Turning to a positive image of garments, the few remaining faithful are told that they will walk with him in white, a powerful word picture of purity and victory, which is the meaning of "white" in the book. There are two ideas in this image: first, the white linen worn by angels and signifying glory and purity; second, the pure white toga worn at a Roman triumph and signifying victory (2 Cor 2:14; Col 2:15). This is an incredible promise for a city that was suffering the effect of military defeat and a church experiencing spiritual defeat. How wonderful to picture oneself walking behind Christ in the ultimate triumphal procession! The reason these few can walk in Christ's victory procession is that they are worthy. They have remained pure; their works are complete in a church increasingly turning apostate. God and the Lamb are worthy of worship in 4:11; 5:9, 12, and the saints here are worthy of reward.

The **eschatological** gift for the overcomer (3:5) flows right out of the commendation of 3:4. In verse 4 it was the few faithful in Sardis. In verse 5, this is then extended to all who will repent and join them in a life of spiritual victory. As victorious conquerors, they will be part of Christ's triumphal procession at the **eschaton**, wearing the white garments of verse 4. As we will see in 17:14; 19:14, the believers will join the angels as part of the army of the Lord of hosts, a major Old Testament title meaning "Lord of heaven's armies," and participate in the final victory over the forces of evil at Armageddon. Still, the primary image here is life in heaven in the glorified body.

Then, as forgiven and kept secure in Christ, their "name will never be erased from the book of life." After the golden calf incident, Moses begs God to forgive Israel, stating he is willing for God to "blot me out of the book you have written," namely the register of the citizens of Israel (Exod 32:32–33; compare Psa 9:5; Isa 4:3). In Jewish tradition this became a heavenly tablet with the names of the righteous (Psa 69:28; Dan 12:1), and such would also contain lists of civic deeds and rewards. The **Hellenistic** world had similar lists, and as the former capital of the Lydian and Seleucid empires, Sardis had been a repository of such records. In both Jewish and **Hellenistic** worlds the erasure of a name would mean censure and exclusion from the community. This is another judicial metaphor: God sits on his judgment seat and has the authority over serious wrongdoers to "blot out" their names from the citizenship records of heaven. In the New Testament, to have names written in the book of life means to be citizens of heaven and children of God (Luke 10:20; Phil 4:3; Heb 12:23; Rev 13:8; 17:8; 21:27). The book of life contains the names and deeds of those who belong to God (Rev 20:12), and only those who are faithful will stay in it. To be erased or "blotted out" is a metaphor for removal and destruction, and is connected with capital punishment in Deuteronomy 29:20.

Finally, the faithful are told that the glorified Christ will "acknowledge that name before my Father and his angels." This alludes to the saying of Jesus in Matthew 10:32, "Whoever acknowledges me before others I will also acknowledge before my Father in heaven." The addition of the angels here continues the judicial imagery, with the angels part of the heavenly council. Christ and the angels stand with the Father as Judge and jury, pronouncing the word of acceptance or rejection. This is the positive side of not being erased from the book of life. The names of the faithful will remain in the heavenly records, and they will be acknowledged before the Father. Those who remain true to Christ have a new identity, a new citizenship, and a new future—eternal life in heaven.

As in 3:6 and the other letters, the risen Lord concludes with the call to listen carefully to the Spirit-led message of this letter. The Spirit not only inspires the words of this letter but also convicts the readers about the letter's demands. Every church must carefully ascertain what aspects apply to their situation and then respond accordingly. Too many churches have, like Sardis, embraced the world's definition of success and ignored the fact that God is displeased with their materialism and worldly practices. The faithful within them must wake these churches up to their true dangerous situation and bring them to repentance while there is still time.

LAODICEA: AN AFFLUENT CHURCH CAN BE DANGEROUS (3:14–22)

THE CITY

The same major Roman road that went south from Pergamum through Philadelphia passed through Laodicea 45 miles later. It was also 100 miles east of Ephesus, near the eastern border of the Roman province of Asia. It was in perfect position to become a wealthy city due to the convergence of trade routes from the east. Sitting on a plateau in the Lycus Valley, it was also politically important as the primary member of a tri-city confederation with Hierapolis and Colossae. Always loyal to Rome, it received many favors and became known for its trade and banking. Its primary problems were twofold—it was earthquake prone, like Philadelphia and Sardis, and it had no water supply, having to pipe it in from several miles away. The city's religion was syncretistic, combining local and Roman gods, and it had a large Jewish population that accommodated itself to **Hellenistic** ways.

JESUS IDENTIFIES HIMSELF (3:14)

Once more the guardian angel is asked to intercede with the church and remind them that they as God's community are a heavenly phenomenon and must answer to heaven for the way they are conducting themselves. In the present circumstances, they are placing their guilt on the angel God has placed over them! The names of Christ here are all the more solemn and important in this light. First, he is the "Amen," an echo of Isaiah 65:16, which twice has "the one true God"—in the Hebrew, "the God of amen"—meaning the faithful God who confirms or verifies what is valid and true. Jesus is the one who authenticates divine truths. He has binding authority, and he alone—in contrast to the Laodiceans—can be trusted to keep his word.

This first title is then defined further in the second, which functions to clarify Jesus as the Amen by stating he is "the faithful and true witness." Every word is an important theme in Revelation. In 1:5, Jesus as faithful witness provides the model for the conduct of the saints in their earthly witness to the world, as exemplified by Antipas in 2:13. In this book, both faithfulness (2:10) and witness (11:3, 17:6) are connected with suffering and martyrdom as the means by which the saints overcome the world. Laodicea was failing in this very area of providing a countercultural witness for Christ.

The third title, "ruler of God's creation," is linked with the Amen in Isaiah, where "the one true God" is followed in the next verse by "I will create new heavens and a new earth" (Isa 65:16–17). God as creator is proof positive that he is indeed the Amen, the one true God. Also, in the letter written to Laodicea's sister church in Colossae, Jesus is described as "the firstborn over all creation. For in him all things were created" (Col 1:15–16). This is an example of the theme of Jesus as God found throughout the book. As in John 1:3 and Hebrews 1:2, Jesus and God together created the world. "Ruler" (Greek *archē*) here indicates not only preeminence but also "source, origin." Jesus is the beginning and source of God's creation. The point

all their worldly wealth was nothing but fool's gold. "Gold refined in the fire" is similar to 1 Peter 1:7, in which the saints who have passed through fiery trials have become pure gold. Christ is then referring to the purifying effects of suffering and a life lived entirely for God. This is true wealth and will never perish like worldly riches do.

Second, the city was famous for its clothing industry and had developed a glossy black wool that was prized throughout the Roman world. The principle here is that, contrary to popular wisdom, clothes do not make the person. Looking good is not the same as being good. You can wear Armani suits and Dior dresses and yet be "shamefully naked" to God. The imagery here is that of exposure, disgrace, and judgment. When God exposes a person's shame in Scripture, judgment always results (Isa 20:1–4; Ezek 16:3; 23:10). White garments, on the other hand, indicate honor, symbolizing righteousness (Rev 3:4–5; 6:11), being washed in the blood of the Lamb (7:13–14), and eternal glory (4:4; 19:14).

Third, Laodicea was famed for its medical center and the eye salve it had developed, but the Christians were blind spiritually. Jesus is telling them that earthly accomplishments are meaningless if they are not right with God. This parallels John 9, which contrasts the man born blind, who was given first physical sight and then spiritual insight, with the Pharisees, who claimed spiritual sight but were blind to the things of God. The key verse is John 9:39: "For judgment I have come into this world, so that the blind will see and those who see will become blind." The Laodiceans needed to be anointed with God's eye salve so they could see their true spiritual condition, repent, and receive healing from Christ.

Christ's Loving Discipline (3:19–20)

The risen Lord begins the next section of the letter with a beautiful declaration: "Those whom I love I rebuke and discipline." This is an important principle in Scripture. We are used to thinking of the wrath of God as the basis of judgment, yet God's love is shown to the spiritually defeated as well as to the victorious. All passages on judgment against God's people, from the 40 years in the wilderness to the exile to discipline in the New Testament, are redemptive in purpose and meant to wake God's people up spiritually and bring them to repentance. For the righteous God's discipline is a purifying process; for the weak it is a wake-up call. Rebuke and discipline build on each other. The first connotes a reproof that points out a problem and convinces the person to act on it. The second refers to a punishment that corrects the error and trains the person in the right way to live for God.

There can be only one proper response for the Laodiceans: to repent and change their conduct. The two verbs, "be zealous (or earnest) and repent," indicate a zeal to get right with God, the sorrow for sin that naturally follows, and a desire to live rightly for God from that time on. The Laodiceans had been blind to their complacent spirituality, immersed in their affluent lifestyle rather than concerned for the things of God. They needed to continue in their enthusiasm but channel it away from the things of this world and toward serving God.

The following verse, 3:20, is one of the most famous passages in Scripture, but it is often misunderstood as referring to evangelism when it really deals with church revival. The picture of Christ at the door is one of a visitor knocking at the door of a house, seeking admittance. Jesus has apparently been standing outside for a while, knocking and hoping the church will open their hearts and invite him deeply into their lives. Perhaps this reflects Song of Songs 5:2, "Listen, my beloved is knocking: 'Open to me … my darling." The loving compassion and deep longing is evident. The challenge comes in the demand for personal response, to hear Jesus' voice, open the door, and invite him in.

The result of letting Jesus in is table fellowship. He comes in to the repentant church's life and dines with them and they with him. Table fellowship was an important part of ancient life, building on the principle, "to share a meal is to share a life." All through the Gospels and Acts, the spiritual life of Jesus and his followers centered on fellowship around the table. The promise here is acceptance, sharing, and blessing, a deep fellowship centered on reconciliation and a new life with God. This is a theological point we would do well to reinstate into our church and family life. The family table should once again be a sacred moment in all our lives. In our overly busy lives, the family often stops communicating, and family meals almost disappear as each one feeds his or her face without sharing with each other. In New Testament times, the meal was family time, and God was considered present at the meal. We would do well to return to this practice and rediscover quality time together.

Challenge to Overcome and Call to Listen (3:21–22)

As in the other letters, Christ challenges the Laodiceans to be a victor over the powers of evil, both the cosmic powers and the earthly powers who serve them, and promises an **eschatological** gift that closely matches the situation and background of the letter. Here the gift arises out of the promise inherent in 3:20—that the faithful will share the glory of Christ. Specifically, the overcomer will "sit with me on my throne," in essence reigning with Christ for eternity.

This motif of reigning with Christ is introduced in the New Testament in Matthew 19:28: "When the Son of Man sits on his glorious throne, you who have followed me will also sit on twelve thrones, judging the twelve tribes of Israel." This authority is extended in 1 Corinthians 6:2–3, "Do you not know that the Lord's people will judge the world? ... Do you not know that we will judge angels?" As we will see in Revelation 7:14, 19:14, the saints at the second coming will join the angels as the hosts of heaven and participate in the heavenly council. In this way, Christ's followers will participate in the final judgment of both the unsaved and the fallen angels. There are, then, three stages in this process in the Bible:

1. Yahweh sits on the throne and judges in majesty;
2. Jesus shares the throne and authority of his Father;

3. the victorious saints also share in the throne of glory and judgment.

All three stages are evident in Revelation. God is on his throne in chapter 4, Christ is on the throne with God in chapter 5, and the saints reign with Christ. This is made clear beginning in 2:26–27, as the faithful conquerors are promised "authority over the nations" to "dash them to pieces like pottery." This will occur after the second coming when the believers join the angels as the armies of heaven (17:14; 19:14) and with Christ crush the army of the beast. Then they will reign with Christ first during the millennial reign (20:4) and then for eternity (22:5). These three stages of reigning are all found in this verse, with the first two inherent in "just as I was victorious and sat down with my father on his throne." When we share in Christ's victory, we share in his authority and reign.

The letters to Sardis and Laodicea provide a serious warning against becoming a secular culture-bound church. It is critical for us to realize, as is clear from 3:22, that the Spirit is using this material to address each and every one of our churches with the danger of this kind of spiritual drift. The question we all need to ask ourselves is, "Do we make Jesus sick to his stomach?" Affluence has made so many of us lukewarm; we have become self-satisfied with our trappings of "success" (big churches, huge budgets) and indifferent to the deeper things of Christ. Popular speakers and writers have shown the ease with which Christian leaders can get inordinately wealthy. For many affluent Christians, Christ and church have become virtual line items on a portfolio. When this happens, we make Christ sick, and he will vomit us out of his mouth! Yet Christ is knocking at the door of our hearts and of our churches. We must repent, open the door, and allow him in to the center of our individual lives and our life together.

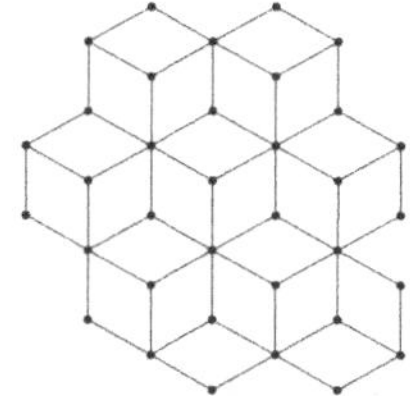

THE THRONE ROOM VISION, PART 1

THE MAJESTY OF GOD

(4:1–11)

The throne room vision of chapters 4 and 5 forms the first of two turning points in the book, the other being the cosmic conflict scene of chapters 12–14. These chapters function as both the concluding scene of the introduction (chs. 1–3) and the introductory scene of the three judgment sets of seven (chs. 6–16). The unifying theme is the throne of God and the Lamb, and the purpose is to establish once and for all the absolute glory and majesty of the Godhead in opposition to earthly powers such as Caesar and Rome.

At the outset John is commanded to "come up" and experience the throne room vision. As readers, we are transported from earthly events in chapters 1–3 to heavenly events, and worship predominates. The worshipers in this vision progress from the living creatures (4:8) to the elders (4:10–11) to "every creature" (5:13), ending with the greatest choir ever assembled. The imagery combines Ezekiel 1 with Daniel 1, the two greatest Old Testament passages on the majesty of God. This vision celebrates creation and redemption, the victory of God and the Lamb over the powers of evil.

JOHN IS CALLED TO ASCEND TO HEAVEN (4:1)

After the letters to the seven churches, John receives a new vision. Previously he had seen Christ walking among the lampstands, the churches (1:12–13), and now he sees the heavenly throne room. His first look shows him "a door standing open in heaven." In Jewish writings, the opening of heaven signified access to God (Psa 78:23; 1 Enoch 14:10–11). In the New Testament, the idea of "heaven opened" indicates that the last days have begun (Acts 7:56, 10:11; 2 Cor 12:1–4). The heavens split apart at Jesus' baptism (Matt 3:16), and in John 1:51 Jesus says the heavens remain open to him. This means that the kingdom has arrived, and the final events are initiated in Jesus' ministry.

As John arrives at the open door, he hears "a voice like a trumpet," which as in 1:10 signifies that the last days are here and that the visitation of God has arrived. An apocalyptic announcement is about to take place. John is called to ascend to heaven, a journey that in apocalyptic literature characteristically leads to a tour of heaven.[1] The "I will give you" of the seven letters is replaced by "I will show you," leading to the revelation or unveiling of divine reality. The content of the ensuing chapters is described as "what must take place after this." This is the same language as in 1:1, 19, with emphasis on the *must* of divine necessity. The events in the central section of the book, chapters 6–16, are dictated by God's sovereign will. He is the "Alpha and Omega" (1:8; 21:6; 22:13), the absolute sovereign over history.

GOD IS ON HIS THRONE (4:2–3)

There is no pause or transition. John is at once transported "in the Spirit," which as in 1:10 points to a Holy Spirit-inspired visionary experience through which God reveals divine mysteries. The emphasis is on the heavenly nature of the scene. In chapter 1 John remained on Patmos for the first vision, but

---

1. See 1 Enoch 1–36; 2 Baruch 22.

now he is observing a vast throne room in heaven. The word "throne" is a major emphasis in the book, and contrasts the throne of God with the throne of Caesar, highlighted here in chapter 4, and the throne of Satan (12:5). It is a symbol for the majesty and authority of the king.

The background to the throne room here is Isaiah 6:1–4 and Ezekiel 1:26–28. This scene is the culmination of all throne room scenes in the Bible and is intended to produce a feeling of awe in the hearer. It is interesting that John does not name God but simply says that someone is sitting on the throne. The reader is to supply that information. God is often described as "sitting on the throne" in Revelation to stress that he is the supreme potentate (Rev 4:3, 9, 10; 5;1, 7, 13; 6:16; 7:10, 15; 19:4; 20:11; 21:5). In the ancient world, the royal throne served as the Bema or judgment seat, so this also stresses his sitting in final judgment on the world.

John describes the majesty and splendor of God via the brilliant colors of three precious jewels that anticipate the more complete list in Revelation 21:18–21. It is important to realize that each jewel is not meant to symbolize a separate spiritual reality, but rather it is the cumulative effect, meant to depict God's glorious majesty and splendor. The first jewel, the jasper, is the primary jewel in 21:11, 18. It refers to an opaque stone that could be red, green, or blue, and could have been an opal or even a diamond. The second, a carnelian or ruby, was a fiery red stone, perhaps the basis for the name "Sardis." The third was "a rainbow that shone like an emerald," a beautiful green in color. It apparently is a halo of radiant light surrounding the throne, yet also adds the idea of God's covenant with Noah in Genesis 9:13–17, in which God promised he would never again destroy the earth with water. God's glory centers on his deep, abiding love for his creation and his people. The God who dwells "in unapproachable light" (1 Tim 6:16) will redeem his creation and his people.

TWENTY-FOUR ELDERS ARE GATHERED AROUND THE THRONE (4:4)

In one sense, chapters 4 and 5 are built around a series of concentric circles of heavenly officials surrounding God's throne. The rainbow is "around" the throne, then the four living creatures, then the 24 elders surround the throne in 4:4, and finally the entire heavenly host encircle the throne in 5:11. This is the imperial court of God, rendering all human royalty paltry in comparison. The point for John's original audience is that God and not Caesar is worthy of worship.

There is debate over the identity of these elders. The key is their twofold description: "dressed in white," with "crowns of gold on their heads." Many believe these are human beings, probably the 12 tribes plus the 12 apostles (= the whole community of saints), because angels are not called elders and do not wear white or gold crowns in Revelation. Others believe these are indeed angelic figures, for in Psalm 89:27; 1 Kings 22:19, and Job 15:8, God sits in a council of angels. Angels are "thrones ... authorities" in Colossians 1:16 and wear white in Matthew 28:3 and John 20:12. The gold crowns would then refer to their royal function under God. In short, the 24 elders/angels form the council of heaven.

Moreover, there are no human figures in this throne room scene, and throughout the book the elders with the living creatures are the worship band of heaven. In 5:8 the elders hold golden bowls with the prayers of the saints; in 7:13–14 they are angelic interpreters explaining the symbols; in 14:3 the 144,000 sing a "new song" before the living creatures and elders. The most likely option is that these are heavenly beings who reign with God and are part of the heavenly retinue standing before his throne. Wearing white means they share the purity and holiness of God, and the gold crowns indicate they play a ruling function in heaven.

The number 24 would allude, then, to the 24 orders of the priesthood in 1 Chronicles 24:4–5 and signifies their priestly ministry in heaven. They are the priests of heaven: leaders of heavenly worship (4:10–11; 5:8), heavenly mediators and interpreters (7:13–14), and those who present the prayers of the saints to God (8:3–4). They serve God "day and night" (4:8) in heaven. The elders are a ruling class of heavenly beings who encircle the throne and lead heavenly praise, thus exhibiting a priestly role.

CELESTIAL PHENOMENA ISSUE FROM THE THRONE (4:5–6A)

Several Old Testament metaphors are combined in these verses. The imagery moves from Sinai to the temple to creation in order to demonstrate more deeply the majesty and mercy of God. First, the lightning and thunder come "out of" (Greek *ek*) the throne itself, recalling the work of God at Sinai (Exod 19:16). In 4:3 we were reminded of the Noahic covenant, here the Mosaic covenant. The sovereign God who created and sustains the world is a covenant God who has made us his own. The manifestation of God in the power of the storm, seen also in 6:12–14; 8:5; 11:19; 16:18–21, was also inherent in the chariot vision of Ezekiel 1:13. This highlights the frightening awesomeness of God. It is this awesome God who is coming to judge and to rule over his creation.

The second part of the scene shifts from the midst of the throne to a position "in front of" it. The seven blazing lamps also stem from Ezekiel 1:13 and signify the powerful presence of God. These are not just lamps but the same "torches" that in Revelation 8:10 are linked with the "great star" that fell from heaven. They often depict the blazing power of a falling star. The storm and the blazing torches are connected in Revelation not just with God's majesty but with the God of judgment and prepare for the outpouring of God's wrath later in the book. The torches are defined as the "seven spirits of God," which as before signify the sevenfold (perfect) Holy Spirit who joins the Godhead as the means by which God oversees and judges his world.

Third, the floor of the throne room is depicted as "like a sea of glass," an allusion to the expanse or firmament that separated the waters in Genesis 1:7 and likely also the bronze sea in Solomon's temple (1 Kgs 7:23–26, also Ezek 1:22). This was a metal basin 15 feet long that held 12,000 gallons of water for the ritual washings of the priests. The crystal-clear glass floor resembles a sea and symbolizes the transcendence and holiness of God. Its transparent nature makes it a repository for the glory of God to radiate through every part of his throne room. Here worship and judgment are intertwined as God's people celebrate his holiness.

FOUR LIVING CREATURES WORSHIP AROUND THE THRONE (4:6B–8)

We now turn back from the appearance of the throne room to its inhabitants. The living creatures form the inner circle ("in the midst of the throne and around" it), and the elders of 4:4 the outer circle. It is best to picture them right next to the throne, surrounding it with their presence. The cherubim of Ezekiel 1, 10 and the seraphim of Isaiah 6 provide the background for these figures (see Ezek 1:5, 12–13; 10:20). Their function in Revelation parallels their use in the Old Testament: They stand guard over the tree of life (Gen 3:24), stand at each end of the ark with their wings outstretched over it (Ezek 25:18–20 = Rev 5:6, 7:11), lead the worship of Yahweh (Isa 6:3 = Rev 4:6–9; 5:8–9), and bear God's chariot through the heavens (Ezek 1:19–21). In short, they lead worship with the elders and participate in divine justice. It seems clear that they are the leaders of the heavenly court and represent the highest order of celestial beings.

Three characteristics are highlighted. First, they are identified with the lion, the ox, the man, and the eagle, building on Ezekiel, where these four also describe the appearance of the living beings (see Ezek 1:5–6, 10–11). One of the most popular understandings of the significance of these animals comes from the church fathers, who linked them with the four Gospels. Augustine, for example, saw Matthew as the lion, Luke as the ox, Mark as the man, and John as the eagle. However, there was no unanimity even among the fathers, and opinions vary considerably. This approach is too fanciful to be at all likely. Others interpret them astrologically as the four corners of the zodiac or Babylonian images of royalty as winged sphinxes. Again, there is too little evidence for such a view. The most viable option is to see this here and in Ezekiel as representing the whole of animate creation, centering on the noblest, strongest, wisest, and swiftest creatures God has made. These creatures sum up all of God's creation, which joins the angelic beings in worshiping God.

The second symbol comes in two parts: the "eyes in front and behind" and "the eyes all around and within." These are drawn from Ezekiel 1:18, where the rims of the wheels of the throne-chariot are "full of eyes all around," depicting the unceasing vigilance of God. The combined picture is of the living creatures virtually covered with eyes. In Ezekiel 10:12, the beings had eyes on "their backs, hands, and wings." All this indicates that nothing can be hidden from God. He sees all and is sovereign over every aspect of the created order.

Third, there are "six wings," drawn from Isaiah 6:2, where two covered the faces of the seraphim, two their feet, and two were used for flying. If the eyes represent vigilance, the wings represent speed. These creatures respond to God's will and carry out his commands with a swiftness and surety that makes them an unstoppable force.

CELESTIAL BEINGS WORSHIP GOD (4:8B–11)

We now come to the first of many worship scenes in the book, which are strategically placed to draw attention to God's sovereignty and the reaction of praise from both heavenly and earthly beings.[2] Praise is the valid response to the God who delivers and vindicates his people and judges evildoers. The worship of chapters 4–5 in particular highlights the unity of Father and Son. The two hymns in chapter 4 worship God, the first two in

2. See "Worship" under "Theology of the Book" in the introduction.

chapter 5 worship the Lamb, and the fifth hymn in 5:13 is sung to the two on the throne together.

The Creatures' Hymn of Praise (4:8b)

The emphasis in 4:8b–11 is on the unceasing worship of God. The Greek of 4:8b literally tells us that the four living creatures "have no rest day and night," emphasizing on their continuous worship. The idea of unending praise was common in Jewish literature (1 Enoch 39:12; 2 Baruch 51:11), as the eternal God is extolled for his majesty and power over creation. In the first hymn, the four living beings celebrate (in order) God's holiness, omnipotence, and eternality. The high point of worship in all of Scripture is the thrice-repeated "Holy, holy, holy" (called the "Trisagion"), found first in the throne room scene in Isaiah 6:3. The repetition brings out the emphatic nature of the worship—God is ultimate holiness, exceedingly great in his nature. The more I have meditated on the nature of God, the more I have realized that the core of his being is holiness, with justice and love two interdependent parts of his holiness. To be holy means to be "set apart," and the emphasis here is on God's separation from the created order. He is wholly other, standing above this world and about to judge it.

God's holiness leads naturally to his omnipotence. Isaiah 6:3 speaks of God as "Lord of hosts," that is, the commander of heaven's armies, while the worship here stresses him as "Lord God Almighty," referring to his sovereign power and lordship over his created universe.[3] The Almighty One is indeed the Lord God.

In the last part of this hymn the living creatures celebrate his eternality, using the title of 1:4, 8 to stress that God controls past, present, and future. God is eternal and sovereign over every moment of human history. He is Lord over creation and time. The emphasis on God as "the one who lives forever and ever" will be emphasized again and again through the book.

---

3. See comment on 1:8.

THE ELDERS' RESPONSE (4:9–11)

The worship scene then shifts from the living creatures to the elders in 4:9–11. The two form an antiphonal hymn, with the living beings celebrating the holiness of God and then the elders providing the refrain on his worthiness to be worshiped. The hymn of the living beings is described as "glory and honor and thanks," with the first two describing the majesty and divine splendor of God along with the prestige and esteem that this glory engenders. The third term depicts the recognition and resultant gratitude on the part of God's people as they experience his glory and honor. "Thanksgiving" is the natural response the saints express when receiving salvation and the bountiful gifts from God.

Two characteristics of God are highlighted in 4:10, and these become major themes throughout Revelation. We have already seen both. First, he "sits on the throne." This is drawn from 4:2 and encapsulates the whole description of the sovereign, majestic God from 4:2–3. He is the great God, king not just over this world but over all of creation and all of time, the one next to whom Caesar pales into insignificance. Second, he is the eternal God, the almighty Lord who eternally reigns. In a very real sense, eternity is the perspective of this whole book, embracing not just God's everlasting majesty but also Christ's eternal glory and reign, the eternal life awaiting the saints, and the eternal judgment of the unbelievers. The elders show their gratitude and worship by prostrating themselves before God. This obeisance in worship is accompanied by complete submission as they "lay their crowns before the throne," a common practice as client kings—the heavenly council here—would demonstrate their allegiance to the emperor. The elders' crowns of 4:4, representing their authority to reign, are now submitted to the great God who alone is sovereign.

The hymn of 4:11 provides a proper climax to the magnificent scene of chapter 4. The hymn of 4:8 is in the third person, constituting praise about God. This hymn is second person, direct worship to God. There is also a political thrust, as the language reflects court ceremony used of Caesar by the Romans ("worthy," "our Lord and God," "glory, honor, and power"). There are two parts of the hymn: the worthiness of God and his creative and sustaining work. The opening, "worthy are you," does not occur in the Old Testament and seems to be drawn deliberately from the acclamation the Roman emperor would receive when entering a city. God is superior to all earthly rulers, and he alone is worthy of worship. This is a point those who wield power today desperately need to remember!

The added "our Lord and God" is quite similar to the Roman emperor Domitian's claim of this very title for himself. It is not the emperor but Yahweh who deserves this title. The ascription of lordship to God (1:8; 4:8; 11:4; 16:7; 22:5, 6) and Christ (11:8; 14:13; 17:14; 22:20, 21) is a major theme of Revelation, centering on their cosmic lordship over creation. The worthiness of God as Lord means that he alone is to receive "glory, honor, and power." The three here are drawn from 4:8, a hymn to the power of Lord God Almighty, and 4:9, the living beings ascribing "glory, honor, and thanks" to God. It functions as a conclusion to the earlier worship scene. Glory and honor refer to the being and character of God while power refers to his actions and sums up his almighty strength exercised in every part of Revelation.

The second half of the hymn celebrates God's power over creation. "You created all things" introduces the creation theology that dominates Scripture and is emphasized throughout this book (see Psa 19:1–2, 33:9; Isa 40:28; Eph 3:9; Col 1:16; Rev 3:14; 4:11; 10:6; 14:7). It is the Creator who has made all things possible, and creation is his loving gift to all of us. In Romans 8:19–22 creation groans, longing to be released from the stranglehold of sin and the decay of this present evil world. In Revelation, one of the themes is not just the final redemption of the saints but also the final delivery and release of creation.

The rest of the hymn further builds upon this theme. Since God is creator of all, every part of his creation derives its very being from his will. Literally, the Greek would be translated, "because of your will they were/have their being." Behind creation is divine providence. In Romans 4:17 and Hebrews 11:3, God by his command created the universe out of nothing; here we are told that the world is sustained by his will and will be both consummated and destroyed at his express command (2 Pet 3:7, 10). Yet that very destruction is a release, making way for the true consummation in the new heavens and new earth of Revelation 21:1.

This vision of the heavenly throne room is certainly one of the most magnificent worship passages in the Bible. There are three primary purposes: First, it tells us that our own worship is grounded in the heavenly worship of God by the heavenly beings. When we worship, God is not interested in the quality of our voices but in the state of our heart. We may sing off-key, but that's irrelevant. Our worship is cosmic, and all of heaven is worshiping with us (see Heb 12:22).

Second, we learn that the incredible splendor of God is in total contrast to the earthly so-called glory of earthly rulers; the truth of the matter is that any glory any of us possess is that glory that we share by being a member of the family of the Godhead. Too often we find ourselves virtually worshiping sports stars, celebrities, or politicians. The queen of England or the president of the United States must bow before the throne of heaven just as the rest of us do.

Finally, this vision of heavenly worship demonstrates that the judgment of God seen in Revelation 6–20 is grounded in his holiness and redemptive work seen in Revelation 4–5. We must recognize that God is Creator and sovereign over his world. Whenever people choose to worship the creation rather than the Creator, as in the imperial cult, it is blasphemy and must lead to judgment. We do not have an equivalent to the imperial cult in our day, but we do worship creation more than the Creator whenever we live for the pleasures of this life more than we live for God.

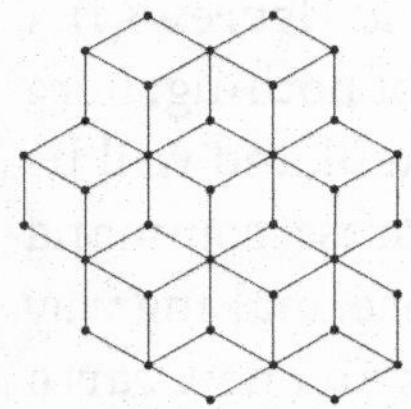

THE THRONE ROOM VISION, PART 2

THE REDEMPTIVE WORK OF THE LAMB

(5:1–14)

The exalted majesty of God in chapter 4 leads naturally to the exaltation of the Lamb and his redemptive work in chapter 5. God is "sitting on the throne" (4:2) and the Lamb is "at the center of the throne" (5:6), stressing their unity—they receive worship together. There is also a strong atmosphere of the imminent end, as the scroll appears in God's hand and awaits one who is "worthy" (4:11; 5:12) to open it and initiate the final events. John weeps because until it is opened, this world of evil cannot be brought to an end. The sheer power of the picture of Christ is overwhelming as it unfolds. Jesus achieves his victory by giving himself to be the slaughtered lamb who then becomes the conquering ram who is at the center of the throne and is God himself. This involves a transfer of authority from God to the Lamb, and the scroll is not only the repository of God's plan for ending this world but is also an official document affirming the Lamb's right to rule.

GOD'S HAND HOLDS A DOUBLE-SIDED SCROLL (5:1)

The one seated on the throne is King of kings, exalted Lord of the universe. His right hand symbolizes power and authority, and the scroll is "on" it, namely, lying on God's open palm. The background is Ezekiel 2:9–10, where a scroll with words of "lament, mourning, and woe" written on both sides of it is in the hand of God and shown to Ezekiel. There and here it is a message of judgment upon those who have opposed God. This kind of scroll was made of strips of papyrus laid end-to-end and glued together, and was the most popular form of writing material for three millennia. Scrolls could be as much as 30 feet long and were normally written on only one side.

What is this document? To answer that question, we must keep in mind three things: It is a scroll, it is written on both sides, and it is sealed with seven seals. Several options have been suggested for its identity. It could be:

1. the Lamb's book of life, with the vast number of names to account for writing on both sides;
2. the Old Testament, with blessings and curses pointing to the covenant laws;
3. a last will and testament centering on the inheritance of the saints, normally sealed with seven witnesses;
4. a divorce bill, borrowing Old Testament imagery about the unfaithfulness of Israel;
5. a doubly inscribed contract deed, sealed with seven seals and with the contents written on the back;
6. a heavenly book containing God's redemptive plan and how God will bring history to a close.

To match the background and purpose of the scroll here, a combination of the last two fits best, with some aspects of the second. The contract deed is the covenant between God and humankind, and the world of evil has refused to keep God's covenant stipulations. They have rejected their contract with God and so are facing the covenant curses. The rest of the book then tells how these curses will take place and traces the judgment of the nations. In this sense, this contract points to the events in the rest of the book that will bring God's plan to completion. God's redemptive plan was made necessary by the effects of sin, and it is anchored in the atoning sacrifice of Christ in 1:5, 5:6, 12; 13:8. The seven seals point to completeness, the fullness of the divine plan. It is perfect, and is to be unveiled at the perfect God-chosen time. The seals must be opened as preliminary events to the unveiling of this final plan.

WHO IS WORTHY TO OPEN THE SCROLL? (5:2–5)

In Ezekiel 2:10 God himself opened the scroll, but here he looks for an agent, and John sees a mighty angel acting as the divinely sent herald. The mighty angel, probably an archangel, appears at critical junctures in Revelation to introduce key events: here, 10:1–2 (the second half of this scroll), and 18:21 (the destruction of Babylon the Great). As a royal herald, he brings a proclamation from the King calling for a worthy agent to instigate the events. As in 4:11 and 5:12, "worthy" is a key term; this worthy agent will be one who can take the place of God in order to "open the scroll and break the seals." Likely this is not a moral or spiritual worthiness so much as it is an inherent sufficiency to stand in for God. Authority is in view here more than virtue.

The problem (5:3) is that no one "in heaven or on earth or under the earth" is worthy to perform the task. This threefold division refers to the whole of creation. "Under the earth" is probably not a reference to the Old Testament saints in the grave; everywhere in Revelation it is used of the underworld, home of demonic forces/fallen angels. This means that neither good angels nor fallen angels, neither saints nor sinners, have the power or authority (implied in *dynatai*, "could" here) to open the scroll.

John therefore "weeps and weeps" (5:4) that the scroll cannot be opened. He weeps because its contents, the events that will end human history and the reign of evil, cannot take place. The language conveys a deep-seated grief for what is lost, for the events that will go unrealized. The final kingdom of God cannot come. It seems a stalemate, but 1 of the 24 elders provides a solution (5:5). He begins by telling John that there is no need for sorrow. The great victory over the powers of evil has already taken place—"has triumphed" is first in the sentence for emphasis. God's Son has provided the central redemptive event of history in his sacrificial death on the cross, and so is the truly "worthy" one to initiate the final events. This is the same verb as the one used to refer to the overcomer/victor in the seven letters of chapters 2 and 3; it means that Jesus' victory is the basis of our triumph.

Two remarkable verses (5:5–6) serve as a transition passage, both concluding the section of 5:2–5 and beginning the section of 5:6–10. On a larger level, these verses also transition from the introductory section of the book (chapters 1–5), introducing the central section (chapters 6–16) by showing how the seals are able to be opened, thus enabling the seal judgments to take place. In fact, many commentators place these chapters with 6–16. What we see in these verses is a brilliant blend of the doctrines of Christ and salvation, repeating the message of 1:5–6. The key themes of Revelation are found right here.

Verse 5 contains two titles, "the Lion of the tribe of Judah" and "the Root of David," that come from major messianic Old Testament texts (Gen 49:9; Isa 11:10). The first refers to Jesus as a lion, the most mentioned animal in the Old Testament (150 times). Genesis 49:9–10 occurs when Jacob gives his patriarchal blessing to Judah and prophesies about the future reign of his greater sons, David and Christ, who like a lion will go up and triumph (49:9) and receive a scepter and ruler's staff (49:10). Genesis 49:8 has a strong military overtone, picturing "your hand on the necks of your enemies." So Judah/Christ is pictured as a young lion growing in strength, capturing his prey, and returning in triumph to reign. The lion is later a symbol for the Davidic throne in 1 Kings 10:19–20 and for Yahweh as Divine Warrior in Isaiah 31:4 and Jeremiah 50:44. Jesus now assumes that role as Divine Warrior and becomes the victor who triumphs. This title celebrates the Messiah's military power and victory over his enemies.

Isaiah 11:1 pictures the coming Messiah as a shoot and then a branch growing out of the "stump of Jesse." In 11:10 this becomes a title, "the Root of Jesse," standing as "a banner for the peoples." The emphasis is on the rise of the Davidic Messiah and the fulfillment of the messianic promises. Yet there is also a military air in Isaiah 11:4, "He will strike the earth with the rod of his mouth," used in Jewish apocalyptic literature for the destruction of the nations.[1] Together these titles picture Jesus as the royal Messiah waging a messianic war against evil and evildoers, with the major weapon being the cross. It is this cosmic victory that enables him to open the scroll.

THE LAMB TAKES THE SCROLL (5:6–10)

The next section begins with one of the most magnificent christological pictures in Scripture, and with 5:5 it takes the shape of a **chiasm**. In this chiasm, the A lines relate to Jesus as the conquering royal Messiah and the B lines relate to his redemptive function as the sacrifice for sin:

A Jesus is the Lion of Judah
    B The Lion is transformed into a Lamb
    B′ The Lamb is slaughtered
A′ The Lamb is transformed into the conquering Ram with seven horns

As we see the lion becoming a lamb rather than vice versa, we realize that Jesus is not awaiting victory; he has already achieved it via the cross. V-Day in Revelation is not Armageddon (16:16). That is merely the final stage of a mopping-up operation. No, V-Day took place at the cross. The victory was not achieved through the powerful claws of the lion but the passive surrender of Jesus' life as the slaughtered lamb. The great victory over Satan has already occurred. The cross is the center of history. Armageddon is the final culmination of a victory already won.

---

1. 4 Ezra 12:32; Sirach 47:22.

The Lamb Described (5:6–7)

The slain lamb is "standing at the center of the throne" with the Father, surrounded by the living beings and angelic elders. The Lamb is the central figure of Christ and salvation in Revelation, indicating that he is the paschal lamb and Suffering Servant of Isaiah 53:7. He also has seven horns in 5:6b, meaning he is not just a lamb but a conquering ram; lambs do not have horns, but rams do. This adds militaristic overtones: in 1 Enoch 90:9–12, the horned ram is a messianic conqueror who leads the people of God to victory. So the Lamb of God is both the sacrificial lamb and the military ram; the second aspect is emphasized later especially in 6:16, which depicts the wrath of the Lamb, and 17:14, which depicts the triumph of the Lamb.

To the seven horns is added "seven eyes," further explained as "the seven spirits of God," which represent the perfect Holy Spirit (see 1:4; 4:5). These are "sent out into all the earth." The Gospel of John depicts the Spirit as being sent by the Father and the Son to carry out their mission to the world (John 14:26, 15:26; 16:7). Here that mission is extended further to include aspects of both redemption and judgment. This is a major theme in Revelation. Despite the fact that the world is deceived by Satan (12:9), follows him (13:3; 16:14), and is soon to come under judgment (3:10), it is still the object of God's salvific love. The "eternal gospel" is proclaimed to it (14:6–7), and the people of the world are called to repentance (9:20; 16:9, 11). Indeed, in 11:13 some survivors of the earthquake "give glory to God"; this is the language of repentance. The Spirit's activity in the world continues during the perilous times narrated in this book, and the goal remains repentance.

In 5:7 the Lamb takes the scroll mentioned in 5:1 as laying in the right hand of God, stressing the divine control of its contents. Now there is a transfer of sovereign authority from God to the Lamb who is already at the center of the throne (5:6). This becomes a type of investiture scene as Jesus steps forward, takes the scroll, and is given control over it. The Son in this sense assumes his royal mantle and proves he indeed is worthy to take the scroll. The Lamb will now execute the divinely mandated plan and bring history to a close.

Worship of the Lamb (5:8–10)

The worship of God in 4:8–11 is now reproduced in the universal adoration of the Lamb, first by the living beings and elders and then in antiphonal fashion by the entire angelic order. As the Lamb takes the scroll, initiating the events that will be launched with the opening of the seals, the worship leaders of the heavenly scene fall down before the Lamb. Prostration is the natural response of both human and angelic beings to the majesty of God and the Lamb.

Each heavenly being has two things—a harp and a golden bowl of incense. The harp, mentioned also in 14:2 and 15:2, is a lyre with 10 or 12 strings, similar to a zither, used in temple worship to accompany hymns. It adds an atmosphere of festive joy to worship. The bowl is a wide-necked golden saucer filled with incense on the table of the bread of the presence in the holy place of the temple, along with gold plates, dishes, and pitchers (Exod 25:29, 37:16). The libation, or drink offering, was poured from a pitcher into the bowl. The angelic beings function here as the priests of heaven and present the sacrifices to God. The incense in the Old Testament signified the "sweet-smelling savor" of the sacrifice and its acceptability to God. Here the incense is "the prayers of the saints," as in Psalm 141:2, where incense symbolized prayer. There is a connection with the prayers of Revelation 6:9–11 and 8:3–4, so the prayers are not just worship but petitions brought before God by the martyred saints for vindication and justice. The trumpet judgments are God's response to these prayers.

The heavenly worship band proceeds to "sing a new song" (5:9). New songs are frequent in the Psalms, expressing a new worship inspired by the mercies of God (Pss 33:3; 40:3; 96:1; 98:1; 144:9; 149:1). In Isaiah 42:10 the new song is **eschatological**, looking ahead to the appearance of the Servant of Yahweh and "new things." There is a new kind of song to celebrate the coming of the new age that is soon to appear.

There are three parts to this new song. They acclaim the worthiness of the Lamb (5:9b), the salvific work of the Lamb (5:9c), and the effects for the followers of the Lamb (5:10). The Lamb is worthy in the same way as God in 4:8, answering the question of 5:2, "Who is worthy to break the seals and open the scroll?" The Lamb through his paschal sacrifice has proven himself worthy and has taken the scroll in order to open it and unlock the final history of this age. The celestial beings are filled with praise that the opening of the seals can now take place. John's weeping can now turn to joy.

The salvific effects are central to the entire book and repeat 1:5–6. In 1:6 the redemptive act was that Jesus "freed us from our sins by his blood," and here the emphasis is that Jesus with his blood "purchased people for God." This language stresses the idea of ransom, that Jesus paid a ransom to free people from slavery to sin. In the book, both sides of redemption are stressed: his blood purchased people (5:9) so as to free them from sin (1:6). In his sacrificial death the greatest emancipation proclamation in human history was made. We have been bought out of sin's slavery so we might enter a new status as slaves of God and through that members of his family, as slaves were in the ancient world. The fourfold formula for the nations ("every tribe and language and people and nation") occurs seven times in the book and is an emphatic way of stressing "all the nations" (see 7:9; 10:11; 11:9; 13:7; 14:6; 17:15). The church is truly universal, bringing together every nation on the planet into a new community of God.

The effects of this salvific work of Christ (5:10) are also drawn from 1:6, and both stem from Exodus 19:6: "You will be for me a kingdom of priests and a holy nation." The church fulfills the promise that God's people would be both royalty and priesthood to the nations of earth. The saints are corporately a nation, and individually priests. As a kingdom they form the people of God, the new Israel experiencing a new exodus.

As priests they serve God in worship and witness. Moreover, as royalty they "reign on the earth," with an inaugurated sense—they reign now in the sense that they belong to God's family, even though it may not seem like it, and in the future their reign with Christ will be complete and eternal (Rev 20:4, 22:5). Note the progression of this theme: First, God and Christ reign (11:15, 17; 19:6); then the victorious saints "reign with him," first spiritually in the present and then literally during the millennial reign (20:4, 6); finally, the saints reign for eternity in the new heaven and new earth (22:5).

THE ANGELIC CHOIR WORSHIPS (5:11–12)

The entire angelic host adds its voice to the adoration of the Lamb. This is the final concentric circle around the throne (with the rainbow, the living beings, and the elders from chapter 4). The vastness of their number is indicated with the "thousands times thousands and ten thousands times ten thousands," drawn from Daniel 7:10, where it describes the attendants to the Ancient of Days. The Greeks did not have a number higher than a myriad (10,000); John could not conceive of a larger number, so this means "an innumerable number," as stressed in Deuteronomy 33:2; Job 25:3; Psalm 68:17; and 1 Enoch 14:22–23. This scene brings out even more strongly the incomparable majesty and splendor of the enthroned God.

The hymn alludes to the core theme of 5:6, the slaughtered Lamb. All the final events in this book are simply the culmination of the redemptive power set in motion by the atoning sacrifice of the Lamb. The is the true victory over Satan and the powers of evil, and this is the absolute proof of the worthiness of the Lamb to set in motion the consummation of human history by opening the scroll.

In the sevenfold acclamation of 5:12, which is repeated in 7:12, the worship of God is extended to the Lamb. The seven can be divided into a pattern of four celebrating the attributes of Christ (power, wealth, wisdom, strength) and three the resultant worship of him (honor, glory, praise). This is another scene that indicates Christ's investiture into his office as Lord and Messiah (see 5:7). "Power" is found often in the worship scenes but is first only here among the hymns, probably because it stresses the power of the sacrificial death of the Lamb to conquer (5:5) the powers of evil. "Wealth" appears in a scene of adoration only here but is used to contrast the majesty of God/the Lamb with the false riches of the world, highlighted especially in chapters 17–18. "Wisdom" looks to Christ as "the wisdom of God" (1 Cor 1:24, 30; Col 2:3), possibly centering on the wisdom of Christ's choice to become the God-ordained sacrifice for the sins of humankind. "Strength" parallels "power" and frames the four attributes by centering on the transfer of might from the Lord God Almighty, the major title for God in Revelation, to Christ. The Godhead exercises its sovereign power to bring this age to a close and defeat for eternity the cosmic powers.

The final three terms describe our proper response of worship to the Lamb. "Honor" is paired with "glory" also in 4:11 depicting the worship of God, so the exaltation and honor of which God is worthy is also extended to the second member of the Godhead. This is an incredible scene, as all the uncountable host of heaven surround the throne and sing their adoration of the true glory of Christ, according him the honor that he is due. The final term, "blessing," occurs in the praise of God (7:12), of the Lamb (here), and of the two together (5:13)—they are one in deserving praise. It communicates the praiseworthiness of the Lamb and develops an image of the basic Jewish benediction, "Blessed be he" (Matt 21:9; 1 John 12:13). This provides a fitting conclusion to the magnificent praise of all of heaven directed to the Lamb.

EVERY BEING WORSHIPS THE ENTHRONED GOD AND THE LAMB (5:13–14)

Now every created being in the universe joins the angelic host to praise God and the Lamb together. As in Psalm 103:20–22, the movement of worship flows from angels to the entire heavenly host to all of creation. It is the culmination of the worship of chapters 4–5, and shows that the God who is worthy in 4:8–11 and the Lamb who is worthy in 5:8–12 are one. "Every creature" refers not just to human beings but includes all the animal kingdom as well. The idea of the universe as in 5:3 includes beings from heaven, earth, the underworld, and the sea. Having the sea mentioned last fits the symbolism of this book, in which the sea represents evil and so belongs with the underworld. The added "all that is in them" stresses every single creature in the cosmos—angels, humans, demons, as well as birds, land animals, and sea creatures. All of creation participates in homage to the Godhead in light of the end of the age. Even demons and sinners reluctantly give homage to the conquering King, as in Philippians 2:10–11.

The hymn itself sums up several themes already found in chapters 4–5. Especially critical is the worship of God with two hymns in 4:8–11, the worship of the Lamb with two hymns in 5:9–12, and the worship of "the one who sits on the throne and the Lamb" here. This is emphasizing the deity of Christ. The actions in the rest of the book will be accomplished by the Godhead acting together. Father and Son end history together, inhabit the new Jerusalem together (21:22, 23), and are worshiped together for eternity.

This is the third of four doxologies in the book, with 1:5–6; 4:9; and 7:12. The four items celebrated in this doxology are items of praise in the previous hymns. In fact, the first three occur in the previous hymn but in reverse order, with "blessing/praise" before "glory and honor," possibly to sum up all the worship scenes as praise scenes. In other words, John is repeating the worship of previous scenes in order to encapsulate them here at the end of this incredible praise session. All of the worship of these first five chapters culminates at this point. "Power" or "might" stems from 1:6 and draws together the two terms for power and strength in 5:12. It is the power of God and the Lamb that has brought about the actions of this book and will produce the final victory for their followers.

Fittingly, the final act occurs when the living beings who uttered the first praise song (4:8) close the worship of 5:13 with "Amen." This does not just conclude this single doxology but provides a fitting end to all the scenes of the throne room vision. It occurs often in Revelation to close worship and functions as an affirmation of the truths celebrated (see Rev 1:6, 7; 3:14; 7:12; 19:4; 22:20, 21). At that the elders "fall down and worship," the proper response to the presence of the Godhead.

The scene in chapter 5 draws together both the Christology and the worship that has taken place thus far. Christ has become the Lion, the royal Messiah, by becoming the slain Lamb. His death on the cross is the true central event of human history, and through his sacrifice the paschal lamb has become the conquering ram who will end this world of evil and usher in eternity. This scene of heavenly worship is also critical when we realize it is taking place at the same time that the persecution of God's people is occurring on earth. The oppression of the saints has a worship aspect to it, because in our suffering we are participating in Christ's suffering (Phil 3:10; Col 1:24), and there are redemptive repercussions when we share with him in this way.

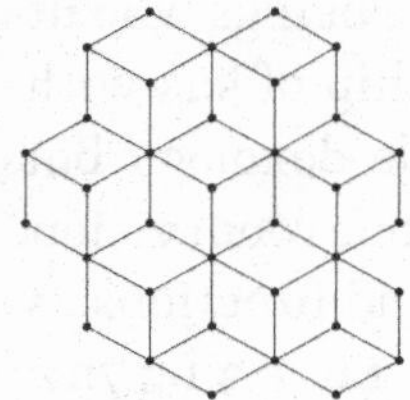

THE FIRST SIX SEALS

(6:1–17)

Before we enter the central section of the book, which deals with the three judgment septets of seals, trumpets, and bowls, there are several preliminary points that will help clarify what these judgments are accomplishing. First, all three sets divide naturally into groups of four and three. The first four judgments fall upon God's earthly creation and the last three are cosmic judgments upon the throne of the dragon/Satan and his minions, as is the pattern in the trumpet and bowl judgments as well.

Second, the seven seals are preliminary judgments that prepare for the trumpets and bowls. These latter two sets closely resemble one another and replicate the Egyptian plagues, with a similar theme—disproving the earthly gods and pronouncing divine judgment upon those who have turned against the one true God. In Revelation these earthly gods are the demonic powers that have turned on their own followers.

Third, there is debate among interpreters about the relationship between the seals, trumpets, and bowls. Many believe that these three sets of judgments should be understood as successive, with the seventh of each set encompassing the next set, which flows out of it. In this case, there would be 21 successive events during the last phase of human history, called "the great tribulation" after 7:14 ("come out of the great tribulation").

One drawback to this approach is that it does not explain the exact repetition in the order of the first four trumpets and first four bowls, which parallel each other in progressing from earthly to oceanic to fresh water to heavenly body judgments (8:6–12 = 16:2–9). It also does not explain the fact that the seals, trumpets, and bowls all seem to end at the **eschaton**. It is more likely that these are not successive events but three parallel cycles that recapitulate one another. This means that they symbolize a series of judgments in which God will be pouring out these natural catastrophes in increasing severity throughout this great tribulation period.

It is also important to remember that the details of these apocalyptic images are not intended to be harmonized with one another. They are meant to be taken as-is, with each vision as a self-contained unit. This means that, despite our curiosity, it is unclear how literal the judgments enumerated here will be. Will every volcano on earth explode, and will a meteor break apart, fall on all the inland waters and turn them to blood? We will find out when they take place.

While the exact form these events will take is mysterious, the overall movement points to a progressive intensification of judgment that affects first a quarter of the people of the nations (the seals), then a third (the trumpets), and finally the whole (the bowls). The cyclical nature of these three sets will be developed as we move through the material in these chapters.

There are seven theological themes that run through the three judgment septets:

1. These judgments are poured out on the earth-dwellers/sinners, and the saints are exempt from them (3:10; 7:1–8; 9:4; 16:2). The emphasis is on the justice of these judgments. The enemies of God receive exactly what they deserve (16:5–7).
2. These judgments are God's response to the prayers of the martyred saints for vindication and vengeance (6:9–11; 8:3–5).

3. God's sovereignty is a key emphasis. This is seen in the oft-repeated phrase "it was given," which amounts to saying that it is God who gives permission (6:2, 4, 8; 7:2; 8:2, 3; 9:1, 3, 5; 13:5, 7, 14, 15). Everything that takes place does so only by divine permission and authorization.
4. While God is sovereign, God does not command evil to operate. Evil acts on its own, comes full circle, and self-destructs (6:1–8; 9:1–19).
5. There is a deep sense of total depravity, as the earth-dwellers, whenever they are given an opportunity to repent, virtually always choose to reject God and follow evil (9:20–21; 16:9, 11).
6. Still, the outpouring of judgment has a redemptive purpose and provides a final chance to repent. This is part of the mission theme in the book (9:20; 14:6–7; 16:9, 11).[1] In 11:13 we see a single instance of repentance.
7. There is a progressive dismantling of creation as the created order is shaken in the seals, then overthrown progressively in the trumpets and bowls, preparing for the final consummation when this world order will be destroyed (20:11; 21:1; see 2 Pet 3:7, 10).

THE FIRST FOUR SEALS REVEAL HORSEMEN RIDING INTO THE WORLD (6:1–8)

The Lamb, the one worthy to open the seals, has taken the scroll. As the seals are opened, they progressively expose and inaugurate God's final plan to rid the world of evil. Yet these are preliminary judgments, as the scroll will not be fully open until all seven seals have been released. When the Lamb opens each of the first four seals, one of the four living beings from 4:6–8 calls forth the famous "four horsemen," showing that every part of these events comes by order from the throne of God. The theme

1. See "Mission and Evangelism" under "Theology of the Book" in the introduction.

of this section is the absolute depravity of humankind. Each of the horsemen demonstrates the descent of humankind deeper and deeper into sin, and together they show the self-destructive nature of sin. Yet three times in this section God gives authority to the riders (6:2, 4, 8), showing God's absolute power over the entire process. Even the forces of evil act only by divine permission.

These four seals follow the pattern of judgments presented by Christ in the Olivet Discourse of Mark 13 and parallels, so Jesus' own teaching was one of the sources behind this chapter. Other sources include Daniel, Zechariah, and Jewish apocalyptic works in general. The imagery of the four horsemen is taken from Zechariah 1:7–11, 6:1–8, where four chariots are drawn by red, black, white, and dappled grey horses. There the chariots go throughout the earth finding "peace and rest," the opposite of the situation here. There the colors symbolize the four winds; here it is death and destruction. Here, the action proceeds from lust for conquest, to civil war, to famine, to death. God is not so much pouring out his judgment as allowing sin to punish itself. This is the true path of depravity.

FIRST HORSEMAN—WHITE (6:1–2)

The worthy Lamb who has taken the scroll from the hand of God now proceeds to open the seals one at a time, acting as the divine Judge beginning the trial proceedings. All of John's senses are involved as he sees the Lamb, hears the command, then writes down the action. The voice is "like thunder" (also 14:2; 19:6), evoking again the manifestation of God in a storm and the Sinai imagery from 4:5–6.

The identity of the first horseman has been variously understood. Some believe that his wearing white and a crown indicates that he is Christ, who will return on a white horse (19:11). Others go the opposite direction and take the figure as the antichrist because of the themes of cosmic war and conquest in 6:1–8, with the horsemen demonic agents of Satan.

The second is more likely than the first, for the evil nature of the action is quite certain. But there is too little evidence thus far to conclude that this is the antichrist. The best option is to see a more general image here, with all the riders relating to the human lust for conquest and its consequences. These are not cosmic but human forces at work. The rider of each horse is described as "sitting," representing the human tendency to sit on our own thrones, setting ourselves up in the place of God (compare 4:2, 3, 9, 10).

The description of the rider resembles the Parthians, a warlike federation of tribes across the Euphrates, the eastern boundary of the Roman Empire. This was the only military force, apart from the Carthaginians under Hannibal, to defeat the Roman legions twice (in 55 BC and AD 62). They were famous for the prowess of their cavalry and their ability to shoot arrows accurately from a galloping horse. Since the rider was given a bow and rode out to conquer, this provides natural background. The crown on this rider would refer to their independence from Rome.

However, this image is not a literal reference to the Parthians. This reference provides background, not the meaning of the passage. Rather, the image of the rider on a white horse points to the propensity of sinful human beings to take things for themselves, to lust for conquest. What is being pictured is the path of human depravity. The "conqueror bent on conquest" introduces the great cosmic war as the final result of the depravity of human beings, murdering and taking over what does not belong to them. Yet three times in this section it is God who gives authority to the riders (6:2, 4, 8). Even the forces of evil act only by divine permission.

Second Horseman—Red (6:3–4)

As with the first horseman, Christ breaks the seal, the living creature gives the command, and the horse and rider appear. Again the sovereignty of God is evident; this is not only judgment but human depravity in process of coming full circle.

With the second horseman, the lust for conquest turns to civil war. Human depravity turns on itself and self-destructs as people kill each other. The second horse is red, the color of "the great red dragon" in 12:3, symbolizing the terrible bloodshed and slaughter that ensues.

The rider is given three things by God: the ability to take peace from the earth, to cause people to kill one another, and to use a sword to accomplish this bloody purpose. God is allowing evil its final freedom to show its true colors and prove once and for all why God must destroy it for eternity. The "large sword" is the symbol of Roman rule—the *ius gladii*, "law of the sword."

Civil war is connoted by the removal of "peace from the earth" and people "slaying each other." These are the "wars and rumors of war" predicted by Jesus in Mark 13:7–8 and that typify human history. This was the greatest fear of ancient dictatorships. Civil war splintered Alexander the Great's empire, and it was the only thing Rome feared. No external army could defeat them, but they nearly self-destructed several times in their history. Examples include the dictatorship of Sulla in the 80s BC, the battles following the death of Julius Caesar that ended the Roman republic in the 44–30 BC, and especially the three different "emperors" (Galba, Otho, Vitellius) who reigned in AD 68–69 following Nero's suicide. Civil war was an oft-repeated tragedy and a constant result of human lust for conquest, as the conquerors turned on one another.

THIRD HORSEMAN—BLACK (6:5–6)

The third and fourth seals denote the effects of war, with the black horse signifying the sorrow and mourning caused by famine. The scales held in the horseman's hand consist of a balance beam with a scale at each end. Their purpose is to ensure justice, as seen in Old Testament texts like Proverbs 16:11: "Honest scales and balances belong to the LORD." Famine caused exorbitant prices leading to food rationing.

Two examples are mentioned: grain supplies and oil/wine. The "voice among" the living creatures stems from the throne room itself and describes the human dilemma. Wheat and barley were the two major sources of food, and Rome annually gave a free portion of grain to the poor to pacify them. Wheat was the better grain, and barley the food of the poor. A denarius was a day's wages, and a quart of wheat was sufficient daily food for one person. This means a man's daily wages could only feed himself, not his family. These were famine prices, 10 or 12 times the normal rate.

Olive oil and wine were also critical staples. The command not to damage or harm the oil and wine has several interpretations. First, it could be a positive indication of social justice, protecting the poor from exploitation by the wealthy. Second, it could seek to protect people from the severity of the famine by ensuring that oil and wine will be kept available. Third, it could describe the terrible conditions at the siege of Jerusalem in AD 70, when starvation prevailed but a group of dissidents stole the sacred oil and wine from the temple for a drinking party.[2]

The best explanation is a combination of the first two. This can be illustrated from an incident from AD 92, when Domitian ordered half the vineyards leveled to increase grain production during a grain shortage. There was such an outcry that he had to reverse himself, for then the oil supply would have been so lowered that the famine would have become worse and been prolonged. We cannot know that this was the situation that prompted the text here, but it is the type of event that often occurred in the many famines of the first century. The primary message is the need to protect the suffering populace from unscrupulous and callous decisions by the powerful in times of tragedy.

---

2. See Josephus, *Jewish Wars* 5.13.6.

Fourth Horseman—Pale Green (6:7–8)

This horse is a yellowish green color, using the Greek term for the color of a corpse. The rider is named Death, with Hades—the grave—following close behind. The rider brings pestilence and death, and Hades follows on foot, scooping the corpses into the grave. Death and Hades are personified here as demonic figures, as they are also in 1:18; 20:13, 14. This means the circle is complete—war leads to civil war and produces famine, pestilence, and death.

God now gives these malignant forces authority to inflict terrible suffering on one-fourth of humankind. These unfortunates were to be killed one of four ways. The first three summarize the four seals—the sword (first two seals), famine (the third), and pestilence/plague (the fourth). The mention of "wild beasts" in 6:8 is due to the Old Testament source for this, Ezekiel 14:21: "For this is what the Sovereign Lord says, 'How much worse will it be when I send against Jerusalem my four dreadful judgments—sword and famine and wild beasts and plague." The wild animals fit the carrion birds that will eat the flesh of the dead armies of the beast in Revelation 19:17–18. The plagues on Israel from Ezekiel 14 will be placed on the nations here.

The result is the death of one fourth of humankind. In today's numbers this would be one-and-a-half billion, more than all the wars of the 20th century combined. It would be impossible to bury that many dead! Death will overtake wicked humanity, and they will not escape the judgment of God. Moreover, they have brought this judgment on themselves; in fact, they have been the instigators and the cause of all the suffering and death. Do we need any further proof of the horror of sin and its consequences?!

THE FIFTH SEAL REVEALS THE MARTYRED SAINTS (6:9–11)

In the first four seals, the emphasis was on the dead from the nations, but now the vision turns to the dead from the saints.

Apparently, the sword given to the armies of the nations in 6:4 was used not only for war but also for persecuting and martyring the believers. Now the scene shifts from the sinners to the saints and from earth to heaven, specifically the heavenly temple. The idea of heaven as a temple is used often in the Old Testament (Psa 11:4; Isa 6:1; Hab 2:20), and in Revelation it is found in 11:19; 14:17; 15:5; 16:7. The altar in Revelation is always in the heavenly temple (8:3, 5; 14:18). The negative judgment of God was emphasized in the first four seals; now the positive justice of God comes to the fore. ***Lex talionis*** is seen throughout Revelation, both in terms of judgment on sinners and as vindication for the persecuted and martyred saints.

At the opening of the fifth seal, John sees the souls of the slain "under the altar." This image stems from the sacrificial system, in which the blood of the sacrificed victim is poured under the altar. These martyrs were sacrificed for God. It is unclear whether this is the altar of burnt offering, favored by the image of the blood poured under it, or the altar of incense, favored by the prayers uttered. I suggest that the two are combined into one altar in this book. As we will see in the altar scenes, the ideas of sacrifice and prayer function synonymously, and there appears to be one altar in heaven.

The believers have been "slaughtered," which is the same term used of the "slain Lamb" in 5:6. This has happened because of "the word of God and the testimony they had maintained," a formula that also occurs in 1:2, 9, and 20:4, and is paraphrased in 12:17 and 14:12. The emphasis is on the participation of the faithful followers in God's presence via their witness. The ongoing effects of their testimony and obedience to God led to their martyrdom, an emphasis that will continue in 11:3–10. The church's response to opposition is not passive flight but active witness.

Now those slaughtered are crying out to God for justice. This is an imprecatory prayer, a cry for vindication and vengeance in the face of enemies. It is similar to many of the psalms that are built on the covenant curses (for example, Pss 12, 35, 52, 57–59).

These enemies of God have deliberately rejected and mocked his covenant with humankind and have turned against God's people. Therefore, they have brought down upon themselves God's curses, and the martyrs are praying for God to fulfill these promises to vindicate his people and avenge them. As in Romans 12:19, the point here is that victims do not seek vengeance but leave that vengeance with God. This emphasis is also seen in Luke 18:7–8, "Will not God bring about justice for his chosen ones, who cry out to him day and night?" This scene is not a low point for ethics but a high point for divine justice.

The prayer begins unusually with "How long?" an anguished plea from a suffering people who are anxious for answers. Yet it also affirms the absolute authority and power of the sovereign Lord who is "holy and true," terms used of Christ in 1:5; 3:7, 14. God is addressed as the master of creation, the Judge who will right a terrible wrong. The question is not whether God will judge the oppressors but how soon. The doom of their oppressors is certain, but the martyrs would like it to be sooner than later. The idea of "judging and avenging our blood" alludes to Psalm 79:10, "avenge the outpoured blood of your servants." The judgment on the sinners is also seen as avenging the blood of God's martyred people. This is an important point, for it can be seen from Revelation 8:3–5 that the trumpet and bowl judgments are in part God's response to this very prayer. This is restated in 16:5–7, when the turning of the oceans and inland waters to blood is given this justification: "They shed the blood of your saints and prophets, and you have given them blood to drink, as they deserve." This is an example of the ***lex talionis*** mentioned above: what they have done to God's people, God will do to them.

God responds to the prayers of the martyrs in two ways in 6:11. First, he gives each one a "white robe." Here, as elsewhere in 3:4–5; 4:4; 7:9–17, these indicate high status, purity, and victory. The martyrs have entered their reward, and God has heard their plea. The answer is coming, but in God's time, not theirs. They must "wait a little longer," for there are events yet to take place before the final victory can be secured. There is a sense of imminent expectation, yet patience is needed. Satan "knows his time is short" (12:12), and the delay is virtually over (10:6). The command to "wait" contains the meaning of resting as well as waiting. With the white robe of glory, they will indeed rest in the glory of heaven as they await the consummation of God's victory on their behalf.

The reference to the "full number" of martyrs in 6:11 is a key element in early Christian expectation, but it seems strange to our modern ears. Called "the messianic woes," it describes the belief that God in his sovereignty had established a certain number of martyrs yet to be killed, a certain amount of suffering to be experienced by his children, before the end of history. This is what Paul was referring to in Colossians 1:24 when he spoke of filling up in his flesh "what is still lacking in regard to Christ's afflictions," by which he meant that his sufferings helped to complete the amount of messianic suffering still to occur before the end could come.[3] Here, this means that God knows each one to be martyred and will vindicate them all at the proper time. The emphasis is on God's omniscience and sovereign control of history, so that the suffering of each one of us is part of his perfect plan. This does not mean God causes this suffering; rather, he knows it is coming and has planned to use it to benefit his faithful and bring them victory.

THE SIXTH SEAL REVEALS THE SHAKING OF THE HEAVENS (6:12–17)

God's response to the "how long" of the martyrs is swift and decisive, beginning with the very next seal judgment. The imminent end of history is pictured in the traditional shaking of the heavens that often in Scripture signals the Day of Yahweh (see Isa 13:9–13, 24:19–23, 34:4; Ezek 32:6–8; Joel 2:30–31). At this time the very ones who have martyred the saints will quake in

---

3. See also 1 Enoch 47:1–4; 4 Ezra 4:35–37.

fear (Rev 6:15–17). The justice of God is uppermost, and he will end this world and right all wrongs in his own time.

The organization of the material is debated, with many thinking the storm here is preliminary, a prelude or anticipation of future events that in effect warns the nations of more to come. However, as said at the beginning of this chapter, it is better to understand the seals, trumpets, and bowls as following a cyclical arrangement. The storm here, then, would be the same storm as in the seventh bowl judgment that takes place at the end of human history (16:18–21). So these cosmic signs herald the return of Christ. At the climax of each set of judgments God brings this world to a close, coming in judgment, partly in answer to the prayers of the martyrs for justice.

COSMIC SIGNS (6:12–14)

Christ breaks the seal, and immediately a terrible shaking and storm erupts. This goes beyond the localized signs around Sinai, for all the earth and the starry heavens are involved. There are three "great earthquakes" in Revelation—here, 11:13, and 16:18—as well as two others (8:5; 11:19). This is a cosmic or universal quake that shakes the heavens and the earth (Isa 24:18–23). The Sinai earthquake just before the giving of the Ten Commandments is the model for all of these (Exod 19:16–18; Psa 68:8), as it signified the holy God coming in judgment (Judg 5:4–5; Joel 2:10). The **eschaton** is the final Sinai deliverance, with the shaking of the cosmos as the initiator of the final events. In Christ's Olivet Discourse it occurs at his return (Mark 13:24–27 and parallels), and here it also includes judgment on the nations and the final deliverance of God's people.

The effect on the heavenly bodies shows that all of creation is involved in the purging of evil from this world. This is the point also of Romans 8:18–22, where creation "groans" in eager longing for its deliverance from the "bondage to decay" that the sin of humankind has brought on it. The darkening of the sun and moon is a harbinger of the fourth trumpet judgment (8:12). "Sackcloth made of goat's hair" was a coarse, thick cloth worn in times of mourning, a natural symbol for this scene preparing for the mortal terror of 6:15–17 below. The blood-red moon is a further sign of judgment drawn from Joel 2:31, also used by Peter in Acts 2:17–21, making this terrible prophecy of doom all the more powerful. This is an example of what could be called "double fulfillment": The Joel prophecy was fulfilled first in the coming of the Spirit at Pentecost, and for a final time at the return of Christ.

The heavenly stars falling to earth pictures a huge meteor shower, stemming from Isaiah 34:4: "All the stars in the sky will be dissolved and the heavens rolled up like a scroll; all the starry host will fall like withered leaves from the vine." In Isaiah it was judgment on the nations, and here this is intensified to encompass the final judgment of all who ever lived. In this the heavens themselves recede like a scroll, "split apart" in the Greek, a poignant image for the end of this world. The universe is depicted as a massive scroll that is unrolled, split apart, and then rolled back upon itself. At Jesus' baptism the heavens were "split apart" (Mark 1:10), signifying the final arrival of God's kingdom and the beginning of the last days. This now completes that image.

Finally, the mountains and islands are removed, possibly by the intensity of the great earthquake. However, in light of its parallel in Revelation 16:20 ("every island fled away and the mountains could not be found"), it more likely means the total disappearance of both. As preparation for the destruction of the cosmos (2 Pet 3:7, 10), the shaking of the heavens will include the disappearance of every mountain and island.

Terror of the Earth-Dwellers (6:15–17)

The previous three verses showed the effects of divine judgment upon the created order. Now, 6:15–17 show the effects on the created beings, in particular the inhabitants of the nations. Many movies, such as *Armageddon* or *Edge of Tomorrow,* have sought to portray doomsday scenarios, but none as frightening as the events of 6:12–14. No wonder the people are cowering in abject terror. This is even more frightening, however, for certainly these hardened sinners would also realize that judgment day has indeed arrived. Yet in this scene also we have God's response to the imprecatory petitions of the martyrs. These are the people who slaughtered them, and the time of their accounting is now here.

The seven people groups listed in 6:15, also in 19:18, allude to the list in Ezekiel 38:2–6 at the destruction of Gog and Magog. As in Ezekiel, these groups who have invaded and plundered the people of God are about to answer to God. The "kings of the earth" refers to the vassal kings who served under the Roman emperor, and we will see them later as "the kings from the east" who join the army of the beast in 16:2 as well as the 10 kings of 17:12–14. The princes, or noblemen, are the civil officials like proconsuls and governors who run the government; this word is used also of the merchants in 18:23. The generals are the military tribunes who were at the top of the Roman army. They controlled "ten centuries," or 1,000 soldiers. The rest of the groups summarize the social classes—the wealthy, the mighty—influential people and landowners—and finally the rest of the populace, "slave and free." The first five groups are the powerful elite who control society, and the last two are the lower classes. All are united in standing against God and are thus objects of his wrath.

In this scene, they are also united in their overwhelming fear. All social distinctions drop away in light of the dismantling of the cosmos and the arrival of God's judgment. Two unusual developments mark the enormity of their terror (6:16). First, they "hide in caves and among the rocks of the mountains." This is a frequent Old Testament image, used of Lot in Genesis 19:30, of the Amorite kings in Joshua 10:16, of the armies of Israel in 1 Samuel 13:6, of David in 1 Samuel 22:1, and especially of Israel itself due to the coming Day of Yahweh in Isaiah 2:10, 19, 21. Those who are in rebellion and sin have a natural desire to flee the wrath of God.

Second, they plead for the rocks to fall on them, to hide them from the face of God. No one in their right mind pleads to be buried in an avalanche; this indicates a virtual insanity of fright. God's "face" is a symbol for his relationship with humanity—his face turns toward us in mercy (Num 6:25–26; Psa 4:6) or away from us in anger (Lev 17:10; Psa 13:1). Here judgment is paramount. "The one who sits on the throne" occurs throughout chapters 4 and 5 and here refers to the throne as the Bema or judgment seat of the King of kings.

"The wrath of the Lamb" is a startling image. It is the opposite of the emphasis on the paschal Lamb who becomes the atoning sacrifice in 5:5–6, as well as the Lamb who is at the center of the throne and worthy of worship in 5:6a, 9. Now he is conqueror (5:5) and judge. A lamb does not exhibit wrath; it just bleats helplessly. But this Lamb has become the conquering Ram (5:6b) and is filled with wrath at sinful humankind; see 11:18; 14:10; 16:19; 19:15. This is the only possible reaction of a holy God toward a world consumed with evil that rejects its redemption in Christ.

The reason for this stark terror is "because the great day of their wrath has come" (6:17). This reproduces the Day of Yahweh passages from the Old Testament, all of which center on divine judgment on an apostate nation and on the rebellious nations (Joel 2:11, 31; Zeph 1:14–16; Mal 4:1, 5). This is the culmination of all of the judgments in Scripture, and the great day refers to the time of Christ's return and the destruction of the world of evil. The natural question in light of this is, "Who is able to stand?" This reworks the language of Joel 2:11 ("Who can endure it?"), Nahum 1:6 ("Who can withstand his indignation?"), and Malachi 3:2 ("Who can stand when he appears?"). When the Lord God Almighty acts in judgment, there will be no opposition. None can withstand it, and both vindication for God's people and judgment upon his enemies will characterize the end of this world.

The events of the seals, trumpets, and bowls will take place as part of the final events of history. It is important to realize that they are aimed at unbelievers rather than God's people. For believers it will be like the plagues on Egypt. Those of us still alive will see them fall on the unsaved, and our task will be to witness to them and try to bring them to repentance and to Christ. We will see human depravity get worse and worse, and many of us will be martyred as unbelievers act out their hatred on us. At that time we must know that our vindication and victory are near at hand, for God will see to it that his justice prevails.

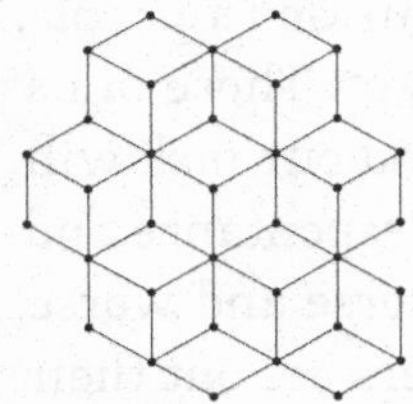

THE SAINTS ON EARTH AND IN HEAVEN

(7:1–17)

Throughout the judgment scenes of chapters 6–16 there are three interludes: 7:1–17; 10:1–11:13; and 12:1–14:20. These are scenes that interrupt the flow of the seals, trumpets, and bowls. They have multiple purposes:

1. the first two occur between the sixth and seventh seals and trumpets and are closely linked to the sixth judgment that precedes each. The third interlude (12:1–14:20) is separate and provides a transition from the trumpet to the bowl judgments, signifying the great conflict between the Satanic realm and God's people.
2. The seals, trumpets, and bowls describe the judgments that are happening to the sinners, while the interludes provide information about the place of the saints in the action of this period.
3. They stress even more God's sovereign reign over the whole process; he is watching over and protecting the saints at every stage.

When we consider the placement of chapter 7, we begin with the question that ends the narrative of the opening of the sixth seal: "Who can stand?" The earth-dwellers or sinners will not stand when the judgments fall, but the heaven-dwellers or saints will stand because they bear the seal of God. Throughout the book, there is an emphasis on the divine protection of God's faithful followers. The promise to Philadelphia in 3:10 that God will keep them from the hour of trial is also highlighted in 8:13 ("Woe" to the earth-dwellers, not the saints), 9:4 ("harm only those who do not have the seal of God"), and 16:6, 19 (judgments only upon the enemies of God's people). Yet note that they are protected from God's wrath, not from the wrath of the beast. They will not suffer from the outpouring of judgment but will suffer persecution, and many will be killed. However, their suffering is their victory. They are protected spiritually but not physically, yet their afflictions are part of the "messianic woes" and controlled by God for their own benefit.[1]

It is often thought that there are two distinct groups in chapter 7: one sealed on earth, referring to Jewish believers (7:1–8), and the other worshiping in heaven, both Jew and Gentile (7:9–17). Yet I will argue below that the 144,000 of 7:1–8 stands for the whole church, not just Jewish Christians, and it is better in this context to see those sealed in 7:1–8 as one and the same with those in heaven in 7:9–17. The purpose of this interlude is to picture the people of God being sealed at their conversion on earth and then worshiping God in heaven after they have died. They are sealed as God's possession and then rewarded with heavenly rejoicing as the fruit of their labor for God.

THE SAINTS ARE SEALED AS GOD'S POSSESSION (7:1–8)

Holding Back the Winds of Destruction (7:1–3)

In the seal judgments of chapter 6 it is clear that the winds of destruction are gathered, but God is not quite ready to proceed. It is necessary first to "seal" his children to protect them. In one sense this is a flashback to their conversion, but it is presented as a global reality; they are in a state of being sealed. So four

1. See the commentary on 6:11.

angels hold back the winds of destruction until God's time to release them. These angels are connected to those in 9:14, alluding to Zechariah 6:5, which speaks of "four spirits in heaven" going throughout the earth. "Four corners" was also an ancient idiom for every part of the earth.

Often in apocalyptic thinking the weather carries out God's will. It was the wind that brought the locusts in Exodus 10:13 and turned the sea to dry land in Exodus 14:21. In Jeremiah 49:36 the winds brought destruction from "the four corners of the heavens." The angels are the royal guards of heaven "restraining" the destruction until God's time. The winds here are prevented from blowing on "land or sea or any tree," the focus of the first two trumpet judgments in 8:7–9. The hot wind off the desert in Palestine was a frequent metaphor for divine punishment (Jer 51:36; Hos 13:15) and the fragility of life (Psa 103:16; Isa 40:6–7). These winds would destroy all commerce and sea trade, thus ending life as people knew it in the first century.

In the second part of the vision (7:2–3) we see why the winds of destruction have been curtailed. "Another angel" appears possessing great authority since he commands the four angels and holds in his hands the seal of God. He arrives from the east, literally "from the rising sun," alluding to Ezekiel 43:2, 4, in which God enters the temple from the east. This signifies the outpouring of kingdom blessings and power, in contrast to the evil powers who parody God and also come from the east (9:14–15; 16:12).

This angel also carries "the seal of the living God," picturing the angel as the divine herald bearing the royal signet ring, used by kings and their officials to authenticate documents, as in the seals on the scroll in chapters 5–6. The seal meant ownership, protection, and privilege; Gentiles viewed those who were sealed as belonging to their patron god. The sealing of the saints is all this and more, meaning God's people are not only his "treasured possession" (Exod 19:5; Deut 7:6; Mal 3:17; 1 Pet 2:9) but also have the Holy Spirit as their seal and guarantee (Eph 1:13–14; 4:30; 2 Cor 1:22). They belong to "the living

God," the covenant God who "never leaves or forsakes" his people (Deut 31:6; Josh 1:5) and is dynamically at work in their lives. As in Romans 8:14–17 this depicts the individual at their conversion being sealed as God's slave/possession and receiving the Spirit.

This mighty angel cries in a loud voice to the four angels who had been "given power to harm the land and the sea." This parallels the four horsemen who had been "given power to take peace from the earth" in 6:4. With them the dismantling of creation was about to begin, as "harm" is stated twice for emphasis. But that initiation of destruction was not to begin yet. The idea of "doing damage to land and sea and trees" points forward to the first three trumpet and bowl judgments (8:7–11; 16:2–4) where this sentence is carried out, but now the emphasis is on restraint, for there is a greater purpose at work: to "seal God's slaves." The personal, loving God will stamp his people as his own to protect them from the unleashing of his destructive power, as promised in 3:10 ("I will keep you from the hour of trial"). The demarcation of the saints as God's slaves fits this image, for they are marked for ownership as God's special possession and are both protected and members of his family, as slaves were in the ancient world.

God's slaves are sealed "on the forehead"—an allusion to Ezekiel 9:4–6, a judgment passage in which six guardian angels appear, five to put to death the idolaters and the other with a writing tablet to mark those who grieved over the apostasy of the nation. The placement on the forehead made it a public proclamation that the person belonged to God. That mark was the letter *tav*, the last letter in the Hebrew alphabet, which in ancient script would appear as an X or T, which to Christians would symbolize the name of Christ or the cross. This is in direct contrast to the mark of the beast in 13:16, denoting the person as belonging to Satan. It is clear that there is no middle ground. You either belong to Christ or belong to Satan, and that will determine your eternal destiny.

SEALING THE TWELVE TRIBES (7:4–8)

The second part of this passage has a strange introduction: "I heard the number of those sealed." Possibly there is an intended link to 6:11, "until the number ... is complete," stressing God's foreknowledge of those sealed. This is in keeping with the number 144,000, the product of 12 x 12 x 1000, indicating completeness. Some have understood the 144,000 as Jewish Christians, the martyrs in this final period of history, or the church as a whole.

The least likely view of these three is that of the martyrs, for this is too limiting in the connection between 7:1–8 and 9–17. The emphasis must lie on the whole group and not just one subsection, as in the "great multitude from every nation" of 7:9. More difficult is the choice between Jewish Christians and the entire church. Certainly the phrasing seems to be Jewish, "from all the tribes of Israel," followed by a list of the 12 tribes. Still, there are other factors that favor a reference to the church. Throughout the book, the emphasis is on all the saints and not just Jewish Christians. For example, in 21:12–14 the 12 tribes on the gates and the 12 apostles on the foundations stress the whole people of God as a unified body. Both groups combine into a single group—the company of faithful overcomers. In the rest of New Testament also, there is quite a bit of material on the church as true Israel: Jesus chose 12 disciples to anchor the origins of the church with the righteous remnant among Israel. The church is "Abraham's seed" (Gal 3:29), "the Israel of God" (Gal 6:16), "the (true) circumcision" (Phil 3:3), and "a chosen people" (1 Pet 2:9).

So the purpose is to stress the comprehensive nature of the church and its continuity with the covenant people of the Old Testament. There is some agreement among scholars that this symbolizes the messianic army. The entire scene with the names and numbering of the tribes has the look of a census, and in Old Testament passages like Numbers 1 and 26 this was done to determine the size of the army and its personnel in preparation for war. The difference is that this army will be militant in witness rather than using weapons and will conduct a spiritual battle to conquer the dragon and the beast. It will achieve victory via martyrdom; see 12:11 and 13:7.

There is no exact match for this list of tribes in the Old Testament. However, the 20 Old Testament lists differ markedly, so this is not unusual. The names here follow the matriarchal order as seen in Genesis 35:23–26:

1. the sons of Leah: Reuben, Simeon, Levi, Judah, Issachar, Zebulun;
2. the sons of Rachel: Joseph, Benjamin;
3. the sons of Zilpah: Gad, Asher;
4. the sons of Bilhah: Dan, Naphtali.

There are two differences—Judah, not Reuben (Jacob's firstborn), is first, likely because the Messiah comes from Judah (Matt 1:3, 2:6); and Manasseh (Joseph's son) replaces Dan, undoubtedly because Dan fell into idolatry (Judg 18; 1 Kgs 12). So this is intended as a warning to the followers of the Nicolaitan heresy (Rev 2:6, 15) and other weak Christians of the dangers of worshiping other gods.

The emphasis, then, is on the completeness of the people of God as the messianic army of Christ. They have been sealed by the Spirit as God's treasured possession and protected spiritually, but not physically, from the evil powers for the purpose of maintaining a militant witness for Christ. They are to call the nations to repentance and by their persevering faithfulness to the Lord defeat the dragon, many through their martyrdom. At Christ's return they will join the angels as the host of heaven.

JOHN SEES A GREAT MULTITUDE IN HEAVEN (7:9–17)

The saints who have been sealed on earth are here seen in heaven wearing the white robes of purity and victory. This first interlude pictures the people of God at the beginning and at the end of their journey. The beginning is their conversion when they are sealed in 7:1–8, and the end is in heaven before the throne in 7:9–17. They celebrate the great victory of God and the

Lamb and then are joined by the heavenly host while they rejoice in their victorious emergence from the great tribulation that ends the reign of evil on the earth.

Scene of Worship (7:9–12)

The believers were numbered in 7:4–8 (and 6:11), but now they form an innumerable crowd, taking their place with the saints from all of history in fulfillment of the promise to the patriarchs that their descendants would be as numerous as the stars of the sky or the sand of the sea (Gen 15:5, 32:12). They are drawn from every nation and language on the earth, stressing once more the universal nature of the church. Here the triumphant saints are celebrating their hard-fought victory won through the intervention of the Divine Warrior. This scene could take place either at the final judgment, when the saints receive their rewards, or at the beginning of eternity in heaven.

The saints are "standing before the throne and before the Lamb," who in an earlier scene were filled with wrath against the earth-dwellers (6:16). This phrase was associated with judgment in chapter 6 and reward in chapter 7. This is the first time anyone other than celestial beings has appeared before the throne; here the "overcomers," virtually a title in the seven letters to the churches, stand in the place of honor to receive their reward. They are given white robes, the garments given to the martyrs in 6:11, and also palm branches, a sign of joy on festive occasions like the Feast of Tabernacles (Lev 23:40–43) or the Triumphal Entry (John 12:13). Like a Roman triumph, victory produces celebration and rejoicing.

The worship of the overcomers (7:10) begins with a loud hymn of praise extolling the salvation God has brought to them. In Revelation, salvation involves the Old Testament sense of victory and deliverance (Psa 3:8; John 2:9; see Rev 12:10; 19:1). Here they praise God for his victory over the powers of evil and the deliverance of his sealed followers. It is his sovereign power, emphasized in the phrase "who sits on the throne," that delivers his people. "Our God" turns this into a covenant formula—

a liturgical worship cry celebrating the covenant God as "our God" who has accepted us as his people. Moreover, the Lamb stands alongside God as Savior of the saints.

In 7:11 "all the angels," the outermost circle around the throne from 5:11, join the multitude of overcomers, and they are joined once more by the elders and living creatures from chapter 4. John is recreating the awesome throne room spectacle so the readers can catch the wonder of their future with God. This group is standing with the overcomers but immediately they prostrate themselves before God, as in 4:10; 5:8, 14. The priestly function of the angels continues as they once more fall down and worship the Godhead.

The hymn that follows in 7:12 has a sevenfold pattern similar to 5:12 and is framed by "amen"—the only hymn in the Bible to do so.[2] In this book, "amen," meaning "so be it," has a liturgical function in affirming the contents before the Lord (1:6, 7; 19:4). The first "amen," then, affirms the hymn of the multitude in verse 10, and the second closes this hymn. The sevenfold praise contains six of the seven from 5:12, replacing "wealth" with "thanksgiving," drawn from the praise of the elders in 4:9. What makes this list of attributes different from those in 4:9, 11 or 5:12–13 is the context celebrating God's great end-time victory over the forces of evil.

It is best to see two word pairs in this hymn—praise/thanksgiving and glory/honor. These introduce the two sections on a note of praise, producing one group of three and another group of four: praise-glory-wisdom, and thanks-honor-power-strength. The two sets praise God for his wisdom and for his might in delivering his people and making them overcomers. This hymn adds to the first one in verse 12 that this will be eternal praise ("forever and ever"), for eternity has now begun.

2. But possibly also Rev 22:20b–21.

Identification of the Saints by the Elder (7:13–17)

John is confused by this vision, so in 7:13 one of the elders asks his question for him: Who are these people and how did they get here? As often in prophetic-apocalyptic writings (Dan 7:15–16; Zech 4:1–2), the elder/angel functions as a mediator and interpreter, explaining key symbols to John. John, aware that the elder intends to explain this to him, says simply, "Sir, you know," and waits for the answer.

The elder first responds that these people have come out of "the great tribulation." This could refer in a general way to an intense period of affliction, but with the definite article "the" it is probably a technical phrase for the last events of history, building on Daniel 12:1—the "time of distress such as has not happened from the beginning of nations until then." It refers to the final war of the dragon and his followers against the saints in chapters 12 and 16. As God exerts his wrath against the world of evil, it retaliates with its own vengeance against the followers of Christ. As in 13:7, God allows the dragon for this short period of tribulation to "conquer" the saints. In Jesus' words, this results in terrible "days of distress unequaled from the beginning, when God created the world, until now—and never to be equaled again" (Mark 13:19).[3]

This victory does not just come from the faithful suffering of the saints but is achieved "by the blood of the Lamb" (see 1:5; 5:6, 9; 12:11). This is the sacrifice of atonement that provided the ransom payment to free the saints from sin (Rom 3:25; Eph 1:7). Christ's sacrificial blood made it possible for these believers to "wash their robes and make them white," an image drawn from the preparation of Israel at Sinai, washing their garments for the appearance of Yahweh on the third day (Exod 19:10, 14). Psalm 51:7 also says, "Wash me, and I will be whiter than snow" (also Isa 1:18). There are two actors here, Christ and the believers,

---

3. In Mark 13, the destruction of Jerusalem is an anticipation of this period.

possibly encompassing both salvation, which comes by the blood, and sanctification, the spiritual growth of the believer.

The elder then turns from prose to poetry in 7:15–17. The redemptive acts of Christ in 7:14 and the faithful response of the people of God in this whole section of 7:9–14 have led to this celebration of the rewards given to the victorious sufferers. There are three parts to these verses: First, there is the presence and service of the saints before God (7:15). The victorious saints now enter their eternal relationship with God, in which they will join the angels as the priests of heaven. At the outset, they stand "before the throne of God," as we already saw in 7:9. They have overcome their earthly afflictions and now are deemed worthy to stand before the throne. This is similar to Ephesians 2:6, "God raised us up with Christ and seated us with him in the heavenly realms." This in turn builds on Ephesians 1:20, "He raised Christ from the dead and seated him at his right hand in the heavenly realms." This is the fulfillment of Psalm 110:1, the primary messianic prophecy of Christ's exaltation ("The Lord said to my lord: Sit at my right hand"). All this means we will share in Christ's exaltation. Now we may share spiritually in the heavenly court, the place of power and victory, but in Revelation this is true with finality. Now the believer sits with God in Christ, but then we will literally stand before the throne!

At this time the saints begin their heavenly duties, to "serve him day and night in his temple." In this passage the throne of God is in the heavenly temple, building on the Old Testament view that God's throne was above the ark in the holy of holies. The verb "serve" (Greek *latreuō*) is a rich term denoting both service and worship, and that is the thrust here. The saints' service to God is an act of worship, as it is today as well. As in Revelation 1:6 and 5:10, Christ has made his followers a royal priesthood, fulfilling Exodus 19:5–6. The priestly activity in heaven is a culmination of earthly service. But this priestly service is continuous ("day and night"), while in the Jerusalem temple priestly activity ceased from the evening service to the morning service.

In a beautiful image, the enthroned God will shelter them with his presence, literally "spread his tent over them" or "tabernacle over them." God "tabernacling" brings up the image of the Shekinah glory (from Hebrew *shakan*, "to dwell") covering his people (Exod 25:8, 29:45; Zech 2:10, 8:3). God not only shelters his people but covers them with his glory. In the New Testament God's Shekinah glory dwells among his people (Rom 9:23; 2 Cor 3:17–18; 12:9). There could not be a stronger image of God's protective presence covering the saints. They will never again fear or experience harm or affliction.

The second part of the elder's hymn is the removal of all suffering (7:16, 17c). This stems from Isaiah 49:10, where the exiles returning from Babylon are told that "they will never hunger nor thirst, nor will the desert heat of the sun beat upon them." Since hunger and thirst were often signs of divine judgment (Deut 28:47–48; Isa 8:21), this is a sign of both forgiveness and reward. All of life's needs will be met; God is supplying a full and rich life. There will also be no more external suffering from nature, such as exposure to the sun's heat, a reference to the Sirocco, the hot east wind from the desert, and to the scorching Mediterranean sun. In our eternal home all such deprivations will be removed, and the believers will experience only joy and peace. This is summed up in 7:17c, "God will wipe away every tear from their eyes." Every hurt and all sorrow—gone forever. While some have limited this to mourning for sin and mistakes, that does not fit this context. These are tears of suffering for both persecution and life's afflictions, drawn from Isaiah 25:8, "the Sovereign LORD will wipe away the tears from all faces."

The final part of the elder's hymn presents the actions of the Lamb and God on their behalf (7:17a–b). There is a rich set of allusions in "the Lamb … will be their shepherd." In the Old Testament Yahweh is "the shepherd of Israel" (Gen 48:15; Psa 80:1), and as in Psalm 23 this pictures God guiding and protecting his flock, leading it to pasture (Jer 50:19) and springs of water (Psa 23:2). In Ezekiel 34:20–24 a future Davidic ruler will shepherd Israel and unify God's people. Here the image is reversed, and the Lamb becomes the shepherd, fulfilling all the imagery noted above. The slain Lamb becomes the conquering Ram (Rev 5:5–7) and then shepherds the new Israel. The Lamb is the Good Shepherd who knows his sheep, calls them by name, and by laying down his life for them gives them life (John 10:3, 11, 14). Jesus thereby becomes "the great Shepherd of the sheep" (Heb 13:20) who is "at the center of the throne" and is "very God of very god," as the Nicene Creed puts it.

The message of the interlude in 7:1–17 must be understood in the context of the persecuted saints and the martyrs of Revelation. Though hated, opposed, and pursued by the nations of the world, God's people have been sealed and belong to him. He is watching over them and protecting them. Even if allegiance to God costs them their lives, that will be their victory. God will vindicate them and they will stand before his throne. Their mission will have proven successful, for people from every nation and language will stand before God and the Lamb (7:9). Moreover, all of heaven will be rejoicing with them and welcoming them into eternity; it will be a scene beyond all imagination, and their worship in heaven will sum up all the worship of history and give it eternal significance.

In the five decades that I have been ministering, each decade I have been told that there were more martyrs and more persecutions of Christians worldwide than ever. While Christians in the United States have been spared this level of opposition, the tide does not appear to be in our favor: Our own nation is turning more and more against Christian values. Nevertheless, this passage shows that no matter how bad it may get for the followers of Christ, it will all be worthwhile. The church will be privileged to stand before the throne in absolute joy and join the angels in priestly worship; all suffering will be removed and the saints vindicated; and the Lamb will become their shepherd and lead them to life-giving streams.

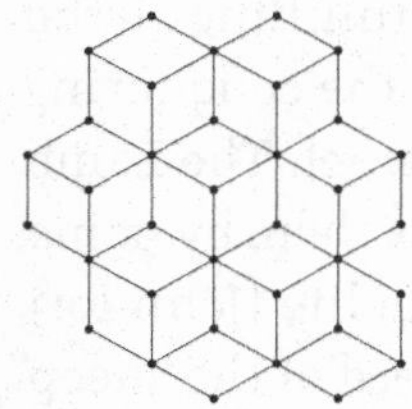

THE SEVENTH SEAL AND THE FIRST FOUR TRUMPETS

(8:1–12)

Both the seventh seal and the seventh trumpet judgments are cut off from the first six by an interlude. One of the reasons for this is to show how the seventh of each is intimately related to the plague judgments that follow. This is especially true here, where the seal judgments are preliminary and prepare for the trumpet and bowl judgments. With the breaking of this last seal the scroll is now fully open, and the way is now complete for the inaugural events that will end this world and initiate eternity. The silence of this judgment is a hushed expectancy for these final events to take place.

THE SEVENTH SEAL IS OPENED AND REVEALS SILENCE IN HEAVEN (8:1)

As he did with the first six, the worthy Lamb opens the seventh seal, completing the task that will allow the events of the end of world history to commence. Yet as the seal opens, a surprising thing happens. Instead of angelic action, as in the earlier seals, a dramatic silence ensues and lasts "about half an hour." There are several differing interpretations of this silence. It could be:

1. a liturgical silence before the prayers are heard;
2. a temporary cessation of revelation at the end;

3. the primeval silence of the first creation returning for the second re-creation of the world;
4. the silence of the condemned as they await judgment; or
5. a hushed expectancy awaiting God's final intervention.

The answer is most likely a combination of several of these. The silence certainly prepares for the prayers of 8:2–5, and as it is the seventh seal, there is a definite connection with the initiation of the final events. Primarily this is a hushed expectancy waiting for God's judgment to unfold; the scroll is now fully open, and all of heaven cannot wait for the final events to take place. Why is there silence at this point? Perhaps because 8:1–6 depicts a sacrificial act, with the incense and prayers of God's people. Priests performed their sacrifices in silence, emphasizing the awe of being in the presence of God. The silence here adds to the worshipful atmosphere of the scene.

THE TRUMPET JUDGMENTS ARE INTRODUCED (8:2–6)

The trumpet judgments flow out of the silence in heaven and inaugurate the final events. They recapitulate the plagues on Egypt of Exodus 7–10, which had two main purposes: to prove the sovereign presence and power of Yahweh and to show the powerlessness of the Egyptian gods. The plagues constituted a cosmic struggle between Yahweh and the powers behind Egypt. The scene here adds a further point: the gods were demonic powers, and the battle was with Satan and his followers, the nations. Also, here there is added material from Sinai, with the fire and the storms, the bitter waters, and the dimming of the heavenly bodies. The stress is on not only judgment but also repentance. Like the bowl judgments, these prove that evil is doomed, yet these also provide a call to repentance (Rev 9:20–21; 16:9, 11). These plagues seek to convert people from idolatry. Further, the trumpet judgments flow out of the prayers that ascend to God and are accepted by him. In other words, they are God's answers to the prayers of the martyrs in 6:9–11 for vindication and justice.

The purpose of this introduction in 8:2–6 is to emphasize the heavenly origin of the trumpet judgments and to show that in sending them, God is responding to the prayers of his martyred followers in 6:9–11. Worship throughout the book of Revelation produces judgment as well as joy, for God in his holiness is characterized by both love and justice, and these are interdependent aspects of his being. God assures his sealed saints that he does hear their prayers and act on them. Throughout this book, worship accompanies the divine judgments. The removal of evil from this world is a holy event, and all of God's followers, angel and human alike, are filled with praise at the destruction of evil forces.

Angels are the agents of heaven and act on God's behalf. The angels "standing before the throne" in 8:2 are undoubtedly the seven archangels of apocalyptic tradition; in 1 Enoch 20:2–8 they are named as Uriel, Raphael, Raguel, Michael, Saraqa'el, Gabriel, and Remiel. Here they are given seven trumpets, making them the royal heralds used in time of war (1 Sam 13:3), at the dedication of the temple (2 Chr 5:12), at the enthronement of the king (1 Kgs 1:34, 39) and often in worship. The Mishnah, an ancient Jewish source, tells us that there were 21 daily blasts in the temple, 48 on feast days (m. Sukkoth 5:5), and the trumpet was the chosen instrument announcing the **eschaton** (4 Ezra 6:23; Matt 24:31; 1 Cor 15:52; 1 Thess 4:16).

After the angels with trumpets appear, another angel arrives in 8:3 to take the next step toward the outpouring of judgment. While some believe this is Christ because of his mediatorial work in bearing the prayers to God, I think that is unlikely. Rather, this continues the priestly task of 5:8 where the elders and living creatures carry golden bowls, or censers, of incense holding the prayers of the saints. This angel stands at the heavenly altar, which, as in 5:8, combines the altar of incense and the altar of burnt offering. This fits the imagery here, for the censer first bears the prayers up to God in 8:4 (the task of the altar of incense), and then is filled with fire as it is hurled to earth in 8:5 (the task of the altar of burnt offering). These are not two separate altars, but one.

The censer was an open-topped pan that was made of bronze in the tabernacle (Exod 27:3) or gold in the temple (1 Kgs 7:50). It would have coals put in it from the altar of burnt offering and then incense to offer prayers before the Lord (Num 16:6–7). The incense combined three aromatic spices: resin and galbanum gum from shrubs and trees, mollusk scent from shellfish, and frankincense, which was also a gum resin. These were ground to powder and placed in front of the altar of incense, symbolizing the prayers of God's people ascending to God (Psa 141:2). The incense would be placed on the coals in the censer and give forth smoke that ascended to God on his throne, together with the prayers of God's people. Note the contrast of the smoke here with the smoke of 14:11 and 19:3, which depicts the torment of the evildoers. Here the smoke is joyous worship; there it is terrifying judgment.

In the temple, the incense was placed on coals in the censer as part of the morning and evening offering, with the ascending smoke signifying God's acceptance of the sacrifice and prayers as a "sweet-smelling" offering (Exod 29:18; Lev 1:9; Num 18:17). That is exactly the image here, as the angel fills the censer with fire from the altar, indicating that God is pleased, and then hurls it down to earth. With the angels, all of heaven is intimately involved in making certain that God receives these prayers for justice. God's response is instantaneous: the trumpet judgments begin as an answer to prayer.

In this way, the priestly angel becomes an avenging angel in 8:5. The Levitical symbolism of 8:3–4 becomes apocalyptic, as fire from the altar is hurled to earth and spawns the storms of judgment. The censer had already held coals to bring smoke from the incense in 8:3; now the angel returns to the altar and takes a second coal of fire from it. The first coals caused the incense and prayers to ascend to God; the second becomes fiery judgment, possibly alluding to Ezekiel 10:2–7, in which coals of fire are taken from the throne and scattered in Jerusalem.

The angel then throws the burning censer to earth, and this initiates another storm **theophany** after 6:12–14, again building on the storms of Sinai. The storms following the seventh seal (here), the seventh trumpet (11:19), and the seventh bowl (16:18) combine earthquake and storm to signify the judgment on the earth, the dismantling of creation that accompanies God's wrath poured out on sinful humanity.

The seven archangels were given trumpets in 8:2, and now they prepare to sound them. The actions of the priestly angel in 8:2–5 are framed by the preparatory action that will inaugurate the next group of seven judgments. The dramatic power of the seals, trumpets, and bowls now resumes after the interlude of 7:1–17 and the events of 8:2–5. The divinely guided movement toward the consummation of world history and the beginning of eternity commences once more.

THE FIRST FOUR TRUMPETS ARE BLOWN (8:7–12)

As stated above on 8:2–6, these trumpet plagues reproduce the Egyptian plagues and like them are directed against the idolatry of the day. This includes not just the Roman Empire but also the pseudo-Christian groups like the Nicolaitan cult of 2:2, 6, 14, 20. The purpose of the trumpets is to prove the absolute sovereignty of God and to provide a final chance to repent. With each plague judgment a further part of the world order experiences partial destruction, using the same 4 (earthly judgment)–2 (cosmic judgment)–1 (**eschaton**) pattern seen in the seal and bowl judgments, with an interlude between the sixth and seventh trumpet (10:1–11:12). The intensification of judgment continues, with the trumpets destroying a third of the earth after the seals destroyed a quarter of the earth.

FIRST TRUMPET (8:7)

With the first trumpet blast "hail and fire mixed with blood" appear in heaven and then are hurled to earth, repeating the action of the angel in 8:5, who hurled the fiery censer to earth. This is built on the seventh Egyptian plague (Exod 9:13–35), in which

God sent hail mixed with lightning and thunder, the worst storm in Egypt's history, destroying all vegetation (Exod 9:18). Hail as judgment appears often in the Old Testament (Josh 10:11; Job 38:22–23; Psa 78:47), but here fire mixed with blood is added from Joel 2:30–31: "I will show wonders ... blood and fire with billows of smoke." The two are often combined in judgment passages (Isa 9:5; Ezek 21:32, 38:22) and might stem from volcanic explosions in the Aegean islands that were said to turn the sky red, or perhaps from the blood-red rain due to red dust particles from the Sahara that still falls today.

As a result, a third of the earth and trees and all the grass are burned up. Why *all* the grass? Probably for apocalyptic effect—nothing will escape this terrible judgment. Also, how does this make sense when taken with 9:4, where the locusts are told *not* to harm the grass? The key is that apocalyptic images are not consistent and should not be harmonized but taken as-is. Each vision is a self-contained unit. Most of us have seen the terrible effects of forest fires, but this goes beyond that. Imagine one-third of the Amazon and the Congo and all the forests of earth—blackened and dead! How long would firefighters and their equipment last in a devastation far beyond anything imaginable?

SECOND TRUMPET (8:8–9)

Now a third of the oceanic waters are turned to blood, intensifying the first Egyptian plague, which affected the Nile (Exod 7:14–21). There it was Moses' staff that caused the event, but here it is "something like a huge mountain, all ablaze ... thrown into the sea." The idea of a mountain uprooted and cast into the sea has roots in the Old Testament (Psa 83:14; Job 28:9; Jer 4:24; Ezek 38:20), and a close parallel exists in Mark 11:23, where Jesus says that true faith can command a mountain to be plucked up and thrown in the sea.

The object like a mountain on fire here can be a volcano or a burning meteor, as in the next trumpet judgment. It is difficult to be sure. The background might be first-century volcanic eruptions like Vesuvius in AD 79, which buried the Roman city of Pompeii, but it is best to see apocalyptic scenarios like Sibylline Oracles 5:158–59: "A great star will come from heaven ... and will burn the deep sea and Babylon itself." This can be combined with Jeremiah 51:25, where Yahweh condemns Babylon, "I am against you, O destroying mountain. ... I will ... make you a burned-out mountain." Rome is called "Babylon" in 1 Peter 5:13 and often in Revelation, so it is best to take this as a symbolic picture of the destruction of Rome, itself symbolized as the empire of the beast in chapter 13.

When the burning mountain is thrown into the sea, the results are particularly devastating. Rome was completely dependent on sea traffic for all its trade and food distribution, so this was even more catastrophic than it appears at first glance. Not only are one-third of all the oceanic waters turned to blood, one-third of all sea life and ships are also destroyed. The sea lanes were called the lifeblood of Rome, for nearly all trade and food items came by ship; the mountains in the north of Italy made land trade very difficult. So this is even more disastrous than the first plague; civilization would cease due to such a terrible event. Still, it is partial (one third), allowing the possibility of repentance and reinstatement.

THIRD TRUMPET (8:10–11)

The plague on the inland waters is another allusion to the first Egyptian plague. This is explicitly a meteor, as a "great star blazing like a torch" tears through the atmosphere as it falls to earth. As in 6:13 falling stars are frequent in apocalyptic to describe the shaking of the heavens and divine intervention in human affairs. Here it is "blazing like a torch," a harbinger of the fiery judgment to come in the "lake of burning sulfur" (19:20; 20:10, 14–15). This burning meteor falls on a third of the rivers and "springs of water," a precious commodity in a land where much of the water stems from natural springs. It is a frequent metaphor for God's gift of life (Prov 10:11, 13:14; Jer 2:13) and provision of "living water" for parched ground (Isa 41:18, 58:11; Joel 3:18).

This star has a name, "Wormwood," a bitter-tasting shrub that was a symbol of bitter sorrow (Prov 5:4) and of judgment and death (Jer 9:15). When it falls on the inland waters, a third of them become wormwood and turn bitter with many deaths. Wormwood itself is not poisonous, but its frequent association with death and sorrow makes it a natural symbol for it. The fiery star turns the water poisonous, a frequent biblical symbol for judgment on sin (Deut 29:18; Jer 23:15). This is a reversal of the miracle of Marah (Exod 15:23) when Moses threw a piece of wood into the bitter water, turning it sweet. Clearly, this is a judgment that would shatter civilization in our day as well. It is hard to imagine a third of even the Great Lakes turned poisonous! Think of the many stories of polluted waste in lakes and rivers multiplied thousands of times.

Fourth Trumpet (8:12)

This replicates the ninth Egyptian plague (Exod 10:21–23) in which Yahweh sent darkness over Egypt for three days, a blackness so dense that no one could move about at all. Here God strikes the heavenly luminaries (in the Greek he "plagues" them). Unlike the exodus event, this plague is partial, lasting a third of each day and night. Every heavenly body is affected—sun, moon, and stars—and they disappear for that time. This is not a solar eclipse or lunar eclipse, however, because the darkness will be total for those periods. There are three emphases: day and night are "alike" (NIV "also," Greek "likewise") in being without light; the darkness lasts a third of the day and of the night; and the darkness is complete—there is absolutely no light.

Darkness is an important apocalyptic symbol. At creation it characterized the chaos of the primal world (Gen 1:2), and throughout Scripture it depicts the world of evil (Job 12:22; John 3:18–21). Darkness is not only central in the ninth Egyptian plague but also in the famous "sun standing still" episode in

Joshua 10:7–14. Joel 2:2 describes the Day of Yahweh as "a day of darkness and gloom" (also Zeph 1:15), and darkness as divine punishment is frequent in later writings (1 Enoch 17:6, 63:6; 2 Enoch 7:1). Jesus describes eternal punishment not only as Gehenna but as "darkness, where there will be weeping and gnashing of teeth" (Matt 8:12; 22:13; 25:30) and depicts the cosmic phenomena at his Second Coming as "the sun will be darkened, and the moon will not give its light." The darkness here prepares for the fifth bowl judgment when the kingdom of the beast is "darkened" and his followers "gnaw their tongues in agony" (16:10).

As in the first four bowls, the purpose of these four trumpet judgments is to reenact the Egyptian plagues by disproving the earthly gods and showing that Yahweh alone is on the throne. God's omnipotence is proven to the world, and the futility of all forces arrayed against him is obvious. Each judgment affects a different part of life—the material world (the first), food supply, trade and commerce (the second and third), heat and light (the fourth). These judgments together demonstrate that the earth-dwellers, those who live only for this world, have chosen foolishly, for only in God can there be true life. The things of this world will always turn on us and leave us unsatisfied and bereft. We dare not depend on them.

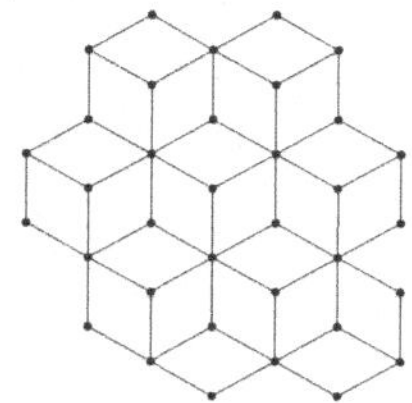

THE FIFTH AND SIXTH TRUMPET JUDGMENTS

(8:13–9:21)

These trumpet judgments are unique as the only judgments preceded by prophetic warnings of woe. The first four centered on the dismantling of creation, but these are cosmic in scope, centering on the demonic powers that turn on their own followers. Those were addressed to nature; these are directed at people. As in the first four seals, God does not need to send these judgments himself; he simply turns the evil forces loose to wreak havoc. The theme once more is the self-destructive power of evil. Moreover, each of the two judgments in this chapter is twice as long as the first four trumpets (8:6–12) put together. The reason is probably that these add an essential component to the theological message—proving to the sinners that the false "gods" they worship are demonic and are not their friends. In fact, their gods want only to torture and kill them!

AN EAGLE ANNOUNCES THE FIRST WOE (8:13)

The judgment theme is heightened by the announcement made by one of the carrion birds that will be invited to the "great supper of God" in Revelation 19:17, 21. This section begins slightly differently than the others, including both "I looked and heard" so as to stress the message of the bird. The bird could be an eagle or a vulture, but the former is more likely, as it is both a biblical symbol and a symbol of Rome—an eagle was on the Roman standard. It was also known for its size, strength, and speed, and was the foremost bird of prey in that part of the world. In all ancient cultures eagles were messengers of the gods, and in Revelation eagles stand for grandeur, power, and a harbinger of judgment (4:7; 12:14).

The emphasis on the eagle "flying in midair" shows the message is delivered all over the world from a point midway between heaven and earth. The other two places announcements from midair take place are 14:6 (the "eternal gospel") and 19:17 (the carrion birds called to the "great supper of God"). The emphasis in all three is the visibility and importance of the event. Human beings must choose between the gospel and the message of judgment. Their decision will determine their eternal destiny.

The eagle's message dominates chapter 9. The threefold "woe, woe, woe" is the obverse of the "holy, holy, holy" of 4:8—God's ultimate holiness that defines his character must produce the ultimate terror of wicked humanity as they face his wrath. God's holiness demands judgment, for sin is abomination and must be destroyed. The Greek *ouai* ("woe") may be onomatopoetic, resembling the sounds an eagle makes. The background for this is certainly the woe oracles of the prophets that depict God's anger and judgment against those who have forsaken him (Isa 5:8–9; Amos 6:1–2; Hab 2:9–10). It does not so much depict sorrow as terror, as it announces "disaster" to come and denotes the total horror felt by those who face it. Once again, the "inhabitants of the earth," or earth-dwellers, are those who have turned from God and live entirely for the things of this world. They are the natural objects of the wrath of God.

THE FIRST WOE ACCOMPANIES THE FIFTH TRUMPET (9:1–11)

The first of the woe judgments tells of a terrifying invasion of supernatural locust-scorpions from the pits of hell (the Abyss) that heap torture on the earth-dwellers for five months. There are two major points: First, the demons turn on their own people and show utter contempt and incomparable cruelty by torturing their very worshipers. Second, God is in complete control and is orchestrating the whole event. In so doing, God proves once more his justice and the necessity of the destruction of evil.

THE DESCENDING STAR-ANGEL OPENS THE ABYSS (9:1)

It is difficult to identify whether this descending angel is good or fallen. Many believe this "falling star" refers to a demonic figure, perhaps Satan himself (if identified with "the king ... the angel of the Abyss" in 9:11), since he is "fallen from heaven" as in 12:5–7, where the dragon is cast to earth. Jewish apocalyptic literature often applies Isaiah 14:12–14, where the king of Babylon is described as the "morning star ... cast down to earth," to Satan.[1] So it would be natural to take this falling star to be a fallen angel.

However, it is equally viable to take this to be a good angel. Nowhere else in Revelation does God use an evil angel to execute his will, with the possible exception of 17:16–17, and it is difficult to conceive of God entrusting the key of the Abyss to the primary inhabitant of the demonic prison house. If we understand the verb as "descending" rather than "falling," the action of the angel here would parallel that of the angel descending with the key of the Abyss in 20:1 to bind the dragon. I believe these are the same angel, which would mean the actions in 9:1 and 20:1 frame the period God has given to Satan and the antichrist to act at this final period of history. This end-time activity encompasses the period of the empire of the beast of chapter 13 and the 3 ½-year "great tribulation" period named in 7:14. So the angel here is another herald sent from heaven to do God's will.

---

1. See 1 Enoch 86:3, 88:1–3; 2 Enoch 29:4–5.

This angel is given a key, another appearance of the verb designating God's sovereign control of the action. This particular key is "to the shaft of the Abyss." The image of the Abyss stems from the bottomless depths of the ocean, and it became an idiom for the place of the dead ("the depths of the earth" in Psa 63:9, 71:20) and the "pit" or prison house for the fallen angels (1 Enoch 10:4–6, 18:9–16; 2 Pet 2:4; Jude 6). In Revelation it is a closed prison, and when opened the smoke as well as the beast emerge (Rev 9:2, 11:7). The shaft is the pit or well that goes down to the prison house itself.

Locust Plague from the Abyss (9:2–6)

Christ has control over the Abyss, and as his representative the angel inserts the key and opens it. This unleashes a huge column of smoke that rises as from a gigantic furnace. This is a frequent image in Scripture, taking place when God descends on Mount Sinai (Exod 19:18, Psa 144:5). Elsewhere, divine wrath is depicted as as "smoke from his nostrils" (2 Sam 22:9, Psa 18:8). This image describes the destruction of Sodom and Gomorrah (Gen 19:28) and the Day of Yahweh (Joel 2:30). Here it also signifies an act of God, a sign of his wrath and coming destruction. It is connected with Gehenna and points to the fires of hell (Rev 19:20; 20:10, 14, 15). The smoke is so dense that it darkens the sun and the sky, echoing the fourth trumpet (8:12) and Joel 2:10, where the sun and moon are darkened at the Day of Yahweh.

Out of the dense smoke locusts fall to the earth (Rev 9:3). Locust swarms are justly known for the devastation they cause. An 1866 swarm was 4 miles long and 100 feet thick. A 1915 swarm in Palestine darkened the sky for five days, completely devastating the land. This scene recalls the locust plague of Joel 1:2–2:11 and also the plague of locusts on Egypt, called the worst in past or future history (Exod 10:14). Locust plagues were frequent in the Old Testament as a sign of divine judgment (Deut 28:38–42; Jer 46:23; 51:14), and in Joel 1–2 a locust plague is a harbinger of the Day of Yahweh. As they ascend from the Abyss, they parallel the ascent of the beast in 11:7; 13:1; 17:8.

This event goes beyond the Old Testament images of locusts. Normal locusts eat only vegetation and do not go after people, but here God does not permit these locusts to eat vegetation (9:4). Instead, they are transformed into creatures "like scorpions" and hurt people, not grass or trees. The vegetation has already been the focus of God's judgment in the first trumpet judgment (8:7); these are directed at humanity. Moreover, these creatures are not natural insects but come out of the Abyss, and so are demonic by nature.

Scorpions are widespread in the Mediterranean world. Their sting is quite severe, even fatal to small children. They were a metaphor for terrible punishment (1 Kgs 12:11, 14) and symbols of demonic powers (Luke 10:19 and here). Here they can only harm the sinners, those without the seal of God, not the saints, as in the plagues on Egypt (Exod 8:22–23; 9:4, 6; 10:23). God's people are protected from the outpouring of divine judgment (Rev 3:10; 7:1–8). Only those who have rejected his offer of repentance (9:20–21) are subjected to this divine retaliation for what they have done to God's people (6:9–11; 8:2–5; 16:5–6). They have the mark of the beast (13:16), not the seal of God.

Yet as in Revelation 6:1–8 and 13:5–8 they "are given" authority/power (Greek *exousia* means both) for their nefarious task. God is the one who gives them authority over the earth-dwellers and power to inflict harm on them. Even the cosmic powers can do nothing unless God permits it. Satan has no autonomy from God and cannot do whatever he wishes.[2]

They are not allowed to kill anyone; that will occur in the next trumpet judgment. Here, they can *only* inflict serious injury ("torment" or "torture") on the unsaved (9:5) for five months. This was both the life span of a locust and the harvest period between the "early and latter rain" (April to August) when locusts tend to appear. Ordinary locust swarms last only a few days, but this is a supernatural event and constitutes a demonic

2. See "The Futility of Satan" in the introduction.

attack. There is emphasis on the torment or agony suffered by the earth-dwellers, a harbinger of the pain to be experienced in "the smoke of the torment" of the eternal lake of fire (14:10–11; 20:10). The torturous agony is caused as they are stung again and again for five months. The scorpion's sting is several times as powerful as a wasp, and it is hard to imagine multiple stings every day for five months. A person would be completely incapacitated for that entire time!

The despair caused by such torment is seen in the statement that the sufferers "long to die" and "seek death." The verb "long for" could almost be translated "they lust after death," and describes an adamant demand that they be allowed to commit suicide. There is great irony here: They took the lives of the martyrs in 6:9–11, and now they want to take their own lives. There are five suicides in the Old Testament—Abimelech (Judg 9:54), Saul (1 Sam 31:4), his armor bearer after he died (1 Sam 31:5), Ahithophel (2 Sam 17:23), and Zimri (1 Kgs 16:18). Job contemplated suicide but decided against it (Job 7:15). In the Roman world it was an honorable death, but in the Bible it constitutes murdering oneself.

However, God will not allow them to die until the right time, in the second demonic invasion of the next judgment. This again is ***lex talionis***, the law of retribution. They have tortured and killed God's people, and now God will allow the demons to return the favor on their own followers. The demons are more than happy to do so. In the Gospels it is clear that demons possess people in order to torture and kill those who are made in the image of God, which is their way of getting back at God (Mark 5:1–20; 9:14–29). They do so again here; this is their true nature.

Description of the Locusts (9:7–10)

This is a complex apocalyptic picture, for John is combining the locusts and scorpions with the horses and warriors of an invading army. These creatures are supernaturally large and incredibly fearsome, drawing images from Joel 1:6–7 and 2:4–5

("A nation [with] ... the teeth of a lion ... the appearances of horses ... noise like that of chariots ... like a crackling fire consuming stubble, like a mighty army drawn up for battle"). Their overall appearance is "like horses prepared for battle" from Joel 2. The head of a locust resembles a horse, and ancient war-horses were fierce indeed, as seen in Job 39:19–25, used in the movie *Secretariat*: "Do you give the horse his strength ... make him leap like a locust, striking terror with his proud snorting?" The added "prepared for war" shows the nature of both these trumpet judgments: the demons are going to war against their own followers.

From the general picture John proceeds to provide the details, moving from the heads to faces, hair, breastplates, wings, and finally tails. The "crowns like gold" on their heads may somewhat resemble the yellow tips of the antennae of a locust but mainly is used as a symbol of the victorious conqueror. This is the Greek *stephanos*, the wreath won by the victor in an athletic contest or a military skirmish; it was often worn by Domitian and other emperors. In Revelation it is worn by the angelic elders (4:4), by Christ at his **Parousia** (14:14), and by the victorious saints (2:10; 3:11; 12:1). For these demonic powers this is a pretentious crown, for they only rule their small earthly kingdom for a short time (12:12). They are usurpers who claim an authority they do not possess.

Their faces are "like human faces," and this, combined with the following "hair like women's hair" (9:8), demonstrates the pretentious desire of these demonic beings to usurp humankind's place at the apex of God's creation. This image also constitutes an imitation of the living creatures of 4:7 ("a face like a man"). These demons had lost their angelic estate in heaven and want it back.

Their "teeth like lion's teeth" returns to Joel 1:6, "the teeth of a lion, the fangs of a lioness." This is also the point of 1 Peter 5:8, "the devil prowls around like a roaring lion looking for someone to devour." They want to destroy all human beings because humans are made in God's image. Therefore, to the demonic horde they are objects of contempt and hatred even if they have rejected God and become followers of Satan. Their war is against all humanity.

Next, they have "breastplates like breastplates of iron" (9:9), a reference to the thorax of a locust, which resembles armor. It also alludes to the practices of the Parthians, who protected their horses with pieces of armor.[3] The breastplate on the horse, as with soldiers, protected both the sides and back and rendered the horse unassailable in the midst of battle. This stresses the invincibility of these terrible creatures.

The "sound of their wings" certainly describes the terrifying sound of a locust swarm. However, the picture is enhanced here, describing the even more terrifying sound of cavalry and war chariots as they hurl themselves into battle, alluding to Joel 2:5, "a noise like that of chariots." Chariots were the single most important key to victory, both in the Old Testament (Judg 1:19; 1 Kgs 10:26; 1 Chr 19:7) and in the Roman world. This adds even more terrifying imagery to the picture of the demons making war on their own followers.

The final word picture returns to 9:5: these creatures have "tails with stingers, like scorpions" (9:10). The Greek word for "sting" (*kentron*) is used in 1 Corinthians 15:55 of "the sting of death," and was used in the first century of the "sting" of the scourge, a vicious whip used to tear a back apart (like Jesus in Matt 27:26). With this the picture is complete, combining the imagery of the locust, the scorpion, and the warhorse to describe the torture caused by the war the demonic forces conduct against the very ones who worshiped them. This is a very important message; those who refuse to turn to God need to understand the true nature and intentions of the gods they have chosen to serve.

3. See commentary on 6:1.

THE KING OF THE DEMONIC SWARM (9:11)

Proverbs 30:27 says that "locusts have no king," but these demonic locust-scorpions do have a king, "The Angel of the Abyss," a title having the Greek article and designating *the* leader of the demonic army. While this could be the angel who opens the Abyss in Revelation 9:1, I argued there the unlikelihood of that connection.[4] That was a good angel, a divine herald acting for God. This is an evil angel, probably Satan himself, with the title stressing his leadership over the denizens of the Abyss. Elsewhere in Revelation the "kings" are earthly rulers who are client kings of the beast and do his bidding (16:14; 17:2, 10–11). This is the demonic king, emperor over the cosmic powers and earthly rulers.

The two names of this demon-ruler are synonyms, with the Hebrew "Abaddon" and the Greek "Apollyon" both meaning "Destroyer." This virtually becomes the title for the fifth and sixth trumpet judgments, in which a third of the earth-dwellers will progressively be destroyed. There is also irony at work, for this being and his false trinity (the dragon, the beast, and the false prophet, 16:13) will be destroyed (19:20; 20:10, 14) along with their followers (11:18, "those who destroy the earth"). In fact, "Destroyer" is a virtual synonym for Hades, as the Old Testament the term often refers to the place of the dead (Job 26:6; Prov 15:11; 27:20). So this "king" is named for the place he rules. The name of one of the chief gods, Apollo, god of pestilence and plague, stems from this term, and the emperor Domitian viewed himself as Apollo incarnate.

THE SECOND WOE ACCOMPANIES THE SIXTH TRUMPET (9:12–21)

The war of the cosmic powers against their own followers will come to completion with this second woe/terror. Torture of all the unsaved becomes the death of a third of humankind. This

4. See commentary on 9:1.

is organized in the same way as the first, with the release of the angels (9:13–16 = 9:1–6), the description of the evil forces (9:17–19 = 9:7–10), and a concluding clarification (9:20–21 = 9:11). Both have demonic cavalry, and both harm with their tails. God is in sovereign control of these woes; the evil forces do his bidding in the long run. Most shocking is the fact that after the demons have produced the greatest death toll in all of history, the unbelievers still reject God and prefer to keep worshiping the very demons who have just tortured and killed them. Is there any greater proof of the insanity of sin?

Introduction/The Second Woe (9:12)

The three "woe" texts (8:13; 9:12; 11:14) show that each is a "woe oracle" like the Old Testament prophetic texts, so these judgments are "woes" or terrors, and each prepares for the others to follow. The emphasis is upon the imminent arrival of the others "soon after this" (see 11:14).

Release of the Four Angels (9:13–16)

This scene begins with a voice "from the four horns of the golden altar that is before God." It may be the voice of the saints praying (Rev 6:9; 8:3–5) but since this is "a (singular) voice," it is more likely the angel who presented those prayers to God on the golden altar in 8:3–5. This is the altar of incense, and the "horns" are the protuberances at the four corners (Exod 27:2, 37:25). Horns are a symbol of power, and on the altar they signify the power of Yahweh. The speaker is not God, but God is speaking through an angelic intermediary, making this a further divine response to the prayers of the saints for justice and vengeance (Rev 6:9; 8:3–4). In 8:5 the first response takes place as the angel hurls the golden censer to earth and initiates the trumpet judgments, and this is the second response, initiating a further stage and releasing the death angels to devastate sinful humanity.

This is the first time an angel sounding a trumpet participates in the event the angel inaugurates (9:14), and that adds power to the scene. Here the heraldic angel "releases the four angels" of destruction. There is some connection to the four angels holding back destruction in 7:1. There the destructive forces are restrained; here they are released. The fact that these "angels" are "bound" favors the view that they are in fact demonic, for Satan is "bound" by Jesus in Mark 3:27. It is likely they are the leaders of the demonic cavalry to be unleashed in 9:16. The place of their binding is the Euphrates, the eastern boundary of the Roman Empire, with the Parthians in the lands to the east.[5] This is similar to 1 Enoch 56:55–57:3, where the "angels of punishment" get the Parthians and Medes to attack Israel. The Euphrates was a symbol of foreign invasion, since so many of the Old Testament invaders crossed it to attack Israel—the Assyrians, Babylonians, and Persians. In Revelation 16:12 the Euphrates is dried up so the "kings of the east" can invade.

In another emphasis on divine sovereignty, God has prepared (another divine passive) these angels "for this very hour and day and month and year" (9:15). In 6:11 the martyred saints are told to wait for the number of martyrs God had predestined to be completed. Here the emphasis is the same, except now it is the exact time for God's punishment to be finished. The divinely chosen moment is the stress in both passages. God's predestined will has chosen this specific point of time (similar to Gal 4:4, "the fullness of time" for the incarnation to take place) to initiate this critical end-time event.

The purpose is also clear: to kill a third of humankind. In 7:3 the four angels of destruction were restrained until the saints were sealed; now it is time to release the forces of death. So this culminates the progress of the trumpet judgments from the dismantling of creation to the death of many due to Wormwood in 8:11 to the torment of the earth-dwellers in 9:5–6 and now to the consummation of all this deadly movement in the death of a third of mankind—in today's numbers, two billion dead, an

5. See commentary on 6:1.

inconceivable number, intensifying the one-third dead of 6:8. Still, we must remember that along with punishment for sins committed, the purpose is also redemptive, to provide a warning to "the rest of humankind not killed" (9:20) that they must get right with God or else. God after releasing the death angels restrains the death toll to one-third to give the rest of humanity an opportunity to repent and turn to Christ for salvation.

The four angels released somehow metamorphose into a horrendous demonic cavalry numbering 200 million strong ("twice ten thousand times ten thousand"). In 5:11 the number of angels worshiping God is "myriads of myriads" (a myriad = ten thousand) referring to an innumerable number of angels, and this doubles that number. The Roman army in the first century was composed of 25 legions or about 125,000, so this was 800 times the size of that, an absolutely unstoppable force. In fact, that was close to the total number of people in the entire Roman Empire. Moreover, these were not infantrymen but mounted cavalrymen, the elite of any legion. This is as imposing a picture as anyone could imagine. John says, "I heard the number," probably because this vision is so astounding that he feels he must tell his readers that this is exactly what he heard.

Description of Demonic Warhorses (9:17–19)

There are close parallels with the description of the locust plague in 9:7–10, both in the description of the warhorses and their supernatural appearance. Both the locusts and the cavalry are demonic in origin and bent on torment and destruction, so they work in concert to bring intense suffering and death to evil humankind. It is likely that both the horses and the riders have breastplates, which fits the Parthian cavalry, with both covered in bright armor and famous for their ferocity in combat. The colors may well indicate the material the breastplates are made of—some made of fire, some of hyacinth, some of brimstone—as well as their colors—red, dusky blue, sulfurlike yellow. Mainly, they correspond to the "fire, smoke, and sulfur" of 9:17b–18 and describe the terrifying nature of this demonic cavalry, filled with fire and devastation.

The locusts have teeth like lion's teeth, but the horses are even more fierce, with heads like "the heads of lions." This is because in 9:19 their power is in their mouths as well as their tails, and it is the mouth that tears apart the prey. Out of their mouths comes "fire, smoke, and sulfur," corresponding to the colors above and showing that these monsters are truly from the pits of hell. In Job 41:19–20 fire and smoke "shoot out" from the mouth of Leviathan, and in Genesis 19:28 Sodom and Gomorrah are destroyed by fire and smoke (also Psa 11:6; Isa 30:33; Ezek 38:22). It is a supreme irony that these demonic forces breathe out the same "fire, smoke, and sulfur" that will become their own eternal torment in 19:20; 20:10, 14. In 9:18 John considers them as three separate plagues (similar to the four in 6:8) that end the lives of a third of humankind. Each has a separate role to play, picturing the siege engines and fiery projectiles of the Roman army.

The tails are "like snakes," for Satan is called "the ancient serpent" in 12:9, 14, 15; 20:2, and that alludes to the "crafty serpent" in the garden in Genesis 3:1–7. Jewish apocalyptic equated that serpent with Belial/Satan in Apocalypse of Moses 16 and 3 Baruch 9:6–8, and the presence of a snake injuring people was a common picture of demonic activity in both Egyptian and Persian religions. The added picture of the head injuring people stems from the warhorse with sharpened teeth that was taught to bite the enemy in the midst of battle.

REJECTION AND REFUSAL TO REPENT (9:20–21)

This concludes not just the fifth and sixth trumpet judgments but the whole of the trumpet judgments, and in fact the seals as well. Each of the trumpet plagues has proven the omnipotence and sovereignty of God as well as both the futility and powerlessness of the earthly gods. The two judgments of chapter 9 have also demonstrated that the cosmic powers despise and hate their own followers and wish only to torture and kill them. The earth-dwellers cannot depend on the things of this world; they will only turn on them and destroy them.

Moreover, we see here that God's actual purpose in unleashing these evil forces was to bring the people to the realization of their folly and give them a final chance to repent. Yet their depravity has such a hold on them that they reject God's message in the plagues. They "refused to repent" (literally "did not even repent"), emphasizing their complete and willful rejection of God. One of the main purposes of the seals, trumpets, and bowls, as we have seen all along, is to provide a final offer of salvation to the nations. Here the emphasis is to prove the hold that the total depravity of sinful humankind has on the people. They have just been given absolute proof of the true intentions of their gods and the end result of worshiping these demonic powers, yet they not only refuse to embrace God's offer of eternal life but prefer "the works of their hands." Most likely this does not refer generally to the things of this world but more specifically to the idols they worship (see Deut 4:28; 2 Kgs 19:18; Isa 17:8).

Demon worship comes to the fore in Deuteronomy 32:16–17, "They made him jealous with their foreign gods and angered him with their detestable idols. They sacrificed to false gods, which are not God" (see also Psa 106:37; Jubilees 11:4). Paul shows two truths about idolatry: First, an idol is nothing; it has no life in and of itself (1 Cor 8:4); and second, "the sacrifices of pagans are offered to demons, not to God" (1 Cor 10:20). In other words, idols are lifeless things made of "gold, silver, bronze, stone and wood—idols that cannot see or hear or walk" (drawn from Psa 115:4–7), but at the same time there are cosmic forces of frightening power behind them. These demons have turned against their own followers, but these foolish people have rejected the God of mercy and preferred to worship the very evil powers that have so mistreated them.

Idolatry is as great a problem today as it was in John's time. An idol by definition is the tendency to turn an earthly object into a god, to worship a created thing rather than the Creator.

Whatever we place at the head of our lives and give priority over God is an idol. The modern world is replete with things that we turn into idols—money, possessions, power, success/fame, sex, pleasure, alcohol, drugs. These things, while not always bad in themselves, when worshiped as idols become the tools of Satan to gain control over our lives. We must be on guard against idolatry in our own hearts, and warn people both inside and outside the church of the control of the cosmic powers in our society. We must turn to the triune Godhead who alone can lift us above addiction to the sins of this world. We must bring others to the alternative universe God is making available and to the salvation in Christ that alone can give them life over the eternal death that awaits them.

The idol worship of 9:20 is followed by the unrighteous deeds of 9:21. Vice lists like this were quite common in ancient writings, and Paul used them frequently to demonstrate the depravity of the pagan world (Rom 1:29–31; 1 Cor 5:9–11; Gal 5:19–21; Eph 4:25–32). The lists here, in 20:8, and in 22:15 stress the depravity of the non-Christian world but also provide a warning to weak Christians—called "cowards" in 20:8—of the danger of giving in to sinful practices. The list here follows the contours of the Ten Commandments, particularly the second (idolatry), sixth (murder), seventh (adultery), and eighth (theft).

The mention of "magic potions" could refer to medicine but more likely denotes the potions used in magic rites. Magic (or sorcery) was widespread in the Roman world, and Ephesus was a center of activity with the temple of Artemis. When the sorcerers in Ephesus burned their magic scrolls in Acts 19:19, this constituted a major victory over the demonic realm. The pagan people believed the gods involved themselves in human affairs and could be cajoled into helping ensure success in business or athletics, in sexual liaisons, healing, or military battles. The message here is that all such practices render one an enemy of God.

The fifth and sixth trumpet judgments are proof positive of two great sorrows regarding the reality of the sin-sick world we inhabit. The first is the sadness of the demonic world under the control of the "Angel of the Abyss" and the focused hatred of these beings who desire only to torture and kill even their own followers. The second is the even greater sadness that depraved humanity is so ensnared and deceived that they fail to realize this truth and rush after sin recklessly. Yet in all this, we can be comforted by the fact that God is supreme. The demonic forces malevolently seek only harm for sinners, but God is giving these people a completely undeserved opportunity to repent and find eternal life. The supreme truth in all this is the redemptive love of God and the justice of his judgments.

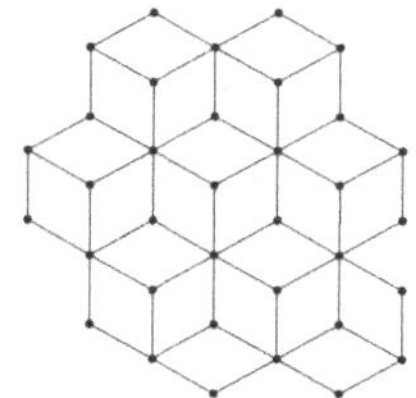

THE LITTLE SCROLL AND JOHN'S COMMISSIONING SERVICE

(10:1–11)

The second interlude (10:1–11:13—the first was 7:1–17) depicts the role of the saints in the last days, including the church age, in three ways: John's commissioning as a prophet (10:1–11), the reintroduction of God's protection of the saints (11:1–2), and the description of the ministry of the two witnesses (11:3–13). The single thread that unites this is prophecy, with the prophetic actions of 10:8–10 and 11:1–2 preparing for the prophetic ministry of the two witnesses in 13:3–6. This is the only place in the interludes where John is an integral part of the action, and he participates as a prophet who is in effect asked to join God's mission to the world, which will involve the two witnesses as well. A second thread here is the "little scroll," that part of the larger scroll from chapter 5 that has not yet come to pass. Here God reveals more regarding the part to be played by the church in these final days of history: bold witness accompanied by intense suffering. They are sealed and protected (7:3–4; 9:4) and constitute God's special possession (11:1–2). At the same time, they are pursued and persecuted by the dragon/beast and their followers (11:7–10), but that very suffering will be their victory (11:11–12).

A MIGHTY ANGEL DESCENDS WITH THE LITTLE SCROLL (10:1–4)

"Another mighty angel" (after 5:2) descends directly from God to carry on the task of the first mighty angel with the scroll. Many believe this angel is Gabriel on the basis of the oath (10:6) and the meaning of his name ("strong man of God"), but that is too speculative. The angel, like most in the book apart from Michael in 12:7, is unnamed. The fourfold description in 10:1 is the most majestic litany of any angel in the book, paralleling Christ in 1:13–16 or God in 4:3, so others believe this is Christ. However, it is difficult to conceive of Christ being described as an "angel" and more likely that this strong angel as the representative of God shares his splendor and might. So he is "clothed in a cloud" like God and represents his Shekinah presence (as in Exod 16:10; Lev 6:2; Ezek 10:4); he has "a rainbow on his head" (like God in Rev 4:3 and Ezek 1:28); he has "a face like the sun" (like Christ in Rev 1:16 and Matt 17:2); and his legs are "like fiery pillars" (like Christ in Rev 1:15). So the angel as the special herald of God and Christ partook of the Godhead's glory and power and signified the deliverance of God's people.

The mighty angel has "the little scroll open in his hand" (10:2). Christ had progressively broken the seals and opened the scroll in chapters 5–6, and now he has given it to his angelic representative to finish the task. Some think the scrolls of chapters 5 and 10 are two different documents, but it is better to see them as one and the same. The first scroll, containing God's plan for ending this age, was progressively opened as each seal was broken, and the contents of it continued to be revealed in the trumpet judgments. So the "little scroll" here refers to the events yet to be revealed in the bowl judgments and the rest of this book. The content of the scroll in 5:1 stems from Ezekiel 2:9–10, and that of 10:2–3 stems from Ezekiel 3:1–3. Both are part of Ezekiel's call and commission, and here they are part of John's prophetic commission.

So now the scroll lies open, and John is to be told in 10:8–11 how the plan relates to the saints still on earth. The scroll was closed in the hand of God, opened by the Lamb, and now lies open in the hand of the angel so as to be related to the church. This is the theme of 10:1–11 (the "sweet" and "bitter" aspects of the coming events for God's people) and of 11:1–13 (the bold witness of the church during these events).

The angel then plants "his right foot on the sea and his left on the land," reminding readers of the Colossus of Rhodes. This was a 105-foot bronze statue of Helios, patron deity of the island of Rhodes. It stood on a pedestal at the entrance of the harbor, symbolizing that Rhodes controlled both land and sea. One of the seven wonders of the ancient world, it was completed in 280 BC and felled by an earthquake in 224 BC. In John's time, the remains of the magnificent statue were still visible. With the angel's feet on land and sea, John was stressing the dominion of God over the whole world.

The angel gives a mighty shout "like the roar of a lion" (10:3), as Yahweh roars in Hosea 11:10 and Amos 3:8. He speaks with the "mighty voice" of God, and then "the seven thunders" respond. This echoes Psalm 29, where God as ruler over creation, as sovereign over "sea and land," speaks like thunder seven times. The thunders always occur in contexts centering on the God of the storms, but they speak only here. This sums up the other storm **theophanies**, celebrating the God of justice and the deliverer of his people.

As elsewhere, John wants to write down the message of the thunders (10:4), but a "voice from heaven" silences his pen and seals the voice of the thunders. This is ironic, for the seals of the scroll are opened while the message of the thunders is sealed or closed. The meaning of this is difficult to ascertain. This certainly echoes Daniel 12:4, where the prophet is told to "close up and seal the words of the scroll until the end" in a context where the end is that final 3 ½-year period at the end of history (Dan 12:11–12). Still, this has led to several theories. One possibility is that God has canceled these judgments so more could be converted. In other words, he has shortened the days for the sake of the elect (Matt 24:22). The problem with this is the seven bowl judgments yet to come. Why aren't they canceled? Others believe these revelations were too sacred to be revealed at this time (2 Cor 12:4), yet it is difficult to explain how these could be more sacred than the others revealed in this book. Perhaps it is the judgments as warning that are canceled to make way for the revelation of the little scroll that will bring history to a close, but the warnings continue in 16:9, 11.

The solution may arise when we recall the influence of Daniel 12:4 and Psalm 29. There may be double meaning in the verb "sealed," meaning first that there will be a specific time when the church will be told the contents of the scroll, but that is not yet; they must await God's will. At the same time, second, the emphasis is on God's complete sovereignty over the events. The message is "sealed" because God controls all aspects and will reveal them to his people in his own time. He is making known the seal, trumpet, and bowl judgments, but all the details are not revealed, so the church must depend on him and him alone. The events are rushing to their conclusion, but God alone will bring about the final close to history, and he will do it in his own time.

THE ANGEL MAKES AN OATH (10:5–7)

The same angel who "stood on sea and land" and claimed the earth for God now raises his right hand and makes an oath, recalling the man in linen in Daniel 12:7 who swore by God that the completion of the divine plan was at hand. Raising the right hand was a common way of taking an oath (Exod 6:8; Ezek 20:5, 15), and here as in Daniel it responds to the basic question already asked in Revelation 6:10, "How long, sovereign Lord?" The answer is always the same: "As long as God chooses—wait on him."

The angel here swears "by him who lives forever and ever" (10:6), echoing the oath form in the Old Testament, "as the Lord lives" (Num 14:21; Judg 8:19; 1 Sam 20:3) and especially Daniel 12:7 that expands the form into "lives forever," thus centering on the eternal God who controls the future as well as the present. Then the angel goes beyond Daniel 12:7 and adds from Psalm 29 the fact that this eternal God is also the Creator of the heavens and the earth and the sea. All three spheres of life in this world are included (heaven, earth, sea = the first four trumpets and bowls), and with each the emphasis is on the creation of "all that is in it," that is, each and every part of creation, animate and inanimate. This angel had placed his foot on sea and land, signifying God's ownership of the whole world, and now he acknowledges God as creator of every part of his created order. This is the angel of Yahweh, Creator of the universe, who now delivers God's message.

The message itself culminates redemptive history. In Daniel 12:5–9 the "how long" question is answered via the "time, times, and half a time" of the final period of human history (see Rev 12:14). The oath is the same here, but the message is more explicit: "There will be no more delay!" In other words, the time of the end of the world predicted by Daniel has now arrived, and nothing can hold it back. Daniel 12:5–10 asks when (Rev 10:6) and what the outcome will be (10:8). Here we are told that the time has arrived, and the outcome will be the beginning of eternity (seen in the seventh trumpet, 11:15–19). The waiting is over, and the hour of vindication and victory is here. The designations for this final three-and-a-half year period will dominate chapters 10–13 (11:2, 3; 12:6, 14; 13:5), showing God is now instigating the final events of the history of mankind, and nothing can delay them.

The angel predicts (10:7) that the revelation of the outcome predicted in Daniel will occur when the "seventh angel" sounds his trumpet (11:15–19). So the seventh trumpet is God's sovereign herald announcing the **eschaton**. At that time "the mystery of God will be accomplished" (fulfilled, brought to completion). "Mystery" occurs four times (1:20; here; 17:5, 7) and is an apocalyptic term designating the divine secrets hidden from past generations and revealed to God's people in these last days. The word "apocalyptic" refers to the process of divine revelation, and "mystery" refers to the content of the revelations.

The major question is what part of the mysteries is being revealed here. Certainly the basic thrust is those events inaugurated by the seventh trumpet, namely the arrival of the eternal "kingdom of our Lord and of his Messiah" (11:15). Yet in what way have they been "accomplished/completed"? The term refers to the consummation of the process that fulfills a plan, in this case God's plan for ending the age of humankind. God's kingdom was inaugurated in the first advent and is to culminate in the second advent. Finally, we are told that this mystery was first announced through God's "slaves, the prophets" alluding to Amos 3:7, which speaks of God's plan revealed "to his servants the prophets." Interestingly, "announced" is the verb form of "gospel." And so the connotation is that this mystery of the final inbreaking of God's kingdom is among the greatest "good news" proclamations ever announced.

JOHN IS COMMISSIONED TO PROPHESY (10:8–11)

The action now returns to the theme of the little scroll in 10:1–4 and its connection with the commissioning of Ezekiel in Ezekiel 3:1–3. There are two levels of meaning. Primarily this denotes John reenacting Ezekiel's consuming of the scroll and thereby initiating his ministry as a prophet. At the same time, the message concerns the church's place in "the mystery of God" soon to take place—it will be "bitter" because it involves much suffering and yet "sweet' because the church will emerge victorious through those difficult events.

The angel who had told John in 10:4 not to write now speaks once more and tells John to prophesy. There is a time to be silent and a time to speak up. Thus the story enters the phase regarding the inauguration of prophetic action. First John is ordered to replicate the work of the Lamb in 5:7–8 and take the scroll from the hand of the angel. For the third time we are told the angel is standing "on sea and land" (10:2, 5, 8), signaling God's dominion over this world. It is time for John as prophet to announce that God is reclaiming his world. The commission of Ezekiel in Ezekiel 2:8–3:3 as prophet to a "rebellious nation"

(Ezek 2:3) now becomes the commission of John to the rebellious nations of his world (and our world).

So John repeats Ezekiel's action and responds immediately, taking "the little scroll" (10:9). The angel repeats the command to Ezekiel by saying, "Take it and eat it." The idea of consuming the Word of God occurs often, as in Psalm 119:103, "How sweet are your words to my taste, sweeter than honey to my mouth," or Jeremiah 15:16, "When your words came, I ate them; they were my joy and my heart's delight" (also Psa 19:10; Prov 24:13–14). When Ezekiel was told to eat the scroll (Ezek 3:2–3), that act constituted his commission to prophesy. John is then told the scroll would be bitter in his belly but "sweet as honey" in his mouth. Ezekiel experienced the sweetness of the scroll but not the bitterness. Still, he was told it contained "words of lament and mourning and woe" (Ezek 2:10) and that Israel would reject the message (Ezek 3:4–7), so Ezekiel left "in bitterness and in anger of spirit" (Ezek 3:14). So in reality Ezekiel also experienced sweetness as well as bitterness.

There is a **chiasm** in 10:9–10. It is "bitter-sweet" in the command of 10:9 and then "sweet-bitter" in the actual ingestion of the scroll in 10:10. This is the key theme of 10:8–11, and understandings differ. In light of its use in Ezekiel in a context of his warning apostate Israel of impending judgment, many are led into seeing the sweetness as the life-giving effect God's word has for those who accept it and the bitterness when the offer is rejected by the nations. Others see the sweetness as the offer of salvation and the bitterness as the message of judgment. There are aspects of both of these here, but it is best to see the larger context in the interlude of 10:1–11:13. This does not just involve John himself as a prophet but must include the church as the focus of the whole passage. The scroll is sweet because God's will always benefits his people, who will be vindicated and rewarded for their sacrifices. It is bitter because in the interim it will bring persecution and great suffering to the saints. So there are two foci: the word as life-giving and yet rejected, and the saints as vindicated and yet hated.

After this parabolic interchange, John receives his direct commission in 10:11. John is told, "You must prophesy again," with the divine "must" (Greek *dei*) showing that John's prophetic ministry is a divine necessity in light of the importance of the message. John had been commissioned to "write down" the visions in 1:11, 19, and in 4:1 he was "shown" the future events themselves. The commission to "prophesy again" builds on both of these and reminds John of his ongoing call to ministry. It especially relates to the visions yet to come in chapters 12–22. John would need this affirmation that God was behind everything he was doing in the difficult days and years ahead—as do we all!

The focus of this prophetic ministry was "about many peoples and nations and languages and kings." The preposition *epi* here is critical and has a double meaning. It is a positive message "about" the nations, addressing the church regarding its witness and the nations regarding their need for repentance. At the same time, it is a message "against" the nations, a message of judgment against those who steadily refuse to turn to God (see 9:20–21). In the context of Ezekiel and of this book, the negative predominates, as seen in the ministry of judgment conducted by the two witnesses in 11:3–6. Still, the positive is important as well, for the nations are the object of God's redemptive mission. There are two additions to the fourfold list (see on 5:9, 7:9): the presence of "many," highlighting the sense of universal witness to all the peoples of the earth; and the presence of "kings," pointing to the "kings of the earth" (6:15; 16:14; 17:10–11) who are the rulers of the nations and persecutors of the saints. The positive side is seen in 21:24, where "the kings of the earth" who have turned to Christ will "bring their splendor" into the new Jerusalem and submit their glorious rule to the King of kings (see 1:5).

Two themes dominate this chapter. The first is God's complete sovereignty over his creation. The mighty angel demonstrates God's omnipotence and control over the cosmos, reclaiming this world for him. Also, the seven thunders show that he is indeed the creator God who proclaims his judgment over his world. The second theme is the prophetic witness of the church. John reenacts Ezekiel's commission as a prophet, and the sweetness and bitterness of both Ezekiel's and John's difficult ministry is passed on to the church. There is sweetness in the knowledge that God will bring his people vindication and victory, and bitterness that the world is rejecting God's offer and turning against his people.

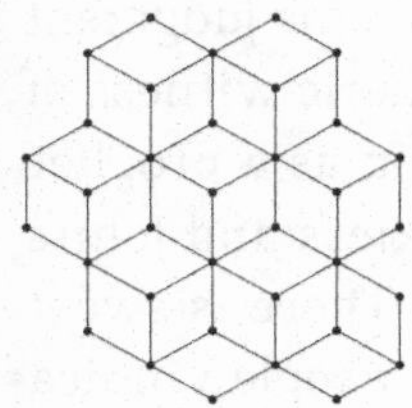

THE ALTAR, WITNESSES, AND SEVENTH TRUMPET

(11:1–19)

This is a complicated chapter, and one of the most difficult of the book. It is complicated in part because it concludes both the second interlude (10:1–11:13) and the section on the trumpet judgments (8:1–11:19). There are three parts to it: the measuring of the altar (11:1–2), centering on divine protection and opposition to the saints; the ministry of the two witnesses (11:3–13), depicting the church's bold witness to their persecutors; and the seventh trumpet (11:14–19), picturing the arrival of "the kingdom of our Lord" (11:15). Two threads hold all three parts together: God's presence with his people and the church triumphing over their enemies. The whole of redemptive history is encompassed in this chapter, and it perfectly encompasses the imagery of the scroll, for its sweetness is seen in 11:1–2 (God's possessive presence with his people) and 11:14–19 (the triumph of God on behalf of his people), while its bitterness is seen in 11:2 (trampled by the Gentiles) and 11:7–10 (the death of the two witnesses).

JOHN MEASURES THE TEMPLE AND THE ALTAR (11:1–2)

Measuring the Inner Court (11:1)

Front and center once again is the divine passive *edothē* ("it was given"), used throughout to designate the divine impetus behind events. God—and by implication, Christ—gives John a measuring rod, a straight hollow reed 10 feet 4 inches long, used for land surveying. The key indicator is ownership; even today if you've ever bought property you've had the property surveyed to indicate the exact land that belongs to you and what belongs to the neighbors.

John is ordered to measure the temple and its environs as well as the people worshiping in it. This picture alludes to Ezekiel 40:3, 5 where a "man whose appearance was like bronze" measured the temple to show what belonged to God. Similarly, in Zechariah 2:1–5 a man measures Jerusalem to demonstrate God's protection and preservation of the holy city. John is asked to measure three things—the temple, its altar, and its worshipers.

"Temple" is *naos*, the term for the sanctuary holding the holy place and holy of holies rather than the temple as a whole. Throughout Revelation, it always refers to the heavenly temple rather than Solomon's or Herod's temples, and that is in keeping with the **eschatological** temple in Ezekiel 40–48. The mention of the altar also fits the inner building or sanctuary. This makes it quite difficult to understand this as the earthly reconstituted temple of the last days; it is a heavenly, not earthly, temple. The temple and the altar should therefore be interpreted as metaphors for the church as the temple of the new covenant (Matt 16:18; 1 Cor 3:16–17; 2 Cor 6:16). The worshipers, then, are the members of the church. The three things measured thus connote the church as a corporate entity (a temple and altar) and as individual members (the worshipers).

When the worshipers are measured, they are identified as belonging to God and protected by him. Their true home is within the temple/church, and they have no part in the world. Instead, they conquer it "by the blood of the Lamb and by the word of their testimony" (Rev 12:11). The message here is intimately tied to and reenacts 7:2–3, the sealing of the saints. So the believers are doubly secure, having been sealed and measured by God.

The measuring is a prophetic acted parable (as in Ezek 40–42) that announces God's ownership and vigilance over his people. Yet clearly this does not protect them from persecution and martyrdom; in 13:7 God "gives" or permits the beast to conquer the saints. However, in that very area the saints actually conquer the beast by giving up their lives (12:11). So they are protected spiritually but not physically. As in 1 Peter 4:13–14, suffering is the path to glory. That suffering, as in Revelation 10:8–11, is their bitterness, but it will produce the sweetness of their final victory over the powers of evil and their vindication by God.

Excluding the Outer Court (11:2)

The second part of this prophetic acted parable is strongly worded, namely the "exclusion" (a strong term used in the Gospels for "driving out" demons) of the outer court. There is double meaning in "outer," for it both denotes the court of the Gentiles in the outer portion of the temple area and also that it is outside God's protective presence. It has been "given to the Gentiles," meaning God has handed over the church to the Gentiles for a period. The central point is the contrast between the inner sanctuary, protected by God, and the outer court, given over to the Gentiles. It is likely that John has in mind more Ezekiel's temple than Herod's, for this reflects Ezekiel's emphasis on a restored temple that will experience once again the presence of Yahweh. God's covenant people both belong to him and are hated by the nations.

The Gentiles will be allowed to "trample the holy city," another symbol for the people of God who are citizens of heaven (Phil 3:20) and aliens in this world (1 Pet 1:1, 17; 2:11). This looks forward to 21:2, 10 when the holy city will be the new Jerusalem, the eternal home for the saints. For a time, God will allow the enemies of his people to persecute them severely, but they will emerge triumphant. Daniel 8:9–14 lies behind this picture. There God allows the little horn to "trample" the "host of the heavens" (God's followers) for a time (also Zech 12:3).

The period God will allow this is designated as "forty-two months," one of three ways this "great tribulation" period (Rev 7:14) is designated—1260 days (Rev 11:3; 12:6 = Dan 12:11), "time, times, and half a time" (Rev 12:14 = Dan 7:25; 12:7), and 42 months (here; Rev 13:5, not in Daniel). This three-and-a-half year period is a common symbol in the Old Testament for a limited time in which God allows Israel's enemies to triumph, as seen in the drought in Israel under Elijah (1 Kgs 17:1; 18:1), the wilderness wanderings (with 42 encampments, Num 33:5–49), and the Daniel material. In Daniel and Revelation it is that period in which for a short time God permits the little horn/the beast to conquer his people. But it is under God's sovereign control and will end in the final triumph of his followers.

THE TWO WITNESSES EXERCISE THEIR MINISTRY (11:3–6)

This next section flows directly out of Revelation 11:1–2. There God gave the outer court to the Gentiles. Here God gives "power/authority to my two witnesses." So the church triumphs by taking the war to the nations but with a new twist—the weapons are not military but spiritual. The people of God fight back with bold witness.

God has chosen two prophetic witnesses to dominate this final period of history. In doing so he has made them his special possession ("*my* two witnesses") and bestowed on them his *exousia*. This, as in 2:26; 9:3, 10, 19, means both "power" and "authority"—authority to prophesy and power to perform great wonders. There is a reversal as well, as God in 11:2 "gives" the church over to be trampled and in 11:3 gives it (the witnesses also symbolize the church) authority to overcome through prophetic witness. The witness theme is very strong in Revelation, grounded in Jesus as "faithful witness" (1:5, 3:14) and the church as witnesses to Jesus (1:9) both verbally (12:11b; 17:6) and through suffering/martyrdom (6:9; 12:11c; 20:4).

Many suggestions have been made throughout history as to the identity of these two—Enoch and Elijah (Tertullian and many church fathers after him), Jeremiah and Elijah (Victorinus), Peter and Paul (Munck), two modeled after Joshua and Zerubbabel (Zahn). Many today believe they symbolize the witnessing church. I believe the best is a combination of two—they do symbolize the church in its witness, suffering, and triumph, but it is also likely they are two actual figures who will appear at the end of history, just as the beast in 11:7 is an actual individual. On the basis of their prophetic ministry in 11:3–6, they are modeled after Elijah and Moses. Like John the Baptist in Luke 1:17, they will come "in the spirit and power" of Moses and Elijah rather than *being* those personages.

They will "prophesy for 1260 days," a variant of the 42 months in 11:2. This must mean that they will minister in that three-and-a-half-year final period, not the church age but that time dominated by the beast or antichrist.[1] Their task will be to lead the church in that final time of universal apostasy that will parallel Israel's national apostasy of the Old Testament prophetic period. As with Elijah, they will be "clothed in sackcloth" to signify sorrow and mourning over the sins of the nations (as in Joel 1:8; Amos 8:10). As in John 3:5–9, this likely also includes a call to repentance, as sackcloth was often worn to signify repentance for sin (see Isa 22:12; Jer 4:8).[2]

John then identifies them (11:4) with imagery drawn from Zechariah 4:2–6 as "the two olive trees and two lampstands." In Zechariah's vision the lampstand is the temple, and the seven lights on it (the menorah) are "the seven eyes of the LORD that range throughout the earth" (Zech 4:10 = the Spirit from Zech 4:4). The two olive trees are "the two who are anointed

1. See the commentary on Rev 11:7.
2. For sackcloth, see the commentary on Rev 6:12.

to serve the Lord of all the earth" (Zech 4:14), namely Joshua the high priest and Zerubbabel the governor. Zechariah's point was that God was in charge of rebuilding the temple and his Spirit would overcome those who opposed it. John is saying here that the Spirit as "the eyes of the Lord" stands over the two witnesses and will overcome all opposition on their behalf. The implicit presence of the Holy Spirit here is likely, buttressing the ministry of the two witnesses.

In light of the two witnesses, John transforms the image of the menorah to two lampstands, possibly referring also to the two churches among the seven who triumphed through suffering: Smyrna and Philadelphia. The "two olive trees" may picture the witnesses/church in its priestly (Joshua) and kingly (Zerubbabel) roles, as in Revelation 1:6, 5:10, 20:6, where the church is made "kingdom and priests" by Christ. Theirs is a twofold ministry—witness to the nations (the evangelistic task) and warnings of imminent judgment (the prophetic task).

Four scenes that reenact the ministries of Elijah and Moses demonstrate the victorious ministry of the church (11:5–6), and all are judgments directed at the sinful nations. The first two are Elijah miracles, and the second pair are Moses miracles. First, the earth-dwellers attempt to kill the two witnesses as they did the martyrs of Revelation 6:9–11. In response, the Elijah miracle of fire from heaven is reproduced (2 Kgs 1); here it is an example of ***lex talionis***, the law of retribution: those who try to kill them are instead killed by them when God causes "fire to come out of their mouths" and devour their enemies. Until their prophetic ministry is completed, God will not allow anyone to harm them. Fire from the mouth is similar to the metaphor of the sword coming from Jesus' mouth (Rev 1:16; 16:13; 19:15) signifying his proclamation of judgment. The fire symbolizes their fiery denunciation of evil and the fiery punishment (20:11–14) awaiting the earth-dwellers.

Second, the power they were given by God in 11:3 allows them "to shut up the heavens so that it will not rain" for this three-and-a-half-year period, reproducing Elijah's miracle of

1 Kings 17–18. The last three miracles parallel the trumpet and bowl judgments, following the threefold pattern of the heavens, the waters, and the earth that characterizes the first four of each. So the two witnesses parallel the seven angels of the trumpets and bowls as instruments of God's judgment on his enemies. As with Elijah, the drought here extends for the entire "time they are prophesying," namely the whole 42 months. The occasion for the judgment in Elijah's time was the idolatry of Israel under King Ahab, and that parallels the idolatry of Revelation 9:20–21.

The two Moses miracles continue the theme of divine retribution from the Elijah miracles. The two witnesses "have power to turn the waters into blood," like the first Egyptian plague (Exod 7:20–21) as well as the second trumpet (Rev 8:8) and the second and third bowls (16:3–4). For the Romans, like the earlier Egyptians, water was a primary symbol of life. This judgment would mean that life is replaced by death. The final of the four miracles is general, referring to Moses' authority from God to "strike the earth with every kind of plague" whenever he wished. This sums up all the Egyptian plagues and undoubtedly refers specifically to the trumpet and bowl "plagues" as well. Like the plagues of Exodus, these will demonstrate the powerlessness of the earthly gods/demonic forces, proving once and for all that Yahweh alone controls the natural world.

THE WITNESSES DIE AND ARE RESURRECTED (11:7–13)

Death and Seeming Defeat (11:7–10)

We now move forward to the close of the three-and-a-half-year period when the two witnesses "have finished their testimony." God will not allow the false trinity (the dragon, beast, and false prophet of 16:13) to have their temporary triumph until this prophetic witness is complete. This is a significant point—while the believers are hunted down worldwide during this "great tribulation" (7:14), the forces of evil will not be able to stop their testimony. As we saw in 11:5–6, their witness has brought judgment upon the nations. The small time God has given Satan and the cosmic powers is now over, but one evil deed is left.

God then allows the beast to attack and kill the two witnesses (11:7). This is also the important point of 13:5–8—the beast in all its evil actions can only do what God permits, and that for only a short time. This is the first appearance of this creature, who will reappear in chapter 13 as the antichrist mentioned in 1 John 2:18. He "ascends from the Abyss," proving his demonic origin. This is a frequent image, the powers of evil ascending from the sea or the Abyss—smoke in 8:4 and 9:2 (the locusts descend in 9:3), the beast here and in 17:8, the beast from the sea in 13:1, the beast from the earth in 13:11. The imagery of the beast alludes to the "little horn" of Daniel 7:7–12 that ascends from the sea to wage war against the saints (Dan 7:3, 21). The four beasts of Daniel 7 prophesy four world empires that would dominate the Jewish people for the next several centuries, culminating in the "little horn" or Antiochus Epiphanes, who in 167–164 BC tried to force the Jews to sacrifice to the Greek gods and precipitated the Maccabean rebellion.[3]

God allows this beast to reenact the Daniel scene above and to "make war" (so also Rev 9:1–11; 12:7, 17; 16:14; 19:19; 20:8) and "conquer them and kill them," language that will be repeated in 13:7. This is part of the martyrdom portrayed in 6:9, and the beast is permitted his moment of triumph, short-lived though it will be. One of the critical themes of the book is the futility of these acts of rebellion against God and his people. In the final war of 19:17–18 there is no battle; the sword comes out of Christ's mouth and every member of the army of the beast is beheaded in an instant. In their suffering and death the believers relive the passion of Jesus and join the "fellowship of his suffering" (Phil 3:10), the "messianic woes" discussed in Revelation

3. Many think these empires are Babylon, Medo-Persia, Greece, and Rome.

6:9. As with Jesus, their death is a cosmic victory over the powers of evil.

The nations show no compassion or honor to the dead. Their murderers cause their bodies to "lie in the public square of the great city" (11:8). To refuse burial to the dead was a great insult (Gen 40:19; 1 Sam 17:43–47), showing the terrible scorn heaped upon these martyrs. The identification of the "great city" is problematic, for everywhere else it refers to Rome (Rev 16:19; 17:18; 18:10–21). Here it appears to refer to Jerusalem, "where also their Lord was crucified." It is clear that the "great apostasy" of Matthew 24:10–12 and 2 Thessalonians 2:3 has taken place, and Jerusalem is under the power of the beast/antichrist. Most likely here Jerusalem and Rome have combined into a single, symbolic "great city," the capital of the empire of the beast. Jerusalem forfeited its place as the holy city when it rejected the Messiah, and its place is taken by the new Jerusalem, the holy city of Revelation 21:2, 10.

This great (apostate) city is "figuratively/spiritually called Sodom and Egypt," referring to its "spiritual state" and what those with spiritual discernment realize about it. Jerusalem is linked with Sodom in Isaiah 1:9–10, Jeremiah 23:14, and Ezekiel 16:46–49. It is like Sodom in its depravity and rebellion against God, and like Egypt in its persecution of the people of God. Final proof of this is the crucifixion of Christ. A people who would put to death the Son of God would hardly have any compunction against killing his two witnesses.

During this time, a religious celebration breaks out as the whole world takes a holiday, looking upon the bodies and rejoicing (11:9). To understand the scene, we have to look ahead to 13:11–18 and the actions of the beast called in 16:13 "the false prophet." He has established a one-world religion centered on the worship of the dragon and the beast/antichrist. He causes all the world "from every people, tribe, language, and nation" to view the bodies, refuse them burial, and rejoice. Like Jesus, the believers are insulted and maltreated to the greatest possible extent. The "three and a half days" is symbolic of the 42 months (three and a half years) of this final period of history.

So the earth-dwellers—the term throughout this book for the unsaved who have only this world—turn this into a religious celebration (11:10). As in John 3:19–20, the people of darkness hate the light. The verbs "rejoice" and "be glad" in this verse have a strong religious connotation, pointing to cultic joy, a virtual religious holiday. This is seen when they "send each other gifts," as in the Jewish Feast of Purim (Esth 9:18–22; Neh 8:10–12 at the reading of the Law) or the Roman festival of Saturnalia. This religious ecstasy is at the demise of the two witnesses in what the nations likely view here as a holy war. John especially describes them as those who had tormented the earth-dwellers, echoing the torment of the locust/scorpions in 9:5. Again the principle of ***lex talionis*** may be implied, for the same term is used in 18:4–8: "Give her as much torment and grief as the luxury she gave herself."

RESURRECTION (11:11–12)

The time for rejoicing on the part of the nations is cut short, for God's sovereignty takes over and ends the festivities after three and a half days, probably paralleling Jesus' resurrection on the third day. At this time "the breath of life from God entered them, and they stood on their feet," an allusion to the valley of dry bones in Ezekiel 37:10: "Breath entered them; they came to life and stood up on their feet." The Ezekiel imagery depicts Israel's return from exile as a valley of dry bones come to life. There is a further allusion to Genesis 2:7, where God breathes life into Adam's nostrils.

As the two are raised and stand up, the joy of the earth-dwellers turns to "great fear," abject terror at the power of God and at their terrible future, possibly drawing from Psalm 105:38: "Egypt was glad when they left, because dread of Israel had fallen on them" (see also Exod 15:16). This terror will lead either to repentance (Rev 11:13; 15:4) or to judgment (18:10, 15), depending on their response.

After their resurrection, they are immediately taken up to heaven (11:11). The bystanders "hear a loud voice"—we don't know whose, whether God, Christ, or an angel. The command, "Come up here," recalls Revelation 4:1 and likely recapitulates Elijah's ascension to heaven in a fiery chariot (2 Kgs 2:11), validating the prophetic ministry of these two as it did Elijah's ministry. They ascend "in a cloud," recalling both Revelation 1:7, Jesus coming back "with the clouds" (from Dan 7:13), and Revelation 10:1 where the mighty angel is "robed in a cloud" (see also Rev 14:14–16). The cloud is a frequent early church apocalyptic image, linked with resurrection (1 Thess 4:17), ascension (Acts 1:7), and the **Parousia** or second coming (Mark 14:62). So the parallel with Revelation 1:7 is uppermost, and this symbolizes their resurrection as part of the complex of events centering on Christ's return.

This could well be the gathering up of the church at Christ's second coming. If the two witnesses are symbolic of the church,[4] that is indeed possible. Many object on the grounds that ascensions to heaven in apocalyptic literature serve to emphasize the vindication of the prophet and thus the church conquering the beast rather than the resurrection of the saints. However, the cloud represents the presence of God in all his glory and majesty, especially at the return of Christ, so it fits well with the theme of the saints' deliverance. The entire context here is resurrection, and so this could well fit the view that this is the catching up of the church (symbolized in the witnesses) to heaven.

This takes place at the end of the three-and-a-half-year period when their prophetic ministry "is finished" (11:7), so at the time when Christ is to return. The main difficulty is in the timing. If this is truly at the end of that "tribulation period" (7:14), how do we account for the events of 11:13 (the earthquake and conversion of many)? In Revelation the only event following

---

4. See commentary on 11:3–6.

Christ's return is the battle of Armageddon, so there doesn't seem to be room for the earthquake, the deaths, and the repentance of many. So it is possible that the resurrection here constitutes a **proleptic** anticipation of the final gathering of the church at the **eschaton** rather than the event itself. The order here seems to be the ascension of the witnesses, the earthquake, the conversion of the onlookers, the return of Christ/gathering of the church, and the aftermath (the events of Rev 20–21). Also, it is indeed possible that 11:11–12 is metaphorical rather than literal language and describes the spiritual vindication of the witnesses/church rather than the event of 1 Corinthians 15 and 1 Thessalonians 4. Still, timelines are distorted in apocalyptic literature, so the view that this is the resurrection of the people of God at the end of history remains a very real possibility and is still my preference.

JUDGMENT AND REPENTANCE (11:13)

After the witnesses are caught up to heaven, another terrible earthquake occurs (as in Rev 6:12; 8:5; 11:13, 19; 16:18), and a tenth of the "great city" (see 11:8) is destroyed. This takes place elsewhere in the Old Testament (Ezek 38:19–20 with Gog and Magog, Zech 14:4 with Yahweh descending onto the Mount of Olives at the Day of Yahweh). Seven thousand die—a tenth of the population of Jerusalem. This is a reversal of 1 Kings 19:18, in which God preserves seven thousand faithful in Israel. Here they perish for their idolatry and rebellion. Still, this is partial judgment along the lines of the one-fourth killed in the seal judgments (Rev 6:8) and the one-third in the trumpet judgments (9:18). These judgments constitute a call to repentance and leave room to get right with God.

After these horrifying events, we are told the survivors "were terrified and gave glory to the God of heaven." The question is whether this action denotes true repentance or the forced homage of a defeated foe, as in Philippians 2:11. Against the repentance understanding would be Exodus 8:19, where the magicians of Egypt confessed that God had indeed sent the plagues, or Daniel 4:34, where Nebuchadnezzar "honored and glorified" God ("God of heaven" occurs three times in Dan 4:37 in the **Septuagint**) without repenting.

However, I believe the evidence for actual repentance in the context of the book is stronger. In Revelation 14:6–7 the angel with "the eternal gospel" calls for the nations to "fear God and give him glory," very similar to the language here. In 15:4 and 16:9, "give glory to God" signifies repentance and the offer of salvation. In 19:5, 7, "fear God" and "give him glory" define the true "slaves" of God. So this language is used in Revelation to designate true repentance and conversion. While the majority of humankind refuses to repent and remains hardened toward God, we see here that there is a portion who realize their sin, understand that the cosmic powers embody pure evil, and turn to God in repentance. It is they who will represent the nations as they bring their honor into the new Jerusalem (21:24, 26) and join the saints.

THE THIRD WOE ACCOMPANIES THE SEVENTH TRUMPET (11:14–19)

The three "woes" (Rev 8:13; 9:12; 11:14) are three terrors that will make clear that God in his wrath will soon bring judgment upon the nations. Yet instead of judgment, this third one is the heavenly celebration at the arrival of the final kingdom of God and the victory of the saints. Yet that very fact is the greatest terror of all for the earth-dwellers. It will spell out the absolute defeat of the forces of evil, for it will designate what they can never have. It is still "judgment," because these wondrous blessings will forever be denied to sinners. At the same time, this astounding vision includes the completion of the wrath of God and the commencement of the judging, rewarding, and destroying in 11:18. So it is doubly a woe—the eternal blessings denied them for eternity and the eternal judgment/punishment that will characterize their eternity.

In other words, we have now arrived at the **eschaton**, the end of the world, further proof of the cyclical nature of the seals, trumpets, and bowls.[5] Many break this central section of the book into two sections, 4:1–11:19 (God's sovereignty in judgment) and 12:1–16:21 (the great conflict between God and the forces of evil), and this is a good way to think of the organization of this section. As such, this passage concludes the judgment section and demonstrates the great victory that God and Christ have won.

THIRD WOE ANNOUNCED (11:14)

The statement that "the second woe has passed" seems incongruous, as so much has occurred since the second woe (Rev 9:12–21). Yet the second interlude (10:1–11:13) is part of the sixth trumpet/second woe, since it noted the suffering of the people of God during the period of the first two woes. The third woe could only commence when the second woe was finalized by the addition of 10:1–11:13. Equally enigmatic is the statement that the third woe is "coming soon." Perhaps the point is speed, so it says "coming quickly." But elsewhere it means "soon" (2:16; 3:11; 22:7, 12, 20), and so the emphasis is on the immanence of Christ's return and the coming of the kingdom.

ANNOUNCEMENT BY HEAVENLY VOICES (11:15)

We are expecting a heavenly judgment to fall, but instead we are treated to the heavenly choir (similar to Rev 7:9–12) of "loud voices" celebrating the victory of God and his people. The silence of the seventh seal (8:1) awaiting the final events has now been reversed and become a mega-symphony of joyous sound as the heavenly choir shouts out the turning point the entire Bible has awaited—the arrival of the eternal kingdom! This hymn is certainly sung at the time of the return of Christ (19:11–12) and takes place in heaven.

The hymn celebrates the reversal of the tragic situation during the age of sin, the reign of "the kingdom of the world."

---

5. See the introduction to chapter 6.

The string of phrases beginning with "has become" looks at the end of history as a complete whole, an accomplished fact. The kingdom is no longer (and will never again be) "of the world," but will forevermore be "of our Lord." Moreover, the oneness motif continues with the definite unity between God ("of our Lord") and Christ ("of his Messiah"). It is the kingdom of the Godhead, and the evil powers, both human and angelic, have been defeated once for all by "the Lord and his Messiah." The heavenly kingdom has replaced the earthly as the one true reality, and the wondrous thing is that now this is the *only* reality. The emphasis in "Messiah" (which has an article in the Greek) is on Jesus' messianic office (as in 12:10; 20:4, 6), and it is the messianic kingdom that is announced here.

The hymn then moves from the fact of the kingdom arriving to the action of Christ "reigning forever and ever." It will be an eternal reign. The eternal nature of God, so stressed in the book (1:6; 4:9, 10; 5:13; 7:12; 10:6), centers on the triune Godhead establishing an eternal kingdom anchored by their eternal reign. The temporary suffering of the saints (6:9–11; 10:9–10) is at an end, leading to their final vindication (6:11; 7:13–17) and resurrection to eternal glory (11:11–12, 15). These promises have now been fulfilled in a final way.

Hymn of the Twenty-Four Elders (11:16–18)

These elders are celestial beings who lead heavenly worship in the book and at the same time are ruling angels "seated on thrones," likely members of the heavenly council (Psa 89:27; 1 Kgs 22:19, Job 15:8).[6] They submit their thrones to him; they "fall on their faces" (contra the client kings of the beast in Rev 17:13), highlighting God's sovereignty and majesty.

The hymn of 4:10–11 celebrated the God who created and sustains this world. This hymn celebrates the God who has ended this world and begun his eternal reign. It begins with

6. See commentary on 4:4.

thanksgiving, building on 4:9 and 7:12. This is the expression of gratitude to the God who has answered prayer, and it is nowhere more appropriate than here since God has now completed his plan of salvation, ended this evil world, and begun his eternal reign.

The thanksgiving proper begins with two of the critical titles in the book. "Lord God Almighty" is the dominant title, appearing nine times and meaning "God has shown himself to be Lord of all by exercising his almighty power." His omnipotence makes him sovereign Lord over all his creation. The most significant element, however, is the transformation of the threefold title from 1:4, 8; and 4:8, denoting the God who controls past, present, and future and is Lord over history. Now the title is twofold and omits "who is to come." There is nothing yet "to come," for history has ended and eternity has begun. A primary stress is still on God's absolute power over and control of the present, even though with Roman dominance it may not seem like it. But the God who was sovereign over past events, which was proven by the Old Testament, is still in control of present events and will lead them to his chosen end. Still, the major thrust is the absence of the future, for with the coming of God's final kingdom the future has become an eternal present!

The reason for this startling truth is "because you have taken your great power and begun to reign." This is a natural movement of thought—the Almighty God "taking his great power" as he overcomes all opposition and establishes his eternal reign. The time of the seventh trumpet actually follows the events of Revelation 19–22, so this hymn celebrates the whole content of this trumpet, the coming of the Day of the Lord.

The second half of the hymn begins with a near quotation of Psalm 2:1, "Why do the nations conspire and the peoples plot in vain?" These are the plots of the nations "against the Lord and against his anointed" in Psalm 2:2 and the book of Revelation. God's response in Psalm 2:4–5 is the basis for the response here: "The nations were angry, and your wrath has come." In the psalm, the Lord laughs and "rebukes them in his anger." Note the interplay between the wrath of the nations and the wrath of God. The first is inconsequential; the second reverses all of history. The anger of the nations is an act of folly and will end in annihilation.

The rest of verse 18 is a **chiasm**:

A The time has come for judging the dead
  B And for rewarding your slaves the prophets
  B′ And your saints and those who fear your name, small and great,
A′ And for destroying those who destroy the earth

This is a stylistic device used throughout Scripture to emphasize two or more points by reversing the order in the second pair. So here the destinies of unbeliever and believer are contrasted. The term for "time" (*kairos*) refers not to chronological time but **eschatological** time, a period centering on the contrast between judgment on the evildoers and reward for the faithful. This "time" flows out of the previous clause and is the result of divine wrath against a world of sin and divine pleasure with those who overcome.

This is why this seventh trumpet is called "the third woe." The judgment of the dead alludes to Daniel 12:2, "Multitudes who sleep in the dust of the earth will awake, some to everlasting life, others to shame and everlasting contempt" (also Isa 26:19, 66:24; Zeph 3:8). They are "the dead" because we are at the end of history, and this is part of final judgment (Rev 20:11–15). The idea of reward for the faithful is explicit in 22:15 but implicit in the section on reward to the overcomers at the end of each of the seven letters in chapters 2–3. Christ spoke of great reward in heaven for the persecuted followers in Matthew 5:11–12 and for the faithful in Matthew 6:1–18. The idea of reward "according to each one's work" is frequent in Scripture and will be discussed at Revelation 22:12.

There are five phrases here for describing those who are given reward: God's slaves, prophets, saints, those who fear God, and the small and the great. The relationship between the five is difficult to ascertain. Four of the five seem to describe the church as a whole, but "prophets" could well describe an office of the church, as in Ephesians 4:11 and perhaps in Revelation. While "prophet" can refer to the Old Testament office (Rev 10:7; 22:6) or to the two witnesses that symbolize the church (11:10), it also speaks of members of an early church office of prophet (16:6; 18:20, 24; 22:9). Here, however, the list seems to be general, and the witnesses/prophets in 11:3–12 describe the church as a whole. The saints are royalty and priesthood in 1:6 and 5:10, and here have a prophetic ministry.

Therefore it is likely that all five describe the church. The people of God are seen first as slaves who belong to God (similar to the Christians as "sealed" in 7:3–4 and "measured" in 11:1–2), and their prophetic witness is described as "the spirit of prophecy" in 19:10. They are "saints" in the sense of being called to set themselves apart from the world and give themselves wholly to God. The combination of "those who fear God" with "both small and great" also occurs in 19:5 and echoes Psalm 115:13, "He will bless those who fear the LORD—small and great alike." The psalm contrasts dead idols with the God of heaven and extols those who fear Yahweh, a warning to the followers of the Nicolaitan cult in Revelation 2:6, 15. The social categories of small and great are frequent in Revelation (13:16; 19:5, 18; 20:12) and stress that all—from kings to slaves—stand equally before God. There are no favorites.

The final clause once more centers on the ***lex talionis***, the "law of retribution": those who destroy God's creation with their sin and their devastation of the earth will themselves be destroyed by God. The destroyers refer to the Great Prostitute in 19:2, who "destroyed/corrupted the earth," and to Babylon the Great in chapter 18, both symbolic of the empire of the beast, the world of sinful humanity. This alludes to God's rebuke of Babylon in Jeremiah 51:25, "I am against you, you destroying mountain, you who destroy the whole earth." The killers of the righteous and despoilers of God's creation will receive the justice they deserve.

COSMIC EVENTS HERALDING THE END (11:19)

Temple scenes frame chapter 11. In 11:1–2 the temple is measured, indicating divine ownership and protection. Now the temple is opened (see also the open door in 4:1), meaning the end of world history has arrived. What is opened here is actually the holy of holies where God sat on his throne above the ark. Both the ark of the covenant (2 Sam 6:2; Psa 80:1, 99:1) and the storm (Exod 19:6–9; Psa 18:13; Isa 30:30) are symbols of **theophany**, God manifesting himself to bring an end to this sinful age and to introduce the eternal age of joy.

As the heavenly temple is opened, the ark "appears/is seen." God is revealing one of the deep heavenly truths, for the ark of the covenant was at the very heart of Israelite religion. It contained the two stone tablets of the Ten Commandments, the jar of manna, and Aaron's rod that budded (Heb 9:4), symbols of God's merciful covenant (the covering of the ark was called the "mercy seat"). This is closely connected with Revelation 21:3, "the dwelling of God is with his people." The ark was so sacred that it was closed off to all via the veil, but now at the end of time it lies open and visible to all. There are no more secrets and nothing closed off from God's people. In 21:9–27, the holy city is symbolized as the holy of holies. We will live for eternity in the holy of holies!

The storm **theophany** occurs often (see 4:5; 6:12–14; 8:5; 16:18–21) and indicates that the awesome God of Sinai (Exod 19:16) is still at work. The addition of "great hail" (as in Rev 4:5; 8:5) may also allude to the seventh Egyptian plague (Exod 9:13–26) and Gog and Magog (Ezek 38:22), highlighting not only the majesty of God but also his judgment, in effect summarizing the trumpet judgments.

Key themes of the entire Bible coalesce in the events of chapter 11. God's ownership and protection of his righteous remnant is a core aspect of the concept of a covenant God, and at the same time the opposition of the nations who trample his people is found throughout Scripture. God watches over his people and keeps them spiritually secure, but he allows the forces of evil to pursue them because suffering is the path to victory. So the saints respond to persecution not by returning evil for evil but with bold witness, as symbolized in the ministry of the two witnesses. Two aspects—prophetic proclamation and victory over their enemies, followed by death and resurrection—sum up the history of redemption. Until the very end, the church father Tertullian's old adage holds true: the blood of the martyrs is the seed of the church. All of this comes to final fruition in the seventh trumpet. This world and the sinful humanity that inhabits it are coming to an end when the eternal kingdom arrives. Evil will be destroyed forever, and the reign of the triune Godhead will inaugurate our eternal glory when we begin our reign with him.

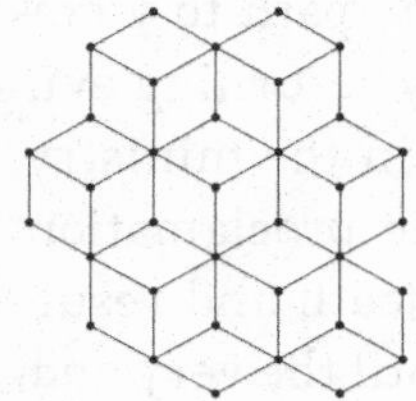

THE DRAGON AND THE PEOPLE OF GOD IN CONFLICT
(12:1–17)

We now enter a new section of the book (Rev 12:1–16:21). The first section of the central portion (6:1–11:19, the first part of chs. 6–16) focused on God's sovereign control of the created order, especially his power over the enemies of his people and the judgments he was pouring into this sinful world. This section contrasts the throne of God with the throne (13:2) and worship of the dragon and the beast (13:4, 8, 12, 14–15). So these chapters trace the great battle between God and the false trinity (16:13). Satan's pretentious assumption of power is central, but it is God who is truly sovereign, and everything the dragon and beast do they can do only because God permits it.

Chapters 12–14 are the third and final interlude tracing the church's involvement in the action of the three judgment sets, this time showing the war between the woman/church and the false trinity (the dragon and the two beasts). This also provides the first extended portrait of the supreme evil being, the dragon/Satan, as well as his purpose and strategy. At the same time, a core aspect here is the futility of Satan, for he is already defeated and cast out of heaven (12:7–9), overcome at the cross (12:11–12), and frustrated in his opposition to the saints (12:13–17).[1] Everything he does is a parody of what God and Christ have already done, from his crowns (12:3 and 13:1 = 19:12), to his mortal wound that is healed (13:3 = the death and resurrection of Christ), to his miracles (13:13), to "the mark of the beast" (13:16 = the sealing of the saints in 7:3).

THE DRAGON OPPOSES THE WOMAN AND HER CHILD (12:1–6)

The story told here can rightly be called an international myth; stories exactly like this are found in virtually every ancient religion, such as Egyptian (the mother goddess Isis pursued by the red dragon Set), Ugaritic (the storm-god Baal defeating the seven-headed serpent Leviathan), Mesopotamian (Marduk, the god of light, kills the seven-headed dragon Tiamat), and Graeco-Roman (the goddess Leto, pregnant with Apollo, pursued by the dragon Python and rescued by Poseidon). It is not unusual for a biblical story to follow such contours; in the Old Testament, Yahweh assumed titles like "Rider on the Clouds" (a title of the Canaanite god Baal; Psa 68:4), and many of the shrines like Bethel were previously pagan and were "baptized" to become Yahweh shrines. One could say that the Bible demythologizes pagan myths by historicizing them—that is, showing that they have now actually happened in history. So the story here is a redemptive analogy with an evangelistic purpose: to show that in Christ all the pagan hopes have been realized.

A GREAT SIGN IN HEAVEN, THE WOMAN (12:1–2)

There is an important contrast between the woman, who in 12:1 is "a great sign," and the dragon in 12:3, who is nothing more than "another sign." The dragon and his cosmic forces are "great" (= "mighty" in 12:3, 9) only in terms of his malignant power and in the realm where he can be called "the god of this world" (2 Cor 4:4). But he is nothing compared to God, and

1. See "Theology of the Book" in the introduction.

Jesus' followers have long been given authority over the demonic realm (Mark 3:15, 6:7). "Signs" here, as in the Gospel of John, refer to divinely sent symbols or signposts depicting heavenly truths and challenging the readers to faith. So the woman and the dragon are signs that alert the reader to the key spiritual conflict of the book.

The woman is "clothed with the sun, with the moon under her feet and a crown of twelve stars on her head." This threefold description stems from Jacob's dreams in Genesis 37:1–9, where sheaves of grain bowed down to him followed by the sun, moon, and eleven stars. Most agree that the sun and moon in that context are Joseph's parents, Jacob and Rachel, while the eleven stars are Joseph's brothers. "Twelve stars" in Jewish literature are usually the 12 patriarchs or tribes. The woman here is likely Israel, while in Revelation 12:17 she represents the church, so overall the woman stands for the whole people of God, Israel and the church.

In Psalm 104:2 Yahweh "wraps himself in light as with a garment," so the image here shows the woman partaking of the majesty of God. The moon stresses the glory of God (Isa 24:23, 30:26). The moon "under her feet" shows she shares his splendor and dominion. A crown, of course, denotes sovereignty, and the "twelve stars" means the church as the new Israel reigns over God's creation. So together these images signify the glory, majesty, and dominion that God has given his people.

The woman is pregnant and about to give birth (Rev 12:2), a reference certainly to the birth of Jesus. Many have from this thought the woman is Mary herself, but this is likely a corporate metaphor for Israel about to produce the Messiah. With the emphasis on "cried out in pain," this is probably the persecuted people of God (in the midst of the messianic woes, as in 6:11) as they tried to give birth to the messianic age. Isaiah 26:18 depicts Israel with child, writhing in labor, trying unsuccessfully to bring "salvation to the earth." This image is altered here to show that with Christ the tension of Isaiah is resolved and salvation has finally come to the earth.

THE OTHER SIGN IN HEAVEN, THE DRAGON (12:3)

The symbol of a great dragon was well-known in antiquity. It depicted a serpent or sea monster usually connected with demonic powers. In Canaan these were the serpent gods who were the enemy of Baal, and in Babylon it was a red serpent that guarded the god Marduk. To the Hebrews there was Leviathan (Psa 74:13–14), the female sea monster Rahab (Job 9:13; 26:12; Isa 51:9), and Tannin (which the NIV translates "monster" in Job 7:12; Psa 74:13). Leviathan is labeled a "dragon" in Job 3:8; 41:1; Psalm 104:26. Since the sea to ancient peoples meant unfathomable depths and the chaos of death, Leviathan/the dragon represented all the terrors of the sea and thus the presence of evil and death. Pharaoh (Ezek 29:3; 32:2) and Nebuchadnezzar (Jer 51:34) are called "sea monsters" because they devoured nations, so this became a symbol also for nations that conquered others and stood against God and his people.

Leviathan is a many-headed beast in Psalm 74:13, so it is natural to see how the dragon image became associated with Satan.[2] In the New Testament the dragon figure is found only in Revelation, though Paul associates the serpent of the garden of Eden with Satan in Romans 16:20 (see Gen 3:15), "The God of peace will soon crush Satan under your feet." The dragon is red, a color associated with dragons in Egypt and Babylon, symbolizing Satan slaughtering the people of God (the "slaughtered Lamb" in Rev 5:6), as in the red horse of 6:4 and the shedding of the blood of the saints in 16:6; 17:6; 18:24.

The dragon has "seven heads and ten horns" like the beast from the sea in 13:1, a common apocalyptic symbol, as in the "many heads" of Psalm 74:13 or the seven-headed monster of Jewish writings. Primarily, the seven heads stem from Daniel 7:4–8 and represent the sum of the heads of the first three beasts plus the four heads of the fourth beast. Unlike the beast from the sea, which has crowns on its horns, the dragon

2. Compare Odes of Solomon 22:5.

has seven crowns on its heads, signifying his pretentious claim to sovereignty. This is not the *stephanos*, the victor's wreath used elsewhere in the New Testament, but the *diadēma* or ruler's crown ("diadem"), used only here, Revelation 13:1 (the false crown of the dragon and the beast), and 19:12 (the true ruler's crown of Christ) in the New Testament. The dragon wants to be worshiped as King of kings but is only "the god of this world" (2 Cor 4:4), and his reign is both temporary and ephemeral. He was defeated once and for all at the cross and "knows his time is short" (Rev 12:12).

The Dragon Goes to War (12:4)

Satan and all the angels were given the same choice as Adam and Eve. Satan chose to rebel against God, seduce one third of the stars, the heavenly host, and try to dislodge God from his throne. So the dragon uses his tail, like the tails of the scorpions in 9:10 and the horses in 9:19, to "sweep a third of the stars" out of heaven to earth. This reenacts Daniel 8:10, where the little horn threw some of the starry host down to the earth and trampled on them. Many see here not a heavenly battle but an earthly one, on the grounds that Daniel 8 is describing the persecution of the Israelites by Antiochus Epiphanes, the little horn, in 167–164 BC.[3] This then would indicate the satanic war against the saints.

However, most Old Testament scholars see the "starry host" in Daniel 8:10 as angels, and the context of Revelation 12:4 is heavenly, not earthly. In Revelation, "stars" generally refer to angels (1:16, 20; 2:1; 3:1), and nowhere else are the believers called "stars." So the picture of Satan throwing a third of the stars from heaven refers to the original heavenly battle detailed below in 12:7–9. So verse 4 here refers to the initial victory when Satan seduced a third of the heavenly host to join him,

3. See commentary on 11:7.

and 12:7–9 tells of the actual battle when they are cast out of heaven and become "fallen angels."

After his partial victory in heaven, the dragon takes the conflict to earth, first against Christ and then against his followers. He "stands in front of the woman" so as to devour the child as soon as it is born. It seems incongruous for a dragon/serpent to be depicted as standing, but this is a common depiction in the ancient world. The primary parallel, of course, is Herod's slaughter of the innocent baby boys under two years old at Bethlehem in Matthew 2:16, echoed in the plots of Jewish leaders in Mark 3:6; John 7:30, 44–48; 8:58–59.

God Delivers the Child and the Woman (12:5–6)

The narrative omits details of Jesus' life in order to center on the drama of life and death itself. This telescoping of events is common in Scripture. The infant is presented as "a male son" in keeping with the stress on the maleness of sacrifices in the Old Testament (Exod 12:5; Lev 1:3; 4:23; 22:19) and also the emphasis on sonship in Jewish circles. "Male" here alludes to Isaiah 66:7 in the **Septuagint**, where it signifies the rebirth of Israel out of the travails of captivity. The salvation and deliverance of the people of God is centered on the coming of the Messiah.

This male child is destined (the Greek word translated "will" often stresses divine necessity) to "rule the nations with a rod of iron." This translation is better than "iron scepter" because it refers to the shepherd's club and is an allusion to Psalm 2:9, quoted in Revelation 2:27 and 19:15 of the shattering of the nations by Christ and his church at his second coming. It pictures the shepherd's club "dashing them to pieces like pottery," a reference to the destruction of evildoers in the battle or Armageddon in 16:14, 16 and 19:19–20.

As the dragon prepares his deadly attack, however, God suddenly snatches up the child to his throne (12:6), a definite reference to Jesus' ascension and exaltation to glory. "Snatches" is a particularly strong verb describing Jesus' ascension to heaven. Satan has tried to "devour" (= Jesus' death) Jesus, but God has "snatched" him (= Jesus' resurrection) from Satan's grasp. This is Satan's defeat. Jesus is not only caught up to heaven but "to his throne" (5:6; 22:1), further emphasizing that Jesus will rule all the nations.

Frustrated at his inability to defeat Jesus, Satan in 12:6 turns his evil intentions to the woman. She has to flee into the wilderness, which some interpret as the flight of Christians from Jerusalem to Pella in AD 66.[4] However, this is a cosmic scene and likely takes place during the three-and-a-half-year final period of history (7:14; 11:2, 3). Still, it also pictures God's protection of his people in the midst of persecution. This echoes the wilderness wanderings when God protected Israel (Exod 16:32; Deut 1:31; 8:3) and the time when Elijah fled to the desert (1 Kgs 19:3–9).

As the dragon pursues her, the woman/church is taken to "a place prepared for her by God," a place of divine comfort where God is nourishing and protecting his beleaguered people. This recalls the measuring of the temple in Revelation 11:1, a sacred place of rest and sustenance in God that echoes the "table ... in the presence of my enemies" in Psalm 23:5. The "1260 days" is the third of five places the final three-and-a-half-year period of history from Daniel is mentioned. All are in Revelation 11–13 (11:2, 3; 12:6, 14; 13:5) and describe that period God has permitted at the close of human history for the false trinity of the dragon, the beast, and the false prophet to do their nefarious work. This points back to Daniel 7:25 and 12:7 as the last act of defiance of the little horn against God and his people. All this means the day of evil is short, temporary, strictly controlled by God, and doomed to end in the false trinity's destruction.

WAR BREAKS OUT IN HEAVEN (12:7–12)

The basic story of the conflict between the dragon and the people of God is told in 12:1–6, and then it is expanded in two ways. First, the conflict of 12:4 describing the battle between

4. As recounted by the church historian Eusebius in *Ecclesiastical History* 3.5.

the dragon and God is filled out with detail in 12:7–9, and then the pursuit of the woman by the dragon in 12:6 is expanded in 12:13–17. In between the two is the hymnic response of the inhabitants of heaven in 12:10–12 to the cosmic victory of 12:7–9.

THE WAR IN HEAVEN DESCRIBED (12:7–9)

In 12:4 this war is seen from Satan's perspective as he sweeps a third of the angelic realm from heaven to earth. Now the whole story is told, and we see how short-lived that seeming victory was. The actual battle was not between God and Satan; Michael and the heavenly host were more than enough to fight and defeat Satan and the fallen angels. There is no dualism in the book between Satan and God; they are not equal. The dragon's adversary is the archangel Michael, and he is the more powerful of the two. In Daniel 10:13, 21; 12:1 he is a "chief prince" or ruling angel who protects and delivers God's people from their enemies. As such, he was viewed in Second Temple Jewish literature as the guardian angel (1 Enoch 20:5) and intercessor (Testament of Levi 5:5–6) of Israel who led Yahweh's host and defeated their enemies for them.

Many who have written on Revelation believe this does not depict the original fall of Satan. Rather, it metaphorically describes the spiritual battle that takes place every day in the life of the believer, as the powers of evil wrestle with God's people. As the saints fight against wickedness here on earth, a heavenly battle is taking place at the same time. This describes the original victory won by Jesus on the cross as well as the daily battles fought by God's people.

While this interpretation is very viable, I believe this is more than purely symbolic and describes the primordial fall of Satan. Isaiah 14:12–15 is part of a prophecy against Babylon and describes the fall of the king of Babylon, but I believe, with many others, that this was drawn from an ancient story of the fall of the dragon: "How have you fallen from heaven, morning star, son of the dawn! ... You said in your heart, 'I will ascend to the heavens. ... But you are brought down to the realm of the dead, to the depths of the pit." There are distinct linguistic connections with Revelation 12:7–9.

The defeat of Leviathan/the dragon is attested in Psalm 74:13–14, and that of Rahab/the dragon in Isaiah 51:9–10. Isaiah 27:1 says God will "punish with the sword … Leviathan the coiling serpent," and several Second Temple Jewish texts speak of the war God wages with the dragon (e.g., Testament of Dan 5:10–13). Second Enoch 29:4–5 tells of the rebellion of one of the archangels on the "second day of creation" and describes how he and his company of angels were cast out of heaven. In Life of Adam and Eve 13:1–2 the expulsion from heaven is linked with the Genesis 6:1–4 incident.[5] The serpent is linked with Satan in Wisdom 2:24 and 3 Baruch 9:7. In light of all this, there are two reasons why this passage most likely refers to an original casting of Satan and a host of angels from heaven at the dawn of history: The Old Testament teaching of the defeat of Leviathan/the dragon at creation, and the Jewish tradition of an original expulsion either at creation or at the incident recorded in Genesis 6:1–4.

The key point is that Satan was not strong enough to succeed in this war (Rev 12:8). This becomes a major point in the ensuing chapters—the futility of Satan. God allows the beast to "conquer" the saints (13:7), but in reality they conquer him by giving up their lives (12:11). As a result, he is filled with frustrated rage (12:12). He may be "ruler of the kingdom of the air" (Eph 2:2) and "god of this world" (2 Cor 4:4), but his authority is restricted to his own followers. He was conquered at the cross and is subject to Christ's followers (Mark 3:15, 6:7). He is defeated by Michael and his forces, and "no place was found for them any longer in heaven" (Rev 12:8). This takes place in three stages, each a "binding" of Satan: at the original expulsion from heaven, in the death and resurrection of Christ, and at the final casting of Satan and his fallen angels into the lake of fire.

5. Also Jubilees 5:1; 1 Enoch 6:1–7:6.

His defeat is complete. He may be "the great dragon," but that is restricted to this world, which is actually his prison (2 Pet 2:4; Jude 6). In actuality he was "hurled to the earth, and his angels with him" (Rev 12:9, referring to that third of the angelic host who became fallen angels in 12:4). His true character is now presented in the most extensive description of him in the New Testament (echoed in 20:2). First, he is "the ancient serpent," the crafty snake (Gen 3:1) who deceived Eve in the garden and defeats the people of God not by overpowering them but by leading them astray. He is not the super-soldier and strong man many think he is, for he has been utterly defeated by the stronger man, Jesus (Mark 3:27). He is the greatest con man who ever lived. The "roaring lion" who wants to devour us (1 Pet 5:8) does so through deceptive temptation.

His identity brings this out—he is "called the devil or Satan." These are Greek and Hebrew synonyms referring to an "adversary" or "evil opponent." At its root this refers to an accuser in a court of law, like the *satan* in Job 1:6–12; 2:1–6.[6] In the New Testament he is the "prince of this world" (John 12:31; 14:30) and the "god of this age" (2 Cor 4:4). He is at heart a liar (John 8:44) and deceiver (Rev 20:3, 8, 10), a destroyer (1 Pet 5:8) and murderer (John 8:44). In fact, he "deceives the whole world," both believers (Matt 6:13; 24:24) and unbelievers (Acts 26:18; 2 Cor 3:12–18). The primary method Satan uses to disrupt the people of God is deceit.

THE HEAVENLY HOST CELEBRATING VICTORY (12:10–12)

The hymns of Revelation function like the chorus of a Greek play, not only celebrating but interpreting the significance of the events. There are three parts to this hymn: rejoicing at God casting down the dragon (Rev 12:10), expanding the sphere of that victory to include the victory over Satan by the saints (12:11), and the effects of the victory on heaven and earth (12:12).

---

6. See commentary on 12:10.

The "loud voice" comes from the heavenly court at the arrival of the messianic kingdom. "Salvation" occurs three times (7:10, here, 19:1) and has its Old Testament connotation of "deliverance" or "victory" of the saints through God. All three bindings of Satan are intertwined and define the extent of that victory—cast out of heaven at creation, defeated at the cross, and cast into perdition at the end of history. This salvation/victory is further defined as "power and kingdom," that strength used by the Lord God Almighty in defeating the dragon and establishing his eternal kingdom. This is that reign of God in which the saints will be royalty (1:6, 5:10) and reign with him (20:4; 22:5).

The reason for this celebration is that the accuser has been thrown down from heaven (12:7–9), developing the meaning of his name ("adversary" in 12:9) and applying it to his primary work of accusing God's people before God day and night. This is language of a prosecutor in a court of law like the *satan* in Job 1:6–12 (accusing Job of serving God for selfish interests) or Zechariah 3:1–2 (accusing Joshua the high priest of the sins of the nation).[7] Victory in the cosmic war involves also victory in God's legal courtroom. As in Romans 8:33, "Who will bring any charge against those whom God has chosen? It is God who justifies."

So God's people have conquered their accuser (Rev 12:11). Satan has initial victory in battle, and is even allowed to take their lives, but this is merely earthly and temporary. In reality, the victory of the saints over him and "the kings of the earth" (here, 17:14) is final and eternal. Note the movement of thought from 12:10 to 12:11: "For the accuser ... has been hurled down, *and* they triumphed over him." This is a two-part thrust—God hurled the dragon out of heaven, and the saints conquered him. In 15:2 the faithful victors stand before the throne and sing the Song of Moses, celebrating their great victory.

---

7. This also occurs often in Second Temple Jewish literature (1 Enoch 40:7; Jubilees 17:15–18:13; Testament of Levi 5:6).

This victory is achieved in two ways: First, "by the blood of the Lamb," as the final defeat of Satan took place on the cross (1:5; 5:6, 9; 7:14). The blood of Christ is the basis of every victory achieved by the people of God. Second, it also takes place "by the word of their testimony," alluding to "the testimony of Jesus" (1:2; 3:14) that became the basis for their faithful "testimony about Jesus" (1:9; 6:9; 12:17; 20:4). The testimony of believers is both a lifestyle of faithfulness to Christ and verbal witness to others. The church during this time of terrible opposition and suffering does not go into hiding but maintains bold witness to the very end.

Their witness is now defined more specifically: "they did not love their lives so much as to shrink from death." This is a major passage that led the Greek *martyria* ("witness") to be used from the second century on for "martyrdom." For the believer, witness involves a willingness to die for Jesus if necessary. As Jesus says in Mark 8:34, "Whoever wants to be my disciple must deny themselves and take up their cross and follow me." Cross-bearing is the essential component of *imitatio Christi* (imitation of Christ); true believers maintain their witness even if it means death.

The final part of the hymn (Rev 12:12) recounts the results of this cosmic victory for heaven and for earth. Because of the arrival of the kingdom, involving both the overthrow of Satan and the victory of the saints, the heaven-dwellers are called to rejoice and the earth-dwellers to mourn. In the Old Testament heaven and earth rejoice together (Psa 96:11; Isa 44:23, 49:13), but the earth has come under the control of evil powers. It must be destroyed (2 Pet 3:7, 10) to make way for the new heaven and new earth (Rev 21:1).

It is likely that all heavenly beings are intended here, as the believers join the hosts of heaven in their joyous celebration of God's final victory over the dragon and his cosmic forces. The phrase "heavens and you who dwell in them" at one level describes all celestial beings as well as humans, but it has a special relevance as a picture of God's people, for it stands in tension with "earth-dwellers" (3:10; 6:10, 8:13) to describe the saints as those who belong to heaven rather than earth. We are the citizens of heaven (Phil 3:10) who are "foreigners and exiles" (1 Pet 1:1, 17; 2:11) on earth. As the old song says, "This world is not our home, we're just a'passin' through."

In contrast, the earth and sea are called on to mourn. These are the regions of evil from which the two beasts emerge in Revelation 13:1, 11. This uses the same term as in the three "woes" of the trumpet judgments (8:13; 9:12; 11:14), describing the stark terror of those facing the wrath of God. Here, however, it is not God's wrath but the devil's anger. As in 12:4, Satan takes the initiative and goes to war, but this time (as in Rev 9) against his own followers. He "goes down" or "descends" on his own—in 12:7–9 Michael casts him down—"filled with fury" (the same term as "wrath"). This is not righteous indignation; it is the opposite. This is frustrated rage at having lost. The final defeat of his evil plots has him livid with anger. He knows he cannot take it out on God, so he plans to vent his hostility on the earth-dwellers, his own people.

There are two reasons for the devil's wrath: He has lost his place in heaven (12:7–9, 10b), and "he knows that his time is short." The same sense of imminence that characterizes the return of Christ (Matt 16:27; 1 Cor 1:7; Rev 22:7, 12, 20) also fits the demise of the devil. I used to think that Satan was the great megalomaniac who thought he could still pull out the victory over God, but I was wrong. He may be supremely evil, but he is not stupid. He knows there is only a short time before he is cast into the lake of fire (Rev 20:10). Out of his frustration he can only wreak as much havoc as he can. He is also aware of the victory God's people have already achieved over him (12:11), so he can only turn on his own people. Why does he hate his own followers? They are still made in the image of God and the objects of God's love (John 3:16). He can still bring pain to God and Christ by torturing and killing these people (Rev 9:1–11, 13–19).

WAR BREAKS OUT ON EARTH (12:13–17)

The wrath of the devil from 12:12 is now turned back against the believers. While 12:7–9 is an expansion of 12:4 (war in heaven), this is an expansion of 12:6, detailing the action of the dragon (the "devil" of 12:12) forcing the woman/the saints to flee into the desert. The theme here is the protection of the woman by God (12:14) and then by creation (12:16), which enrages the dragon further as he leaves to make war on her offspring (12:17), leading to the strategy he devises to destroy God's people, told in chapter 13.

Pursuit by the Dragon (12:13)

Initially defeated when he is unable to kill the Christ child (12:5) and is "thrown to the earth" (12:7–9), the dragon makes the best of his situation by going after the woman who had given birth to the child, and she is forced to flee (12:5, 6). The moment he reached earth, he immediately turned his fury on the woman/the church. The verb has a double meaning, as Satan both "pursued" and "persecuted" God's people. The image of the woman fleeing as she is pursued is an example of the exodus motif in the Bible, recalling the picture of Israel fleeing the chariots of Pharaoh—who is called the dragon "Rahab" in Isaiah 51:9–10.

Care and Protection of the Woman (12:14–16)

In 12:6 the woman "flees into the wilderness to a place prepared for her by God," and in 12:14 we are told how she gets away. God gives her "the two wings of the great eagle," recalling Old Testament examples of eagles as divinely sent agents who rescue his people (Exod 19:4, 32:10–11, again recalling the exodus). It is important to realize that she is not passive here (delivered by the eagle), but active (given the wings to fly away herself). In Isaiah 40:31 the faithful are told they will "soar on wings like eagles"; they will rise above their earthly trials with the strength God supplies.

The wings allow her to "fly to the place prepared for her in the wilderness," language that recalls 12:6 (see the discussion there). God has provided a refuge to protect her. Note the imagery of God as heavenly Father caring for his children. She is "nourished" there, the same verb that in 12:6 depicts the physical needs of God's beleaguered children. This recalls Jesus' words in Matthew 6:25: "Do not worry about your life." The desert is often seen in the Old Testament as a place of refuge and provision (Exod 16:32; 1 Kgs 19:3–9).

God will watch over her for "time, times, and half a time" (1 + 2 + ½), a variation of the "42 months" (Rev 11:2; 13:5) and "1260 days" (11:3; 12:6). It is an allusion to Daniel 7:25; 12:7, a reference to the three-and-a-half-year period in Daniel (and Revelation—see Dan 9:27) when the saints will be handed over to the "little horn" who will oppress them (Dan 7:25). God will keep her "out of the serpent's reach" for that time. By using "serpent" here, there is emphasis on the wiles of the devil, as in the Lord's Prayer: "lead us not into temptation" (= "give us the strength to overcome temptation").

In 12:15 a specific example of her protection is provided. The serpent's connection with Leviathan, noted in the comments on 12:7–9, returns as the serpent "spews water like a river." He is sending a flood—a twofold flood of lies and of persecution. Satan's use of lies and deception is part of end-time activity in Matthew 24:24 ("signs and wonders to deceive, if possible, even the elect"), John 8:44 (Satan a liar), and 2 Thessalonians 2:9–10 (counterfeit miracles). In Revelation this may allude to the false teachers (Rev 2:22, 14–15, 20–23). The flood as persecution echoes Psalm 18:4, 32:6, 69:2; and Isaiah 43:2.

When Satan tries to drown the woman, another miracle occurs in 12:16 as the earth "opens its mouth and swallows the river." Creation now comes to the aid of God's people. There are several possible Old Testament allusions here. The best is probably Israel's rescue from Pharaoh's chariots, as the Song of Moses celebrated in Exodus 15:12, "You stretched out your right hand and the earth swallows your enemies." Similar language is used of God taking the lives of the sons of Korah in Numbers 16:32, where "the earth opened its mouth and swallowed them" (also Psa 106:17). So this flood is both internal (conflict caused by the lies of the false teachers) and external (pressure caused by persecution).

RAGE AND PURSUIT BY THE DRAGON (12:17)

Here the dragon is filled with wrath once more, this time at his further defeat by God and creation in 12:15–16. Both words for anger are used in the context (*thymos* and *orgē*), and together they connote an intense, passionate anger focused specifically on the woman that leads him to go to war against the rest of her offspring. There are three defeats of the dragon in chapter 12—the snatching up of the Christ child (12:5), the expulsion from heaven (12:8), and the attempt to drown the woman (12:15–16). Now he attempts a fourth offensive against "her offspring." There may be double meaning of the woman and the offspring. They could refer to both: 1) the ideal church in heaven (the woman, 12:1–2) and the earthly church (the offspring, 12:17); and 2) the woman as the church of John's day and the offspring as those who will come to Christ in the future, namely the converts down through the ages as well as in the final period depicted in chapters 10–13.

These Christ followers who are the object of the dragon's wrath become victors when they "keep God's commands and hold fast their testimony about Jesus." This is one of the core phrases in the book for describing the perseverance of the saints, building on 1:2, "the word of God and the testimony of Jesus Christ" (see 1:9; 6:9; 19:10; 20:4). The key to victory in this book is clear—obeying God and witnessing to Jesus. This obedience and faithfulness in 14:12 is the way we avoid the same terrible fate as the followers of the beast. The believer is accountable to God to maintain an ethical path through life modeled after Jesus.

It is impossible to read Revelation 12 and not be convinced of the reality of spiritual warfare. Many of us might like to be Switzerlands and remain neutral in this war, as if we could ignore Satan and be certain he would thereby ignore us. But Satan is real, and so is his hatred for every one of us! To be neutral is to lose. Satan the great red dragon tries in every way to thwart the plan of God, both broadly in redemptive history and narrowly in each of our lives. He was soundly defeated at his original rebellion and at the cross, yet he continues to work very hard at his nefarious plots, and often he succeeds. The path to victory over our adversary is quite clear. We must absolutely depend on Christ, drawing strength from the Spirit and obeying God in all we do. When we do that, we cannot lose. The forces of evil will distract us with earthly trials and persecution, but so long as our eyes are fixed on Jesus, we will overcome.

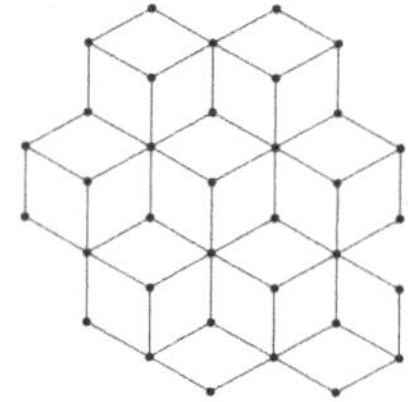

THE BEASTS FROM THE SEA AND THE LAND

(12:18–13:18)

Satan's strategy for conducting his war against the woman and her offspring (12:17) is now presented. It centers on the other two members of the false trinity, the beast from the sea (13:1–10) and the beast from the earth (13:11–18). The first beast is the military and administrative head of the empire, and the second beast is the head of the one-world religion centered on worshiping the beast and the dragon (the "false prophet" in 16:13). The dragon gives the beast his authority and his throne (13:2), so the beast in effect is his "son," a parody on Christ as Son of God. As such, the beasts conduct the final war against God and his people and demand universal worship. This is what Satan attempted in the original rebellion when he was thrown out of heaven (12:4, 7–9), and to the original readers this would depict the imperial cult demanding worship of the emperor. Throughout this chapter I will be noting a series of parodies or great imitations, as the dragon and the beast copy what God has already done. This is also present throughout the book, for if Satan wants to do anything right, all he can do is parody what God has done perfectly. Thus in this chapter there is a false trinity, a fatal wound healed (= the death and resurrection of Christ), and a mark of the beast (= the sealing of the saints in chapter 7).

THE DRAGON EMPOWERS HIS AGENT, THE BEAST FROM THE SEA (12:18–13:4)

The Emergence of the Beast from the Sea (12:18–13:2b)

Translations differ on the best way to handle the statement that the dragon stood on the shore of the sea, which I have labeled 12:18. Some include it in 12:17 (ESV); others fold it into 13:1 (NIV, NASB). I agree with the latter placement, for it introduces the emergence of the beast from the sea in 13:1.

All of this chapter, then, is the result of the wrath of the dragon in 12:17. The war on earth of 12:13–17 continues; we saw the intentions and initial action in 12:13–17, and now we see how those intentions are carried out. The dragon "stands at the shore of the sea," ready to call forth his associate in evil. "Stands" is actually the third verb in the sentence of 12:17–18, "The dragon was enraged ... and went ... and stood." Still, the subject matter introduces 13:1. The scene alludes to Daniel 7:3, where the four beasts "came up out of the sea," and recalls Revelation 11:7, where the beast "came up from the Abyss."

He stands on the shore in order to call forth his agent for the final battle (13:1), the military and administrative head (the king, in effect) of his empire.[1] As stated in the commentary on 12:7–9, the dragon is Leviathan, the sea monster of the deep, and the sea in Revelation symbolizes the realm of evil. So it is natural that the beast emerges from the sea. This is a dramatic scene, picturing the beast emerging slowly: first the horns, then the heads with the crowns, and finally the body.

This description highlights the close connection between the dragon and the beast: both are sea monsters, and both have "ten horns and seven heads." The order here reverses the order

---

1. In the ancient world it was common for the king to lead his forces into battle.

of the dragon in 12:3, for the beast has his crowns on his horns, symbolizing military prowess.[2] The dragon is the emperor of the underworld, the beast the military arm who will lead the final battle. All this shows that the beast is united with the dragon, and this is the first parody or great imitation in chapter 13: the dragon usurps the role of God the Father, the beast the role of God the Son, and with the second beast (13:11–18) they form the counterfeit trinity.

In addition, the heads and horns allude to Daniel 7, with the seven heads the sum of the heads of the four beasts in Daniel 7:4–8 and the ten horns the horns of the fourth beast, signifying ten kings who follow him (Dan 7:7, 20, 24). In Daniel 7:23–25 the ten kings and another ruler (the little horn) blaspheme the Most High and persecute the saints. This also parallels Revelation 17:12–14 and shows that this beast is the antichrist of early church tradition, the one who will try to usurp God's authority and power at the end of history (2 Thess 2:1–12; 1 John 2:18; 4:3).

However, this identification is debated; many, particularly in the amillennial tradition, believe this is not a singular figure but a symbol of all the opponents of Christ and the church down through the church age. For Revelation's original audience that would mean the Roman Empire embodied in the emperor as the "god of this world." This is partly correct, but I maintain that this beast is also an actual figure that will appear at the end of history, like the two witnesses in Revelation 11.

In Judaeo-Christianity the antichrist "legend" began with the little horn of Daniel 7, who sets up "the abomination that causes desolation" and persecutes God's people (Dan 11:31; 12:11). This figure became the prototype of the supreme opponent of God on earth. In Second Temple Judaism of the intertestamental period there were two types of anti-messiah

2. These crowns are "diadems," the ruler's crown; see commentary on 12:3. The horns recall the "seven horns" of the Lamb in 5:6.

figures—an external tyrant who stands against the saints (embodied in the "beast from the sea") and an internal false teacher who deceives the people (embodied in the beast from the earth or false prophet of 16:13). Psalms of Solomon 2:25–26 speaks of empires that opposed God and his people, and Ascension of Isaiah 4:1–13 describes Beliar descending as a "king of iniquity" against Israel.[3]

Jesus and the early church inherited these ideas from Daniel and late Judaism and developed them into the "man of lawlessness" (1 Thess 2:1–13) and the "antichrist" (1 John 2:18; 4:3). From these two texts, there is no question that the early church expected an actual person to appear.[4] The figure of the beast here closely fits this figure expected by Judaism and the early church. Certainly, just as the two witnesses also symbolize the church, so the beast symbolizes the Roman Empire and its emperor in their desire for deification and world domination. However, the two beasts are also two actual persons who will appear at the end of history and establish the one-world empire called Babylon the Great (Rev 18).

This beast has "a blasphemous name" on each head, depicting his blasphemous claim to deity and desire to supplant God as an object of worship. These names allude to the titles of deity ascribed to the emperor under the imperial cult, such as "lord," "savior, "son of god," "our lord and god."[5] This imperial cult especially proliferated in the province of Asia where the seven cities resided. Sacrifices were offered to Domitian, who was thought to be the person who united the human and the divine—a definite parody of Christ.

As the head and torso appear, animal characteristics prevail (13:2a). These are apocalyptic symbols that portray the horror

3. So also 4QTestimonia 22–24; Sibylline Oracles 3:63–74; Apocalypse of Elijah 3:5–13.

4. 1 John 2:18, "as you have heard that the antichrist is coming."

5. See "Historical Background" in the introduction.

of the beast, for it is the embodiment of all that is evil.[6] It builds on the four beasts of Daniel 7:4–7, where four successive empires are seen as resembling a lion, a bear, a leopard, and a beast with iron teeth and ten horns. In Daniel they are consecutive empires, but here they coalesce into one being who sums up all the evil empires of history. All the animals are predators, and each does not have individual significance. Rather, they together portray the destructive power of evil as embodied in the beast/antichrist.

AUTHORITY OF THE BEAST (13:2C)

As God "gives" or authorizes activity (*edothē*, 6:2, 4, 8; 7:2; 8:2), so the dragon "gives" to the beast his own "power and throne and great authority." Once more Satan both parodies God and usurps God's sovereignty in his own pretense to reign over creation. First, he gives the beast his "power," namely strength to perform miracles and accomplish great things. All the actions that lead the church to submit and worship him stem from that power. Second, he gives "his throne," namely dominion and sovereignty over this world (but only over this world!). Third, the dragon gives "great authority," echoing Daniel 7:6, where the third beast, the leopard, received "authority to rule." There is a progression of authority from the dragon to the first beast (here) to the second beast (Rev 13:12) and then to the ten kings who serve the beast (17:12–13). But this power and authority are temporary (13:5) and surpassed by the authority God gives to the avenging angels (14:18; 16:8; 18:1).

FATAL WOUND HEALED (13:3A)

One of the seven heads of the beast receives a fatal wound that is healed, another great imitation copying the death and resurrection of Christ. This is repeated twice more in 13:12, 14, so it is a major emphasis in the narrative. Since it is "one of the

6. They are also a parody of the living creatures in 4:7.

heads" that is mortally wounded, it is common to link this with the Roman Emperor Nero, who committed suicide in AD 68 after it was proven he had set the fires that destroyed much of Rome. The chaos that reigned after his suicide almost became the death-knell of Rome, with three upstart pretenders (Galba, Otho, and Vitellius) claiming the throne in a single year. The recovery of the empire under Vespasian seemed miraculous. In the 70s a rumor arose that Nero had come back to life and was going to lead an army of Parthians to destroy Rome. This became known as the *Nero redivivus* legend and likely forms part of the background to chapter 13. However, there is certainly more than this. The church did not believe the beast was Nero but that he was a Nero-like figure. The early church did not take this association with Nero further, and it was never more than background for the beast/antichrist theme. In the beast's claim to be "god of this world" alongside Satan, he recapitulates the death and resurrection of Christ.

Universal Worship of the Dragon and the Beast (13:3b–4)

As a result of the counterfeit resurrection, the whole world is "filled with wonder" and follows the beast. This is another parody, for the same term is used of the reactions of the onlookers to the miracles of Jesus (Matt 8:27; Mark 5:20). The nations are easily deceived, as in Revelation 13:13–14 and 16:14, and begin to follow and worship the antichrist. This is the heart of idolatry, to worship the creature rather than the Creator.

In worshiping the beast, they also worship the dragon who had "given authority to the beast" (13:4). This is not just practiced by the pagans in the imperial cult but also by weak Christians like those in the Nicolaitan cult (2:6, 14–15, 20–25). The one-world religion is occult demon worship; this will be a frequent refrain in the following chapters, separating the "true worshipers" (14:7; 15:4; 19:4, 10; 22:9) from false ones. In Scripture idols are not just dead images; demonic powers are behind them.

These idolatrous worshipers make two liturgical affirmations. First, they say, "Who is like the beast?" a parody of the acclamation of Yahweh (Exod 8:10; Psa 71:19; Isa 41:7, 46:5). God alone is incomparable and worthy of worship. Second, they acclaim, "Who can wage war against it?" This looks back to Revelation 12:7, where the question is answered: Michael and his angels "make war" and cast the dragon and his fallen angels out of heaven. In fact, in 12:11 the saints are able to conquer the dragon, yet the unsaved world flocks after him and utters these very lies in worship. Truly, the "god of this age has blinded the minds of unbelievers" (2 Cor 4:4).

God Permits the Beast's Activities (13:5–8)

The key to this section is the phrase "was given," communicating God's control over all things and meaning "God allows/authorizes." The dragon and the beast can do nothing without permission from God. Every action of the antichrist here is introduced by God giving his permission.

God Allows Blasphemy and Slander (13:5–6)

In 13:2 the beast had "a mouth like a lion," and now we see it roars words of blasphemy, with authority to do so for 42 months. In Daniel 7:6 the third beast "was given authority," and in 7:8 the little horn utters "great things." These two images are combined here, and the antichrist "speaks great blasphemies" with authority. This boastful speech characterized the little horn (Dan 7:11, 20), and this was addressed especially "against the Most High" (7:25). The word for "blasphemy" is the same term as "slander," and it refers to religious slander of God, here the dragon and beast claiming the name and worship of God for themselves. This pretension to greatness is exposed by all the emphasis throughout the book on the great acts of God (Rev 8:8, 10; 12:14; 18:21; 19:17). The authority of the beast/antichrist is severely limited. God *allows* it for only "forty-two months," the period already seen in 11:2, 3; 12:6, 14. At the end of this period, the witnesses/church will arise, Christ will return, and the forces of evil will be destroyed. God is in control, not the antichrist. He may claim divinity, but his reign of infamy will last only a short time, so long as God permits.

When he "opens his mouth to blaspheme God," he centers on three things: God, his name, and his tabernacle: the heaven-dwellers. Jesus says in the Lord's Prayer that the goal of every believer is to keep God's name sacred (Matt 6:9), also a major Old Testament theme (Exod 20:7; Psa 111:9; Isa 5:16; Ezek 20:41). Profaning the name is the heart of blasphemy. The saints as "heaven-dwellers" means that even though they still live on earth, they belong to heaven, and it is their true home.[7] They are identified here as God's *skēnē* or "tabernacle,"[8] paralleling Revelation 11:1, where they are linked with the temple and altar. In chapter 21 the new Jerusalem is not just a place but a people, for they are sacred repositories of God's presence. In 21:3 the new heavenly reality is described: "Now the dwelling (*skēnē*) of God is with his people, and he will live (*skēnē*) with them." When God's people are slandered, God is blasphemed, for he "tabernacles" in them.

God Allows the Beast to Conquer the Saints (13:7a)

In 11:7 the beast ascended from the Abyss and made war against the two witnesses, conquering and killing them. This is repeated here. Since the witnesses symbolized the church, this is connected, for God gives permission to the beast to do exactly that to the saints. This also alludes to Daniel 7:21, where the little horn "wages war" and defeats the "holy people." Yet only in Revelation 11:7 and 13:7 are the saints "conquered," and in 12:11 we see that in reality it was God's people, not the false trinity, who were victorious when they lost their lives. This is one of the supreme paradoxes. When Satan takes the life of a believer, Satan is the one who is defeated, for martyrdom is the supreme

---

7. See commentary on 12:12a.
8. The NIV erroneously makes them separate.

victory over the cosmic powers. This follows the pattern set by Christ. When Satan took control of Judas to lead Christ to the cross, he participated in his own defeat. When he "conquered" Christ, he was conquered by Christ!

God Allows the Beast to Receive Universal Worship (13:7b–8)

The authority God allows the beast may be temporary (13:5b), but it is worldwide: over "every tribe, people, language, and nation." This fourfold list is used often to stress the involvement of every group in the world in the events of Revelation (see 5:9; 7:9; 10:11, and others). This is a major reason I cannot hold the preterist position—the action does not center only on first-century Palestine but on every part of the world.[9] The beast has total control, and the nations obey his every whim. Still, a limitation is implied: His influence is restricted to the earth-dwellers, and he has no ultimate power over God's people. As Jesus says in Matthew 10:28, "Do not be afraid of those who kill the body." As we have seen throughout the book, martyrdom is actually a victory over Satan.

The unsaved world does not just bow to the beast's authority; "all worship him," meaning not only all nations but every person in them. This goes beyond the imperial cult, which never attained universal acceptance. This has to refer to the future, to the final events of history. It is a parody of Daniel 7:14, in which "one like a son of man … was given authority … all peoples, nations, and those of every language worshiped him." Again, the antichrist demands and receives the universal worship that belongs only to Christ.

John now adds a significant comment, that their "names have not been written in the Lamb's book of life." The book of life is mentioned five other times in Revelation (3:5; 17:8; 20:12, 15; 21:27). As noted in the comments on 3:5, such lists recorded the

9. See "Methods of Interpretation" in the introduction.

citizens of a city and the civic deeds they have done. Here it refers to the heavenly book in which the names of the righteous, the citizens of heaven, were kept (Dan 7:9–10; 12:1). It stresses the security of the believer who belongs to heaven no matter what the forces of evil do. These people are earth-dwellers who have no access to heaven or to eternal life. They are doomed.

Moreover, this is "the Lamb's book of life," made possible because in his mercy he "was slain from the creation of the world." It was the death of Christ that made salvation possible, the blood of Christ that became the atoning sacrifice for sin. This is the main title for Christ in Revelation (28 times), and the phrase "slain Lamb" is taken from 5:6, stressing the great victory and his worthiness to open the seals. The final victory over evil is not future (Armageddon) but past (the cross).

Moreover, Christ's death was preordained "from the foundation of the world." Some think this modifies "book of life written," as it does in 17:8, but the word order here favors it modifying "slain Lamb." God's redemptive plan was established even before this world was made. God's foreknowledge was aware of what it would mean to create humankind. He knew of the fall into sin and the implications for humankind. They could not pay for their own sins, and the only result could be their eternal destruction, unless ... God paid the price himself, for it had to be a perfect sacrifice to atone for sin. Thus when God decided to create humanity, he already knew he would have to send his Son to die for their sins.

John Points Out the Significance for Believers (13:9–10)

John interrupts his narration of the cosmic war to provide a prophetic warning to believers. He begins with the challenge from the seven letters, "Whoever has ears, let them hear," repeating Jesus' frequent call (Mark 4:9, 23; Matt 11:15, 24:15; Luke 8:8). This commands the readers to pay special attention and to obey the injunction that is coming. The Christians of John's day and of our day had better listen carefully to this critical message.

The four-line proverbial saying is made up of two couplets centering on the danger of captivity and death by sword. There is no verb in any of the lines, and the reader should supply, "It is God's will that ..." for each line. It alludes to Jeremiah 15:2, "Those destined to death, to death; those to the sword, to the sword." In Jeremiah the context is judgment on Israel. Here it is the opposite, the persecution of the saints. Still, the point in both is that God's people must yield to God's will. The judgment oracle of Jeremiah has been transformed into a prophetic call for God's people to join in Jesus' "fellowship of suffering" (Phil 3:10) and be willing to follow his model, as in 1 Peter 2:23: "He entrusted himself to him who judges justly."

Captivity and death have often been the lot of the saints, as with Smyrna in Revelation 2:10: "The devil is about to throw some of you into prison. ... Be faithful to the point of death." In the final days under the antichrist, this will become a universal experience of the church. Jesus' words in Matthew 24:21 ("distress unequaled from the beginning of the world to now—and never to be equaled again") likely use the destruction of Jerusalem as a **proleptic** anticipation of this final "great tribulation" (Rev 7:14).

The message is difficult but clear. While believers decry evil and refuse to follow the wicked injunctions of the beast, they must passively accept their lot of suffering. This is an important correction for those who see the book of Revelation as a call to active, violent opposition against evil regimes. We are the messianic army of Christ and we will fight back, but our weapons "are not the weapons of the world" but have "divine power to demolish strongholds" (2 Cor 10:4). The saints fight back with bold witness, as in Revelation 11:3–6, and accept whatever happens to them as God's will: "If to captivity, to captivity; if to the sword, to the sword." It is Yahweh who fights the war; our task in it is to be faithful and persevere in witness.

John ends 13:10 with a comment that summarizes all the perseverance passages of the book. The call to passivity mandates "patient endurance and faithfulness," with endurance a dominant ethical demand in the seven letters (2:2, 3, 19; 3:10). It is deepened and defined carefully in the command to faithful living (1:5; 2:10, 13; 17:14). The saints are victorious by "not loving their lives even to the point of death" (12:11) and by trusting God to defeat the forces of evil on their behalf (6:11).

A Second Beast, the False Prophet, Praises the First Beast (13:11–18)

As stated in the introduction to 12:18–13:18, Satan parodies the Godhead and produces his own false trinity—the dragon (himself), the beast from the sea (the antichrist), and the beast from the earth (the false prophet, 16:13). He uses these creatures to gain control of the nations, to create a one-world government centered on the antichrist and a one-world religion centered on the false prophet. The first beast gains a universal following by parodying the death and resurrection of Christ. When this antichrist returns from the dead, his associate, the false prophet, uses the world's wonder to forge a new world religion reproducing the imperial cult and centered on the universal worship of the dragon and the beast. So while the first beast represents political power, the second beast is the head of a new religion. For John's original readers this would point to the imperial priesthood of Rome, and the Asiarchs who both controlled Graeco-Roman religious life in the province of Asia and promoted the imperial cult.

The Beast Described (13:11)

Like the first beast (13:1) this beast ascends, but now it comes "from the earth," echoing the four kingdoms of Daniel 7:17. The two beasts are obviously connected closely. This second beast parodies Christ as the Lamb with seven horns in Revelation 5:6 by having "two horns like a lamb." This fits Jesus' warning against false prophets who "come to you in sheep's clothing, but inwardly they are ravenous wolves" (Matt 7:15). It also alludes to Daniel 8:3, where the "ram with two horns" is the Medo-Persian Empire in its opposition to God. The horns of the false trinity (Rev 12:3; 13:1, 11) describe the might of the evil powers in defiance of God and his will. Moreover, this second beast also "speaks like a dragon," a further parody of Christ, who speaks with the authority of God (John 5:25-30; 7:16–18). The same lying words used by the dragon and the antichrist to deceive the world (Rev 12:9; 13:5–6) will characterize the false prophet, fulfilling the prophecies of 2 Thessalonians 2:3 (the "great apostasy") and 1 John 2:18 (the "many antichrists").

The Work of the False Prophet (13:12)

The central verb in the rest of Revelation 13 is *poieō* ("do, make"), used nine times in 13:12–16 to describe the incredible activity of this beast on the dragon's behalf. The dragon gave his authority to the first beast, and now "all authority" is transferred to the second. There is a distinct chain of command, and the purpose is to enslave the whole world in their falsehoods, primarily to "make" every person "worship the first beast." The verb "make" is *poieō* and indicates an activity designed to cause people to do something, in this case worship the false trinity. The basis of this worship, as in 13:3–4, is the healing of the mortal wound, that imitation of the greatest miracle of all, the resurrection of Christ. As Christ's resurrection launched Christianity, so its copy will launch this new blasphemous counterfeit religion.

The Imitation—Great Signs (13:13–14a)

The next activity of the false prophet is to "perform" (*poieō*) spectacular but counterfeit miracles that mirror those of Elijah and Christ as well as the two witnesses of 11:5–6. Moses was viewed as a miracle-working prophet (Exod 4:17; 7:9–10; 10:1–2), and Elijah and Elisha were justly famed for their incredible miracles. John's Gospel centers on the "sign" miracles of Jesus, as the wonders he produced "signified" the essence of who he was. The signs here are true miracles but performed to support a lie, that the false trinity is the true Trinity. Deuteronomy 13:1–4 and 2 Thessalonians 2:9 speak of miracles used by false teachers in the service of their lies.

Here the second beast parodies Elijah, who calls down fire on Mount Carmel in 1 Kings 18:36–39 and has God send down fire on the soldiers sent by Ahab to arrest him in 2 Kings 1:10–14. This miracle occurs validly twice in Revelation, with the two witnesses (Rev 11:5) and at the destruction of Satan's army (20:9). The false prophet brings fire down "in full view of the people," not in service of God but to deceive the people into worshiping a false god. It is not a religious act but a public relations performance with an evil purpose behind it.

However, God is in actual control, as seen in another instance of *edothē* ("was given") in 13:14 to mean God permits the beast the power to perform the miracle. Since the sinners have rejected God's offer and refused to repent, God is "giving them over" (as in Rom 1:24, 26) to the deceptions they clearly prefer. If they want to worship the very demonic powers who have tortured and killed their friends and neighbors (Rev 9), God will allow them to experience that delusion in all its terrible force.

THE IDOL SPEAKS (13:14B–15)

As a result of these deceptive powers, the earth-dwellers obey the false prophet and erect an idolatrous image. This echoes Daniel 3:1–6, where Nebuchadnezzar constructs a 90-foot gold idol and commands the nations to worship it. Under the imperial cult a great number of statues of the emperors were placed in temples, and Ephesus alone had temples dedicated to Julius Caesar, Augustus, and Domitian. The temple of Domitian contained a statue of him 22 feet high, and this could well provide the background for the image here. Moreover, under the teaching of the Nicolaitan cult noted in Revelation 2:2, 3, 14–15, many so-called Christians participated in this practice of venerating the emperor.

After the idol is erected, God allows (another "was given"; see comments on 13:5–8) the false prophet to "give breath" to the image and "make it speak" (13:15). This is another parody, this time of the raising of the two witnesses in 11:11, when "the breath of life" entered them. In the ancient world some temples would have pulleys or tubes attached to the idols, and the priests would use ventriloquism to make it seem like the idols were speaking. That is not the case here. Life is breathed into the idolatrous statue, and it speaks. It was popularly believed in the first century that the gods did inhabit their idols, and rituals existed to call forth the spark of the divine in them. The Roman world was enamored with magicians and rituals. But the antichrist will go beyond such deeds and will bring these things to pass in reality.

The primary thing the now-living image will proclaim is a new state religion. Nebuchadnezzar in Daniel 3:6, 11, 15 demanded worship of the dead idol on penalty of death, leading to the famous incident of the three young men in the furnace. This image makes it a capital crime to refuse to participate in the worship of the beast/antichrist. This did not occur under Domitian, but 15 or so years later, in AD 112, a Roman official named Pliny the Younger wrote a letter to Emperor Trajan saying he had executed Christians who had refused to offer wine and incense before a statue of the emperor.[10] The whole of the province of Asia was expected to participate in the imperial cult, but it never became a capital crime. Under the antichrist, it does so.

The Mark of the Beast (13:16–17a)

The eighth and final use of *poieō* occurs here, as the false prophet "makes" all people (believer and unbeliever alike) receive a mark to identify their allegiance to the antichrist. As in 6:15 and 19:18, all the social categories are noted to stress the universality of this new law. The first pair stresses the social side, the second pair the economic side, and the third pair the societal side. Both the haves and the have-nots must receive the mark.

Two rules define the new demands. First, the mark is to be on the forehead or wrist, Satan's counterpart of the seal of

10. Pliny the Younger, *Epistles* 10.96.

God in the forehead in 7:3. Both God's seal and the antichrist's mark signify ownership, so these unfortunates are now Satan's property. In Deuteronomy 6:4, 8 the Shema was placed on the hands and foreheads of God's people, the basis for the phylacteries worn in Christ's day and today.[11] Then in Ezekiel 9:4, the Hebrew letter *tav* was placed on the foreheads of the faithful to show they belonged to Yahweh. In Roman practice religious tattoos were often worn to indicate a person's patron god. It signified both the rejection of former loyalties and absolute acceptance of the new allegiance. There will be no neutrality; one either belongs to Christ or to the beast. To take the mark will mean final rejection of Christ. As in Mark 3:28–29, Hebrews 6:4–6 and 1 John 5:16 (the sin that leads to death) it will constitute final apostasy from Christ: the unpardonable sin.

Second, "no one can buy or sell" without the mark. In Smyrna and Philadelphia, economic persecution had left believers poverty-stricken (Rev 2:9; 3:8), and at Pergamum and Thyatira the guild structure of the trades placed enormous economic pressure on Christians. This is the ultimate expression of this tactic. Starvation awaits those who refuse the mark. Believers will lose their jobs, their homes, and their places in society; then they will be hunted to the death. This was true at times in the first century; it is true in many places today; and it will universally be the case in the final period of history.

The Number of His Name (13:17b–18)

The mark is further linked with the "name of the beast" and then with "the number of its name." When believers see Christ in eternity, "his name will be on their foreheads" (Rev 22:4), so once more the antichrist is parodying Christ. The "number of his name" refers to the ancient practice of gematria. The letters of the alphabet were also used as numbers, with the first nine

---

11. These were leather pouches containing passages from Exod 13 and Deut 6.

letters of the alphabet being the numbers 1–9, the second nine letters 10–90, and so on. So every name and word had a numerical value when you added up the total of the letters in the word. For example, ABC would be six (1 + 2 + 3).

There has been so much wild and wooly speculation on the number 666 through the centuries that John's opening observation is perhaps more needed today than it was in his time: "This demands wisdom." John adds that it also demands understanding. This alludes to Daniel 12:10, "those who are wise will understand," and is similar to Jesus, who in the Olivet Discourse, after prophesying the abomination, says, "Let the reader understand" (Matt 24:15; Mark 13:14). So John commands the readers to exercise extreme care and divinely guided wisdom in interpreting this number.

There are several possible options:

1. The names of world leaders, so long as we remember it is a 1st-century, not 21st-century, name—not Hitler or Mussolini or any other modern figure but Julius Caesar or Vespasian.
2. Apocalyptic riddles with symbolic significance; for example, the name Jesus (*Iēsous*) in Greek adds up to 888 (*I* = 10, *ē* = 8, *s* = 200, *o* = 70, *u* = 400, *s* = 200).
3. A symbol for the antichrist—since 6 is the number of finite man, 666 would symbolize humankind in ultimate sin and rebellion against God.
4. A triangular number, the sum of 1–36 (= 666) with 36 the triangular number for 1–8 (the beast as the eighth king).

The most oft-cited solution falls under option one above, and it may well be the most likely. The name "Nero Caesar" in one Hebrew spelling (*qsr nrwn*) adds up to 666, and this is supported by the alternative number 621 in a few ancient manuscripts, which is "Nero Caesar" in Latin; this would show it was the understanding in some quarters of the church. A second and very good possibility combines the second and third options above. The use of the threefold 666 as a counterpart and foil for the three "holies" of 4:8, and the gematria of the name of "Jesus" (888) would contrast the absolute imperfection of the antichrist (666) with the completeness of 777 and the absolute (beyond) perfection of Jesus as holy and as 888. Both these options fit well in the context, and I cannot choose between them.

In this chapter we have seen that, as Satan's original rebellion was likely a self-centered desire for adulation and power, this has continued down through the ages. For his final effort he can only emulate God's perfect work, so everything he does is a parody of God's actions. He establishes a false trinity that appears on earth for the final period of history—the dragon (functioning behind the action), the beast/antichrist, and the second beast/false prophet. John's readers would have seen this taking place in the imperial cult with its economic and religious pressure on Christians, and it has also been exemplified in the false teachers and anti-Christian tyrants throughout the church age. At the same time, this will culminate in a final "great tribulation" (7:14) at the close of human history, when the antichrist appears and establishes an "unholy Roman Empire" with the false prophet the head of a "one-world religion" that deifies the dragon and the beast and persecutes the church all over the world. Christians will not just be marginalized; they will be hunted down when they refuse to take the "mark" that means final rejection of Christ (as in Heb 6:4–6).

This has important implications for the present. In our time there are many "antichrists" (1 John 2:18) who twist Christian belief and turn the world against the church. I believe these end times are near, and we must remain ready for ever-greater pressure and ever-increasing persecution of God's people. Things are not getting better, and we must take our stand right now. Yet we do so in the certain knowledge that our final victory is certain, for God is still sovereign even if it seems like evil is taking over.

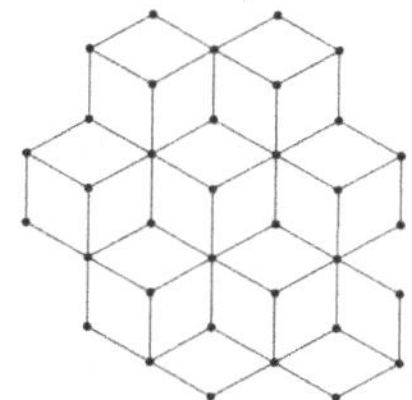

THE DESTINIES OF SAINTS AND SINNERS CONTRASTED

(14:1–20)

The entire book thus far has been organized as a series of scenes juxtaposing the heavenly with the earthly. The vertical realm centers on the presence of God and the Lamb with the saints, and the horizontal realm centers on Satan and the cosmic powers with their followers, the earth-dwellers. Yet it is clear that the conflict has already been decided, for Satan is filled with frustrated rage, and God is sovereignly in charge of everything including the forces of evil. This chapter portrays this powerfully and applies it to the issue of eternal destiny. The final interlude in the book (Rev 12–14) contains two sections: chapters 12–13 detail the war the false trinity wages against God and his people, and chapter 14 describes the actions of God in response, centering on the **eschatological** futures of the people of God versus the people of this world. There were three parts in the first half of the interlude (12:1–17; 12:18–13:10; 13:11–18), and three parts in this second half (14:1–5, 6–13, 14–20).

THE 144,000 SING WITH THE LAMB (14:1–5)

This provides another glimpse (after 7:9–17) into the glory awaiting those who faithfully respond to the oppression and temptation that has overtaken them (12:15; 13:9–10). They have chosen between the mark of God (7:3–4) and the mark of the beast (13:16–18), and that meant a choice between death in this world (to reject the mark of the beast was to be executed) and death in the next (to accept the mark of the beast meant to die for eternity). They have chosen God and Christ, so they are on Mount Zion worshiping with Christ rather than in the beast's "great city" (11:8) worshiping the false trinity.

THE LAMB ON MOUNT ZION WITH THE 144,000 (14:1)

While the dragon stands on the shore of the evil sea awaiting the emergence of the beast (12:18), the Lamb is standing on Mount Zion awaiting the victorious saints. Is this an earthly or a heavenly scene? Since the sound comes "from" heaven, it is best to see this as earthly, but Christ does not descend until the **Parousia** (19:11–16), so this seems to be a flash-forward either to the millennial period of 20:1–6 or the new Jerusalem of 21:1–6. It is an earthly scene anticipating a future reality.

Zion in the Old Testament Prophets referred not only the temple mount but the location where the Messiah would gather his people to himself, the capital of the renewed kingdom of God to be established by the Messiah (Joel 2:32; Isa 24:23; Mic 4:1–8). Jesus stands as the Divine Warrior in the place of deliverance and glory. The 144,000, as in chapter 7, are the whole people of God and on their foreheads have "his name and his Father's name," a complete contrast with the "mark of the beast" (Rev 13:16). This combines the promises of 2:17 (the Pergamum Christians given "a white stone with a new name written on it") and 7:3 (the "seal on the foreheads"). As in chapter 7, this means they are God's special possession and are secure under his vigilant care. They are his people and bear his name as his slaves and bride!

THE SAINTS SING A NEW SONG (14:2–3)

While the earth-dwellers are plotting their final war with the false trinity in chapter 13, the saints are singing of their great victory with the Lamb in chapter 14. Harps and hymns are also found in 5:8–9 and 15:2–4; all three are songs of joy at the great victory Christ has wrought at the cross and at the end of history. John combines three images to show the volume of the joyous praise—"roar of rushing waters" (the crashing surf), "loud peal of thunder" (a storm like 6:12–14), and "harpists playing harps." This last image is separated from the first two and emphasized, with a "harp" a 10- or 12-stringed lyre used in temple worship (Psa 33:2; 57:8). The combination of the loud singing and the harps emphasizes the tremendous joy and worship in this scene.

Their hymn was a "new song" (14:3) like the one in 5:9. This could even be the same song, as both are celebratory hymns rejoicing in the purchase of the redeemed by the blood of the Lamb. Since the song must be learned, it is likely that the heavenly choir is singing and the saints are trying to learn it. The song is sung "before the throne and before the four living creatures and the elders," going back to the throne room scene of chapter 4 and depicting the high worship of heaven. This explains why it can only be learned by the 144,000 redeemed—the conquerors who have overcome the spiritual wars of earth and emerged triumphant. It can only be sung by the faithful who have overcome temptation and opposition.

The Triumphant Character of the Redeemed (14:4–5)

These two verses provide important challenges to the Christians of John's day and our own. This is how God expects his true followers to live. The description of the redeemed is presented in three pairs: The first two center on their purity and relation to the Lamb, while the third is a concluding statement on ethical blamelessness. The first pair uses strange language, and it sounds on the surface like John is describing a group of celibate Christians, perhaps a monastic sect living an ascetic lifestyle. But the language is too strong for that, for if the clause "not defile themselves with women" refers to celibacy, it would entail a serious denigration of marriage, an attitude missing from other passages on celibacy in the New Testament (Matt 19:12;

1 Cor 7:1, 32). It is better to see this as a "bride of Christ" metaphor (see Rev 19:7–8; 21:2), building on Israel as the virgin bride of Yahweh (2 Kgs 19:21; Isa 37:22; Amos 5:2) and the church as a "pure virgin" in 2 Corinthians 11:2.

So this is figurative, referring to a refusal to participate in immorality, and, in fact, in worldly pursuits of any kind. The idea of "remaining virgins" is meant spiritually for men as well as women, referring to those who keep themselves pure from sinful pleasures. It is also possible that this refers to faithful believers as soldiers in a holy war, since they were required to keep themselves chaste (Deut 23:9–10; 1 Sam 21:5; 2 Sam 11:8–11). There is an emphasis on the messianic war as holy war in several places like Revelation 2:27 ("dash [the nations] to pieces like pottery") and 19:14 ("the armies of heaven ... dressed in fine linen, white and clean").

The second pair of descriptions concerns their relationship to God and the Lamb. The first is a virtual definition of faithfulness, to "follow the Lamb wherever he goes." It is the heart of discipleship in the Gospels (Mark 1:18; 8:34—70 times in Jesus' teaching). "Wherever he goes" implies *imitatio Christi*, involving the surrender of everything and a willingness to die as in Revelation 12:11 ("did not love their lives so much as to shrink from death").

The second item in this pair has two parts: 1) "purchased from among humankind," building on 5:9; 14:3. This uses the language of redemption, referring to the purchase of freedom from the slavery of sin via the ransom-price of the blood of Christ, to describe freedom from sin and presentation to God; 2) "offered as firstfruits to God and the Lamb," a sacrificial image describing the saints as the first parts of the harvest offered to God to signify that the entire crop was dedicated to him (Num 18:12; Deut 18:4; Lev 23:9–14). Christ as "firstfruits" in Romans 8:23 and 1 Corinthians 15:20 guaranteed that the redeemed would follow him in resurrection. So perhaps this connotes the conversion of the nations as the great harvest of God.

The third pair depicts the redeemed as blameless in their ethical conduct. It is interesting that out of all the ethical aspects, John centers on "no lie." He is not referring to all lies but has in mind primarily the lies of the false teachers, specifically the Nicolaitan cult. In Revelation 2:2 their so-called "apostles" are proven to be "false," and in 3:9 the Jewish persecutors are labeled "liars." In 21:8, 27; 22:15 liars are excluded and thrown into the lake of fire. When they have conquered such falsehood, among other things, the Christians are considered "blameless," another sacrificial term depicting the sacrifice as perfect and acceptable to the Lord (Exod 29:1; Lev 4:3). Here it refers to an absolute commitment to God, a total walk with Christ, and a commitment to sound doctrine.

THREE ANGELS URGE REPENTANCE AND ISSUE A WARNING (14:6–13)

These angels progressively announce a final opportunity to repent. At the same time, they provide a final warning of the danger of refusing to do so, namely 1) the imminent fall of "Babylon the Great," which is Rome (called "Babylon" in 1 Pet 5:13), the empire of the beast; and 2) the eternal torment awaiting the unrepentant.

THE FIRST ANGEL WITH THE ETERNAL GOSPEL (14:6–7)

"Another angel" appears in Revelation 14:6, and probably is meant to take the reader back to the seven angels of the trumpet judgments as an introduction to the proclamations here. This first angel is "flying in midair" and speaking "in a loud voice" like the eagle proclaiming the woes in 8:13. So this angelic herald makes an announcement to the whole world. The picture is of an angel moving from nation to nation crying out the demand to repent.

This first proclamation of judgment is markedly different from the next two, for it entails an offer of salvation. The angel is carrying "the eternal gospel," but it is a very different gospel than elsewhere in the New Testament. It does not mention

Jesus and his sacrifice for sin, nor is there a direct call to repentance as in 9:20; 16:9, 11. Rather, the nations are called upon to "fear God and give him glory" in light of the coming judgment.

It is possible that there is no offer of salvation here but rather a declaration of judgment (the negative side of the "eternal gospel"). However, it is more likely that a final chance to repent is being given to the nations. It is unlikely that "fear God and give him glory" is a statement of forced homage. In Revelation it is far more positive, reflecting covenant language in the Old Testament (fear god—1 Sam 12:14; Psa 34:11; Isa 11:3; give him glory—1 Chr 16:24; Psa 22:23; Isa 42:12) and redemption language in the New Testament (fear God—2 Cor 5:11; Phil 2:12; 1 Pet 1:17; give him glory—Rom 15:6, 9; 1 Pet 2:12). In Revelation 15:4 the victorious saints sing, "Who will not fear you, O Lord, and bring glory to your name?" In 16:9 the sinners "did not repent so as to give him glory," virtually defining repentance as glorifying God. In 19:5, 7 "those who fear him" sing, "Let us rejoice and be glad and give him glory." Thus in Revelation "fear God and give him glory" are code words for repentance and conversion.

The added "the hour of his judgment has come" provides the reason ("because, for") for responding to the gospel and repenting. This could be translated, "has already arrived," and so emphasizes the imminent expectation of the Day of the Lord. The "hour" in Revelation often speaks of the final outpouring of judgment (9:15; 14:15; 18:10, 17, 19). The certainty and imminence of final judgment makes the call to repentance all the more critical; opportunities are running out, and one's eternal destiny is at stake.

The final aspect of the eternal gospel is the result of repentance, the worship of God. The homage and praise called for centers once more upon the God of creation "who made the heaven and the earth and the sea and the springs of water." Creation theology is found throughout the book, saying that the God who created this world and sustains it will end it as his sovereign will dictates (3:14; 4:7, 11; 5:13; 10:6; 12:16). The fourfold list reiterates the focus of the first four trumpet (8:6–12) and bowl (16:2–9) judgments. So these sum up the effects of God's wrath. The purpose of the three judgment septets (seals, trumpets, bowls) is still to prove his omnipotence, disprove the earthly gods, and give the nations a final chance to repent. The core of worship is God's holiness, and that means reflection on his love (seen in the story of redemption) and his justice (the destruction of sin). When God destroys his tainted creation (see Rom 8:18–22), he will bring his eternal new creation, the new heaven and new earth, into being. That is indeed worthy of worship!

THE SECOND ANGEL PREDICTING DESTRUCTION (14:8)

The second angel follows the first, drawing a close connection between the two announcements. This one describes what the judgment in 14:7 entails. The doublet "fallen, fallen" stresses the absolute certainty of the coming destruction. The language is derived from Isaiah 21:9, where a messenger in a chariot cries, "Babylon has fallen, has fallen," followed by an announcement of Babylon's gods "shattered on the ground." Not only will the empire be destroyed but so will its idols, here even more so than in Isaiah. Rome, the Babylon of John's day, would see its "greatness" shattered because of its hubris and pride. This prophecy about the violent passing of "Babylon the Great" will be unpacked in detail in chapter 18.

The reason for this total destruction is that this unholy Roman Empire of the antichrist "made all the nations drink of the wine that leads to passion for immorality." "All the nations" refers to the peoples of the world led astray by the immorality and idolatry of Rome. The imagery of "drinking the wine" depicts their participation in a lifestyle of debauchery, including the spiritual adultery of idolatry. The primary difficulty is the last part, which reads literally, "wine of the wrath of adultery." The genitive *tou thymou* ("of wrath") could be descriptive, leading to the NIV translation "maddening wine," or it could be result, "wine producing passion [another meaning of the term] for adultery." The latter fits the context better. Babylon/Rome got them drunk with passion for licentious pleasures; now she will pay the price for her sins. This alludes to Jeremiah 51:7: "Babylon ... made the whole earth drunk."

The Third Angel Pronouncing Judgment On Those Who Follow the Beast (14:9–11)

The third angel now unpacks the judgment proclaimed by the second. The order is reversed here, as the reason for judgment (14:9) comes before the judgment itself (14:10–11). The first part of the message details the reason for judgment and effectively sums up chapter 13—"If anyone worships the beast and its image and receives its mark on their forehead or on their hand" (also 15:2). The false prophet forces this worship on penalty of economic sanctions and death, but here the penalty for obeying the demand to worship the antichrist is far more severe—eternal torment. The guilt of the nations is firmly established. The alternative is also abundantly clear: worship God and suffer earthly death or worship the beast and suffer eternal death.

The results of the premise (14:10) expand on the second angel in 14:8. Those who drink the cup of "passion (*thymos*) for immorality" (14:8) will now drink a second cup filled with "the wrath (*thymos*) of God" (14:10). This is a "taste of new wine," but not one that has a pleasant bouquet! Note the wine in this second cup is "full strength." Wine with a meal would always be watered down anywhere from one-to-one to one-to-three (one part wine to three parts water). They would drink undiluted wine only when they wanted to get drunk. So God in effect is saying, "You want to get drunk on your pleasures? Okay, I will get you really drunk!" Note that "God's fury" (*thymos*) is poured into "the cup of his wrath" (*orgē*). Both words for anger (they are synonymous here) are used to stress the severity of God's displeasure and of the coming judgment.

The rest of this passage (14:10b–11) shows how terrible the results of God's wrath will be. The imagery is incredibly severe. When these hedonists fall down dead drunk this time, they will never get up. The results are eternal. Theirs will be a "torment with burning sulfur," looking ahead to the fiery "lake of fire" that will constitute eternal judgment (19:20; 20:14, 15). Sulfur, or brimstone, was a type of asphalt found in volcanoes that produced intense heat and became an image for terrible suffering under divine judgment (Isa 30:33; Ezek 38:22). The sentencing will take place at the Bema or judgment seat of God "in the presence of the holy angels and of the Lamb" who will form the council of heaven (see Rev 4:4). They are not mere witnesses; this is the heavenly court meeting in judicial proceedings, and they will participate in carrying out the sentence (Dan 7:9–12; Luke 12:9; see also 1 Enoch 14:19–23).

The severity of the punishment is further stressed by the added, "the smoke of their torment will arise forever and ever," alluding to Edom's destruction in Isaiah 34:9–10, "Edom's streams will be turned into burning pitch ... it will not be quenched night or day, its smoke will rise forever." Since smoke can be either a positive or a negative image in Scripture, there may be a double meaning: a sign of their torment but also a "sweet-smelling incense" (see Rev 8:4; 15:8) rising to God. This image will be seen again, as the heavenly multitude in 19:3 sings, "Hallelujah! The smoke from her goes up forever and ever." This may seem overly harsh to us, but we must remember that the destruction of both evil and the wicked who live for it is necessary for a holy God. When all the saints see the full effects of evil, they will rejoice at its annihilation from this world.

The final point is that the sinners will have "no rest day and night," also going back to Isaiah 34:9, 10: "not quenched night or day." This is the reverse of the "day and night" worship of the living creatures (Rev 4:8) and the "day and night" service before the throne of the victorious saints in 7:15. These people have "worshiped the beast and his image" on earth, and now they will suffer eternal torment with the beast in the lake of fire.

Ethical Conclusion—Call For Endurance (14:12–13)

After the prophetic announcements of 12:1–14:11, John now contextualizes the material, relating the implications for his readers. This builds on 12:17 ("keep God's commandments and hold fast their testimonies"), 13:10 ("This calls for patient endurance and faithfulness"), and 13:18 ("This calls for wisdom"). It is another call for perseverance that is one of the primary themes in the book.[1] Every term in 14:12 occurs in one of these three passages.

This is the last of seven times "patient endurance" occurs in Revelation (1:9; 2:2, 3, 19; 3:10; 13:10; 14:12). It is the key ethical term in the book and commands God's people both to wait on the Lord and to overcome evil. The rest of the verse is in effect a definition of "endurance," depicting it in terms of obedience and faithful living. Keeping God's commandments, as in 12:17, means to understand them, follow and obey them, and to "guard" (part of the meaning of the term) them in a world that prefers darkness over light. This is a corporate concept; all in the church must be vigilant to help each other keep God's commandments.

The second aspect can be translated "maintain your faith in Jesus." "Faith" occurs in 2:13, 19; 3:10, and "faithful" in 1:5; 2:10, 13; 3:14; 17:14; 19:11; 21:5; 22:6. While the term could refer to doctrine ("the Christian faith"), it more likely connotes a faithful Christian walk, remaining faithful to Jesus. Together, the whole of 14:12 demands that the believers maintain their allegiance to Christ and overcome the pressures of the world to conform to its sinful lifestyle.

Those who faithfully persevere in Christ and refuse to give in to the world's pleasures can expect severe opposition and persecution, even to the point of martyrdom. So in 14:13 a "voice from heaven" directly from God reassures the readers. In 10:4, 8; 11:12, it also denotes a message straight from God with no mention of an angelic herald. The command to "write this" echoes 1:11, 19; 19:9; 21:5, and emphasizes further that John

---

1. See "The Perseverance of the Saints" under "Theology of the Book" in the introduction.

is merely the channel and these are God's words to the church. This is the second of seven beatitudes in the book (with 1:3; 16:15; 19:9; 20:6; 22:7, 14) and proclaims God's special **eschatological** blessings on those who will die for Christ.

Martyrdom is addressed often in the book (6:9–11; 7:14; 12:11; 13:7, 15; 16:6; 17:6 18:24; 20:4; 22:14) and builds on Jesus' teaching that following him involves a willingness to die (Mark 8:34). Throughout church history "the blood of the martyrs is the seed of the church," in Tertullian's words, and so it is here at the close of history. Martyrdom means victory, a conquering of Satan by participating in "the fellowship of Jesus' suffering" (Phil 3:10) where we reenact Jesus' cosmic victory via his death.

At the same time this blessing cannot be restricted to those who give their lives for Christ but encompasses all "who die in the Lord." To die in the Lord means to remain faithful to the very end, to make Christ the sphere of your life. The important addition of "from now on" teaches that this refers not just to the final period of history but to all the saints down through the ages who remain true to Christ. The period of testing has started, and God's people must steel themselves for the difficult days ahead. The Christian life was never meant to be easy; it will always involve sacrifice and suffering and demand a life of continual faithfulness.

To demonstrate the importance of this concept, the Holy Spirit makes his first direct comment in the book (see also 22:17). He solidifies the critical exhortation to remain true to Christ in the midst of hard times. The Spirit is the revelatory source of the seven letters ("hear what the Spirit says to the churches" in each letter) and the heart of prophetic activity in the book (11:11; 19:10), the one who brings the visions to John (Rev 1:10; 4:2; 17:3; 21:10). The Spirit's *nai* ("yes") is the functional equivalent of "amen" (1:7; 5:14; 7:12; 22:20) and means the Spirit is affirming the special blessings awaiting those who "die in the Lord."

Ahead for those who live faithfully and especially for martyrs lies an eternal "rest from their labors." Those who reject Christ "have no rest day and night" (14:11), while the martyrs are told to "rest awhile" (6:11) as they await their final vindication. The "rest" here is that eternal rest with God in heaven, the Sabbath rest promised to the faithful (Heb 4:1–11). The "labors" refer to the faithful lives lived for Christ, that perseverance under pressure that is the mandate of Revelation 14:12–13.

This includes the idea of reward for their victorious lives, seen here in "their deeds will follow them." Their "deeds," or "works," include not only good works but their lives of faithfulness and service to God and the church. Judgment according to works is an important doctrine found often in Scripture (2 Chr 6:23; Psa 62:12; Jer 17:10; Matt 16:27; Rom 14:12; 2 Cor 5:10; 1 Pet 1:17) and frequently also in Revelation (2:23; 18:6; 20:12; 22:12). This is ***lex talionis***: We receive from God what we have done in our lives and conduct. For the Christian it means everything we have done for God and for others will come with us into eternity and be our reward.

But we must distinguish "judged by works" from "saved or justified by works." The latter is heretical and goes against Ephesians 2:8–9, which states that we are saved by grace and not by works. We are justified only by the atoning sacrifice of Christ on the cross, but at the end of our lives we will give account to God and be judged or rewarded according to our deeds. Our service and good deeds are in a sense banked in heaven earning interest, and we will enjoy our "retirement benefits" for all eternity!

THE EARTH IS HARVESTED (14:14–20)

The judgment prophesied in 14:8, 10–11 is now spelled out in detail using the imagery of the harvest of judgment in the Day of Yahweh passage from Joel 3:13: "Swing the sickle, for the harvest is ripe. Come, trample the grapes, for the winepress is full" (also Isa 17:5; Jer 25:30; Hos 6:11). The imagery here depicts the grain harvest (14:14–16) and the grape harvest (14:17–20) as pictures of the gathering of the saints and the sinners for judgment à la the parables of the wheat and the weeds (Matt 13:24–30).

THE GRAIN HARVEST (14:14–16)

There is debate whether the one "seated on the cloud" in 14:14 is an angel or Jesus himself. In this context where all the other harvesters are angels, and with the figure of 14:15 called "another angel," this could well be an angel. However, it is more likely Jesus, for the one on the cloud is "like a son of man" (from Dan 7:13), and in Revelation Christ is the Son of Man (see Rev 1:7, 13).

This Son of Man has three characteristics. First, he comes "on a cloud," echoing Daniel 7:13, where he "comes on the clouds of heaven." Here the cloud is not a chariot but a throne he is seated on, echoing Joel 3:12, "There I will sit to judge all the nations on every side." The cloud depicts the Shekinah presence of God dwelling among his people (from the Hebrew *shakan*, "to dwell"), and white in Revelation symbolizes purity, glory, and victory. The clouds in 10:1; 11:12 signify salvation, but here judgment is more likely (as in 1:7). Judgment dominates this section, and both saints and sinners will stand before the Bema or judgment seat of God and give account for their lives. Second, he has a "crown of gold on his head," a *stephanos*, which was a victory wreath in athletic contests and a sign of victory for a general or sovereignty for a ruler. In Revelation (see 4:4; 9:7) it has a ruling function; here it signifies royal authority and divine glory. This "one like a son of man" is a sovereign about to judge his world. Third, the Son of Man has a "sharp sickle" in his hand, and as in Mark 4:29 it stands for the judgment of God in this final harvest. The sharpness of the sickle highlights the finality and power of this final judgment.

In 14:15 another angel (after the three in 14:6–13) appears from the temple of heaven where God has his throne (7:15) and sends forth his judgments (11:19; 15:5–8; 16:1, 17). The two harvests are directed from the heavenly temple. God's holiness (4:8) demands justice as well as mercy, and both will be exemplified here. The angel brings orders to Christ from the throne commanding him to "take your sickle and reap." The swinging of the sickle is a decisive act, ending the season of humankind on earth and gathering the sheaves for the final harvest.

It is common to understand both the grain and grape harvests as judgments of the lost, but I follow a minority who see the grain harvest as the gathering of the redeemed. The imagery of judgment is missing here, such as the burning of the branches in John 15:6 or the trampling of the threshing floor in Matt 3:12 and Luke 3:17. There is no hint of final destruction like there is in the next scene (Rev 14:19–20). I contend that 14:15 depicts the harvest of the saints and 14:17–20 the harvest of the sinners. This fits Jesus' teaching that also juxtaposes the two, as in the parables of the wheat and weeds (Matt 13:36–43) and the good and bad fish (Matt 13:47–50, see also Matt 9:37–38; John 4:34–38). The "harvest of the earth" (the grain harvest) in Revelation 14:15–16 is the same event as described in 11:11–13, the resurrection of believers to glory (1 Cor 15:51–52; 1 Thess 4:13–18).

The Grape Harvest (14:17–20)

Another angel now comes out of the temple like the one in 14:15, meaning he is sent from the enthroned God. Like Christ, he has a sharp sickle for the harvest. Then there arrives still another angel, this time "from the altar." As in 6:9 and 8:3, the heavenly altar combines the altar of burnt offering with the altar of incense, and there is again a connection with the prayers of the saints for vengeance and vindication (6:9–11). As in 8:2–5 these prayers have reached God, and he sends his angel to initiate once more his response of judgment upon the oppressors. This angel has "charge" (*exousia*, "authority") of the fire, certainly fiery judgment linked to the coal of fire in 8:5 and the "fire and sulfur" of 14:10. As the angel fills the censer with fire in 8:5, inaugurating the trumpet judgments, so the angel here has authority to initiate the final fiery judgment.

This angel commands the first angel to "take your sharp sickle" and harvest (14:18). In Joel 3:13 the reason for the grape harvest is that "the winepress is full and the vats overflow," and here it is because "its grapes are ripe." The time is up, and the harvest must take place. So the angel obeys, swings the sickle and "gathers its grapes" (14:19). As in 12:7–9 these are the hosts of heaven, the angel-warriors who carry out God's judgment on the earth. None escape, and all humanity is gathered to the judgment seat. As in John 15:6, the avenging angel cuts down every vine and casts its grapes into the great winepress of God.

The "great winepress of God's wrath" echoes Isaiah 63:3, "I have trodden the winepress alone. ... I trampled them in my anger." Winepresses in ancient times consisted of two vats, an upper one where the grapes were trodden down and a lower one where the juice was collected. The ritual of pressing the grapes was a joyous occasion; while this is a gruesome image here, the destruction of evil it represents will be a wondrous thing and occasion hallelujahs (Rev 19:3–4). The angel executes the harvest, God is the judge, and Christ executes the penalty, as in 19:15, where the returning Christ "treads the winepress of the fury of the wrath of God Almighty."

The judgment takes place "outside the city" (14:20), referring to the great city of 11:8, Jerusalem. To be executed outside the gate is to be cut off from the covenant people (Heb 13:12; Rev 22:14–15). These sinners have no part with God or his people; they are God's enemies, cut off from any hope of salvation. Moreover, Jewish tradition said the final destruction of God's enemies would be near yet outside Jerusalem (Joel 3:2, 12; Zech 14:4–5; see also 2 Baruch 40:1–2).

In this final battle, a terrible outpouring of blood will ensue, flowing out of the vat of the great winepress "as high as the horse's bridles." In 1 Enoch 1:3 the final war will be so terrible that a "horse will walk through the blood of sinners up to his chest" (see also 4 Ezra 15:35–36). In Revelation 19:17–18 the carrion birds are invited to "the great supper of God" to feast on the flesh of the army of the beast. The bloodbath will flow for a distance of 1600 stadia, or about 180 miles (300 kilometers). That would be the length of Palestine, picturing the carnage of battle as a lake of blood five feet high for the length, and likely breadth, of Palestine. This symbolizes the completeness of the judgment of God ($4^2 \times 10^2$), stressing the finality and terrible scope of God's righteous wrath against those who have defied God and so mistreated his people.

If all we had was Revelation 12 and 13, we would feel despair, for the false trinity sounds invincible and is implacably determined to destroy us. Chapter 14 comes as a breath of fresh air, for we see that Satan is not in charge; God is. While the world of unbelievers worships the beast, God's people worship the Lamb on Mount Zion. While the false prophet makes being a Christian a capital crime, God sends forth his angels of destruction upon the enemies of his saints. Yet there is still hope for the world, for along with the angels of judgment God sends out the angel with the "eternal gospel" to offer salvation to the unsaved. So once more it is all about choice: the decision to turn to Christ or to turn away from him and move toward destruction.

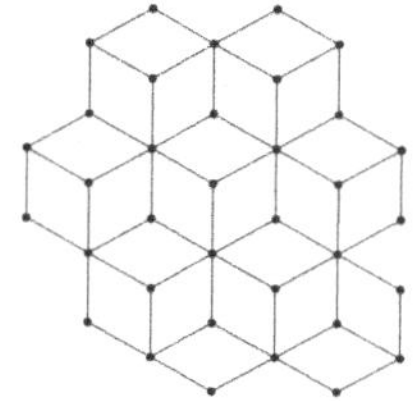

INTRODUCTION TO THE BOWLS

ANGELS WITH THE FINAL PLAGUES

(15:1–8)

After the second interlude with its message regarding the great conflict between the forces of good and evil (Rev 12–13) and the coming final harvest of the righteous and the wicked (Rev 14), John returns to the judgment septets, moving into the final set: the bowl judgments. The emphasis once more is upon the absolute sovereignty of God and the necessity that the nations come to repentance. The narrative begins with the introduction to these judgments in 15:1–8 (paralleling 8:2–5), as the angels prepare to pour out the bowls with the plagues (15:1, 5–8) and the victorious saints celebrate the saving deeds of Almighty God and sing the song of Moses (15:2–4).

ANGELS ARRIVE WITH THE PLAGUES (15:1)

In 12:1 the first great sign appeared in heaven, the "woman clothed with the sun." Now another great sign appears, but in addition it is "marvelous" or "wondrous." This evokes the image of the "marvelous deeds" of God in the Old Testament, and the emphasis is on God's incredible act of bringing history to a close. The sign itself is the seven angels bearing the seven last plagues, reenacting once again the plagues on Egypt in Exodus. The angels do not actually act until 15:7, so this is preparatory and functions as a title for the whole of Revelation 15–16. "Plague" is also used in 9:18, 20 of the trumpet judgments and in 11:16 of the judgment miracles of the two witnesses. The Exodus plagues were signs of God's power in judgment to the Egyptians and of God's mercy and deliverance to the Israelites. They function in the same way here, with the added emphasis that they provide a final opportunity to repent.

These seven plagues are "last" not because they end the series in the visions but because they are the last judgments of history. John adds, "because with them God's wrath is completed." Revelation 10:7 says "the mystery of God is completed" at the sounding of the seventh trumpet, and in both places it means God's plan has now been finalized and the **eschaton** has arrived. The "wrath/anger of God" is found often in the book (6:16–17; 11:18; 14:10; 15:7; 16:1, 19) and has now culminated in these final judgments. We must remember that a holy God is not only loving but just. When his justice is mocked and flaunted, he must respond with wrath. Sin demands judgment; it must be destroyed.

THE VICTORIOUS SAINTS SING BY THE SEA (15:2–4)

In a scene reminiscent of 7:9–17, the saints are in heaven standing beside "a sea of glass," which in 4:6 means standing before the throne itself. The imagery is borrowed from three places: Genesis 1:7 (the firmament of the waters at creation); 1 Kings 7:23–26 (the bronze sea in Solomon's temple); and Ezekiel 1:22 (the expanse above the living creatures). It symbolizes the majesty and splendor of God, and with the added "glowing with fire" (literally "mixed with fire") there is a further connotation of divine judgment in the scene. In a sense this pictures rivers of fire—in the manner of the lake of fire—flowing from the throne and depicts the fiery destruction of evil. The sea as a place of evil with Leviathan in it (Psa 73:13–14) has been swept clean by the fires of God, and it has now become a sea of glass before God's throne.

The believers stand on the crystal sea as conquerors, having emerged victorious over three things—"the beast and its image and the number of his name" (also Rev 14:9). These are drawn from 13:1–2 (the beast), 13:14 (his image), and 13:17–18 (the number of his name), and stress personal conflict (the beast), religious pressure (his image), and economic persecution (the number of his name). The theme of victory is found throughout the book, beginning with the "overcomers" of the seven letters (and also 5:5; 6:2; 11:7; 12:11; 13:7; 17:14). This presents the people of God as victors over temptation, the pressures of the world, and the cosmic powers. When the beast takes the life of a saint (13:7), he is actually conquered by the believer who yields his life (12:11). Their death is their final victory! The saints are rejoicing in this victory in the hymn here.

In their hands are the "harps of God," and this stresses that they are playing and singing for God, in worship of him. As with the elders in 5:8 and the 144,000 in 14:2, the presence of harps brings out the Old Testament imagery behind the worship scene. They sing "the song of Moses" (15:3), reenacting the victory over the Egyptian armies as fulfilled in the final victory over Satan and the antichrist. As God delivered Israel from the Egyptians through the Red Sea, so has Christ delivered his people from the dragon with his blood (12:11). Thus like Moses after the exodus from Egypt (Exod 15; Deut 32), the saints sing a song of victory. In fact, there are elements of both Exodus 15 and Deuteronomy 32 in the hymn here. Liberation and restoration are the primary themes in the new exodus experience celebrated in this passage. This song of Moses is also a "song of the Lamb" because the final victory was won by Christ on the cross, and that is the true exodus—deliverance for all eternity from the power of sin by the blood of Christ.

The first half of the hymn (15:3b) praises God for his wondrous deeds of salvation. No details of the marvelous acts are provided here because they were recounted in chapter 14. This hymn focuses on the characteristics of the God who has conquered the evil forces on behalf of his people. The first line celebrates the "great and marvelous" works, reflecting Psalm 111:3 in the **Septuagint** ("Great and majestic are his deeds"). The same great deeds that took place in Exodus 15:1 when he hurled horse and rider into the sea have occurred again when he hurled Satan out of heaven and will take place when he hurls the enemies of his saints into eternal punishment. These are the wondrous deeds of the Lord God Almighty (Rev 1:8; 16:14; 19:15), as God proves himself to be sovereign Lord by exercising his omnipotence and controlling events in earth and heaven.

While the first line centers on his works, the second celebrates his ways. The first focuses on praise, the second on justice. "Just and true" alludes to Deuteronomy 32:4 (the other song of Moses), "his works are perfect and all his ways are just." Deuteronomy 32 details the sovereign justice of Yahweh and warns rebellious Israel of his justice and wrath. In it the covenant God brings a lawsuit against those who thwart his will. The people of this world who have broken covenant with him will discover the truth of his warnings and the justice of his punishment. They will realize the truth behind the parallel statement in 16:5 and 7, "You are just in these judgments ... because you have so judged. ... Yes, Lord God Almighty, true and just are your judgments" (also 19:2). We are at the heart of the theme of the righteous justice of God in this book.

The title "King of the nations" relates another important theme in which the nations come and worship God (15:4). There is movement from sovereign judgment to the promise of salvation, taken from Jeremiah 10:7, "Who should not fear you, King of the nations?" (also Psa 22:28, 47:8; 1 Chr 16:31). Only God is King of the nations (not Caesar), and only Christ is "King of kings and Lord of lords" (Rev 17:14; 19:16). There is double meaning here, looking back to God as sovereign judge (15:3) and forward to God as merciful and righteous redeemer (15:4b).

The first part of 15:4 consists of rhetorical questions that provide the focus for the rest of the hymn. The first, "Who will not fear you?" also stems from Jeremiah 10:7. When a person truly comes to understand God's sovereignty and power, fear is the natural response. Jeremiah 10 concludes the section on impending judgment due to national apostasy, and 10:7 is part of a diatribe against idolatry (Jer 10:2–16), so the fear of God is set in contrast to the "senseless and foolish gods" of the pagans. God is incomparable, and Jeremiah 10:6 (= Exod 15:11) is part of the theme in the hymn here, "No one is like you, LORD; you are great, and your name is mighty in power." In light of the imperial cult in John's day, the idea of the incomparable greatness of God could be seen as central to the next few chapters.

Building on this is the second half of the rhetorical question, "and bring glory to your name," drawn from Psalm 86:9 ("All the nations ... will come and worship ... they will bring glory to your name"), which parallels both Exodus 15:11 and Jeremiah 10:6–7 with its worship of the incomparable God. This is part of the mission theme in Revelation.[1] While the majority of the earth-dwellers will be obdurate and face the wrath of God, some will indeed respond to God's call to repentance (and the church's witness) and convert to Christ; they will "fear and glorify" God (see the "eternal gospel" of 14:6–7).

The last three lines of the hymn are "because" clauses telling the reason why the nations must fear and glorify God. First, only he is holy, echoing Psalm 145:17 in the **Septuagint**, "The LORD is righteous in all his ways and holy in all his works." Only he among the gods is holy, meaning he stands apart and above all earthly forces. This goes back to the "holy, holy, holy" of Revelation 4:8; God is ultimate holiness, and that defines his true character.

The second reason all should fear and glorify Yahweh is because "all the nations will come and worship" him. This is startling in a context of judgment, but throughout this book judgment provides the basis for the call to salvation, as in 14:7, "Fear God and give him glory, because the hour of his judgment has

1. See "Theology of the Book" in the introduction.

come."[2] One of the purposes of the seals, trumpets, and bowls is to disprove the earthly gods and call the people to repentance, to make them realize they must choose between the God of mercy and the God of judgment.

The final ground for the glory and fear of Yahweh is because "your righteous acts have been revealed." Most likely "righteous" here carries both its meanings of righteousness and justice. Justice and judgment are central in 15:3b ("just and true"), and God's salvific deeds are central in 15:4 (fear God and give him glory). So this sums up both aspects of this hymn: God's justice and his righteousness. It celebrates the revelation of God's righteous deeds in pouring out his judgments and through them calling the nations to repentance, thereby resulting in the salvation of many (as in 11:13).

SEVEN ANGELS EMERGE FROM THE HEAVENLY TEMPLE (15:5–8)

Preparatory Events (15:5–6)

As in 11:19 the temple opens, and the scene is theologically linked to the tearing of the veil at Jesus' death (Mark 15:38) where it signified the opening of the holy of holies by Jesus' death. In these last days, access to God becomes open to all. In Revelation 11:19 and here it signifies the end of human history and the arrival of the end of the world. In this context it leads into the final set of judgments that mark the culmination of the days of humankind (15:1, "with them God's plan is completed").

Emerging from the heavenly temple (15:6) are "the seven angels with seven plagues" (see 15:1) who will carry out God's judicial sentence on the nations. The connection with the Egyptian plagues continues, but there is also an echo of Leviticus 26:21 in the **Septuagint** ("I will also bring on you seven plagues"), part of the covenant blessings and curses there. The nations have broken covenant with God and must face the consequences.

2. See also the commentary on 1:7; 5:9.

It is interesting that the angels have the plagues in their hands before they are given the bowls (15:7). The content of the bowls is more important than the bowls themselves.

The angels are "dressed in clean, shining linen," the garment worn by priests (Lev 16:2, 23). Once more the angels have a priestly function, caring for and using the temple vessels as God directs. The pure linen connects them to the bride of Christ in Revelation 19:8 and the armies of heaven in 19:14. Clearly these are heavenly garments befitting the purity and glory of celestial beings. The "golden sashes around their chests" are the same as those worn by the "one like the son of man" in 1:13. As emissaries of Christ, they share his elevated status.

The Commissioning of the Angels (15:7–8)

The four living creatures were the innermost circle of the heavenly beings around the throne in 4:6–7. They combine the features of the seraphim of Isaiah 6 and the cherubim of Ezekiel 1 and appear to be leaders of the heavenly court. They guide heavenly worship in Revelation 5:6–7; 7:11; and 14:3; send out the four horsemen in 6:1–8; and cry out "Amen, hallelujah" in 19:4. Here they serve as angelic heralds mediating God's judicial penalty on the evildoers. The giving of the bowls functions as the commissioning of the seven angels to God's service.

Here the living creature acts as an emissary of God and gives each angel a golden bowl, possibly the same censer from the table of showbread we saw in 5:8. This signifies 1) that the outpouring of judgment is a sacred offering to God; and 2) that the action comes as a result of the prayers of the saints from 5:8; 6:9–11; and 8:3–5. The golden bowls link divine retribution with the prayers for vindication.

Yet the bowls are more than this. They are "filled with the wrath of God" rather than incense, so they are likely also linked to the bronze sprinkling bowls of Exodus 27:3; 38:3 (made of gold in 2 Chr 4:8), used to sprinkle the sacrificial blood. This further makes the judgments a blood-filled sacred offering to God. God's anger was poured out on the nations in Revelation

6:15–17 and 11:18; drunk full-strength by the immoral in 14:10, 19; and completed in the events of 16:1, 19; 19:5. God is described as the one "who lives for ever and ever," with his eternality part of his sovereignty over creation as well as his majesty on his throne or Bema (judgment seat).

As the bowls are filled with wrath, the temple is filled with smoke in 15:8. Smoke in the Old Testament symbolizes the awesome presence of God, as in the cloud of smoke at Sinai (Exod 24:15–16), the cloud that was the Shekinah in the exodus (Exod 14:19, 24), and the cloud that filled both the tabernacle (Exod 40:34–35) and the temple with his glory (1 Kgs 8:10–12; Isa 6:3–4; Ezek 10:2–4). Three images emerge from these passages—smoke, glory, and power—and these are found in the added comment that the smoke came "from the glory of God and from his power." Judgment is closely linked with the presence, glory, and power of God, and these are all connoted by the bowl judgments.

The final comment flows out of the aura of Shekinah glory behind this—"no one could enter the temple" until the judgments were over. This calls to mind two of the passages above. In Exodus 40:35, "Moses could not enter the tent of meeting," and in 1 Kings 8:11, "The priests could not perform their service," both because the glory of the Lord had filled the temple. The presence of God and his Shekinah glory have caused the cessation even of temple worship. Due to his awesome holiness, majesty, and power, no human presence or activity dare take place. Until the judgment of God in the seven plagues is completed, all other events, even the temple service, can only wait. This is similar to the seventh seal, the half hour of silence awaiting the final events in 8:1.

This idea of judgment is a serious and somber issue, and it seems to conflict with the idea of a loving, merciful God. Yet in Revelation the justice and love of God are intertwined, and one cannot exist apart from the other. A holy God must judge sin and sinners, and this includes the vindication of the saints for all they have suffered. Here "the wrath of God is complete"

(15:1), and this signifies the removal of evil from the world. This chapter signifies not only judgment but the celebration of the saints over the victory, namely the saving deeds of Almighty God as he rids the world of sin and redeems his people. "All nations will come"—finally, a racial reconciliation that will last for eternity! Divine judgment is an essential part of God's majesty and of his saving work.

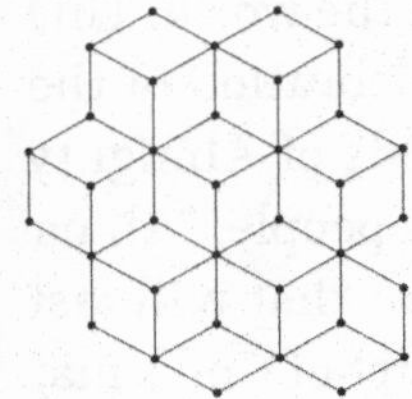

THE SEVEN LAST BOWL JUDGMENTS

(16:1–21)

As mentioned in the introduction to 6:1–17, the seal, trumpet, and bowl judgments are characterized by a progressive intensification in the severity of the penalty. The seals destroyed a quarter of the earth, the trumpets a third of the earth, and now the bowls affect the whole earth. Moreover, while the seals and trumpets punished the earth-dwellers indirectly, the bowls are poured out directly upon the sinners. As with the seals and trumpets, the bowls are organized according to a 4 (poured out on the earth) + 3 (cosmic judgments on the beast) pattern. The action moves from natural disasters (the first four = the trumpet judgments) to direct judgment on the throne of the beast (the fifth) to preparation for the final battle (the sixth) to the storm that begins the final destruction of the empire of the beast (the seventh).

The themes continue from earlier chapters—the wrath of God, the justice of God's retribution, and the final chance for repentance—but now it all ends. There is no more future, for Christ is now to return and eternity to begin. Once more the issue of symbolic vs. literal is huge. These are highly symbolic, but at the same time the pictured events are intended to get us (like the readers in the first century) to imagine what such terrible judgments would look like. As with the seals and trumpets, while we may be tempted to harmonize these apocalyptic images with one another and figure out how one relates to the next, they are not consistent. Each vision is a self-contained unit. God is not telling us how this will work out in actuality. Some we can imagine literally happening, like the boils, and some happened before, like turning the water to blood. With respect to others, like a darkness that causes intense pain or mini-novas reaching earth and incinerating people, we wonder if they are more symbolic. We will not know for sure about any of them until these events actually happen. For now, we are primarily meant to see their theological significance.

THE BOWL PLAGUES ARE POURED OUT ON THE NATURAL REALM (16:1–9)

THE HEAVENLY COMMAND (16:1)

The "loud voice from the temple" occurs only here and in 16:17, stemming from the temple scene of 15:5–8 and continuing the emphasis on this as a sacred scene. It alludes to Isaiah 66:6 in the **Septuagint**, in which Isaiah tells the righteous remnant to "hear the voice from the temple" as the Lord "repays his enemies." This is probably God himself speaking and commanding the angels to pour out the seven bowls containing his wrath. The wrath of God describes the contents of the bowls, and "pour out" is a technical verb for the drink offering (Exod 30:18; Lev 4:7, 18) or for sprinkling the blood in the covenant rite (Exod 24:6, 8). Jeremiah prays that God would "pour out his wrath on the nations" (Jer 10:25), so this depicts God's wrath as a sacred drink offering and an act of temple worship.

THE FIRST BOWL: TERRIBLE SORES (16:2)

The wording "went and poured out" continues the sense of this judgment as a drink offering to God. The first bowl is poured out "on the earth." The judgment falls only on those "who had the mark of the beast and worshiped his image" (also in 14:11; 20:4), continuing the theme that only the sinners, not the saved, are affected (3:10; 7:3–4; 9:4). This is part of the exodus motif that the people of God are spared from the outpouring of wrath (Exod 8:22–23; 9:4, 6). As mentioned in the introduction to Revelation 6, note the intensification of the seals (a quarter of the people) and trumpets (a third of the people), as the whole earth is affected. This reproduces the sixth Egyptian plague, in which terrible boils broke out on both people and animals (Exod 9:9–11). These are also the same as the sores that plagued Job (Job 2:1–13), but now it is the unrighteous who suffer. These are abscessed, ulcerous sores, handled today by antibiotics but a huge problem then. Still, medical supplies today would also be exhausted quickly, as those affected would be unable to walk, sit, or lie down without intense pain, and life in effect would come to a screeching halt.

The Second Bowl: The Sea Turns to Blood (16:3)

In the second trumpet a burning mountain fell on the sea, and a third of it turned to blood (Rev 8:8–9). This plague (15:1) is much more severe, for now all the oceans "turned into blood like that of a dead person." Death becomes a worldwide phenomenon, and "every living thing in the sea died." The sea was the lifeblood of Rome, for its food supply but even more for commerce, since the majority of trade goods came by sea. This is tantamount to the destruction of all civilization. Such a disaster would bring down any economic system, today or in the first century. It is impossible to imagine the trillions of fish in the oceans of the world lying on top of a sea of blood. While apocalyptic imagery is symbolic, and there is certainly symbolism here, we must also remember that this took place literally at the exodus. This may well be both.

The Third Bowl: The Inland Waters Turned to Blood (16:4)

This is actually closer than the second bowl to the first Egyptian plague, but again it is much more intense, as every lake and river in the world is turned to blood. The terseness of the wording here makes the universal nature of the judgment all the more powerful. The simple "they became blood" is all the more frightening for its simplicity of expression. It alludes to Psalm 78:44, "He turned their rivers to blood." I live near Chicago among the Great Lakes, and it is hard to imagine them turned completely to blood. The devastation is beyond imagination.

A DOXOLOGICAL HYMN ON DIVINE JUSTICE (16:5–7)

In 16:5–7 an angel sings a doxological hymn. The central theme is the righteousness (*dikaios*) of God, but this Greek word also means "justice," so this is affirming that the righteousness of God mandates the justice of divine punishment (see Psa 9:4, 8; 2 Chr 12:6; Neh 9:33). This could also be called a "vindication hymn," for there is equal stress on the avenging of the blood of the saints.

The speaker is labeled "the angel of the waters," using the common apocalyptic symbol of angels controlling the natural elements, not the Graeco-Roman gods. All ancient people were animists, believing that each member of the pantheon was in charge of a particular aspect of nature: Poseidon was god of the sea, Aphrodite was goddess of love, and so on. In Revelation 7:1 angels were in charge of the four winds, and in 14:18 there is an angel over the fire. This was probably the angel(s) who turned the water into blood in the previous judgments.

The angel sings in 16:5, "You are righteous/just in these judgments." Throughout the Old Testament the rightness of God's judgments is stressed. The judgment of the nations results from God's holiness, and so they are at all times "just and true" (15:3; 16:7; 19:2). God is "righteous judge" (Psa 7:11; 67:4; Isa 11:4; 2 Tim 4:8), and this is the message behind this hymn. The title that follows ("O Holy One") is another major assertion of the book, for every single act of God in Revelation flows out of his holiness (Rev 4:8; 6:10; 15:4). He is set apart and stands above the events of this world, yet his holiness demands that evil be removed from it. God's holiness and his righteousness work together throughout Scripture (Deut 32:4; Psa 145:17; Jer 38:23), and both demand his just judgments to bring rightness back to his creation.

The next title pictures God as Lord over history, built on the threefold title of 1:4, 8; 4:8 ("the one who is and was and is to come"). As in 11:17, the third element is omitted. There is no longer any "to come," because the final act of God has been inaugurated and the future has now arrived. God's eternal reign has begun. Here the reason is that the final judgment has come. In the bowl judgments the final events of history have been enacted, and "future" is no more.

In 16:6, the hymn identifies what caused God's mighty hand to fall on the enemies of God's people: "they have shed the blood of your holy people and your prophets." This goes back to 6:9–11, 15–17, for these are the sinners who martyred the saints there. "Shed" is the same verb as "poured out" in 16:1–4, where it was used of the pouring out of the bowls as a sacred offering to God. So the blood of the saints here is depicted as a sacrificial offering to God, exactly like the image of the souls under the altar in 6:9. This is an example of the motif of ***lex talionis*** in Revelation: They poured out the blood of God's servants, so God is pouring out his judgments on them.

The mention of "the holy ones/saints and prophets" parallels 18:24, where again it is the shedding of their blood that is highlighted. The early church believed that Christian suffering became not only a sharing of Jesus' suffering but also sharing with the prophets of old (as in Heb 11). The whole people of God, the saints, as well as the prophets of both the Old Testament and New Testament (both are intended), participated with Jesus in a "fellowship of suffering" (Phil 3:10). These are the holy people of God whose lives are so cruelly forfeit, and God will avenge their blood. He will repay and give "them blood to drink, as they deserve." In Isaiah 49:26 God told Israel, "I will make your oppressors eat their own flesh; they will be drunk on their own blood" (also Psa 79:3, 12; Jer 32:18). "As they deserve" recalls Revelation 4:11 and 5:12 on the "worthiness" of God and the Lamb to be worshiped, for it uses the same term, *axios*, and can be translated, "as they are worthy." The vindicating God is worthy of worship; they are worthy of drinking blood.

Finally, the altar responds (16:7) and affirms the justice of God's response. In 6:9 the souls of the martyred saints cry out from under the altar, then the voice from the horns of the altar commands in 9:13–14. Now the altar itself speaks. The emphatic *nai* ("yes") confirms the rightness of the judgment in 16:6 and anchors it in the person of God as "Lord God Almighty," the primary title in the book (nine times; see 15:3). This affirms him as the omnipotent Divine Warrior and Lord of the universe. Also, in 15:3 the saints sing out, "Just and true are your ways," while here the altar proclaims, "true and just are your judgments" (see also 19:2). The reversal of the order is deliberate and adds emphasis to both aspects. The true nature of God's actions are grounded in his very nature as true, and this means that every judgment of this book is absolutely just.

THE FOURTH BOWL: THE SUN SCORCHES PEOPLE (16:8–9)

Earlier in Revelation the sun symbolized the majesty of God in Christ (1:16), a mighty angel (10:1), and the woman/church (12:1). In the new Jerusalem there will be no more sun (21:23; 22:5). In the fourth trumpet (8:12) and here, the sun is directly involved in the judgment of sinners. In this instance we have a massive solar flare or mini-nova as God "gives" (another instance of *edothē*; see 6:2, 4, 8) the sun power to "scorch people with fire." The saints were promised they would never again face the sun's "scorching heat" (7:16), but their persecutors face much more than a sunburn!

The most grievous aspect is not the punishment but their reaction to it. As they are severely burned, they respond not with repentance but instead "curse [literally 'blaspheme'] the name of God." This fiery judgment is a particularly severe warning, and when they not only reject it but blaspheme in return, their guilt is obvious. This term is used only two places in Revelation—here and in 13:1, 6 (the beast)—so they are depicted as joining the antichrist in blasphemy. This is the very God who "has authority over the plagues," namely who proved to the nations his power and justice via these judgments. So when they refused to "give him [the] glory" (14:6–7) he alone deserved, there was nothing left but the great white throne judgment of 20:11–15.

THE BOWL PLAGUES ARE POURED OUT ON THE BEAST'S THRONE (16:10–21)

The Fifth Bowl: The Beast's Throne in Darkness and Pain (16:10–11)

In 13:2 the dragon gave the beast/antichrist "his power and his throne and great authority." Yet it was a finite and temporary gift, for the dragon knew "his time is short" (12:12), and in 16:17 at the seventh bowl the throne of God will counter, "It is done!" This event in fact inaugurates the demise of the antichrist's throne. The antichrist's kingdom is short-lived, and the darkness into which it is plunged is a foretaste of the eternal darkness awaiting it. The readers of John's day would have seen this throne and kingdom to be the Roman Empire, so we are to think of the antichrist's reign as the revival of an unholy Roman Empire.

The beast's kingdom is "plunged into darkness" in 16:10, reenacting the ninth Egyptian plague of total darkness covering Egypt for three days (Exod 10:21–29). As such it intensifies the fourth trumpet judgment, in which darkness reigned for a third of the day and night (Rev 8:12). It was called "a darkness that can be felt," in which "no one could see anyone else or leave his place" (Exod 10:21, 23). The results of this bowl judgment are even more intense, for this darkness produces torment as people "gnaw their tongues in agony." This is closely connected to Jesus' metaphor for eternal punishment—"darkness, where there will be weeping and gnashing of teeth" (Matt 8:12; 22:13; 25:30). These are idioms for intense pain, and the purpose here is to provide a harbinger of the final judgment.

Yet again the sinners "blaspheme the God of heaven" and "refuse to repent" (16:11). As Pharaoh continually hardened his heart against God, so the earth-dwellers become more and more adamant in their hatred of God and his people. The pain did not drive them to their knees but stiffened their spines against God. Note the emphasis upon "their deeds" (NIV, "what they had done"). As in 2:22 ("their works") and 9:20 ("the works of their hands"), this focuses not just on their mindset but on the actions that result. People's thoughts always flow out into the way they live their lives. God will *act* on the basis of the way people have *enacted* his laws in their lives.

THE SIXTH BOWL: PREPARATION FOR THE FINAL WAR (16:12–16)

This bowl consists of the drying up of the Euphrates (16:12), the gathering of the kings of the earth for a final battle (16:13–14), a parenthetical warning from Christ (16:15), and the gathering of the kings for Armageddon (16:16). It somewhat parallels the sixth trumpet, in which four angels bound at the Euphrates were released, resulting in the horde of demonic horsemen (9:13–19). The Euphrates is called the "great river" because it was the largest river in that part of the world (2,000 miles long). Here the Euphrates dries up, reenacting the drying up of the Red Sea so Israel could cross to safety (Exod 14:21–22; see also Josh 3:13–17). Isaiah saw in this a prophecy that the Euphrates would dry up to allow the righteous remnant to escape their enemies (Isa 11:15–16; 44:27). The Euphrates was the eastern boundary both for the land God gave Israel (Gen 15:18; Deut 1:7–8) and for the Roman Empire.

Euphrates dries up (16:12). Rather than the demonic horsemen of chapter 9, the drying up of the Euphrates here allows "the kings of the east" to cross. Geographically, these would be the Parthians, a series of warlike tribes that inhabited the territory of ancient Babylon.[1] First-century readers would be thinking of a Parthian invasion of Rome, a possibility that would strike

1. See commentary on 6:1–2.

fear into all Romans.[2] However, this is not an invasion, for these kings join the forces of the antichrist against the Christians, likely alluding to Gog and Magog in Ezekiel 38–39 (see Rev 20:7). This is not a war against Rome; it is just the opposite. These kings cross the boundary not to destroy Rome but to join Rome. The kings from the east coalesce into the kings of the whole earth, and this becomes preparation for Armageddon (16:16).

So the message is symbolic, describing the final war that is the subject of this judgment in 16:14, 16. It depicts the entire world joining the antichrist in his war against the followers of Christ, and these kings here become the 10 kings of 17:12. The positive crossing of the Red Sea as a deliverance of God's people is reversed here in the drying up of the Euphrates to make way for an invasion that seeks the annihilation of God's people.

False trinity calls rulers (16:13–14). Here, in a sense, the false trinity finally reacts to the series of divine judgments poured out upon their empire. They are now gathered together for the first time. The dragon (12:3–9, 13–18) is Satan, the supreme antagonist of God and his people. The beast (13:1–10) is the antichrist, the earthly persona (in effect, son) of the dragon. The false prophet (13:11–18) is the religious head of the new occult one-world religion intended to focus all humanity on allegiance and worship of the dragon and the beast. This is the "great apostasy" of Mark 13:6, 22; and 2 Thessalonians 2:3. Jesus predicted false prophets as signs of the end of the age in Matthew 24:11, 24 (see also 2 Pet 2:1; 1 John 2:18; 4:3).

In calling the world's rulers to join them, the false trinity sends "three impure spirits that looked like frogs." Frogs were unclean creatures featured in the second Egyptian plague (Exod 8:1–15). The mouth to the ancients symbolized royal proclamation, so this is an official summons from the counterfeit "king of kings" to the world's rulers. These are the "kings" who

---

2. Note the *Nero redivivus* legend discussed in the commentary on 13:3.

commit adultery with the great prostitute (17:2) and reign under her rule (17:18), the "ten horns" who submit their authority to her (17:13).

The purpose is to "gather them for the battle," namely the cosmic war (19:19—there will be a second battle after the millennial reign, 20:8). This end-of-the-world battle was predicted in the Old Testament (Ezek 38–39; Zech 12–14; Joel 2:11; 3:2) and here is described as "the great day of God Almighty" (also Rev 6:17, "the great day of their wrath"). It is "great" because it culminates the plan of God that existed "before the creation of the world" (Matt 25:34; Eph 1:4; Rev 13:8; 17:8). Then Almighty God will prove his sovereign power and bring this world to an end.

Christ issues a warning (16:15). The importance of this warning is seen in the fact that Christ the Lamb speaks directly and abruptly to them. It is undoubtedly occasioned by the unparalleled danger the saints are facing in light of this final war. Alertness is desperately needed, and the danger of failing to persevere has reached new depths. The image of Christ "coming like a thief" is a New Testament theme (Matt 24:43; 1 Thess 5:2–4; 2 Pet 3:10) stressing the unexpected nature of the second coming and the danger of being unprepared.

This is the third beatitude, after 1:3 and 14:13. The problem is like that of the two weak churches: spiritual sloth as at Sardis ("stays awake" = 3:2) and shameful nakedness as at Laodicea ("remains clothed" = 3:18). Both images are spiritual failures and demand readiness for Christ's return. This warning pictures the sinful churches being exposed by God, with nakedness a symbol of judgment. This imagery is found in the Old Testament: Isaiah went about "stripped and barefoot" as a prophetic parable of the judgment Israel was facing (Isa 20:1–4), and Ezekiel depicts Israel as an adulterous wife about to be handed over to Assyria to be stripped naked for her sins (Ezek 23:29). So the believers are warned to remain faithful to Christ and remain ready for his return.

Kings gather (16:16). The false trinity called the kings and their armies to the final battle in 16:13–14; now they gather at the place for the battle. "Armageddon" literally means "Mount" (*har*) "Megiddo" (*megiddon*), but the problem with identifying this place is that there is no "Mount Megiddo." Megiddo is an ancient city in northern Palestine in the Valley of Jezreel or Esdraelon. It is ringed by hills, but it is only a city and a plain. Many suggestions have tried to make "Armageddon" a literal reference to this place, such as that this is a general reference to the whole area, not just the town. But it is hard to imagine how an army the size of the one described here could ever gather in so small an area.

So most likely this is symbolic. The symbolism might be based on the etymology of the word itself, perhaps "mountain of assembly" (= Mount Zion in Isa 14:12–14) or "marauding mountain" (= Babylon). But that is rather speculative. Instead we should begin with the connection of Megiddo with warfare, since so many battles were fought there (Judg 4–5, 7; 1 Sam 31; 2 Kgs 23; 2 Chr 35). It is also associated with the obstinate opposition of the world to God and his people, with the primary background being Gog and Magog (Ezek 38–39) and the mourning of the apostate nation in Zechariah 12:9–14, who here represent all the nations who have broken covenant with God. Thus the message in the name "Armageddon" would be that all who stand against God will mourn as they face God's wrath. It stands for the assembly of all the sinful nations arrayed against God and his people as they come together in defiance to make war against God and the Lamb.

The Seventh Bowl: Cosmic Judgment (16:17–21)

This bowl effectively brings history to a close and concludes both the time of silence at the seventh seal (8:1) and the arrival of the final kingdom in the seventh trumpet of Revelation 11:15–19. It is likely that the storm **theophany** of this judgment is the same one as that in the sixth seal (6:12–14).

This bowl is poured out "into the air" and completes the earthly judgments on the land (16:1–2), water (16:3–4), fire (16:8), and air (16:17). The voice comes "from the throne," which makes this the only place where heaven, temple, and throne are juxtaposed in judgment. This is the supreme **eschatological** moment when all the forces of God come together to finalize God's plan for this world and remove evil so that eternity can begin.

The voice of God from the throne proclaims the **eschaton** in electrifying simplicity with one word in the Greek: *gegonen*! This term means "it has happened" or "it has come to pass," and God's final kingdom has now arrived. This culminates the process launched with Christ's cry on the cross, "It is finished" (John 19:30). The stages of inaugurated eschatology, the initiation of the end-times process, have now been consummated. This does not mean that there are no events yet to take place, for there is still the return of Christ, his earthly reign, final judgment, and the coming of the new heaven and new earth, namely the events of Revelation 19–22. That final end is stated in 21:6 when God repeats, "It is done." The two declarations frame the final events. The declaration here in 16:17 concludes the judgments that initiate the end (the seals, trumpets, and bowls), and 21:6 concludes the **eschaton** itself with the new creation.

Following the announcement of the end, there is a storm **theophany** and earthquake in 16:18–19a. A **theophany** is a manifestation of God in which he physically appears in an event. This is also called "the shaking of the heavens" (see the commentary 6:12–14) and takes place often in Scripture, with the seminal event at Sinai (Exod 19:16–18) and several repetitions (Isa 13:9–13; Ezek 32:6–8; Joel 2:30–31). This is the last of several cosmic storms in Revelation (4:5; 8:5; 11:19) and has the most extensive coverage of the four. The lightning, thunder, and earthquake are part of the Sinai imagery and a new exodus theme, with this signifying the launch that leads to the final exodus at the return of Christ.

This is the first time an earthquake is called "great" in the book, though the hailstorm in 11:19 was "great." The comment that nothing "like it has ever occurred since humankind has been on the earth" is reminiscent of the Olivet Discourse, when Jesus spoke of the days of tribulation as "unequaled from the beginning, when God created the world, until now" (Mark 13:19). Both go back to Daniel 12:1 in the **Septuagint**, "a tribulation such as has not happened from the beginning of nations until now."

The earthquake is so severe that "the great city split into three parts" (Rev 16:19), recalling 6:14 where it shook "every mountain and island from its place." As I said at 11:8, the great city is an amalgamation of Rome with apostate Jerusalem and in essence is the capital city of the antichrist's empire. Primarily it is Babylon/Rome (as in 18:10, 16, 18, 19, 21). The "three parts" indicates the totality of the devastation, and the added comment that "the cities of the nations fell/collapsed" shows the worldwide impact of this judgment. It anticipates the great white throne judgment of 20:11–15 as every city and person of the evil empire "falls," as in the fall of Babylon the Great in 14:8; 18:2–3.

The reason for the complete destruction of the seventh bowl is given in 16:19b: "God remembered Babylon the Great" and her crimes against everything holy and good. In Scripture, to remember is to act. God in this sense has those crimes brought to his mind by the angels who bear the bowls and bring the prayers of the saints to him (8:2–5). As God remembers the suffering of his people and the depraved deeds of the nations, his wrath is kindled (14:10–11) and pours forth in just retribution (16:5–7; 18:6). The sins of Babylon the Great are being paid back in full.

The effects of the cosmic storm continue unabated in 16:20–21. As already noted, this recapitulates the storm of the sixth seal, where "every island and mountain were removed from its place." Here the islands "flee" and the mountains "disappear." This continues in 20:11, where we are told, "The earth and the heavens fled from his presence, and there was no place for them." Such disappearances are common in apocalyptic literature (Isa 2:12–18; 45:2; 1 Enoch 1:6–7; 4 Ezra 15:42) and make way for God's restoration of peace and order in his creation.

The hailstorm in 16:21 provides another judgment motif (8:7; 11:19), drawn from the seventh Egyptian plague and signifying divine judgment on the enemies of his people (Exod 9:13–35, see Josh 10:11). These hailstones weigh about 100 pounds, which would be a hailstone 17.6 inches in diameter. The Guinness record for the largest hailstone in recorded history is 2.25 pounds on Bangladesh on April 14, 1986, and the largest in US history fell on Coffeyville, Kansas on Sept 3, 1970 (1.671 pounds, 5.26 inches in diameter). If a literal event, this is the worst storm in the history of the world.

Yet once more the sinners refuse to repent (see Rev 2:21; 9:20–21; 16:9, 11). Instead, they blaspheme God for the judgment he has sent. Their blasphemy is because "the plague was so terrible," that is, the pain was incredibly severe. They focused not on the message regarding their own guilt or on the proof of God's sovereignty and power, but only on their present pain. They are still narcissists who care only about themselves and their pleasures. So they blame God and not their own actions that lay behind the just penalty for their sins. Here are no more opportunities to repent. They are at the end of their ropes, and destruction is their only future.

As the final of the three judgment septets, the bowl judgments intensify the seals and the trumpets and end at the **eschaton**. Here the justice of the divine judgments is evident, as the world that has turned against God and his people receives exactly the justice it has earned with its vile deeds. God is in charge and allows evil to come full circle, participating in its own destruction. Still, God gives all humankind an opportunity to repent; he is merciful as well as just. These judgments are redemptive in that, like the Egyptian plagues, they disprove the earthly gods and show that God alone is sovereign. There is salvation only in him. Now God's earthly judgment is complete, and all that remains is the final destruction of the evil empire. The Day of Yahweh and of the Lamb is soon to arrive.

This final set of seven judgments culminates and intensifies the others, affecting the whole earth and bringing to completion the earthly judgments of God. It contains the same themes as the others—the absolute justice of God, his sovereignty over creation as he dismantles his created order and makes way for the "new heaven and new earth" of 21:1, the redemptive nature of his judgments as they give the sinners a final chance to repent, the total depravity of those who refuse to repent. So the central portion of the book (Rev 6-16) comes to an end, and the final events are initiated. All that remains is the final destruction of the evil empire of the beast (chapters 17–18) and the final events that end world history and lead into eternity (chapters 19–22).

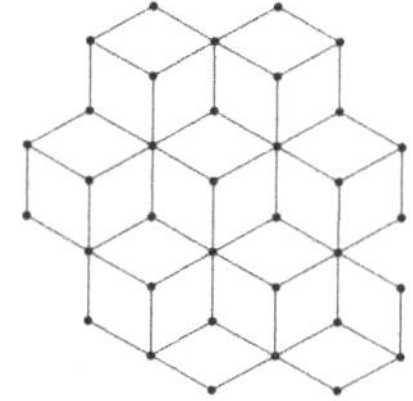

THE GREAT PROSTITUTE ON THE SCARLET BEAST

(17:1–18)

The theme of God's just judgment upon the evil nations has been strongly featured in the three judgment septets of the seals, trumpets, and bowls. They moved forward in a progressive intensification pattern of one-fourth (the seals) to one-third (the trumpets) to affecting the whole world (the bowls). Here that judgment is spelled out in greater detail. The destruction of the evil empire, implicit especially in the bowls, is central to 17:1–19:5.

John uses two metaphors for Rome, the empire of the beast—the great prostitute in chapter 17, and Babylon the Great in chapter 18. In both chapters, the narrative proceeds from the reasons for their destruction, emphasizing especially the economic exploitation of the surrounding nations as a major factor in her guilt. Yet at the same time there are some differences. Chapter 17 has a mediating angel explaining the meaning of key symbols in the book, and chapter 18 features the funeral laments of the kings, merchants, and sea captains. In both, Rome's depravity is uppermost, and her guilt has brought divine punishment upon her head.

AN ANGEL INTRODUCES THE GREAT PROSTITUTE (17:1–2)

This material is tied to the bowl judgments in that the angelic guide is "one of the angels having the seven bowls." The judgment of this chapter is an extension of the bowl judgments, especially of the last two as leading to the destruction of the evil empire. This intro will be repeated in 21:9, and points to an important contrast between the great prostitute and the bride of the Lamb. The unholy one leads to final judgment, the holy one to the wedding feast of the Lamb (19:9). "I will show you" appears often (1:1; 4:1; 21:9, 10; 22:6, 8, 10) and always refers to the divine revelation of visionary realities, often via angelic interpreters.

Here it is the judgment of the "great prostitute," who is "great" because she symbolizes the empire of the beast. Scripture frequently uses the image of a prostitute to describe the immorality and idolatry of apostate Israel and the nations (Jer 3:1–3; Ezek 23; Hosea in nearly every chapter; Isa 1:21; 23:15–17). Sinful humanity plays the harlot in that it not only commits licentious behavior but also leads others into doing so. There have been many suggestions as to the basis for this figure, like the cult leader Jezebel in 2:20 or Cleopatra or the goddess Roma. While the latter is a possibility, the image is too general for an individual and is clearly the Roman Empire as a whole in all its alluring depravity.

The prostitute is pictured "sitting on many waters." This echoes Jeremiah 51:13, which describes Babylon as "you who live by many waters," alluding to the ancient city's location on the river Euphrates with a series of canals and irrigation streams from the river. The "many waters" are defined in 17:15 as the many nations under the control of Babylon/Rome. To "sit upon" a nation is to conquer and gain control over it.

In 17:2, the "kings of the earth" are the rulers over these nations. The indictment that they "committed adultery" (= idolatry) with the great prostitute is a key phrase in 18:3, 9; and the idea of one nation committing adultery with other nations is frequent in the Old Testament (Isa 23:17; Nah 3:4). The populace of these nations have become "intoxicated with the wine of her adulteries," language reminiscent of 14:8, 10 ("the wine of passion for adultery"). This also alludes to Jeremiah 51:7, which depicts Babylon as making "the whole earth drunk," resulting in God making them really drunk "with the wine of my wrath." The charge is that Rome has subverted the nations religiously, politically, and economically with promises of luxury and power.

JOHN DESCRIBES THE GREAT PROSTITUTE (17:3–6A)

This is the third of four times in the book John is "carried away in the Spirit" (with Rev 1:10; 4:2; 21:10), referring to the visionary experience that God sent him via the Holy Spirit. This builds on Ezekiel's many references to being empowered by the Spirit (Ezek 2:2; 3:12; 8:3; 11:1; 37:1; 43:5). John was taken to God's throne in Revelation 4:2 and to a high mountain in 21:10, but here he is taken into the wilderness or desert. In the Bible the desert can be positive, a place of divine comfort and protection (1 Kgs 19:4–6; Isa 40:3; Mark 1:35, 45), or negative, a place of testing and difficulty (the 40 years in the wilderness; Psa 95:7–11; Isa 21:1–10; Jer 51:36; Matt 4:1). In Revelation it is positive in 12:6, 14 (the woman in the wilderness) and negative here and in 18:2 ("a dwelling for demons").

As John arrives he sees "a woman sitting on a scarlet beast." While the beast is the political ruler of the empire,[1] the woman/great prostitute stands for the blasphemous religious and economic system that seduces the nations into its blasphemous lifestyle. The description of the beast as "scarlet" highlights the luxury of the Roman Empire, seen also in the "purple and scarlet" clothing of the woman in 17:4 (also 18:12, 16). The added material on the "blasphemous names" and the "seven heads and ten horns" is drawn from the emergence of the beast in 13:1.

---

1. See the commentary on 12:18–13:10.

Their presence here prepares for their interpretation in 17:9–14. As in 13:4, 8, 14–15, this stresses the pretense of the beast setting itself up as "the god of this world" (2 Cor 4:4).

The vast luxury and moral corruption of the woman is described in 17:4. Only royalty and the supremely wealthy could wear purple or scarlet garments in the ancient world, for the dyes were inordinately expensive. In addition, she is "glittering with gold, precious stones, and pearls." This is the kind of opulence we see on the red carpet of Hollywood openings, and in the great prostitute's case it is a sign of her moral bankruptcy.

However, the more serious indictment follows. She holds in her hand "a golden cup ... filled with abominable things and the filth of her adulteries." All her wealth is detestable to God, and it is compounded by a licentious lifestyle. As with 17:2, this is taken from Jeremiah 51:7, where Babylon is "a gold cup in the LORD's hand" that has "made the whole earth drunk." The depravity of the nation provides the contents of that cup, and it has led them not to true pleasure but rather to the wrath of God. "Filth" refers to that which is unclean and further highlights how abhorrent the actions of these nations are to God.

The great prostitute has a "name written on her forehead," paralleling the seal of God on the saints in 7:3, 4 and the mark of the beast in 13:16. It defines who she really is and the god to whom she belongs. Roman courtesans would often place their names on their headbands, so this divulges her true identity. Some versions make "mystery" (see on 1:20) part of her name (KJV, NIV 1984), but most today consider it further identification, "a mysterious name" (NRSV, ESV, NLT, NIV 2011). That is more in keeping with the use of the term in Revelation (1:20; 10:7). God is unveiling new divine truths about the last days. The mystery is the name "Babylon the Great," how it is a great prostitute and symbolizes the empire of the beast.

Rome is Babylon because, like Babylon, Rome conquered Israel, destroyed its temple, and led the world into its depravity and opposition to God (1 Pet 5:13; see also 2 Baruch 11:1). She is also "the mother of prostitution and of earth's abominations."

In the New Testament "son of" is used to describe a person's primary characteristic (for example, "son of righteousness"). Calling a person "mother of" means it not only characterizes them, but that they also reproduce it in others. Rome was not only a prostitute and an abomination, but she had her own children (the conquered nations) and made them as depraved as she was. Apostate Israel is at times depicted in the Old Testament as a mother who prostitutes herself (Isa 50:1; Hos 2:2–7).

In 17:4 the woman held a gold cup and was drunk with idolatry and immorality. Now in 17:6 she is also "drunk with the blood" of the saints. This is a frequent Old Testament metaphor (Isa 49:26; Jer 46:10; Ezek 39:18–19) and depicts the savage joy with which armies would slaughter anyone in their way. In Revelation 13:7 God allowed the antichrist to make war against the saints and conquer them, and this describes the results of that carnage. There are four things Babylon/Rome focuses on here: idolatry, immorality, luxury, and persecution.

Still, as in 12:11 where God's people conquer Satan by "the word of their testimony," they emerge triumphant. Their sacrifice has taken place because they "bore testimony to Jesus." Throughout this book these two themes merge and mingle: 1) Satan, his cosmic powers, and their followers pursue, persecute, and martyr the believers unmercifully; yet 2) with God's protective presence, the undergirding strength supplied by the Spirit, and their own faithful endurance, the saints are victorious. The reason is that in this very persecution they have united with Jesus in "the fellowship of his suffering" and thereby share in his victory. At no time are the followers of Christ hiding in forests or caves. Rather, they engage in in fearless witness and conquer the evil powers.

THE ANGEL INTERPRETS THE VISION (17:6B–14)

As this vision closes, John is "amazed" and quite confused. This Greek term for wonder is used often for people's reaction to miracles (Mark 5:20; Matt 15:31). He had been told he would see Babylon's judgment, but instead he saw her luxury, glory, and seeming triumph. Most would feel admiration and even coveting at the thought of such wealth, so John is perplexed like Daniel was at his vision (Dan 7:15).

John's Confusion Leads to the Angel's Explanation (17:6b–7)

John is overwhelmed, so the angel from 17:1, 3 explains the scene. First, he questions John's wonder/perplexity. God is sovereign and alone is truly majestic, and he has already predicted the demise of this so-called mighty empire. By definition, her "glory" is merely temporary, so why the confusion? The solution is obvious: The angel will explain the mystery (see on 17:5) regarding the meaning of the woman and the beast. Interestingly, the explanation focuses on the beast, its heads, and its horns, and the woman herself is interpreted last (17:18). The woman's downfall is explained in 17:16 in a reenactment of the civil war motif from the second seal (6:3, 4) as the beast and kings turn on her and destroy her.

The Interpretation of the Beast (17:8)

Each of the angel's interpretation is introduced by the phrase "which you saw," referring back to the vision in 17:1–6a. The description of the beast is a parody of both God and Christ. In 1:4, 8; 4:8, 11:17, and 16:5 God is called "the one who was and who is and who is to come," referring to him as Lord over time and history. Now the beast "once was, now is not, and yet will come up out of the Abyss." The beast along with the dragon demands worship as "the god of this world" (2 Cor 4:4, see also Rev 13:4–15). Moreover, the "once was and now is not" also parodies the death and resurrection of Christ. Christ in Revelation 1:18 states, "I am the Living One. I was dead, and now look, I am alive forever and ever." The beast imitates this in 13:3, 12, 14 in the fatal wound that was healed.

The phrase "was and is not" points forward to the "eighth king" explained in 17:11, referring to the antichrist who "was" with Satan, "is not" here right now, but "will come" at the end of history (1 John 2:18). He will assume power and take on the pretense of divine attributes, but he is the opposite of divinity. For the third time he is said to "come up out of the Abyss" (Rev 11:7; 13:1). In keeping with "once was and is not," this ascension has not yet occurred but is "about to" (in the Greek) happen in the imminent future.

In one sense this could refer to the ongoing ascensions of anti-Christian rulers and false teachers throughout history, but primarily it points to the final appearance of the antichrist at the end of history. But his destiny is settled, for as he ascends, the beast is going to "go to his destruction," alluding to the rise and fall of the little horn in Daniel 7:11, 17–18, 23, 26. In Daniel and here the demonic powers behind the little horn/antichrist will temporarily prevail over the saints, but his predetermined end is destruction. The false trinity "knows [their] time is short" (12:12), and the frustrated rage they feel fuel their evil efforts. They know it will all come to naught, but it is all they can do. At least they can temporarily enjoy the pain their terrible deeds bring to God and his people.

In another reflection from 13:3, 8, the earth-dwellers are even more astonished than John because they don't just hear about the death-resurrection of the antichrist, they will see the beast that "once was, now is not, and yet will come." They will be present when that event takes place, and they will watch the rise and career of this arch-nemesis of the believers.

The reason they are so easily deceived is then explained. Their "names have not been written in the Lamb's book of life," a statement taken from 13:8. They are not citizens of heaven and have rejected God's offer of salvation, so they are easily led astray by falsehood. In 13:8 "from the creation of the world" modified "the Lamb slain," but here it modifies "the book of life" and refers to the sinners whose names were kept from the book of life from eternity past. In the same way that God has kept his followers secure, he has known his enemies from the beginning of time. They will never have any peace or security for all eternity.

The Interpretation of the Seven Heads (17:9–11)

As he moves into even more difficult material, the angel states, "This calls for a mind with wisdom." This repeats the call for wisdom in 13:18 (the number of the beast) and calls the reader to seek divinely given wisdom and understanding. The astonishing nature of the antichrist and the events he will initiate demand that the reader turn to God for help, a fact that is often stressed in the Bible (Dan 1:4, 17; 9:22; 11:33; Mark 13:14).

The angel identifies the seven heads with "seven hills or mountains," often used as a euphemism for Rome because it was built on seven hills. In Domitian's time a festival called the *Septimontium* celebrated this fact. In 17:1 the woman was said to sit on "many waters" (= the inhabitants, 17:15), meaning she ruled over them. Here she sits on the seven hills, meaning she is enthroned on Rome.[2]

The seven hills are identified with seven kings (17:10), usually linked with Roman emperors, but the numbering is very difficult to understand (we need "wisdom"): "Five have fallen, one is, the other has not yet come" is obviously a parody exactly like 17:8 of the title for God. If this refers to emperors, it means five have died, and the present one will soon be superseded by a seventh whom God will allow to reign for a time. This is based on the added point, "he must remain for a little while," with the "must" (*dei*) indicating divine necessity. Then there will arrive "an eighth king" who "belongs to the seven and is going to his destruction." This last is clearly the beast/antichrist of 17:8. This numerical riddle is probably built on the *Nero redivivus* legend (see on 13:3), with the beast killed and rising from the dead leading to universal worship by the nations. This unholy king is also "of the seven," meaning he emerges from the previous seven kings. So the numbering is 5 + 1 + 1 + 1, but it is hard to fit this into the list of emperors:

2. See 1 Enoch 24:1–25:3, where the seven hills become the throne for the Lord of glory.

Emperor	Reign
Julius Caesar	died 44 BC
Augustus	27 BC–AD 14
Tiberius	14–37
Caligula	37–41
Claudius	41–54
Nero	54–68
Galba, Otho, Vitellius	68–69
Vespasian	69–79
Titus	79–81
Domitian	81–96
Nerva	96–98
Trajan	98–117

First we must date the book either to the time of Nero or that of Vespasian or Domitian. In the introduction I favored Domitian as the most likely.[3] Then we must decide whether to begin with Julius Caesar or Augustus. Most go with Julius Caesar, who called himself *imperator,* and Augustus (who was his nephew Gaius Octavius) idolized him.

If we date this in the time of Nero it is simple, for Nero was the sixth emperor (= the "one who is"), and the revived Nero would be the "eighth king" who returns as the unholy emperor or beast. But there are problems dating this book during Nero's reign, so that is unlikely. Others take this not as kings but empires, with five previous empires (perhaps Egypt, Assyria, Babylon, Persia, Greece) and Rome being the sixth then with the seventh and eighth being future empires. But if the beast is an individual more than an empire, this approach too falls short, for these would need to be individual kings.

3. See "Date" in the introduction.

Probably the best option is to take the numbers as apocalyptic symbols (like "Armageddon" in 16:16), with the seven (5 + 1 + 1) meaning that the world kingdoms (and kings) are complete; the time for the nations is over. This fits the use of sevens throughout the book to indicate completeness. The 5 + 1 + 1 may also indicate emperors and not just empires. However, the numbering does not indicate specific emperors but a symbolic reference to the belief that Roman tyranny was temporary and soon to end. The beast/antichrist is the eighth emperor who will reign at the end of history, and at the time of writing he had yet to appear. He will be a Nero-like figure, evil in his character and doomed in his destiny to destruction.

THE INTERPRETATION OF THE TEN HORNS (17:12–14)

The 10 horns of the beast (13:1) builds on Daniel 7:7–8, 20–25, where it depicts 10 kings from the final kingdom, with the little horn (= the beast in Revelation) arising from these 10 horns. In John's day, these kings would be "client kings" under the Roman emperor who ruled the 10 provinces that made up the Roman Empire. Only Herod the Great and his grandson Agrippa I were allowed by Rome to be labeled "king," but all of them aspired to it. These 10 kings represent the world's rulers who will give their allegiance to the beast.

This passage expands the scene that began in 16:12, when the Euphrates dries up so the "kings of the east" can come and join the beast/antichrist. Then in 16:14 the false trinity called the other rulers from the nations to make war with them. So the whole world joins the army of the beast. Yet the beast/antichrist is not really in charge, for the actual source of that authority is God who gives them power "for one hour," used also in 18:10, 17, 19 to symbolize the swiftness of the destruction of Babylon the Great (see also 8:1). Their power will be very short-lived and will last the three and a half years of that final period of history (11:2, 3; 12:6, 14; 13:5).

These 10 kings will be united by a single purpose (17:13), to yield their "power and authority to the beast." They are of one accord in following the antichrist and give him absolute allegiance and support, accepting every decision he makes. So there are four groups in the evil empire—the antichrist, the 10 kings who fawn over his every move, the rest of the world's rulers who join them (16:12, 14, 16), and the earth-dwellers who worship him.

That single purpose is revealed further in 17:14, where their unified intention is to "wage war against the Lamb," a reference to Armageddon (16:16). In 12:17 and 13:7 they "wage war" against the saints, referring to the intense persecution and martyrdom of this "great tribulation" period (7:14). Now these 10 kings prepare for the final event of that period, the "great day of God Almighty" (16:14; see 6:17). However, the victory will not be theirs but belongs to the Lamb, who has seven horns, transforming him into the conquering ram (5:6). Thus they now face "the wrath of the Lamb" (6:16) who will now "triumph over them." That victory is instantaneous in 19:19–20 because the Lamb is "Lord of Lords and King of kings," a title used of Yahweh in Deuteronomy 10:17 and Daniel 2:37, 47 in the **Septuagint**, transferred to the Lamb here and in 19:16.

Not only will the Lamb be victorious, but the people of God will be victorious with him. In Revelation 2:26–27 these "overcomers" are promised that they will accompany him and shatter the nations "like pottery" (from Psa 2:9; see also Rev 19:15). So the saints will participate in the final war. They will form part of the Lord's army and will accompany Christ back to earth (19:14), probably alongside the hosts of heaven (the angelic army implicit in the title "LORD of hosts" in the Old Testament). They have conquered the dragon spiritually in 12:11, and now will conquer him with finality in that ultimate victory over the evil forces in 19:19–21.

CIVIL WAR BREAKS OUT, AND THE GREAT PROSTITUTE IS DESTROYED (17:15–18)

In this section the angel describes both the identity and the fate of the great prostitute, beginning with the waters on which she sits. The waters are the peoples of the nations, described in the typical fourfold "peoples, multitudes, nations and languages" (see 5:9; 7:9; 10:11 and others). So the prostitute "sitting" means she rules over all the people of the world (see on 17:1). This woman represents the "great city" controlling the world (17:18).

Now we see the true feelings of the beast/antichrist for the harlot (17:16). This follows the civil war motif of the second seal (6:3–4) as the beast and kings turn on the great prostitute and destroy her. It also follows the fifth and sixth trumpet judgment of chapter 9 where the demonic powers turn on their people to torture and kill them. The cosmic powers have no love for their own followers, for they are still made in the image of God and loved by God. In harming their followers, they are getting back at God. This is the true nature of evil: It never builds up; it only destroys. So the evil powers destroy the great prostitute. This **eschatological** civil war is predicted in Ezekiel 38:21, where as part of the judgment of Gog "every man's sword will be against his brother."

The reason for this betrayal is stated in 17:16. The beast and 10 kings "hate the prostitute," and this leads them to turn on her. This kind of civil war was a great fear of Rome. No external army could defeat Rome, but Rome several times nearly self-destructed in civil wars. The latest before the time of Revelation took place in AD 68–69, when three generals (Galba, Otho, Vitellius) one by one brought armies into Rome to take it over after the suicide of Nero. Then the great general Vespasian left the Jewish war to his son Titus, brought his legions to Rome, and saved it.

The evil powers first "bring her to ruin," with this verb a cognate of "desert," meaning laying waste or depopulating a city. Then in a series of destructive steps, they "strip her naked, ... eat her flesh, and burn her with fire." This is built on Ezekiel 23:25–29, detailing the destruction of Jerusalem at the exile by telling the story of two harlot sisters (Samaria and Jerusalem) who are indicted for their sins and then punished. The harlot Jerusalem is stripped and consumed by fire. Here John adds the image of "devouring her flesh," a symbol of the total annihilation of the harlot-city. Being "stripped naked" pictures the exposure of their evil deeds (see the "shameful nakedness" of Laodicea in Rev 3:18). The image of "burned with fire" may go back to Leviticus 21:9, where a priest's daughter who became a prostitute was to be "burned in the fire." All three are images of sins exposed and the terrible penalty sin exacts.

The false trinity will destroy the great prostitute because "God has put it into their hearts to accomplish his purpose." It seems startling at first but is in keeping with the core theme of the book—the absolute sovereignty of God over all things, including the demonic realm.[4] The verb "put" is actually the word for "given," that verb that emphasizes divine control. When these kings submit "their royal authority" to the beast and obey his orders, they are actually fulfilling God's purpose. Even the evil intentions of the cosmic powers ultimately serve the larger purposes of Almighty God to carry out his judgments on the sinful nations.

The ultimate purpose follows: that "God's words are fulfilled." There are three levels in which this takes place: 1) fulfilling the prophecies of Daniel 7, 10, 12 regarding the destruction of the little horn/beast/antichrist (also Rev 10:7, the completion of "the mystery of God"); 2) keeping the promise of 6:10–11 that God would "avenge the blood' of the martyrs when the "full number" of those to suffer was completed; 3) keeping the promise of 17:1 that John would see "the punishment of the great prostitute."

The final point (17:18) defines the woman as "the great city that rules over the kings of the earth." We have already seen in 16:19; 18:10–21 that the "great city" is Babylon/Rome, the capital city of the beast. Note the **inclusio**—the first thing John sees (17:1) is the last to be interpreted. It is last in order to provide a

4. See "Theology of the Book" in the introduction.

transition to chapter 18, which will center on the judgment of Babylon the Great.

This is a prophecy about the final Babylon, the unholy Roman Empire established by the antichrist to rule sinful humankind. This will be the final stage of the many evil empires and anti-God rulers and false teachers down through history, but this depravity is soon to end for all eternity. We are living in the world that will produce this final evil. We face daily the atmosphere of anti-Christian sentiment that will produce the final antichrist, and so we, like those addressed originally by John, must become "overcomers" and rise above the sins of our world to live fully for Christ. False teachers exist all around us, and we are called by God to speak and live truth in the midst of such falsehood.

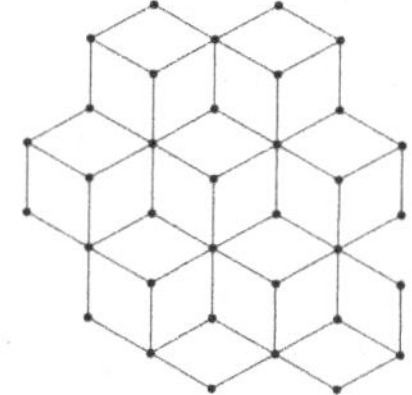

THE FALL OF BABYLON THE GREAT
(18:1–24)

The destruction of the great prostitute was noted in 17:1, 16, and now that judgment is expanded into a full-fledged vision. Earlier the evil "great city" was condemned for her idolatry and immorality, but here a further sin is highlighted: the economic exploitation of the world. John uses every Babylon polemic in the Old Testament and adds those against Nineveh and Tyre as background. There are three major sections to chapter 18: 1) an announcement of Babylon's demise is followed by a command to believers to flee in light of the judgment (18:1–8); 2) Three laments or funeral dirges are pronounced by the three groups most affected—the kings, the merchants, and the sea trade (18:9–19); and 3) the heavens and the saints are called to rejoice over her downfall (18:20–24).

AN ANGEL ANNOUNCES THE FALL OF BABYLON (18:1–3)

In 18:1 John sees another angel, after the one from chapter 17, "descending from heaven," in contrast to the beast who "ascends from the Abyss" in 17:8. There are two further contrasts: First, he possesses "great authority" while the beast only has a derived authority given it by the dragon (13:2) and God (13:5). Second, he illuminates the earth with his splendor (or "glory"), while the members of the false trinity have no glory in this book. The term is never used of them. The angel reflects the glory of God (as in 10:1), implying he comes directly from the divine presence. This echoes Ezekiel 43:2, which says that "the land was radiant with his glory" as God in solemn procession entered the renewed temple through the east gate. This passage is fulfilling that prophecy, and now it includes judgment, putting an end to evil.

In a loud voice this angel repeats the cry of Revelation 14:8, "Fallen! Fallen is Babylon the Great!" It alludes to Isaiah 21:9, where a messenger in a chariot makes this announcement and adds, "all the images of the gods lie shattered." The judgment on the empire includes the destruction of its idols, especially the idol set up of the antichrist in Revelation 13:14–15. This event was foretold by Isaiah.

The desolation of Babylon/Rome/the empire of the beast is described in three parallel lines. It depicts a ghost town, a deserted city inhabited by demons and unclean birds, taken from Isaiah 13:21–22; Jeremiah 50:39; 51:37 (Babylon); but also Zephaniah 2:14–15 (Assyria) and Isaiah 34:11–14 (Edom). First, "she has become a dwelling for demons." This is natural because demons are said to inhabit desert areas (Isa 34:14; Matt 12:43). The meaning of this is clarified in the other two lines. She is "a haunt [literally, 'prison'] for every impure spirit," building on the biblical view that demons are chained in the prison-house of darkness (2 Pet 2:4; Jude 6). Finally, she is "a haunt for every unclean bird … every unclean and detestable animal." This echoes the presence of scavenger birds in Isaiah 13:21 and prepares for the carrion birds invited to the "great supper of God" in Revelation 19:17–18, 21. The point is that Babylon will become a dead ghost town with no inhabitants, an unclean place unfit for life.

The reason for this (18:3) is the depth of her depravity, again expressed in three poetic lines. First, as in 14:8 and 17:5, she is not just filled with sin herself but has gotten the nations drunk on "the wine that leads to passion for her adulteries."[1] They have freely participated in her debauchery and so will perish with her. In 14:10 it was said that this willing life of immorality would result in "drinking the wine of the wrath of God"; so also here (see Isa 51:17; Jer 25:15–18; Zech 12:2). In the second line, not only the nations but also their rulers have imbibed in immorality (which includes religious apostasy/idolatry) with her. The third line adds the "merchants" and moves into the economic side of her depravity. The sin of excessive luxuries and economic exploitation of the unfortunate is frequently condemned in Scripture. For the Roman elite gross consumption was the order of the day, and the empire's economy was at all times intended to support the ruling class. The lament for Tyre in Ezekiel 27:12–25 is important background, and I will discuss this extensively in 18:11–13 below.

A HEAVENLY VOICE COMMANDS BELIEVERS TO LEAVE (18:4–8)

THE COMMAND TO LEAVE (18:4)

Voices from heaven have spoken in Revelation 10:4, 8 and 14:2, 13 and always carry direct messages from the throne itself. The command "Come out of her, my people" demands that true Christians separate themselves completely from her depraved society; this command is frequent in Scripture (Isa 52:11; Jer 50:8; Ezek 20:41; 2 Cor 6:14, 17). Here it means to leave the city lest they be destroyed with the pagans (Jer 51:45, "Run for your lives!"). In its spiritual sense this is the definition of holiness: to separate from the things of the world. The danger is that they "share in her sins" and thereby "receive … her plagues." This is God's law and in the Roman world is ***lex talionis***, the law of retribution. What you do has consequences, and divine as well as human law says you receive just recompense for your actions (good or bad).

1. See the commentary on 14:8.

The Basis of Judgment (18:5)

The reason for removing oneself entirely from such sinful pleasures is the depth of Babylon's depravity: "her sins are piled up to heaven" (Jer 51:9), literally "touched the sky." This is reminiscent of the tower of Babel that attempted to reach heaven (Gen 11:4), and states that the sins of the nations are a vast heap that have piled up to God himself. Therefore "God has remembered her crimes," and when God remembers, he acts. For the righteous, he works on their behalf (Pss 105:8–11; 111:5–6); and for sinners he acts in judgment (Psa 109:14; Jer 14:10). When the just God "remembered Babylon" in 16:19, he gave her "the cup filled with the wine of the fury of his wrath." The wrath of God is a judicial response to the crimes of the wicked.

His Just Judgment Explained (18:6–8)

This section too is dominated by the ***lex talionis*** and says that God will repay Babylon in kind for her sins. Imagine a courtroom, as the divine Judge reads the verdict and Babylon stands before the Bema (judgment seat), receiving her just recompense. The swift severity of the sentence begins this section: "Pay back to her as she has given" (recalling Jer 50:29 of Babylon); "Repay her for her deeds; do to her as she has done." The same verb is used in both parts: "Pay her what she has paid others." This is a frequent scriptural emphasis, and the basis of the doctrine of reward and punishment—what you do to others, God will do to you.

The second and third lines are more difficult to interpret: "Pay her back double for what she has done. Pour her a double portion from her own cup." This does not sound just, so some think this refers to a full or complete requital for her crimes, with "double" a metaphor for full recompense rather than twice the penalty. Yet at the same time a double penalty was required for some crimes, such as stealing an animal (Exod 22:4, 7, 9), and the prophets called for double retaliation on occasion (Isa 40:2; Jer 16:18, 17:18). So either way, this call for a double portion of judgment stresses again the severity of her crimes.

The next two verses (18:7–8) provide two examples of this "cup" of sin. First, she has "glorified herself" rather than God. Scripture is replete with passages that condemn arrogance, like Luke 14:11, "Those who exalt themselves will be humbled" (also 2 Sam 22:28; Prov 3:34; Isa 2:12, 17; 1 Pet 5:6). A primary emphasis in Revelation is that all glory belongs only to God. Second, she is characterized by "sensuous luxury," a term that connotes both sensuous living and inordinate opulence. This has been true of virtually all empires throughout history, but Rome has always been considered the archetype for such misuse of power for pleasure.

This is portrayed clearly in her boastful claim, "I sit enthroned as a queen." Note the startling contrast—a prostitute claiming to be a queen! The sense of entitlement and the desire to exploit the rest of the world to achieve unprecedented wealth and a licentious lifestyle typified Rome. Consider Messalina, the wife of Claudius, whose sexual appetite was so prodigious that she would at times become a sacred prostitute in one of the temples. Bacchanalia was the order of the day among the Roman elite.

To this is added, "I am not a widow, I will never mourn." In the Roman world a widow was not supposed to remarry and would often have to stay with the husband's family. They often had only their dowry to live on, as the estate would go to the sons in order to carry on the family dynasty. So widowhood was greatly feared. For the early church, ministry to the many penniless widows was particularly important (Acts 6:1–7; 1 Tim 5:3–16; Jas 1:27). So her arrogant boast is that she will always sit on the throne and never have to suffer grief and dependence like a normal person.

Because of all this, her guilt is established. She has condemned herself in God's court of law. Thus the sentence of Revelation 18:8 is a just legal decision. "*Her* plagues"—those she has brought upon herself—will now overtake her like a swift flood. Moreover, they will come "in one day," echoing Isaiah 47:9, where the judgment of Babylon was to come "suddenly, in an instant." The four plagues enumerated ("death, mourning, famine ... consumed with fire") have all been seen before: "mourning" in Revelation 18:7, "death" and "famine" in 6:8, "consumed with fire" in 17:16.

These apocalyptic judgments are the proper recompense for the enormity of her crimes. The principle is important—let none of us think we will get away with flaunting our self-centered pleasures before a holy God. Every act we do (good deeds as well as evil) will be justly repaid. Lust for power and for pleasure must come full circle and self-destruct. Even more so, the judgment for sin is guaranteed by Almighty God. As in 18:8, "mighty is the God who judges her." There is a direct contrast with the pretentious "mighty city" of 18:10; God alone is truly mighty, and he is the sovereign Judge.

THREE LAMENTS ARE SUNG OVER BABYLON THE GREAT (18:9–19)

These funeral laments are given by the three groups who have profited the most from the largesse of Babylon/Rome: the kings who gained power and wealth; the merchants who shared the worldwide markets she created; and the seamen who carried her cargo over all the world. They have now lost all that Rome had provided, so their sorrow is not for Rome but for their loss. The laments are built on Ezekiel 27, the lament over Tyre, that great maritime and commercial giant of Ezekiel's day. We see in this the ultimate end of worldly pursuits—temporary pleasure and profit end in total loss.

Lament of the Kings of the Earth (18:9–10)

These kings and sister nations have shared Babylon's adulterous way of life (both immorality and idolatry) as well as her luxury (see 14:8; 17:2, 4; 18:3; 19:2). They have lost their paramour and are bereft. These "kings" are the ruling class of the other nations, and they like Babylon have grown fat on the poverty of their people (Ezek 27:33). The sin of economic exploitation is a disgrace of nations today as much as in Roman times, and the message here is that there will be a future accounting with God.

So these kings see "the smoke of her burning," a frequent image of judgment in the book (Rev 9:17–18; 14:11; 18:18). They lament the destruction of their gravy train and so "weep and mourn over her" (Ezek 27:35). But they do so only as they "stand far off and cry." They distance themselves as far as possible from the burning city. They cry for their loss but want nothing to do with the punishment. Naturally they are completely "terrified at her torment," saying in effect, "Better them than us." They were guilty of the same sins and so wished not to be noticed.

Their cry is stereotypical. The three "woes" by these groups parallel the three "woes" of the trumpet judgments (8:11; 9:12; 11:14; see also 12:12). There it was a pronouncement of judgment; here it is a cry of sorrow and horror at the judgment that has already occurred. Once more Babylon is the "great city" (11:8; 16:19; 17:18); the earthly rulers have been seduced by the pretentious majesty of this depraved and doomed empire.

"One hour" connotes an immediate response. The suddenness of the judgment is reminiscent of the instantaneous judgment on Nebuchadnezzar when he was "immediately" driven insane by God in Daniel 4:33, and even more of the writing on the wall in Daniel 5 when Belshazzar was slain and his kingdom lost in one night. The instantaneous destruction here prepares for the similarly immediate annihilation of the army of the beast at Christ's return in Revelation 19:19–21.

Lament of the Merchants (18:11–17a)

These are the wholesale dealers who traveled the Roman roads, making fortunes in the agoras/marketplaces in every city. Their sorrow, like the sorrow of the merchants of Tyre (Ezek 27:27, 36), was at the loss of trade and profit. The amount of trade was staggering, with enormous profits from Africa, Egypt, India, China, and Europe.

The list of cargoes in 18:12–13 demonstrates the kind of wealth involved in the lucrative trade. It builds on Ezekiel 27:12–24 (15 of the 29 items), but is exclusively Roman and organized by types of cargo. For the most part it lists goods that were exclusively for the Roman elite and rarely if ever touched by the common people. The purpose is to show why God's wrath has descended on such materialistic ostentation and self-centered ways of living. If we read through the list and see how many of these unimaginably luxurious (to the first century) items (or their equivalents) we ourselves have in our homes, it would be very convicting of our own materialism!

1. *Precious stones and metals*. Gold, then as now, was the most important metal, so prevalent as a sign of wealth (ceilings, buckles, jewelry) that many Romans began to turn to silver. Both gold and silver were imported from Spain. Silver became a status symbol, with couches, baths, and other luxury items being made from it. Precious stones came mostly from India and including those in the lists of 4:3, 21:19–20. Pearls were considered the most luxurious jewel and came from the Red Sea. They were enormously expensive, and there came to be so many worn by women that they became a symbol of decadence.
2. *Luxurious fabrics*. "Fine linen" describes the clothing of the wealthy. A dress from a famous garment center like Scythopolis could cost 7000 denarii (roughly equal to $280,000 today); purple or scarlet garments were particularly expensive (see 17:4). The purple dye came from the murex, a tiny shellfish that produced a drop at a time, so incredible numbers were needed for a single garment. In order of price, silk (from China), linen, or woolen garments were plentiful for the elite.
3. *Expensive wood and building materials*. Citron wood, from a North African tree, was the most expensive of them, known for its beautiful grain patterns, and tables made from it could cost millions. Other "costly woods" could be

maple or cedar. Ivory was used in sculptures and idols as well as furniture. "Brass" or "bronze" was used in shields or furniture, but especially statues. Iron from Greece and Spain became weapons and also statues. Marble was from Africa, Egypt, and Greece and was used for buildings as well as plates, jars, and baths.

4. *Spices and perfumes*. Cinnamon came from Africa or the Orient, used as a spice, perfume, incense, and a flavoring for wine. "Spice" was amomum from India, used to make hair fragrant. "Incense" blended several ingredients for both religious and home use. Myrrh from Somalia was quite expensive for perfume or medicine. Frankincense was another perfume, given with gold and myrrh to the baby Jesus, paying for the family's sojourn in Egypt (Matt 2:11).
5. *Food Items*. These were mainly staples and not expensive, but Rome was famous for its extravagant banquets, importing expensive delicacies like nightingale tongues or the breasts of doves. A single banquet could cost the equivalent of millions of dollars. Wine came from Sicily or Spain, and olive oil from Africa and Spain. Wheat was imported from Egypt and given free to about 200,000 citizens of Rome (called "the grain dole," estimated at 80,000 tons) to keep them happy. The rest of the empire suffered greatly to supply all this.
6. *Animals and slaves*. This does not list animals transported for the games (lions, elephants, and so on) or meant for food (beef was not a popular meat), but those animals used for work. The slave trade was immense. There were an estimated 10 million, or close to 20 percent of the population of the Roman Empire. The status of the wealthy was connected to the number of slaves they owned. In the first century BC war produced most of the slaves, but in the time of Jesus and Paul it was debt. Rome plundered the world for slaves as well as for goods.

The merchants' grief over the fall of Babylon is entirely for their losses. There is no remorse, only sorrow for what has been taken away. "The fruit you longed for" refers to all these luxuries that are now gone. The splendor of these expensive goods has vanished and is "never to be recovered." They are gone forever, a warning to any society (like ours!) given over to the folly of conspicuous consumption. The old adage, "You can't take it with you," is still oh so true. Like the kings, the merchants too will "stand far off" because they want nothing to do with the punishment of Babylon. They share the guilt of Babylon/Rome, for they have "gained their wealth from her," but they neither acknowledge their part in her sins nor have any sympathy for her plight. There is nothing but a self-centered sorrow at all they have lost.

Their mourning in 18:16 also parallels that of the kings. "Woe, woe great city" is found also in 18:10, 19 and expresses horror at the destruction of the world's capital city that is now a wasteland (18:2, 22–23). The description of her luxurious garments is a near-verbatim copy of the description from 17:4. The kings mourn the loss of her power, the merchants the loss of her ostentatious wealth. The extravagant lifestyle of this wicked empire has been found wanting, judged, and destroyed forever (see Jas 5:2–5). The sudden destruction of all this ("in one hour") parallels the effect of death on every one of us. The possessions we may spend our lives acquiring will be taken from us in an instant.

Lament of the Sea Captains and Sailors (18:17b–19)

Virtually all of Rome's wealth came by sea, so the inclusion of these next groups is natural, building on Ezekiel 27:29, "all who handle the oars ... the mariners and all the sailors." There are four groups: the "sea captain" is the one who commands the ship rather than the owner (listed in 18:19); those who "travel by ship" are the passengers and merchants; the "sailors" are those who sail the ship; and "all who earn their living from the sea" are possibly fishermen and merchants. These are mostly the shipping magnates rather than small shipping companies, the lords of the sea who forced out small competitors and gained favorable tax status from Rome.

Like the kings and merchants, they too see "the smoke of her burning" and stand "far off." They remember the glory days when they cried, "Who is like the beast?" (13:4) and "Who is like this great city?" (here, echoing Ezek 27:32 on Tyre). They go further in their sorrow, throwing "dust on their heads" as a sign of mourning (Josh 7:6; 1 Sam 4:12; Job 2:12). They too decry the destruction of the "great city" but center on their own losses. Again, they are lamenting not Rome but themselves; they have lost their livelihood. Those who "became rich through her wealth" are especially the owners of the cargo ships but would include everyone involved (sailors, merchants, fishermen). Babylon's sudden ruin is their ruin; their future has gone with the destruction of the "great city."

A MIGHTY ANGEL ANNOUNCES BABYLON THE GREAT'S FINAL DOOM (18:20–24)

THE CALL FOR THE HEAVENS AND THE SAINTS TO REJOICE (18:20)

Note the absolute contrast between 18:19 and 20. Those who have joined with and profited from Babylon's destruction mourn her passing and are filled with terror ("woe"), while those who are faithful to God are filled with joy that the name of God has triumphed and his people vindicated. Thus both the inhabitants of heaven and the saints on earth are enjoined to "rejoice over her." At first glance this reaction seems offensive; aren't we supposed to pray for the lost rather than feel jubilant over their fate? This will be even more evident in the "hallelujah" hymns of 19:1–5. Yet we must remember that this refers to those have rejected God with finality, committing the "unpardonable sin" (Mark 3:28–30; Heb 6:4–6; 1 John 5:16) when they took the mark of the beast (Rev 13:16). The rejoicing takes place because God's justice is being served; those who rejected him with finality and oppressed his people are receiving the just recompense they have brought upon themselves. This is the theme of this verse.

There are two groups who are called to rejoice, building on Old Testament passages where heaven and earth are called to celebrate God's righteous deeds (Psa 96:11; Isa 49:13; Jer 51:38). The "heavens" are the celestial beings of this book, the angels, elders, living creatures, and possibly the saints who have died and are in heaven. Those on earth are the "heaven-dwellers" of Revelation 12:12, with the threefold designation "saints, apostles, prophets." The "apostles" are certainly the Twelve of the Gospels and Acts, the "twelve foundations" of Revelation 21:14. The "prophets" here are probably not the Old Testament prophets (if so, we would expect the order to be reversed: "prophets and apostles") but New Testament prophets like those of Revelation 11:18, 22:9. In Ephesians 4:11 these are listed as officers in the church.

God's justice is the reason for the jubilation, another example of the ***lex talionis*** theme (see Rev 6:9–11; 11:5, 18; 14:8, 10; 16:5–7; 18:6). Like 18:6, this is a legal scene, and the saints and angels watching divine justice at work celebrate the just penalty handed down by the Judge of all. These who have committed the "eternal sin" (Mark 3:29) and taken the lives of God's people ("the judgment she imposed on you") will now suffer that same punishment, "as they deserve" (16:6, see Gen 9:5–6; Deut 19:16–19). The joy is not over the souls lost but over the vindication of God's people and the honor of God's name, emphasized in the Lord's Prayer of Matthew 6:9: "May your name be honored/made sacred."

The Destruction of Babylon (18:21–24)

For the final time a "mighty angel" acts (Rev 5:2; 10:1–2). In his previous two appearances he bore the scroll containing God's plan for ending this world and exemplified the authority of God over his creation. Now he picks up "a boulder the size of a huge millstone," a stone so large it had to be turned by a donkey (Mark 9:42), weighing several tons. In a prophetic act (as in

Rev 10:8, 10; 11:1–2) he casts it into the sea. This is similar to the scene where Jeremiah ties "a stone to the scroll" and throws it into the Euphrates, saying, "So will Babylon sink to rise no more" (Jer 51:63–64). In these final days of this age, "Babylon will be thrown down, never to be found again." Her violent demise is still future ("will be thrown down") and will occur in two stages: civil war (Rev 17:16) and total destruction at the return of Christ (19:11–21). She has been judged (18:20), and her just punishment is imminent (here). The terrible violence of her destruction is prophesied in the casting of the millstone and will take place at Armageddon (16:16; 19:19–20) and the final judgment (20:13–15).

The last phrase, "never to be found again," provides the model ("never ... again") for the five details used to flesh out the terrible nature of that judgment in 18:22–23a. These five losses build on the merchants' lament of 18:14, "all your luxury and splendor have vanished, never to be recovered." First, all music and musicians are gone, those artists who brighten everyday life and bring joy to humdrum existence (Isa 24:8; Ezek 26:13). Second, the craftsmen and trades that make city life possible have departed forever, removing the economic substrata of the empire and demanding the end of civilization. Moreover, this was a major source of oppression against Christians, who were ostracized from the trade guilds due to their refusal to worship the patron gods of the guilds. So once more this destruction constitutes just payback.

The last three are likely derived from Jeremiah 25:10, "I will banish from them the sounds of joy and gladness, the voices of bride and bridegroom, the sounds of millstones, and the light of the lamp." The third is the disappearance of the millstones, meaning that there will be no food supply, probably related both to business (the production of food) and family life (the "hand mill" noted in Matt 24:41). Without food there is no life and no joy in life. Fourth, "the light of the lamp" switches from day (the millstone) to night. These are not torches outside the house but the small lamps of the home, thus referring to the simple joys of family life. They too are to be seen no more. Finally, "the voice of the bridegroom and bride" provide the strongest metaphor yet for the "joy and gladness" (Jer 25:10, where it is first in the list) of life. This provides a further contrast between the destinies of sinner and saint. The nations will never again know the celebration of a wedding, while God's people will become the "bride of Christ" (Rev 19:7–8; 21:2, 9).

The reasons for the terrible judgment on Babylon are presented again in 18:23b–24. In ancient law courts the crimes were read aloud as the sentence was carried out. That is the point here. In the lists of sins in this chapter (also 18:2, 3, 7) there are five primary types: idolatry, immorality, economic tyranny, sorcery, and murder. The last three are stressed here. The merchants of 18:11–17a encompass types three and four, and so are described here as "important people" but also as sorcerers (see below). The elite of Rome were the senatorial families but also many in what was called the "equestrian class," made up of wealthy families with land holdings and including the wealthy merchants. Rome both dominated and exploited its subject peoples for their resources, and the merchants distributed that wealth. In Isaiah 23:8 the merchants of Tyre are called "princes ... renowned in the earth." They live their lives worshiping success and trying to get ahead. God is out of the picture, and this could be called "economic idolatry," a sin many of us are also guilty of committing (see also Jas 4:13–17).

They were also the "sorcerers" who "led the nations astray." Magic was a huge enterprise in the Roman Empire, and Ephesus with its temple to Artemis was a leading city practicing sorcery. The creation of a universal demand for ostentatious luxury was a type of sorcery, and the people were definitely deceived. If anything, this type of economic "magic" describes our modern mindset even more than in the first century, for the deception perpetrated by the advertising industry is even more universally successful today. This includes immorality as well, for blatant sexual innuendoes are rife in TV commercials.

Finally, Babylon is condemned for murdering the saints. The mention of those "slaughtered on the earth" goes back to 6:9 and the cries of the "slaughtered souls" to God. The mention of the "prophets and saints" revisits the list in 18:20.

Like the original readers of Revelation, we live in a narcissistic culture, a society of greed whose credo is, "I can do whatever I want, and my rights trump everyone else's." This culture is the heart of the evil empire of Babylon the Great, and it describes the American way as well. As it was in the first century, it is still easy for us to go along with the prevailing culture and live like our friends do, but there are consequences to such hedonistic acts. The stakes are a lot higher than we think, and we will pay the piper in the end. The punishment the great prostitute faced was inevitable, and that is exactly what will happen to our selfish way of life. Pleasure-seeking societies always self-destruct, and we must heed the command and warning of 18:4: "Come out of her, my people, lest you share in her sins!"

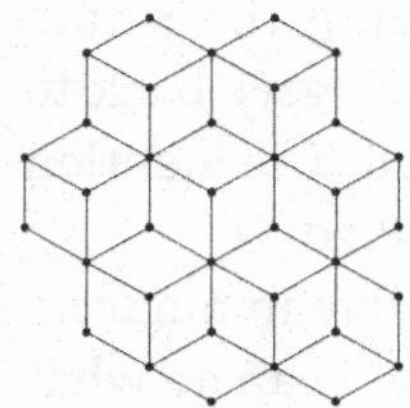

THE FINAL VICTORY
THE END OF THE EVIL EMPIRE AT THE PAROUSIA
(19:1–21)

The first stage of the great victory, the destruction of the evil empire, Babylon the Great, was the subject of 17:1–19:5. There we saw the "what"; here we see the "when": this will happen at the return of Christ. In the New Testament there are two aspects of his return, the "catching up" (popularly called the "rapture") of the saints (Mark 13:24–27 and parallels; 1 Cor 15:51–52; 1 Thess 4:13–18) and the judgment of the sinners (Matt 13:24–30, 25:31–46; 1 Thess 5:1–11; 2 Thess 2:1–10; 2 Pet 3:10–13). The wedding feast of the Lamb (Rev 19:6–10) belongs with the first aspect, and the **Parousia** (19:11–16) with the second aspect. The destruction of the sinners takes place in three stages: the coming of Christ on the white warhorse with the armies of heaven in 19:11–16, the invitation of the carrion birds to the "great supper of God" in 19:17–18, and the final battle in which the army of the beast is annihilated in 19:19–21.

HEAVEN REJOICES AT GOD'S JUST JUDGMENT (19:1–5)

Hymns of Praise by the Multitude (19:1–3)

These first verses (19:1–5) actually conclude the section on the destruction of the evil empire (17:1–19:5) and expand the call to the heavens and the saints in 18:20 to rejoice in that just penalty on the world of evil and its inhabitants. God's righteous judgment can only be greeted with praise by the jubilant multitude of heavenly inhabitants, which probably includes saints as well as celestial beings (see 7:9). "Hallelujah," meaning, "praise Yahweh," is drawn from the Hallel psalms, Psalms 113–18, and its use as a title for several others (Pss 106, 111, 135, 146–50). This word had a special place in the cultic life of Israel, expressing jubilant joy, and that is the tone here.

The hymn of praise begins with the celebration of the salvation or deliverance of God's people from the evil powers as God demonstrates his glory and exercises his power on behalf of the saints. "Salvation" also refers to the "victory" of God achieved through his almighty power, resulting in his glory (see 7:10, 12; 12:10). The reason for this joy (19:2) is a virtual quotation of 16:7, "true and just are his judgments." This act of judgment is "true" because it is based on his covenant faithfulness, applying the covenant curses to those who have flaunted his grace and mercy. It is "just" because it is based on his holy character that must destroy all that is evil. These sinners have brought his righteous judgment down upon themselves. The evil deeds of this unholy empire demand such an extreme penalty.

The legal basis is that the great prostitute (see Rev 17) has "corrupted the earth with her adulteries," stressed in 14:8 ("made the nations drink the wine that leads to passion for immorality," also 17:2; 18:3, 9). This harlot-empire has seduced the nations by employing Satan's great weapon, deception (12:9; 20:3). Now she has paid the price for her sinful folly. In addition, God is "avenging on her the blood of his servants," returning to 6:9–11 and the imprecatory prayers of the saints for vengeance and vindication. These prayers were partially answered in the seals, trumpets, and bowls (see 8:2–5; 16:5–6), and are now fully answered in the destruction here, which includes both Armageddon and the last judgment of 20:13–15.

In 19:3, the heavenly multitude adds a refrain to the worshipful praise of 19:1–2. A second "hallelujah" celebrates the extent of the punishment, reflecting 14:11 (and Isa 34:9–10), "the smoke of her torment ascends forever and ever." Also, "the smoke of her burning" in 18:9, 18 describes the devastation caused by the final war. This "smoke of torment" is the polar opposite of the "smoke of incense" describing the sweet-smelling prayers of the martyrs in 8:4 and the "smoke from the glory of God," the Shekinah, that filled the temple in 15:8. When God creates a soul, he is creating an eternal being, and thus the punishment and torment must be "forever and ever."

Concluding Affirmation by the Elders and Living Creatures (19:4)

The elders and living creatures are the celestial worship leaders in the book (4:8–10; 5:8, 11, 14; 7:11–17; 11:16; 14:3; 19:4). Once more (4:10; 5:14) they "fall down and worship" God. Prostrating oneself is a more serious form of worship, symbolizing total surrender. The emphasis is on God's complete sovereignty, symbolized in "who was seated on the throne." Their refrain is not a second hymn but a solemn affirmation of the previous hymn, meaning, "So be it, praise Yahweh." The "amen, hallelujah" is taken from Psalm 106:48, where it follows a prayer for deliverance from the nations. Here that deliverance has already occurred, and this is thanksgiving for God's mighty act.

Refrain: The Voice from the Throne (19:5)

This is the third group after the multitude in 19:1–3 and the celestial worship leaders in 19:4. Now the scene shifts to earth, and the voice from the throne addresses the saints on earth for the refrain. The voice in this verse is not God, for it commands them to "praise *our* God." This is probably similar to "the voice from heaven" in 18:4 and is an angelic herald bringing a divine message. "Praise our God" is a near translation for "hallelujah" (= "praise Yahweh") and commands the believers to engage in joyous doxological praise. There are three descriptions of the saints in this verse:

1. "his servants" (*douloi*) refers once again to the "slaves" of God (1:1; 2:20; 7:3; 11:18; 22:3, 6) who are his special

possession, as in the imagery of them as "sealed" in 7:3-4 and "measured" in 11:1-2.

2. "You who fear him" (11:18) is a critical part of the perseverance theme and means more than reverence. This refers to that healthy fear of the holy God who is Judge and rewards both saint and sinner "according to their works" (2:23; 14:13; 18:6; 22:12).
3. The "small and great," also in 11:18 and 20:12, reflects Psalm 115:13 and means all stand equally before God and have the privilege of worshiping him.

THE MULTITUDE PRAISES GOD'S REIGN AND JOHN IS COMMANDED TO WRITE (19:6-10)

This is the second half of the new "hallel psalms" of Revelation (19:1-10), with the first half (19:1-5) concluding and celebrating the destruction of Babylon the Great (17:1-19:5), and the second half (19:6-10) initiating the final chapter, the **Parousia** and final war that destroys the empire of the beast (19:6-21). This will be the greatest celebration of them all, when the saints become the bride of the Lamb.

The "great multitude" began the first half of these hallelujah choruses (19:1), and it begins the second half as well. As they sing, the incredible volume of their heavenly hymn resembles the sound of waves crashing on the shore and a huge thunderstorm (1:15; 14:2-3). The great volume fits the stupendous message. Wedding songs are known for their exuberance.

Then follows the basis for praising Yahweh: He is "Lord God Almighty" (1:8; 4:8; 11:17), stressing his omnipotence and lordship over his creation, and he has "begun his [eternal] reign" (see 11:17). The time of evil is forever over, and God is on his throne in his heaven. Thus the people of God must "rejoice and be glad" (19:7), for joyous worship is the only proper response to all that God has done. This call is frequent in Scripture (Psa 31:7; 118:24; 1 Chr 16:31; Matt 5:12), and it naturally leads to "giving him glory," the praise and honor due him especially in light of experiencing God's reign and taking part in the wedding supper of the Lamb.

The further reason for this joy and praise is not only the beginning of God's eternal reign but the incredibly joyous event that initiates that reign—"the wedding of the Lamb has come." Note the contrast between the great prostitute in chapter 17 and the bride of Christ here and in 21:2, 9. The imagery of Israel as the bride of Yahweh (Isa 49:18; 54:5; 61:10; Jer 31:32) and of the church as the bride of Christ (Mark 2:19–20; 2 Cor 11:2; Eph 5:25–27) is behind this. In Hosea 2:16–20 God tells Israel that if she returns, "you will call me 'my husband,'" and "I will betroth you to me forever"; and Paul speaks of presenting believers "to one husband, to Christ" as "a pure virgin" (2 Cor 11:2). They are the betrothed (19:7) who become the bride and wife (21:2, 9) of Christ.

Yet this goes even further, for this describes the "wedding supper of the Lamb" (19:9). This is the same event as the "messianic banquet" elsewhere, as in Luke 14:15, "Blessed is the one who will eat at the feast in the kingdom of God," or Matthew 8:11, "Many will come from the east and the west, and will take their places at the feast with Abraham, Isaac and Jacob in the kingdom of heaven" (also Luke 22:30). The idea of the messianic feast stems from Isaiah 25:6, "On this mountain the Lord God Almighty will prepare a feast of rich food for all people." It was developed further during the intertestamental period, as in 4 Ezra 2:38, "Rise and stand and see at the feast of the Lord the number of those who have been sealed" (also 1 Enoch 62:14; 2 Baruch 29:8; Testament of Isaac 6:22; 8:6). So this was a well-established expectation in Judaism.

The "bride has made herself ready" builds on 7:14, "they have washed their robes and made them white." Christ has purchased his followers with his blood (1:5; 5:9), and he expects them to put that into practice and live faithfully for him (2:10; 13:10; 14:12). He purifies us, and then we live pure lives (14:4, "they remained virgins"). This builds on Ezekiel 16:8–14, where God prepares Israel with wedding jewelry and garments to be his bride, but it adds the imagery of the bride making herself ready, which we will see in the next verse refers to the righteous deeds they perform.

The wedding day has arrived, so "God gives" (the divine passive *edothē*, "was given," see Rev 6:2, 4, 8) the bride her wedding gown. The "fine linen" is the luxurious linen of 18:12. Compare the garish ostentation of the great prostitute in 17:4 with the simple beauty here. These garments are "bright and clean/pure," symbolizing the bride's spiritual purity and victory (the meaning of white, pure garments in the book), like the armies of heaven in 19:14 that wear "fine linen, white and clean" (from Isa 61:10).

These garments are defined as "the righteous acts of God's holy people." There could well be a double meaning here—the righteous works of God on behalf of his people, namely redeeming, strengthening, and vindicating them, followed by their righteous deeds in response for all he has done. The victory of the saints takes place as they "overcome" their temptation, trials, and the actions of the cosmic powers against them (emphasized at the end of each of the seven letters in Rev 2–3).

A command to write is then given in 19:9–10. This command has been given several times, always at key junctures of the book (1:11, at the start of each of the seven letters, 14:13; 21:5). This is the fourth beatitude (see on 1:3) and introduces another image for the wedding. In 19:7 the saints are the bride, while here they are the invited guests. These are not two separate groups, and mixed metaphors like this were common in the ancient world. Those invited were the people who heeded the call of the gospel and became believers. This parallels 17:14, "his called, chosen and faithful followers." The verb is *kaleō*, translated "invited" here but the same term as "called" in 17:14. It likely combines the idea of an invited guest with connotations of election: These converts are those "called and chosen" by God.

The angel concludes with, "These are the true words of God," a saying that will be repeated in 21:5 and 22:6. This is similar to the "trustworthy saying" in 1 Timothy 1:15; 3:1; 4:9;

2 Timothy 2:11; Titus 3:8, an affirmation pointing to a particularly important truth. It likely refers to this whole section (Rev 19:6–10) as well as the beatitude. They must realize how true and crucial the wedding supper is. As the inaugural event of the **eschaton**, they must make certain they are indeed among the invited. Remember that half the bridesmaids in the parable of the 10 virgins in Matthew 25:1–13 were not allowed to enter the banquet.

John's natural response is to fall on his knees in worship (19:10). But he was standing before an angel, not God or Christ, and that was tantamount to idolatry. So the angel immediately says, "Don't do that!" What follows is an important reminder to all of us in an age when angels are often elevated to near-godlike status in some circles. He tells John he is not a quasi-divine figure but actually "a fellow servant with you" and all believers who "hold to the testimony of Jesus." Angels are celestial beings but are not above us in the hierarchy of created beings. They are parallel to us and in some ways serve us as messengers of God throughout Scripture, as seen in several Jewish writings.[1] The idea of angels as "fellow slaves" means that like us they serve God and belong to him. In the army of Christ the two will stand together (Rev 17:14; 19:14), and that will continue through eternity. "The testimony of Jesus" is a semi-technical phrase (1:2, 9; 12:17) describing the official witness to the world about Jesus, a task that belongs to angels as well as human believers.

This testimony or witness is further defined as "the Spirit of prophecy," a phrase that is difficult to understand. It could mean that the witness about Jesus forms the "essence" (rather than "Spirit") of prophecy or perhaps refers to Jesus' own witness as the essence of prophecy. Also, it could refer to the Holy Spirit who undergirds our witness and inspires this prophetic witness. Because of the importance of the Spirit in his prophetic role in the letters to the seven churches as well as in 14:13;

1. Apocalypse of Zephaniah 6:11–15; Ascension of Isaiah 7:21–22.

22:17, the third option is best. This means that the Spirit is not only behind the visions of this book but also active in empowering this prophetic witness through the church to the world.

THE CONQUERING CHRIST ARRIVES WITH THE ARMIES OF HEAVEN (19:11–16)

Throughout this book Christ is presented as conquering ram and Divine Warrior (1:14–16; 5:6b; 6:16; 11:15; 14:14; 17:14), and this imagery culminates in this passage. The **Parousia** of Christ is seen from the perspective of the conquering King come to destroy his enemies and establish his reign. The characteristics of the rider on the white horse (19:11–13) lead to his actions (19:14–16). Of the two aspects of the second coming passages—the "rapture" of the church and the judgment upon sinners—this section entirely centers on the second.

The opening two pictures govern the whole. As in 4:1 (also 11:19; 15:5, where the temple is opened), John sees "heaven standing open," meaning God is about to act in this world in a decisive way. This was a significant motif for the early church (Mark 1:10; John 1:51; Acts 7:56; 10:11; 2 Cor 12:1–2, building on Ezek 1:1), meaning that the consummation of God's acts in history is imminent. The **eschaton**/end has arrived. The second is the appearance of the rider on the white horse, building on the ancient tradition that the conquering king rode a white horse into battle, signifying his invincibility. The earlier rider (Rev 6:2) brought war to this world, and this ultimate rider will bring the war that ends all wars. Now comes the sevenfold description of this rider:

1. He is called "faithful and true," building on his character as "faithful witness" in 1:5; 3:14 and as true to his calling and purposes in 3:7, 14; 19:11. The final war is mandated because Christ is faithful to his divine destiny and true in his judgments (16:7; 19:22, "true and just are your judgments"). Not only his character but also his words are "faithful and true" in 21:5; 22:6.

2. As the Warrior Messiah he "judges and makes war in justice/righteousness," with this double meaning intentional. He is just in his judgment and righteous as he goes to war against God's enemies. As God always judges "in righteousness" (Psa 7:11; 50:6; 96:13; Isa 11:4), so also his Son will dispense justice via his own righteous standards. Accordingly, the Godhead makes war against the forces of evil, cosmic and human (2:16, 26; 6:16; 17:14; 19:14–16). Of all the holy wars, this is the pinnacle—the true war to end all wars.
3. As Judge and Divine Warrior, his eyes are "like a blazing fire," repeating the description in 1:14; 2:18 and recalling Daniel 10:6 ("his eyes like flaming torches"). There it introduced "the man dressed in linen" as he prophesied regarding the "great war" (Dan 10:1). The image stresses the penetrating vision that discerns all and the fiery judgment that results. God knows all, which means he will miss nothing as he dispenses justice.
4. As royal Messiah Christ has "many crowns," and this is the "diadem" (*diadēma*) or royal crown rather than the victor's wreath (*stephanos*) found elsewhere in the New Testament for "crown." This word only occurs in two other places in the New Testament (Rev 12:3; 13:1), contrasting the pretentious "crowns" of the dragon and beast with the true crowns of Christ here. The false trinity again is guilty of the great imitation, for they are mere pretenders trying to claim a crown that can never be theirs.[2] Jesus wears many crowns because he is King of kings (19:16), and his rule is absolute and eternal.
5. He has "a name written on him that no one knows but he himself," building on 2:17 where the victorious saints are promised "a new name written that no one knows." Isaiah 62:2 tells Israel, "You will be called by a new name that

2. See "The Futility of Satan" in the introduction.

the mouth of the LORD will bestow" (see 65:15), and Christ tells the Philadelphian church, "I will write on them the name of my God … and my new name" (Rev 3:12). This is probably not the name of Yahweh, for that is not new (Phil 2:9); it is more likely this is a name hidden until the end of this evil age, when we will see the triune Godhead in all their revealed glory. At the second coming we will first learn the new name of Christ (here) and then will be given our new name (Rev 2:17).

6. As Christ rides the white horse, he is "dressed in a robe dipped in blood." The blood could be the blood of Jesus as atoning sacrifice (1:5; 5:9; 7:14; 12:11), or the blood of the martyrs sacrificed for him (6:10; 16:6; 17:6; 18:24; 19:2). Yet the context is military, so this is better seen as the blood of his enemies, a reference to his total victory over the enemies of God and his people. The image goes back to Isaiah 63:3, where it is combined with the winepress image of the wrath of God (see Rev 14:10). It continues the theme of ***lex talionis***: The terrible crimes of these evil people must be answered with divine retribution.
7. His name is called, "the Word of God," paralleling the famous *logos* sayings of John 1:1–18 and found often in Revelation (1:2, 9; 6:9; 17:17; 20:4). In John, Jesus as the Word connotes the idea of Jesus as living Revealer of the Father, while here he is the authoritative Word, the proclaimer of salvation and of divine judgment. The spoken message is both military and forensic, both the sentence of guilt and the carrying out of the punishment. As such it is linked with the "sword from his mouth" in 19:15, the instrument of proclaiming and executing divine justice.

On the basis of his character, Christ performs four works in 19:11–16. They are both judicial ("he judges") and military ("he makes war"). Since he is "faithful and true" to his calling and to his role as the Word of God, both dimensions are necessary. He must act in accordance with his character as Judge and Warrior Messiah.

1. The "armies of heaven" follow after him, "riding on white horses and dressed in fine linen." These are the hosts of heaven, undoubtedly composed of angels ("hosts" in the Old Testament refers to the angelic heavenly army—Josh 5:13–15; 2 Kgs 6:17; Psa 103:20–21; Zech 14:5) along with the saints (see Rev 17:14). Like the Divine Warrior (19:11) they ride white horses, which is remarkable since in the ancient world only the conquering king did so. They are all pictured as conquerors, as they are called in the seven letters. They also wear fine linen like the bride in 19:8; the image of white linen depicts the Roman triumph and pictures the believers as already triumphant.
2. In 19:15 there comes from his mouth the "sharp sword" mentioned in 1:16; 2:12, 16, the symbol of Roman might and authority over life and death. These passages say that Christ alone is final authority, echoing Isaiah 11:4 (the justice with which Yahweh will rule the world) and 49:2 (the power of his word to deliver Israel and "strike the nations"). Here it signifies Jesus' proclamation of judgment on the forces of evil and the execution of that judgment in the destruction of the nations.
3. Then the Warrior Messiah will "rule them with an iron scepter," referring to Psalm 2:9, used also in Revelation 2:26–27 to depict the image of the shepherd's club that will "shatter the nations like pottery." This is not Christ *governing* the nations (with a royal scepter) but the conquering King *destroying* the nations (with a shepherd's club).
4. Finally, he will "tread the winepress of the fury of the wrath of God Almighty," combining the great winepress of 14:19–20 with the cup of God's furious wrath of 14:10 and 16:19. These are frightening pictures of absolute destruction, alluding to the winepress of Isaiah 63:1–6. The shedding of their blood is just payment for their slaughter of the saints (Rev 6:10; 16:6; 17:6; 18:24; 19:2) and is carried out by God Almighty, whose omnipotence guarantees that justice will be done.

The final point occurs in 19:16 and returns to the characteristics of Jesus Messiah: the name written "on his robe and on his thigh." Most likely this does not refer to two places but one, that spot on his robe at thigh level. This is where his sword would rest and where it could be seen as he rode a horse. There follows the fourth title of this section (with 19:11, 12b, 13b), summarizing the effects of the others. It is not Caesar but Christ who is truly "King of kings and Lord of lords" (the title already given to Jesus in 17:14). For Rome this meant Caesar was lord over the client kings in control of the provinces, but for Jesus it means he is Lord of the universe. Christ is sovereign over all, and he is now proving this by destroying the world of evil and the cosmic forces over it. The Warrior Messiah is God himself!

CARRION BIRDS ARE INVITED TO ANOTHER MESSIANIC BANQUET (19:17–18)

Now the vision switches from the returning Christ to the armies arrayed against him. As Christ descends from heaven with his celestial army composed of angels and saints, we turn to the situation on earth. There enters "an angel standing in the sun." Like Christ in 1:16, the mighty angel in 10:1, and the woman in 12:1, this angel is imbued with the radiant character of God. The message is gruesome and powerful, assuming the outcome of the battle before it is even joined. The carrion birds—eagles, vultures, hawks, and so on—are invited to "gather together for the great supper of God."

The implication is that there are two messianic banquets: the wedding feast *with* the Lamb for the saints and the terrible feast *on* the sinners by the carrion birds. The believers will partake of the greatest banquet in history, and the unbelievers will become the greatest banquet predators ever seen. This image is drawn from Ezekiel 39:17–20, where the birds and wild animals are invited to feast on Gog. There it took place after the battle was won, while here the invitation occurs before the battle even begins.

THE SWIFT BATTLE AND ITS AFTERMATH (19:19–21)

The false trinity began preparing for this battle in the sixth bowl of 16:13–16, sending out demonic spirits to call the nations to war. Now the kings and their armies who responded (they all did) are "gathered together to wage war," so the scene is set for the final battle. There will be no more atheists, for the world will recognizes the truth about the second coming. The beast will tell them that the conflict between God and Satan is real, but will convince them that the combined might of the world's armies under his generalship cannot lose. So they are waiting for Christ and the saints to come, thinking that their victory is a sure thing. There are many passages that describe the final **eschatological** war in the Old Testament (Isa 31:4; 59:17–20; 63:1–5; Ezek 38–39; Dan 12:1–3; Joel 3:9–16; Zech 12:3–9; 14:2–9) and in the New Testament (Luke 17:30; 21:27–36; 1 Thess 5:1–3; 2 Thess 2:8). This passage culminates the others.

Yet there is in reality no battle. The armies of the antichrist are waiting in 19:19, but when the sword of judgment comes from the Lord's mouth (19:15), the battle is instantly over and all the evil forces are dead on the battlefield. In 19:20 the beast and the false prophet are captured. The armies of Christ seemingly take no part in the fighting, because there is no fighting! It is over before it even begins. The part the saints play in shattering the nations (according to 2:26–27) is apparently to accompany the Warrior Messiah as he single-handedly decimates the enemy.

In language drawn from 13:12–15 and 16:14, we are told the reason why these two members of the false trinity had to be taken and their armies destroyed: the counterfeit miracles of the false prophet had deceived the sinful world and led them first to take the mark of the beast and then to worship his image. They had led the world in rebellion against God and then to commit final apostasy and idolatry. The guilt of the wicked nations is absolute and final. They have committed an "eternal sin" (Mark 3:29), and there is no more hope or mercy. These legal charges against them necessitate final judgment.

After the utter defeat and the indictment, the verdict is made and the sentence carried out (19:20c–21). As the dragon was thrown to earth (12:9), the beast and false prophet are thrown into the "lake of fire that burns with sulfur." It is important to realize that they are thrown in alive, indicating *conscious* punishment. The destiny of sinners, who are also thrown into the lake of fire in 20:14–15, is not soul sleep or annihilation but eternal, conscious torment in the lake of fire. The horror of the punishment is obvious, and one of the purposes of 19:6–20:15 is evangelistic. Unbelievers need to think carefully about their eternal destiny before rejecting Christ!

The idea of a lake of fire occurs only in Revelation in Scripture, and the background is complex. The antecedents appear to be Sodom, which was destroyed by fire and sulfur (Gen 19:24), and the Gehenna of the Gospels with its imagery of fiery punishment (Matt 5:22–30; 10:28; 18:9; 23:15). The depiction of this as a "lake of fire" is a natural extension. In the Old Testament, Daniel 7:9–11 speaks of a "river of fire" flowing from the throne of God, and in Jewish apocalyptic literature 1 Enoch 90:24–27 depicts the wicked thrown into "a fiery Abyss and burned." Other apocalyptic works speak of a great river of fire (2 Enoch 10:2; Sibylline Oracles 2:196–209), so this image of a fiery lake becomes a natural next step in the imagery.

After the fate of the beast and false prophet, the destruction of the armies in 19:21 demonstrates clearly the effects of the sword from Christ's mouth. As stated earlier, this pictures first the proclamation of guilt and the legal punishment effected by the crimes and then the sentence as it is carried out. The declaration and the execution of the sentence are both part of the imagery. Every member of the army of the antichrist is killed, and the promise made to the martyrs in 6:11 has been fulfilled.

The feast promised to the scavenger birds in 19:17–18 is now here. All the birds that come are able to "gorge themselves on the flesh." This is a further example of ***lex talionis***, the law of retribution. In 11:7–10 the beast slays the two witnesses and then refuses them burial. Now the Lord shows them the same indignity and degradation. The ultimate humiliation in the ancient world was to be denied burial. God is turning upon their own heads what they have done to the martyrs.

Revelation 19:1–21 shows us that there are only two kinds of people in the world: those who follow Christ and those who reject Christ. Both will participate in great banquets: believers will feast at the wedding supper of the Lamb, and unbelievers will *be* the feast, eaten by the carrion birds. The event that will end world history is the battle of Armageddon, but there will be no battle; every soldier of the beast's army will be destroyed as Christ comes to exercise judgment and vindicate his people. The second coming of Christ, the event Christians have been awaiting for over two thousand years, will finally take place when he comes as the Divine Warrior, the conquering King, to destroy the enemies of God. Evil is doomed, and those who turn from God to embrace wickedness will face the divine wrath. As we look ahead to this moment, we must acknowledge that there is no issue more serious than this: to decide whether we want to follow Christ or take our chances with the ways of the fallen world. If we believe Christ's assurance that the end of world history will come in this way, the choice is clear.

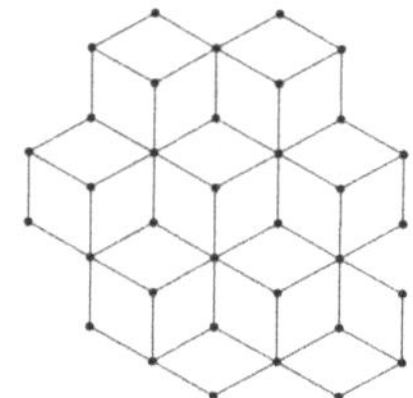

THE THOUSAND-YEAR REIGN AND FINAL JUDGMENT

(20:1–15)

There is nothing explicit about the earthly reign of the Messiah in the Old Testament, but there are several passages on the coming kingdom of God on earth, and these provide the background for the concept of a "millennial" reign of Christ (Psa 72:8–14; Isa 11:6–9; Zech 14:5–17). The early rabbis had such a concept, with lengths ranging from 40 years (built on the wilderness wanderings) to 400, to 4,000 years. The early church debated "chiliasm," their term for the thousand (Greek *chilias*)-year reign, for the first three centuries until Augustine won the day for the amillennial position. The premillennial position did not reappear until the Pietist movement of the 1700s and the Plymouth Brethren movement in England in the 1800s.

Three positions have dominated the scene. To take them in chronological order, premillennialism (the dominant view in the early centuries) believes Christ will return to earth, destroy the army of the beast, and then reign on earth for a lengthy period (seeing the thousand years symbolically), leading into the final judgment and beginning of eternity. The amillennial position denies any earthly reign and says the thousand-year period symbolizes the church age. Postmillennialism believes that this will be a period of triumph for the gospel and a time of peace that will precede the second coming. As we go through 20:1–10 I will try to highlight which sections favor one or the other view. Overall, premillennialism takes the symbols more literally and amillennialism takes them more symbolically.

This passage is part of 17:1–20:15, which centers on God's final judgment and destruction of the evil forces that have dominated this world since Adam and Eve. There is an A-B-A pattern: the judgment of the sinners (19:11–21; 20:11–15) and vindication of the saints (20:1–10) have been promised since 6:9–11, and now that promise is realized. Whichever position we prefer for this passage, all recognize the structure: the opening event (the binding of Satan, 20:1–3); life during the earthly reign (20:4–6), and the aftermath (final defeat of Satan, 20:7–10).

Three themes stand out:

1. The judgment of the dragon, anticipated throughout the visions, now occurs. It takes place in two stages. First he is bound/jailed in the Abyss for the thousand years (20:1–3) and then defeated and cast into the lake of fire (20:7–10).
2. The defense of the justice of God in Revelation culminates here. The nations have rejected every attempt to bring them to repentance, and now those who are not part of the beast's army live through the millennial period. Yet in all that time of experiencing Christ's benign rule, none of them repent, and as soon as Satan is released, they all flock to join him. This proves the depths of depravity and necessitates the final judgment of 20:11–15.
3. The final vindication of the saints, in which God avenges their blood (20:7–10, 11–15, see 6:9–11) and gives them glory (20:4–6), occurs now. The saints reign with Christ and share his authority (fulfilling 2:26–27, 3:21). The promises come to reality, and this provides a bridge to the full realization of these promises in the new heaven and new earth of 21:1–22:5.

CHRIST REIGNS FOR A THOUSAND YEARS (20:1–10)

THE BINDING OF SATAN (20:1–3)

The same angel as in 9:1 descends from heaven with a key to the Abyss. In 9:1 the star/angel opened the Abyss and initiated the time of the false trinity's short period of ascendancy over the nations. Now he will close the Abyss, ending that period. God, not Satan, determines the time and the extent of the false trinity's power over this world. The Abyss is the prison-house of demonic spirits (2 Pet 2:4; Jude 6) where they await their final destiny. The key here is the fourth in Revelation (with 1:18; 3:7; 9:1), demonstrating God's control over his created realm. The angel has not only a key but also a great chain in order to bind Satan all the more securely. This intensifies the prison imagery. The Gadarene demoniac was strong enough to break his chains (Mark 5:4), but the size of the great or large chain will not allow that here. Satan is triply bound: a jail, a chain, a key to lock him in!

The angel then seizes the dragon (20:2), in a sense grabbing him by the scruff of his neck, showing the dragon's utter powerlessness. The rest of the verse records the indictment and repeats the list of evil titles from 12:9.[1] The names are official, in a sense picturing the legal sentence being read in God's law court. The dragon is guilty because he is "the ancient serpent," Leviathan, the serpent of the garden. He stands before God without excuse, for he is the devil or Satan, the adversary who accuses God's people day and night (12:10) and seeks to deceive them into sin.

Therefore, he must be bound in his prison "for a thousand years." "Bound" and "thrown" are normal language for an official arrest and incarceration. It recalls Mark 3:27, where Jesus is the stronger man who enters Satan's fortress and binds him. Jesus considered his exorcisms a "binding of Satan" and of his demonic realm. This passage borrows that imagery and also

1. See the commentary there.

recalls Isaiah 24:21–22, where God declares his victory over the evil powers of heaven and earth: "They will be herded together like prisoners bound in a dungeon; they will be shut up in a prison and be punished after many days." There it was the pantheon of pagan gods that was brought down; here it is the fallen angels.

The "thousand years" is an apocalyptic number. There are various periods for God's final reign found in Jewish literature. In 1 Enoch 21:6 it is 10 million years, while in 4 Ezra 7:28 it is 400 years, and the rabbis varied from 40 to 7,000 years. This thousand-year period could stem from reflection on Psalm 90:4, "a thousand years in your sight are like a day." Jubilees 23:27–28 says that in the messianic kingdom people will live for a thousand years. The question for us is whether this should be seen as a literal period of time or a symbolic use of numbers. Numbers in Revelation tend to be symbolic, and that is likely the case here. As the half-hour in Revelation 8:1 and the hour in Revelation 18:9–19 refer to very short periods, this likely connotes a lengthy period of time. Note the contrasts between the short period of the antichrist's reign (42 months) and the very long period of Christ's reign here.

As Michael threw the dragon out of heaven in 12:9, so the angel now throws Satan into the Abyss (20:3). There is great emphasis on the extent to which Satan is sealed in his prison, intensifying the idea that he is locked in his cell and connoting an absolutely secure situation. Satan will not only be thrown into his jail cell but shackled to its wall with the chain, then locked into that cell with the key. The purpose is to ensure that Satan cannot "deceive the nations anymore." In 12:9 the primary purpose of the dragon was to "deceive the whole world" (also 13:14; 18:23).

There is debate over the nature of this binding of Satan. The amillennial position takes this as a description of the church age, saying that Satan is restricted from stopping the missionary enterprise of God's people. He can deceive the unsaved but cannot keep them from responding to the gospel.

Certainly this view is viable, but I maintain that the language of binding here is much stronger than this. It says here that Satan will not be able to "deceive the nations," yet that is exactly what he does in this present age. During the time of the millennial reign, Satan will not be present and will be kept from deceiving the nations. In this present age, he is only restricted with respect to believers; he has full control over the unbelieving nations. He "blinds their minds" (2 Cor 4:4), traps them (1 Tim 3:7), and devours them (2 Pet 5:8). In Revelation 20:1–10 he does not deceive anyone until the period is ended (20:7–8). Therefore, this is not the partial binding of the present age but the full binding of a future period after Christ returns.

Who are "the nations"? Most likely they are the same as in the rest of the book—the unsaved people among the earthly nations. Those who were killed in 19:21 constituted the army of the beast. The rest of the unbelieving world who were not part of the army will live through the battle and be present for the millennial reign of Christ. They are the people/nations over whom the saints will reign with Christ.

Note how Satan's release is phrased: "afterward he *must* be set free for a short time." God has determined that there has to be a final appearance of Satan, referring to the event in 20:7–10. We are not told why it is necessary, yet it is understandable. God's purpose is to prove the extent to which total depravity controls the unbelievers. For the entire "thousand years" the nations—the earth-dwellers who were not part of the beast's army and did not die in 19:21—will dwell under Jesus' benign rule and will not experience the evil machinations of Satan. Yet the moment Satan is released they are deceived all over again and flock after him. Thereby they prove the eternal hold that sin has over them and demonstrate the necessity of eternal punishment at the final judgment of 20:11–15. This millennial reign is the final proof—the judicial evidence—of the guilt of sinners.

The Thousand-Year Reign of the Saints (20:4–6)

Literally 20:4 reads, "And I saw thrones, and they sat on them, and judgment was given to them." Who are "they"? It could be the heavenly tribunal, the elders on thrones in 4:4 and 11:16; or perhaps the martyrs, now vindicated (6:11; 16:6; 18:20, 24) and reigning with Christ. Yet if we see 20:4 as a whole, it would refer to all the saints, with the martyrs a special subset within the larger group. A reference to all the saints who have refused to worship the beast makes more sense, and this would include not just the tribulation saints but also all believers throughout history who have refused to worship false pretenders who give themselves god-like status. In 3:21 Christ promises the overcomers "the right to sit with me on the throne" (see also 2:26–27; 3:12; 5:10), and this fits Matthew 19:28 ("sit on thrones judging the twelve tribes") and 1 Corinthians 6:2–3 ("the Lord's people will judge the world" and "judge angels"). The martyrs are the primary group in Revelation 20:4, and in the larger context (such as 20:9, "the camp of the saints") all who have remained faithful to Christ are included.

As they sit on the thrones, God gives them "authority to judge," alluding to Daniel 7:22 in the **Septuagint**: "Judgment was given to the saints of the Most High." This builds also on the passages noted in the previous paragraph, and many believe this means not only judging but also ruling over the nations. For this period, the saints will govern the nations under Christ. These victorious Christians have done three things for Christ: They have been beheaded/martyred, they have refused to worship the beast, and they have refused to accept his mark. The reason for all of this is repeated from 1:2, 9 (also 6:9; 12:17; 19:10)—"their testimony about Jesus" and "the word of God." They have maintained their witness and remained faithful in the face of incredible persecution. They have earned the right to sit on Christ's court and help adjudicate God's laws in this final period before the last judgment.

The next part is also at the heart of the millennial debate. John says they "came to life" (Greek *ezēsan*). If this means they have been raised bodily from the dead, then this indeed does occur after Christ's return. This is clearly the meaning in 20:5 (the "rest of the dead" coming to life) as well as passages on people returning to life (Matt 9:18; John 11:25; Rom 14:9). It refers to Christ's resurrection in Revelation 1:18; 2:8 and the beast's coming back to life in Revelation 13:14. Those who hold the amillennial view say this refers to either the new spiritual life after conversion, the exaltation of the saints to heaven after death, or the intermediate state. Yet the verb regularly in the New Testament refers to physical life and better fits the idea of bodily resurrection. So this pictures the saint's resurrection at the second coming and then their reign with Christ for the "thousand years." This is another of the primary purposes of this millennial period—the vindication and exaltation of those who lost all for the cause of Christ.

John now tells us in 20:5 that "the rest of the dead," most likely the unbelievers, "did not come to life until the thousand years were ended." Most versions correctly recognize this verse as a parenthesis addressing the situation of the sinners who have died, namely those who died in the battle of 19:19–21 (Armageddon) and the unsaved dead throughout history. This means that when unbelievers die, their next conscious moment will be when they face God at the last judgment, unlike Christians, who go immediately to heaven to be with the Lord.

In 20:5b John returns to the subject of the exalted saints in 20:4 and states that their "coming to life" is "the first resurrection." While some see this as the moment after death when believers go to heaven in the intermediate state, it is closely connected to 20:4, namely "coming to life and reigning with Christ." Thus it refers to the resurrection at Christ's second coming when the saints receive their resurrection bodies (1 Cor 15:51–52; 1 Thess 4:13–18). So believers experience the first resurrection while unbelievers experience only the "second death" (20:6). This is the point of John 5:29, which speaks of Christians "rising to life" and of non-Christians "rising to judgment."

In 20:6 the fifth beatitude (1:3; 14:13; 16:15; 19:9) addresses the blessed state of those who share, or have a part in, the first resurrection. This is the only beatitude in the New Testament with a second adjective ("blessed and holy") describing the true nature of the "saints/holy ones" who have been set apart from this world for God and thereby inherit eternal life. Christ and God are "holy and true" (3:7; 4:8; 6:10), and the saints share their holiness in this life and for eternity. There is a further contrast between those who have a part in resurrection life and those who have no share in "the tree of life and in the holy city" (22:19) but instead have a part in the lake of fire (21:8).

There are three characteristics of those who partake of the first resurrection:

1. The "second death has no power over them," namely eternal death in the lake of fire. Believers experience the first death, which ends their earthly existence, but receive the crown of life rather than the second death (2:10–11). For them death is "the last enemy" that is destroyed (1 Cor 15:26, 54–55). For the faithful, the second death is powerless.
2. They will be "priests of God and of Christ," as in 1:6; 5:10 (from Exod 19:6) and a significant theme in the book (7:15; 22:3). Angels are the priests of heaven, and the saints will join them in serving God for eternity. We have a priestly role now as we faithfully worship God and witness for Christ to the nations. As Christ is the "priest-king," we share in that as his "kingdom and priests" (1:6).
3. The faithful "reign with him for a thousand years," repeating 20:4 and a foretaste of our eternal reign (22:5). So the destiny of the believers is to worship the Godhead as priests and rule with them as royalty.

The Release of Satan and the Final Battle (20:7–10)

There are five aspects of to this scene: the release of Satan, his deception and gathering of the nations, his army surrounding God's people, their destruction as fire descends from heaven, and the casting of Satan into the lake of fire. God is absolutely sovereign, and he orchestrates the events. The scene is built on Gog and Magog in Ezekiel 38–39, the model for the final **eschatological** war in Judaism.

Satan is not released until "the thousand years were over," as was said in 20:3. This is evidence for the premillennial position, for it is clear Satan was not allowed to deceive the nations *at all* during that period. He is "released from his prison" on parole, and it is clear from 20:3 ("must be set free") that this is part of the divine plan, allowing a final period of deception to prove the extent of human depravity. Now the time of deception begins anew, and every unbeliever among the nations immediately flocks to Satan. It is as if for the entire time they were under Christ's rule, they longed for Satan to return. They have never responded to the gospel during that lengthy time, and now they demonstrate once and for all the depth of their depravity. Their sin is eternal, and so eternal punishment is the only valid option.

In 20:8 Satan goes out with a twofold purpose: to "deceive the nations" and to "gather them for battle." As in 12:9 and 20:3 it is clear that Satan does not overpower people—he deceives them with lies that convince them to follow him. His ultimate purpose is to gather the armies of the nations for the final battle, a last-ditch effort to snatch victory out of defeat. He goes out to "the four corners of the earth," namely the whole world, to unite all the nations for war. Their number is "like the sand on the seashore," a common image for an innumerable host (Josh 11:4; 1 Sam 13:5).

The nations are identified here as "Gog and Magog," a reference to Ezekiel 38–39, where Gog (the king of the northern lands) and Magog (= "the land of Gog") come to wage war against God's people. With a similar order of events to Revelation, the coalition of nations comes to destroy them (Ezek 38) yet are destroyed themselves (Ezek 39), followed by the glorified people of God enjoying the **eschatological** temple (Ezek 40–48). John sees the millennial events as a fulfillment of that prophecy. Gog and

Magog symbolize all the nations uniting to oppose Christ and his followers. God here, as in Ezekiel, is a covenant God who is faithful to his beleaguered people and will deliver them from their enemies.

The purpose of Satan's strategy is another important part of the millennial debate—"to gather them for battle." The wording is taken verbatim from Revelation 16:14 and leads many to posit that 20:8 describes the same battle as 16:14, and thereby that 20:1–10 is cyclical, describing the church age. If this is true, 20:7–10 depict the battle of Armageddon that ends the church age, and 16:14–16; 19:11–21; and 20:7–10 portray the same event. However, when you look at the details of 19:11–21 and 20:7–10, the only real similarity is that one clause. In chapter 19 Christ returns, the beast leads the war, and only the beast's army is destroyed by the sword from Christ's mouth. In chapter 20 Christ has been reigning on earth a thousand years, the war is led by Satan, and all the sinners are destroyed, this time by fire from heaven. The details are too different and more likely are describing two battles separated by "a thousand years."

The massive host of unsaved humanity now marches across the earth to "surround the camp of God's people" (20:9). This includes every unbeliever who lived through the millennial period. The language indicates a military attack with armies coming from all around the world to strike at the saints. The "camp of the saints" recalls the camps of the 12 tribes around the tabernacle during the wilderness wanderings (Exod 33:7–11; Num 2:1–34). This pictures God's people once more hunted down yet protected by God even from a vast, seemingly invincible foe. The camp is situated in "the city he loves," namely Jerusalem. In 11:8 Jerusalem was an apostate city and with Rome became the capital city of the beast. Now it has been reinstated to the sacred city it was in the Old Testament.

As in 19:19–21, the enemy comes to do battle, but there is no battle. The evil intentions come to naught, for God takes over, sends fire from heaven, and consumes the armies of Satan. The "ascent" of the unbelievers (translated "marched" in the

NIV) against the saints is more than matched by the "descent" of the fire from heaven, echoing the fire in 2 Kings 1:10, 12 that consumed the soldiers who opposed Elijah as well as the fire sent down upon the soldiers of Gog and Magog (Ezek 38:22; 39:6). So the enemies of God and his people are consumed by fire, a foretaste of the eternal punishment that awaits them in 20:13–15.

Now God turns his attention to "the devil who deceived them" (20:10), with "devil" the Greek translation of the Hebrew *satan*.[2] In 19:20–21 the two other members of the false trinity, the dragon and the false prophet, were thrown into the lake of fire. Now the founding member, the devil/Satan, follows them into eternal punishment. There are three stages by which the lake of fire is populated: first the two beasts (19:20–21), then Satan (20:10), and finally their unbelieving followers (20:13–15). So now the devil is "thrown into the lake of burning sulfur," paralleling the punishment of Gog in Ezekiel 38:22: "I will pour down torrents of rain, hailstones, and burning sulfur on him." Satan is aware of his certain defeat, as in Matthew 8:29 where the demons ask, "Have you come here to torment us before the appointed time?" and in Revelation 12:12 where we are told that Satan "knows his time is short."

In conclusion, while the amillennial view is viable, it is my firm opinion that the language and details of 20:1–10 best fit a premillennial perspective. We dare not be dogmatic about the issue, though, for this is the only biblical passage that clearly discusses the event, and Old Testament passages like Isaiah 11:6–9 or Zechariah 14:5–17 can be made to fit whatever position we choose. Nevertheless, it is still an important question, and I feel the evidence is sufficient to support an earthly reign of Christ between his return and final judgment.

The purpose of this earthly reign of Christ is twofold: the vindication and exaltation of the saints, providing an important transition from their earthly suffering to their heavenly

2. See the commentary on 12:9.

glory; and the final proof of the eternal nature of the depravity of the sinners, who even after experiencing Satan for a single lifetime and Christ for 14 lifetimes (70 years x 14 = 980 years) flock after Satan the moment he is released. This then leads to the necessity of eternal punishment in 20:11–15. The truth is that even after a billion years those who are controlled by sin will still hate Christ!

The implications for us are critical. Those who choose the world throughout their lives and plan to make a last-minute decision for Christ so as to get into heaven are deluding themselves. Every day they turn from Christ further hardens their hearts, and if they have time at the end of their lives to make a decision, it will be governed by a lifetime of rejecting Christ. For those of us who are Christians, this millennial period will be a glorious time of enjoying Christ's presence and getting to know the countless believers from throughout history.

GOD JUDGES FROM A GREAT WHITE THRONE (20:11–15)

THE GREAT WHITE THRONE (20:11)

This episode begins similarly to 4:2, with a heavenly throne and God seated on it. This scene also culminates 19:11–21, where Christ came to earth in order to defeat and destroy the forces of evil. Now that purpose is brought to completion in the last judgment. The throne is central throughout the book, connoting God as sovereign Lord over his creation. Here the throne is also the Bema seat, where the King acts as Judge over his kingdom. Only here is there a further description of it. It is the "great" throne in that it is not immense but also majestic beyond description. When we think of the spectacular thrones uncovered through archaeology and those of our day (like the Queen of England), we must realize how insignificant they are compared to the eternal throne of God. It is also "white," which throughout Revelation symbolizes purity, holiness, and triumph (1:14; 4:4; 6:11; 7:9; 14:14; 19:11).

Before the new age can begin, this present age must come to an end. So "earth and sky flee from his presence, and there [is] no place for them." This builds on Isaiah 51:6, which says, "The heavens will vanish like smoke; the earth will wear out like a garment" (also Psa 102:26; Ezek 32:7–8). The event is described in 2 Peter 3:7, 10, "The heavens will disappear with a roar; the elements will be destroyed by fire, and the earth and everything in it will be laid bare." Romans 8:18–22 tells us that creation itself longs for this day. It is groaning, filled with frustration because of the sin and decay humankind has brought upon it. God's creation longs for the day when it will be refashioned and become what God originally meant it to be, part of "a new heaven and a new earth" (Rev 21:1). So here they flee (6:14; 16:20) because there is no place for them. They are filled with sin and therefore have no place in the presence of God. As in 16:20, total destruction is connoted, and in 21:1 the new heaven and new earth are able to descend "because the first heaven and the first earth have passed away."

THE JUDGMENT OF THE RIGHTEOUS (20:12)

The identity of "the dead" in 20:12 is debated, and the majority of scholars take the whole of 20:12–13 as the judgment of sinners. Yet I believe this follows the pattern of the harvest scene in chapter 14, where I argued that the grain harvest (14:14–16) is the saints and the grape harvest (14:17–20) the sinners. In favor of the dead in 20:12 being the righteous would be 1) they are "standing before the throne," paralleling Christ in 5:6 and the saints in 7:9; and 2) the opening of the book of life takes place here but not in 20:13, connoting that their names are written in it in contrast to the sinners (20:15). If Daniel 12:1–2 is behind this image, this would mean, as it does there, that "everyone whose name was found written in it will be delivered ... to everlasting life." Against such an understanding would be that the righteous "came to life" before the millennium in 20:4, while here they are "the dead, great and small," which could be taken to mean they are the unbelievers of 20:5. But the dead in 20:12–13 could be those who have experienced earthly death, with 20:12 being those who "came to life" in 20:4 and 20:13 being "the rest of the dead" in 20:5. So my view is that 20:12 is the judgment of the righteous, a judgment of rewards. The group of the dead in 20:12 is the same group that came to life before the millennium in 20:4 (the righteous), and the dead in 20:13 are the "rest of the dead" from 20:5.

The "books" (containing the deeds of the righteous) are opened before the council of heaven and the "Ancient of Days" (from Dan 7:10), and the saints give account to God (Heb 13:17) in order to be approved by him (2 Tim 2:15). Next we have another book opened, namely "the book of life." The first books contain the deeds of believer and unbeliever alike; this book contains the names of the citizens of heaven, those who have eternal life, built on Daniel 12:1–2 (noted above). Elsewhere it is used negatively, stressing those *not* in the book (Rev 3:5; 13:8; 17:8; 20:15). Here it is those who are in the book, those who belong to heaven and are God's special people.

Here those who have life are "judged according to their works." This is a virtual definition of the issue of rewards in Scripture. All that we have done for God and for others will be returned to us and will be ours for eternity. In Luke 16:9–13 this is pictured as a return on investment, with our deeds placed in the bank of heaven and then given to us when we enter heaven. This theme is found often in the Old Testament (Job 34:11; Psa 28:4; Jer 17:10; Ezek 18:20) and New Testament (Matt 16:27; Rom 14:12; 2 Cor 5:10; 1 Pet 1:17). It is important to separate this from justification by faith. Ephesians 2:8–9 makes it clear that we are saved by grace, not by works. However, believers will at the end of our lives "give account" to God (Heb 13:7) and repent of unconfessed sin as well as receive our rewards for what we have done for God and others.

The Judgment of the Sinners (20:13–15)

The "sea" (12:12; 13:1) along with "death and Hades" (1:18; 6:8) both personify the realm of evil in Revelation. The sea is said to be destroyed in 21:1, yet it gives up its dead here. This is in keeping with apocalyptic symbolism, in which each vision is intended to be taken as a self-contained unit. The sea is the realm of evil, and it surrenders its dead for final judgment. This is the "second resurrection" implied in 20:5, as the unrighteous dead now come to life to give account to God. When they stand before God, ***lex talionis*** functions once more, and they are "judged according to what they have done" during their earthly lives (the same as the righteous in 20:12). This has led many, such as Dante in *The Inferno* or Milton in *Paradise Lost*, to posit degrees of punishment in hell to parallel the degrees of reward in heaven. This cannot ultimately be proven, but on the basis of this passage it must remain a possibility. However, this is not the same as the doctrine of purgatory, for which I see no evidence in the Bible.

After the final judgment takes place, the evil powers join the false trinity in the lake of fire (20:14). First, "death and Hades," personifying the demonic forces, are cast into the fiery lake. As Paul says in 1 Corinthians 15:26, "The last enemy to be destroyed is death"; this includes both physical death and the purveyors of death, the fallen angels. The added note here, "The lake of fire is the second death," clarifies 20:6, "The second death has no power over them" (the righteous). Eternal punishment is reserved for the hardened sinners and is powerless over believers, who will inherit eternal life. So at this point all the evil powers—the false trinity and the demonic realm—are forever removed from contact with the people of God. God has eradicated evil for all eternity!

In 20:15 we return to "the book of life" and to those whose "names are not found in it." The final stage in the removal of evil is the casting of unbelievers into the lake of fire. We must understand that the "second death" (20:6) does not constitute death in the same way as earthly death, that is, the cessation of earthly existence. There is no end of life here but rather ongoing conscious punishment. Yet it is still death, because there is no experience of goodness or of God to be had for the rest of eternity. They have no part in God's people and no future with God. A holy God must eradicate evil and since created beings are eternal, this must mean everlasting punishment.[3] The idea of fiery judgment occurs in Daniel 7:9–11 (the beast "thrown into a blazing fire") and Isaiah 66:24 ("the fire that burns them will not be quenched"). There is no biblical answer as to how literal this fire is intended to be. The image so permeates Scripture that the default position is that it is literal, but we must await the final judgment to know for sure.

The entire Bible has looked forward to this sequence of events that will end the reign of evil and transition into the eternal reign of the triune Godhead. The same is true of the final judgment of the evil powers and the sinners who follow them. All of us, saint and sinner alike, will face God, give account of our lives, and be judged or rewarded on the basis of what we have done. Divine justice demands this, and the end of evil is necessary before eternity in the heaven of goodness can begin. Sinners, the fallen angels, and Death and Hades itself, must be thrown into eternal darkness and torment to make way for the joy and blessedness of the "new heaven and new earth." Moreover, it is clear this cannot be annihilation but conscious torment for eternity (Rev 14:10–11; 19:20; 20:10; 20:13–15).

We speak of "getting ready for retirement," saving funds that will take us through our twilight years. How about preparing for our eternal "retirement" and taking eternal rewards with us into our heavenly existence? Everything we do now for God, the church, and others will become our eternal reward. I challenge you, the reader, to live for eternity and not just for the present.

3. Since animals were part of Eden and are mentioned often in Old Testament passages depicting the future world, it is likely that animals will be in heaven. However, there is no biblical evidence that animals have eternal souls.

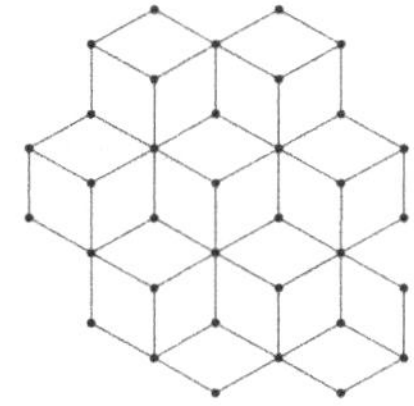

A NEW HEAVEN AND A NEW EARTH
(21:1–27)

From the moment Adam and Eve lost their place in the garden/paradise, the divine plan and all of Scripture have been focused on the moment when sin will be eradicated and God's creation can return to its original purpose. Not just the book of Revelation but all of Scripture has prepared for the events of chapter 21. The weaknesses of the seven churches are now overturned in the strengths and perfection of the holy city, the new Jerusalem; the visions of the book, centering as they have on the vindication of the saints and just punishment of the sinners, now culminate in the vision of the perfect goodness of the citizens of heaven. The spiritual peace and joy of the earthly kingdom has been a foretaste of what is now revealed: the far greater glory of God's whole and holy people as they enter eternity. God's plan of salvation now reaches its final stage, and the saints, who spiritually experienced God's presence in their earthly life, now bask in his real presence and have eternal peace and joy with him.

This chapter is organized like chapters 12–13, with a thesis paragraph in 21:1–8 (the descent of the holy city) followed by two expansions of this opening vision, viewing the new Jerusalem as an eternal holy of holies (21:9–27) and then as the final **eschatological** Eden (22:1–5). As with the previous visions in the book, this one is likely symbolic, with the descent of the new Jerusalem signifying the arrival of the new heaven and new earth and the initiation of eternity with God. The new Jerusalem is the reality that finalizes the hopes of God's people and rewards them for all they have endured for him.

JOHN SEES THE NEW HEAVEN AND NEW EARTH (21:1–8)

This is a transition passage similar to the Hallelujah Choruses of 19:1–10. It concludes the visions of 19:11–21:8 and introduces the heavenly visions of 21:9–22:5. As such it bridges from the earthly scenes to the heavenly, culminating the scenes of the **eschaton**—the **Parousia**, Armageddon, millennium, and last judgment—and initiating the final scenes that depict the eternal state of God's people.

THE BASIC VISION (21:1–2)

Isaiah concludes his prophecy with the promise that God will make a "new heaven and new earth" (Isa 65:17; 66:12); and 2 Peter 3:13 states that the fiery destruction of the old earth would lead to a "new heaven and new earth." Sin has so sullied God's first creation that it must be replaced, and Romans 8:18–22 states that creation itself longs for that day when it will be recreated anew. Two ideas existed side by side in Judaism, one teaching a renovated, transfigured earth (Jubilees 1:29; 4:26; 1 Enoch 45:4–5), and the other the destruction of the present world and a brand new creation (1 Enoch 72:1, 83:3–4; 2 Baruch 44:12). This and 2 Peter 3 likely follow the second tradition, with God creating a new order and a new world. We know little of what form it will take. With a physical resurrection and the imagery of a "new earth" with streets and so on, some aspect of physicality seems indicated. But we will have to wait and see what exactly it will be. All we know for sure is that it will be wondrous beyond imagination! The absence of any sea in 21:1 means the complete absence of evil. Sin and all its manifestations in the demonic forces and the wicked nations will be gone forever.

With the new heaven and new earth in place, then "the holy city, the new Jerusalem" will "descend out of heaven from God" (21:2). The earthly Jerusalem had apostatized by crucifying the Lord (11:8), opposing the two witnesses (11:2), and joining Babylon the Great as the "great city" (11:8; 16:19; 17:18). Now it has returned to Christ (20:9) and is once more the "holy city." In Isaiah the new, glorified Jerusalem will become the world's religious center (Isa 2:1–5) with Yahweh its Redeemer (59:20) and become "Jerusalem, the holy city" (52:1). There will be a "new exodus" with the garden of Eden restored (Ezek 36:35) and God's sanctuary reestablished: "My dwelling place will be with them. I will be their God, and they will be my people" (Ezek 37:27). In the New Testament this theme is continued in Galatians 4:26 ("the Jerusalem that is above") and Hebrews 12:22 ("the heavenly Jerusalem").

In John 1:51, Jesus said that in his coming to earth his disciple Nathanael would "see heaven open, and the angels of God ascending and descending on the Son of Man." In other words, Jesus is Jacob's ladder, and he has brought heaven down to earth (see Gen 28:12). In the new heaven and new earth the two are finally completely united. There will never again be an earth "down here" and a heaven "up there." The heavenly temple of Revelation 7:15; 11:19; 14:15–17 has descended in the form of a city and has become the eternal home of the saints.

In its beauty and joy the city is "prepared as a bride beautifully dressed for her husband." The church is "the bride of the Lamb," with her dress constituting her "righteous deeds" (19:7–8). Here the holy city is like a bride, echoing Isaiah 54:5–6, where Zion is the wife of Yahweh with precious stones (54:11) and "garments of salvation" (61:10). In a very real sense the new Jerusalem is both the place the saints will reside for eternity and a symbol for the people themselves, describing their future state as well as their future home.

THE VOICE FROM THE THRONE (21:3–4)

The throne-room voice, likely an angelic herald with a message from God, interprets the meaning of the heavenly city, drawing upon Old Testament motifs. The covenant of Sinai is fulfilled as the holiness code from Leviticus 26:11–12 comes to fruition: "I will put my dwelling place among you. ... I will walk among you and be your God, and you will be my people." This covenant promise reverberated through the Old Testament (Exod 29:45; Jer 31:33; Ezek 37:27 [the verse behind the wording here]; Zech 2:11). "The dwelling of God" is a virtual translation of the "Shekinah" (from Hebrew *shakan*, "to dwell"), typified in the pillar of fire by night and the cloud by day of the exodus as well as the cloud that filled the tabernacle. This primary covenant reality is consummated here in the eternal communion established between God and his people. God no longer dwells high and lifted up above his people but now "tabernacles" in their midst.

The rest of Revelation 21:3 expands this basic idea in two ways. First, "they will be his peoples." The text here is plural, meaning that in heaven all ethnic and racial discrimination will disappear. The peoples of the world will become one, and we will treasure each other's cultures (see also 21:24, 26). The new covenant passage of Jeremiah 31:33 (= Heb 8:10) says, "I will be their God, and they will be my people." This passage was partially fulfilled in the church as the melting pot for diverse people groups (Eph 2:14), and now it is completed absolutely for all eternity. Only in the eternal reality can this be fulfilled in a final sense. Second, "God himself will be with them and be their God." This too was fulfilled partially in the church as new Israel. But all the covenant promises in the Old Testament and New Testament were experienced at the spiritual level only. In heaven the full physical reality will finally take place. Moses could not look on the face of God and live, but there we will look on his face and walk hand-in-hand with him.

After depicting the core meaning of the new Shekinah experience, John describes the benefits associated with this new reality (21:4), centering on the peace and joy the saints will have with our God. First, God will "wipe every tear from their eyes," reproducing 7:17 (looking back to Isa 25:18; 30:19; 35:10). All of life's sorrows (the result of sin) will be gone forever. Second, there will be "no more death or mourning or crying or pain," for the debilitating effects of sin and suffering have been removed from us. Not only does creation "groan" in the midst of its infirmities, but we too "groan inwardly as we await our adoption as God's children," referring not to conversion but to "the redemption of our bodies" at our translation to heaven (Rom 8:22–23). This hope has comforted the saints down through the ages, and John is describing the moment when that hope becomes reality.

All this has taken place because "the old order of things has passed away." The "former things" consist of the "crying and pain" of finite life characterized by "death and mourning." These present realities have no place in the new world. This was the hope of the heroes of the faith in Hebrews 11, whose faith centered on "a city with eternal foundations, a city designed and built by God" (Heb 11:10 NLT). They were looking for "a better place, a heavenly homeland" (11:16), and now that homeland has arrived.

God Describes the New Heavenly Order (21:5–6)

In Revelation 21:3 the angelic herald spoke from the throne, but in 21:5–6 "the one seated on the throne" speaks for the first time. Likely his statement applies to all the visions of the book and not only the immediate context. There are five elements of the speech:

1. "I am making everything new" is virtually a title for this section on the new heaven and new earth. The verb "making" is used often for God's act of creation (14:7) and redemption (1:6; 3:12; 5:10), and this is a new creation in which heaven and earth are amalgamated into a single place where the redeemed will spend eternity. The old order, tainted by sin, is gone forever and replaced in keeping with Isaiah 65:17, "See, I will create new heavens and

a new earth. The former things will not be remembered, nor will they come to mind." Today there is an inaugurated aspect to this: Every Christian is now a "new creation" in preparation for the final "new creation" in eternity.

2. As in Revelation 1:11, 19; 14:13; 19:19, John is ordered to "write down" the message, pointing to its great importance for the church. The reason for its critical nature is that as in 1:11, 19 it is "trustworthy and true," pointing to the truthfulness of this crucial message from God. The church must trust them and heed them, for they stem from the faithful and true God who has given his people this new creation.
3. At the seventh bowl judgment (16:17) a voice proclaimed, "It is done," pointing to the finalization of God's plan contained in the scroll of chapters 5 and 10. In 21:6 God repeats that message, meaning that God's history of salvation has now been accomplished and the final age has begun. There have been three stages: at the cross Jesus said, "It is finished" (John 19:30), referring to God's redemptive plan centering on his atoning sacrifice. Then Revelation 16:17 pointed to the **eschaton** that ended this present evil order. Finally, here this statement means that all of human history, including the destruction of this evil world and the new creation of the eternal home, has now taken place.
4. All of these divine actions are anchored in the character of God as sovereign over history, seen in the repetition of 1:8, "I am the Alpha and the Omega, the Beginning and the End" (also 1:17; 2:8; 22:13). The whole of Revelation is framed by this central theme, building on "the first and the last" of Isaiah 44:6; 48:12. All of history has been under his control, so the readers can be assured even in this time of evil that God remains sovereign over all.
5. John finally declares the future blessings engendered by the divine control of history, and it finalizes those in 21:4. The "thirsty" are those who have persevered and

remained faithful to Christ. In the new Jerusalem the Lord will give them the free gift of the "water of life," paralleling John 4:10–15; 6:35; 7:37–39. This stems from Isaiah 55:1, "Come, all you who are thirsty, come to the waters," and it repeats Revelation 7:17, promising that the Lamb "will shepherd them and guide them to the springs of living water." So this is an invitation to all readers to assuage their spiritual thirst in Christ with the promise that they will never thirst again.

THE CHALLENGE TO OVERCOME AND NOT BE A COWARD (21:7–8)
John now interrupts his presentation of the vision to address the readers, who are warned to recognize the difference between faithfulness and compromise, to be a conqueror rather than a coward. The opening challenge to "be victorious" was the concluding thought in the letters to the seven churches, leading to the **eschatological** promises to these overcomers. Ironically, as the beast conquers them by taking their lives (13:7), they conquer him by yielding their lives. As a result, they "inherit all this," referring not only to the promises in the seven letters but also to all the blessings of the new heaven and new earth in 21:1–22:5. The "inheritance" is the rewards awaiting the faithful (Acts 20:32; Rom 8:17; Gal 3:29; 4:7; Eph 1:14; 3:6; Titus 3:7; 1 Pet 1:4).

The greatest blessing of all is the incredible reality from Revelation 21:3, "I will be their God, and they will be my children." This sums up the Abrahamic covenant (Gen 17:7) and the Davidic covenant (2 Sam 7:14) and points to the adoption language of Romans 8:14–17, "Those who are led by the Spirit of God are the children of God." Now the full adoption has occurred, and what we experience now is a foretaste of that eternal joy.

In complete contrast to those who inherit those blessings, the sinners will be cast into the lake of fire (21:8). This seems out of place, since the punishment has already taken place in 20:13–15. However, this is an excursus warning the readers and so is not part of the narrative. The list of sins is a vice list common in the

Roman world, in the New Testament (Rom 1:29–31; Eph 4:25–32; Jas 3:14–16; 1 Pet 4:3, 15), and in this book (Rev 9:21; 22:15). The list here sums up the sins of the book and proves the depravity of the unbelievers.

"Unbelievers" are those who refused to repent and remained opposed to God (9:20–21; 14:6–7; 16:8–11). This list enumerates the sins that send unbelievers to the lake of fire. The "vile" acts are the abominable actions that result from unbelief (17:4–5; 21:27). The "murderers" are those who have killed the saints (6:9; 9:21; 13:7, 10; 17:6). The "sexually immoral" were part of the Nicolaitan cult (2:14, 20) and constituted most of the unsaved (9:21; 14:8; 17:2, 4; 18:3, 9). "Magic" or sorcery was an inherent part of Roman religion, centered in Ephesus (Acts 19:13–20), and is noted in Revelation 9:21; 18:23; 22:15. "Idolatry" is a major theme of the book and is at the heart of the core sins (2:14, 20; 9:20; 13:4–15; 22:15). "Liars" are often condemned and primarily referred to the lies of the false teachers and pagan religion (2:2; 3:9; 14:5; 16:13; 19:20).

Special consideration must be given to the "cowards," a term found only here in the New Testament. There is a specific contrast between the conqueror who inherits eternal life and the coward who spends eternity in hellfire. The list that takes up most of 21:8 describes the wicked unbelievers, but the coward is likely the weak quasi-Christian who fails to persevere and gives in to the false teachers and the pressures of the world; they "fall away" (as in Heb 6:4–6; Jas 5:19–20; 1 John 5:16). The readers are told to make a choice whether to overcome and follow Christ or to *be* overcome as a coward, thereby joining the unbelievers in eternal damnation.

THE NEW JERUSALEM IS A HOLY OF HOLIES (21:9–27)

After the introductory vision of 21:1–8, John gives the reader a detailed look at the city of God, moving from its descent (21:9–10) to its beauty (21:11) and foundations (21:12–14), followed by its measurements (21:15–17), its precious jewels (21:18–21), and its inner purity (21:22–27). The absolute contrast between the empire of the beast and that of Christ, seen in the parallels with 17:1–19:5 (e.g., 17:1–3 with 21:9–10), are evident. The readers are warned to choose their allegiances very carefully, for eternity is at stake. Many of the images are taken from the temple vision of Ezekiel 40–48, yet one contrast is striking. Everything in Ezekiel centers on the temple, but in the new Jerusalem there is no temple (Rev 21:22). The city of God is a temple—in fact, the holy of holies—in and of itself. God's Shekinah has been expanded to include the entire dwelling place of the people of God, heaven itself. We will spend eternity in the holy of holies!

An Angelic Guide Transports John (21:9–10)

There are three parallels between these two verses and 17:1–3: It is one of the angels with the bowls that again shows John the vision; the angel says, "Come, I will show you…," becoming John's heavenly guide; then in both places we are told, "Then he carried me away in the Spirit," highlighting a new vision and the centrality of the Holy Spirit in the process. The contrast between the empire as a harlot and the holy city as a bride becomes all the greater.

As mentioned above (on 21:1–2), the new Jerusalem is not only a place but also a people. The city of God is the place where the saints will live for eternity, yet it is wholly composed of the people themselves. In 21:2 the new Jerusalem is "like a bride"; here it is the bride and even more. It is "the wife of the Lamb," culminating all the Old Testament and New Testament imagery noted in 19:7. The ceremony has taken place, and Christ and his church will spend eternity as husband and wife. The sacrificial death of the Lamb and the victory this wrought over the cosmic powers have made this possible.

With this the angel "carries [John] away in the Spirit" (21:10), as in 17:3, referring to the visionary state. But here, unlike 17:3, John is taken not into the desert but to "a mountain great and high," possibly alluding to Mount Sinai where God gave Moses the Torah (Exod 19–20) or to Mount Nebo where Moses was shown the promised land (Deut 34:1–4). In addition, this reflects

Ezekiel 40:1–2, where the vision of the new temple took place on "a very high mountain." Restating 21:2, the "holy city" descends "out of heaven from God." Jewish tradition placed the final city of God on a mountain (Isa 4:1–5; Mic 4:1–2; 1 Enoch 18:8; 24:1–3), and it is possible this pictures the new Jerusalem nestled on Mount Zion. It descends from God, emphasizing that the merciful God who gave his people salvation is now giving them an eternal dwelling place.

The Appearance of the City (21:11–21)

The new Jerusalem shines, and in 21:11 its luminescence is caused by "the glory of God." This refers to his Shekinah glory residing among his people and filling the holy city in the same way that it covered Mount Sinai in Exodus 24:15–17 and filled the temple in 1 Kings 8:10–12 (also Isa 6:1–4; Ezek 43:2–5). The divine glory gives the city a "brilliance" or "radiance" that is blinding in its intensity, as in Ezekiel 43:2, "I saw the glory of God coming from the east … and the land was radiant with his glory." This dazzling beauty is then likened to "a very precious jewel like a jasper, clear as crystal." As said in the commentary on Revelation 4:3, a jasper was either an opal or a diamond, likely the latter in terms of being "clear as crystal." It is the primary jewel of the book, making up the walls in 21:18 and the first of the foundation jewels of 21:19–20. In all these passages the jewels symbolize the glory of God in all its majesty, radiance, and purity.

In 21:12 the new Jerusalem is described like one of the major fortified cities of the ancient world, with "a great high wall" (not described until 21:17–18) and gates that provided entry into the city. However, all evil and danger have been removed, and there is no longer a need for walls and gates to protect the citizens. This may well be the reason for the details here, to remind the readers of the eternal security God's people will enjoy. The walls and gates symbolize the incredible safety God now provides. It is a "great high wall" because of the size of the city and the greatness of the glory of God, so its purpose is not defense against danger but because it contains 12 gates and provides entrance to all the people of God down through history.

Ancient Jerusalem had five gates, but this is a megacity, and there are three gates on each of the four sides (21:13). This pattern is taken from Ezekiel 48:30–35, but in Ezekiel each gate is named after a tribe; here it simply states that the gates as a whole are named after the 12 tribes. In Ezekiel each gate provides an exit for each tribe to go out to its assigned territory in the promised land, but here these gates provide an entrance to all humanity, the people who have inherited the city (Rev 21:3, 7). Let me be clear: The names of the tribes on the gates do not represent all of humanity, but Israel—the covenant people of the Old Testament. God's intention, as in the Abrahamic covenant, is that Israel would provide a "blessing" to the nations (Gen 12:3) and make access for them to enter God's dwelling place. The people of God in this way provide access to the people of the world so they might repent and gain entrance to the holy city. They can enter the new Jerusalem from every part of the compass. The order here (east, north, south, west) reverses Ezekiel's order, but most likely the emphasis is not on the order but on the entrance effected. There are "twelve angels at the gates," linked with the watchmen on the walls of Isaiah 62:6. However, these angels are not guards against threats but guardians like the angels of the seven churches, representing God's new relationship with his people.

Next (21:14), there are 12 foundations of the wall. In the ancient world these were large stones chosen for their beauty and strength, like the foundation stones of the temple (1 Kgs 5:17). While the gates contained the names of the 12 tribes, these were inscribed with "the names of the twelve apostles of the Lamb." As with the tribes, the emphasis is not on the individual apostles but on the Twelve as a symbol for the church. In Ephesians 2:20 the church is "built on the foundation of the apostles and the prophets." "Lamb" occurs seven times in this section, and in a very real sense the holy city is his city, made possible by his atoning sacrifice that alone allows people to enter. The presence of the 12 tribes and the 12 apostles together on the walls unites the two covenant groups into a whole people of God who together provide entrance into the eternal city.

In 11:1–2 John took a rod and measured the temple, altar, and worshipers to show they belonged to God. In 21:15, the angel who talked with John in 21:9 uses a gold rod to "measure the city, its gates and its walls." A gold rod is appropriate for a "city of pure gold" (21:18) whose streets are of gold (21:21). The gates are not measured but are probably included in the walls. In Ezekiel 40–48 the man dressed in linen several times measured Jerusalem and its environs (Ezek 40:5–9; 41:5, 13; 42:16–17 and others), signifying God's ownership and protection. Here it indicates God's final and eternal presence, guaranteeing the absence of all tears, pain, and suffering for his people.

Like the temple in Ezekiel 42:15–20 and 45:2, the city is laid out "like a square" (21:16). The Ezekiel temple was 850 feet (500 cubits) square, the very dimensions of Herod's temple. Here these measurements are incredibly exaggerated. In Ezekiel the temple is a square (length and width measured), but here it is a perfect cube with the same dimensions for length, width, and height. The perfection of this city is another degree greater than that of Ezekiel. Also, Ezekiel describes a temple, while here it is a heavenly city, and there is no need for a temple (21:22) because the entire city constitutes a temple. The cube shape matches the holy of holies of the Jerusalem temple (20 cubits each direction; 1 Kgs 6:20). The unbelievable measurements multiply Ezekiel's many times, 12,000 stadia (nearly 1500 miles) in each direction, meaning a volume of 3,375,000,000 cubic miles. As the 1600 stadia of 14:20 was the length of Palestine, this is the length of the Roman Empire from Spain to the Euphrates! This is definitely a city large enough to house all the saints down through the ages from "every tribe, language, people, and nation" (5:9; 7:9).

After measuring the city, the angel measures the wall (21:17), and it is "144 cubits [216 feet] thick," which seems vast until you realize it is a wall 1500 miles long. This seems small for a city this size, but we need to realize these measurements are apocalyptic symbols. Both 12,000 stadia and 144 cubits are multiples of 12 and 10, linked with the 144,000 of 7:4; 14:1 to signify the perfection and wholeness of both the people of God and the holy city in which they will spend eternity. The great size and beauty of the city matches the splendor of the people who will call it home. John emphasizes that the angel is using a "human measurement," thereby stressing that these are human standards meant to be understood by the readers.

The use of gold, precious jewels, and pearls in 21:18–21 is an echo of Isaiah 54:11–12, where God promised to rebuild Jerusalem with "stones of turquoise ... sapphires ... rubies ... sparkling jewels, and ... precious stones." The desolate city is transformed into a city decorated with gold and jewels, the bride of Yahweh. These precious stones for John symbolize the grandeur and majesty of God's throne room in heaven (Rev 4:3–6) as well as the new Jerusalem as a whole, and the city reflects the majesty and splendor of God himself. Since the wall was measured in 21:17, the description begins with it, and it is constructed with "jasper," the diamond used to describe the radiance of the city in 21:11. The beauty of the wall partakes of the glory of God (see 4:3).

The city itself is constructed of "pure gold, as pure as glass," exactly like its main street in 21:21, reflecting 1 Kings 6:20–22, where Solomon overlaid the interior of the sanctuary and its altar with gold. This goes beyond Solomon, for the city is not overlaid but constructed of pure gold. The impure gold of this finite world is insufficient, for nothing impure can be allowed in the new Jerusalem (Rev 21:27). Moreover, this is transparent gold (like the "sea of glass" in 4:6). The glory reflected from solid gold is inadequate, for the floors and walls of the heavenly city must radiate the glory of God rather than reflect the glory of impure metals.

The vision now turns to the foundation stones (21:19–20) that are described as precious jewels. These stones in 21:14 were inscribed with the names of the 12 apostles, so the glory and majesty of God signified in the precious stones of 4:3–6 are now extended to his people. The list of 12 jewels decorating the foundations has been variously understood as a general depiction of the glory of the people of God, as a reversal of the list of 12 jewels linked with the 12 signs of the zodiac in ancient Egyptian and Arabic lists, or as paralleling the list of the jewels on the breastplate of the high priest in Exodus 28:17–20; 39:10–13. A comparison of the three lists is essential:

Exodus 28, 39	Revelation 21	Zodiac
ruby	jasper	amethyst
topaz	sapphire	jacinth
beryl	agate	turquoise
turquoise	emerald	topaz
sapphire	onyx	beryl
emerald	ruby	chrysolite
jacinth	chrysolite	ruby
agate	beryl	onyx
amethyst	topaz	emerald
chrysolite	turquoise	agate
onyx	jacinth	sapphire
jasper	amethyst	jasper

At first glance the zodiac hypothesis seems impressive, and it would fit the anti-magic stance of Revelation. However, there is no real evidence that such a list existed in the first century. The more likely possibility is the jewels of the high priest's breastplate, for eight of the twelve match up perfectly, and there is evidence that the other four are equivalent stones under other names (the NIV has equated the names). In Exodus the jewels represent the twelve tribes, while here they point to the twelve apostles (= the church). So the twelve jewels highlight the priestly nature of the church, the end-time Israel (see Rev 1:6; 5:10; 20:6). The first view is also basically correct but should be subsumed into the priestly option.

Jewels as a symbol for God's people are used frequently, as in Isaiah 54:11–13 where the restored Jerusalem will be made of costly jewels, and Ezekiel 28:13 where they adorn the king of Tyre as he arrogantly sets himself up as the god of his people (note also the jewels of the great prostitute in Rev 17:4). With these jewels the contrast between the harlot and the bride continues.[1] So Revelation builds on a lengthy tradition depicting the majesty of the celestial city and the glory of the people of God who inhabit it.[2]

Then the 12 gates are described (21:21; see 21:13). While the foundations are 12 different jewels, each gate consists of one colossal pearl. Pearls were part of the list of jewels in 18:12, and there I noted the inordinate worth of pearls in the ancient world. Since the walls were 144 cubits thick, the gates would be the same. These are definitely apocalyptic pearls! Finally, the "great street," like the city as a whole in 21:18, is made of "gold as pure as transparent glass." In 22:1, 2 the "river of the water of life" flows from the throne down the center of this main thoroughfare, and the transparent gold once more means the glory of God radiates from the central street. Unlike Babylon/Rome, where the streets signify pure evil (see 11:8), this street signifies the purity and glory of the Holy God emanating from his people.

The Conditions in the City (21:22–27)

The rest of chapter 21 provides a glimpse of life in the new Jerusalem as typified by holiness, glory, and joy. It consists of a series of negative statements telling what earthly elements cannot have any part in the city (21:22, 23, 25, 27) interspersed with the glory of the nations entering the city (21:24, 26). Together they describe the conditions that will characterize the new Jerusalem.

Jewish writings always centered on the heavenly temple in discussions of the new Jerusalem (see commentary on 3:12;

---

1. See commentary on 21:9.
2. See also Tobit 13:7–8; 2 Baruch 6:7–8; 4QpIsa.

21:1–2), especially Ezekiel 40–48, where the temple is the entire focus. This, then, is surprising, yet it is understandable in light of the emphasis on the holy city being depicted as the holy of holies. In other words, the *entire* new Jerusalem is a temple, so there is hardly any need for a temple in it. The primary feature of the temple was God's residence (the Shekinah, from the Hebrew *shakan,* to dwell) there; this is what made the temple sacred. In the new Jerusalem he resides among his people, so the entire city becomes the holy of holies where God makes his home.

The reason there is no temple is "because the Lord God Almighty and the Lamb are its temple." In Exodus 40:34 the book ends with the statement, "Then the cloud [symbolizing the Shekinah] covered the tent of meeting, and the glory of the LORD filled the tabernacle." In the final temple city, the new Jerusalem, that glory permeates the entire city in such a way that Yahweh *becomes* the temple. The Shekinah (from the Hebrew *shakan,* "to dwell") is God and his glory "dwelling" among the saints. So here "God's dwelling place is now among the people" (21:3). God in his sovereign power and the Lamb in his redemptive presence constitute the temple of heaven.

In Isaiah 60:19 the glory of **eschatological** Zion is depicted this way: "The sun will no more be your light by day, nor will ... the moon shine on you, for the LORD will be your everlasting light." With "the glory of God" radiating through the city and giving light, there is no need for mere created light. James 1:17 calls God "the Father of the heavenly lights," and 1 Timothy 6:16 says God "lives in unapproachable light."

The light of God and the Lamb is so intense that "the nations will walk by its light" (21:24), culminating the theme in Revelation on the conversion of the nations (see on 1:7). This is not universalism, for the majority will not be converted and will face eternal punishment (see on 1:7). But one of the purposes of the seals, trumpets, and bowls was to convict the nations of their sins and bring them to repentance, alluding to Isaiah 60:3, 5, 11, "Nations will come to your light. ... Your gates will always stand open ... their kings led in triumphal procession."[3] This finalizes the procession of the nations to Zion in Isaiah, as Israel was to be "a light to the Gentiles" (42:6; 51:4) so that the nations will be drawn to the light (49:6; 55:5; 60:1, 3). Thus those among the nations who repent now enter the celestial city.

The kings who were "led in triumphal procession" in Isaiah 60:11 thereby "will bring their splendor into" the holy city. The imagery in Isaiah is of military victory, with the kings of the nations marching in display behind Yahweh's victorious chariot. John has transformed this imagery from military triumph to that of conversion and worship (though Isaiah has both, with the nations "coming to the light" in 60:3), as the kings enter the celestial city and "bring their *doxa* [glory, splendor] into it." The earthly glory that the royalty and the nations possessed is now returned to the One who gave it to them in the first place and who alone is "worthy" (Rev 4:11; 5:12) of it. The kings earlier gave their allegiance to the beast (16:12–13; 17:2, 18; 18:3, 9) and were destroyed with those armies (19:21). Yet God's mercy extends to all and ultimately triumphs over evil. Thus some have indeed repented and been redeemed.

The allusion to Isaiah 60 continues as the gates are "never shut" (Isa 60:11 adds, "Your gates will always stand open"). In ancient times the city gates were closed at night to protect the citizens and keep unwanted visitors outside. Now God is in control, and all evil has been destroyed. There are no hostile armies, and many among the nations now have entered the celestial city as fellow believers. Moreover, "there will be no night there," since the light of the glory of God is at all times radiating through the city (21:23). The light of day is an endless delight, and both danger and darkness are gone forever.

As a result, the nations can freely enter (21:26) and bring their "glory and honor" into the new Jerusalem (expanding 21:24).

---

3. See "Mission and Evangelism" under "Theology of the Book" in the introduction.

This may connote the idea of bringing gifts to God, common for official pilgrimages in the ancient world, for instance, in the homage and gifts brought to the baby Jesus by the magi in Matthew 2. In Revelation, honor always belongs to God in worship (Rev 4:9, 11; 5:12–13; 7:12), so the image is of the royal caravan making pilgrimage to the holy city to worship God. We might picture such earthly worthies as the queen of England and the president of the United States on their knees before God's throne. They will honor and glorify God and the Lamb for all eternity.

The eternal city is to be pure, a sacred space. Therefore, "nothing impure [can] ever enter it" (21:27). This reverses 3:20, where Christ knocks in order to "enter" our church. Combining the two, we will be able to enter the holy city when we have invited Christ to enter our hearts. The means for doing so is spelled out in 22:14—those who wash their robes will be allowed to enter the gates into the city (see Matt 5:20; 7:21; 18:23). There are three groups that cannot enter:

1. The impure or unclean are those that characterize the empire of the beast, such as unclean spirits (the term in Mark for demons) as in Revelation 16:13 or impure actions such as the immorality and lies of 21:8. Maintaining ritual purity was part of the holy lifestyle in Leviticus 11:44–45, and unclean things are an abomination to Yahweh (Lev 11:40–43; Deut 7:25–26; 14:3).
2. Those who perform shameful acts are excluded. The Greek term can be translated "abominations," referring to things absolutely detestable to God, like the actions of the great prostitute in Revelation 17:4–5, and this certainly includes the vice list of 21:8. Holiness characterizes the new Jerusalem, and there can be no place for anything unholy.
3. Deceit is excluded, referring to the lies/falsehood of the unbelieving and persecuting Jews (3:9), the Nicolaitan cult and its false teachers (2:2), the false prophet (13:14; 16:13; 19:20), and church members who disprove their

> profession of faith with their evil conduct (the "cowards" of 21:8). They all follow Satan the great deceiver (12:9; 20:3). In contrast the saints have "no lie found in their mouths" (14:5).

The saints are the only ones allowed to enter the celestial city, for their "names are written in the Lamb's book of life." This is the last of six places the book of life is mentioned, twice stressing those in it (3:5; 21:27), three times those not in it (13:8; 17:8; 20:15), and once its use at the final judgment (20:12). It is the Lamb's book, made possible by his death (13:8) and containing the register of the citizens of heaven (compare Psa 9:5; 69:28; Isa 4:3; Dan 12:1).

So much has been written about heaven down through the centuries, yet the only extended biblical description is found only here in Revelation 21. The most important thing about it is that it will realize the greatest promise of all—we will dwell with God face to face. Moses could not look on him and live; we will not only look upon him but walk with him hand in hand. Moreover, all our suffering will be over; there will be no crying or tears or pain—only joy as we inhabit our perfect eternal body. What we think of today as pure luxury will be commonplace, as the description here shows. But unlike the luxury of the great prostitute in Revelation 17, this luxury will not be wrung from the blood and sweat of those who have been crushed by injustice. Instead, God will give it to those who have loved him even to the point of death (12:11).

It is impossible to imagine the beauty and the glory and the bliss of our eternal heavenly existence. Human minds cannot begin to think of the wonders of heaven. If we think of the most glorious life possible and multiply it a million times, that is a mere approximation of what will be ours. The angels will be or next-door neighbors, and the Old Testament heroes as well as the apostles will live just down the street. This chapter is nothing more than a slight picture of what awaits us!

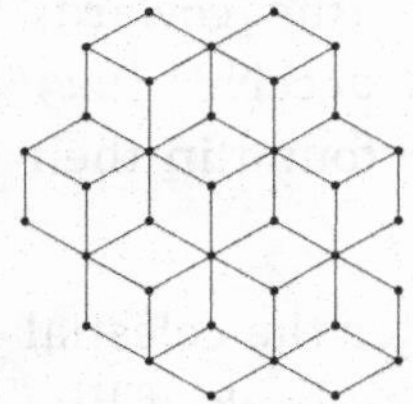

THE FINAL EDEN RETURNS TO THE FAITHFUL

(22:1–5)

The visions conclude by returning to the first creation and the garden of Eden. God's intention in creating the first garden was to provide a "garden of delight" (the meaning of *eden* in Hebrew) as a reward for the covenant with Adam and Eve. These first inhabitants were not only to enjoy it but were to care for it as a service to God (Gen 2:15). Their whole existence was oriented to God, which explains why they were not to partake of the tree of the knowledge of good and evil (Gen 2:17). To do so would be to replace God with self and one's own knowledge. They did partake of it and lost their place in paradise (the **Septuagint** term for the garden). Following this, the Jews believed the garden was taken up to heaven to await the faithful (2 Baruch 4:3–7; Testament of Levi 18:10–11). The vision here shows its descent to the renewed earth to be returned to God's people.

THE RIVER OF LIFE FLOWS FROM THE THRONE (22:1–2A)

In Revelation 21:9 the angel showed John the bride, the new Jerusalem. Now the angel shows John the second part of the vision of heaven, "the river of the water of life." In Genesis 2:10 a river flowed from Eden to "water the garden," but life was restricted to the tree of life (Gen 2:9; 3:22–24). In the regained Eden here, the tree of life stands on both sides of the river (22:2), and the river itself consists of the water of life. Moreover, in Genesis the river flowed "from Eden," while here it flows "from the throne." Eden has become one with the city, building also upon Ezekiel 47:1–12, where the life-giving presence of God infuses the river as it flows from the temple to replenish everything it touches (see also Psa 64:4; Isa 35:6–9; Jer 2:13; Zech 14:8; John 4:10–14; 7:37–39).

The source of this river is the Godhead, the "throne of God and the Lamb." Once more Revelation stresses the oneness between God and the Lamb (3:21; 4:9–11; 5:9–13; 6:16; 7:10; 11:15; 14:4; 20:6; 21:22) and the deity of Christ.[1] The throne (45 times in the book) centers on the sovereign rule of God as protector of his people, and as in 7:9–17 they "stand before the throne" and enjoy his presence.

This great river flows "down the middle of the great street" (22:2) that is constructed of "gold as pure as transparent glass" (21:21), so the street and the river are the primary thoroughfare and determine the movement in the holy city. The picture is powerful. The main street is a superhighway, but in the middle of the highway is not a median but the great river of Eden, and on both banks of the river in the middle of the thoroughfare is a multiple tree of life. In the original garden there was a single tree of life, but now life fills the new Eden.

THE TREE OF LIFE IS PRESENT, AND THE CURSE IS REMOVED (22:2B–3A)

Clearly the major characteristic of the new Jerusalem is life, seen in both the "water of life" and the "tree of life." Adam and Eve surrendered life when they chose the fruit of the tree of knowledge of good and evil, and they were expelled from the

---

1. See "Doctrine of Christ" under "Theology of the Book" in the introduction.

garden as a result. In Genesis 3:22 the tree is the source of eternal life, so Adam and Eve had to be banished lest they attain immortality in the midst of their sin. Now that (eternal) life is returned to God's people. Eden has been restored and is far greater than it was in Genesis 2–3, for life permeates the whole new creation. In Ezekiel 47:12 "fruit trees of all kinds will grow on both banks of the river" (also Prov 3:18; 11:30; Isa 35:6–9), and that is the case here. Like the original Eden abundant fruitfulness flourishes, and now that fruit is not just physical but spiritual/eternal life. The promise of Revelation 2:7 to "eat from the tree of life" is now fulfilled.

These multiple trees of life produce "twelve crops of fruit, yielding its fruit every month." The promise that fruit will be provided every month of the year is incredible. Fruit in our world comes only once a season, though modern shipping can make it seem as though it comes more often. This adds to 21:4—there will be "no death, mourning, crying, pain," and now also no more hunger. Yet there is more: the leaves will "heal the nations," another allusion to Ezekiel 47:12. But in Ezekiel it is national Israel that is healed, while here it is all the nations, further material on the conversion of the nations (1:7; 5:9–10; 7:9; 11:13; 14:6–7; 15:4; 21:24, 26). This does not mean healing for illnesses is still needed. Rather, it symbolizes that healing has already taken place. There will be no hunger and no sickness in the new Jerusalem.

Zechariah 14:11 says, "There will no longer be a curse, for Jerusalem will dwell in security" (NASB). This refers to the covenant curses, which are no longer needed. Christ atoned for the sin Adam and Eve brought upon humanity, and the evil that resulted has been done away with for all eternity. Those among the nations who found healing in Christ are now forgiven and adopted as God's children. There is forgiveness and absolute security in the eternal city.

GOD'S PEOPLE HAVE A NEW RELATIONSHIP WITH GOD AND THE LAMB (22:3B–4)

Throne scenes frame the description of the new Eden (22:1, 3b). Everything the garden city means—eternal life, abundant provisions, complete healing, absolute security—flows out of the sovereign presence of God and the Lamb. Since the triune Godhead is present, "his slaves will [worship and] serve him" (with *latreuō* meaning both "worship" and "serve" here). The emphasis on *douloi* ("slaves") in the book (1:1; 7:3, 15; 11:18; 19:2, 5; 22:6) defines the divine/human relationship. We have been purchased by his blood and belong to him as his special possession. As such we are members of his family and protected by him. In response we worship him and offer him priestly service. As in 7:15, we "stand before the throne and worship/serve him day and night in his temple." The saints are priests of God in 1:6; 5:10; 20:6, and that is the defining activity of God's people for eternity. This was to be the work of Adam and Eve in the first garden, and now it will be the privileged task of the saints in the final Eden.

The joy of God's people is not just in service; they will "see his face." This represents the final of four stages in the Bible:

1. Moses could not look on God's face and live (Exod 33:20).
2. Christ the Word was the Shekinah encased in human flesh, so to look upon Jesus was to behold the face of God (John 1:14, 18).
3. In our present existence as citizens of heaven (Phil 3:20), we sit beside God in Christ (Eph 2:6–7) and "see the Lord" spiritually (Heb 12:14).
4. In the celestial city God will be physically with us (Rev 22:4), and we will look upon his face literally. Moreover, "his name will be on [our] foreheads," fulfilling the promise of 3:12 ("I will write on them ... my new name") as well as 7:3 ("put a seal on the foreheads of [my] slaves") and 14:1 ("his name and the name of his Father written on their foreheads").

We are God's for eternity, and we will share his "new name."

GOD GIVES LIGHT (22:5)

To sum up the meaning of the visions of 21:1–22:5, John repeats images from 21:25, 23 and 20:4c, respectively. "No more night" and "no light" from either lamp or sun bring together the negative side, the effects of sin upon life in this world—night, shut gates, danger, impurity, shame, deceit, lies. As stated above, God's Shekinah glory radiates through the city, and it will perpetually be day as "the Lord God [gives] them light." As in Isaiah 60:19, "the LORD will be your everlasting light" (also Num 6:25; Psa 118:27).

In light of the divine presence and the royalty that the saints share with Christ, "they will reign forever and ever." There are three stages in this: in this present world we are royalty and priesthood in Christ (1 Pet 2:9); we will reign/rule with Christ during his millennial reign (Rev 20:4); in the new Jerusalem we will reign eternally as a member of the royal family (here). This fulfills Daniel 7:18 ("The saints of the Most High will receive the kingdom and will possess it forever") and 7:27 ("Then the sovereignty, power, and greatness of the kingdom under heaven will be handed over to the holy people of the Most High"). Of course, this can hardly be meant literally, for heaven will consists of only angels and saints; we will not reign over the celestial beings, for we are all "fellow servants" (19:10; 22:9). This likely means we will participate in the rule of Christ over the eternal kingdom, as Adam was to rule over the original Eden.

In 21:9–27 heaven is described as a city that becomes the holy of holies in heaven. Here heaven is described as the final garden of Eden, a compilation of this world's most beautiful gardens. If Adam and Eve had not sinned, this would have been theirs. The emphasis is on the utter magnificence of heaven, the extent to which it fulfills all the deepest longings of the human heart. God will provide for us and care for us for all eternity. Our needs will be met, our hurts healed, and our sins forgiven. In an eternal sense, we will have everything we have ever wanted or needed. Imagine spending eternity in a garden that combines Keukenhof, the tulip garden of Holland, with

Butchart Gardens on Vancouver Island in Canada, with the Queen's royal garden on the grounds of Buckingham Palace. Take all the beautiful gardens in the world, put them together, and still they won't hold a candle to the new garden of Eden in heaven.

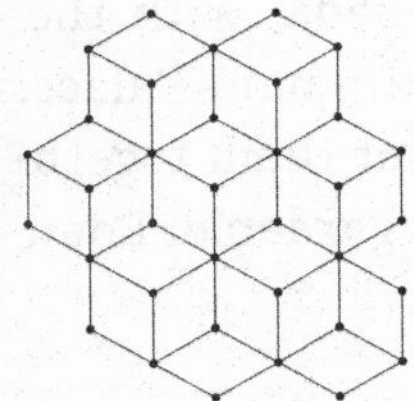

EPILOGUE TO THE BOOK

(22:6–21)

The epilogue consists of a series of utterances that at first seem haphazard but actually coalesce along two major themes—the authenticity of the prophetic visions, (22:6, 8, 16, 18–19) and the nearness of the return of Christ (22:7, 10, 12, 20). There are two primary speakers: an angel who gives three commands (22:8–11), and a series of seven sayings by Christ (22:12–19).

THE BOOK IS AUTHENTICATED (22:6–7)

Likely the speaker is the same angel who spoke in 21:9, and he is drawing together 19:9 and 21:5 on the God-given trustworthiness of these visions. This prophetic message parallels Christ who is "faithful" (1:5; 3:14) and "true" (3:7, 14; 19:11). Since God and Jesus are the true source (1:1; 22:16), these writings are completely reliable and must be obeyed.

God is called "the Lord, the God of the spirits of the prophets," meaning that the prophetic message of John stems from the Lord God. It is debated whether "spirits" is the prophetic spirit or the Holy Spirit. It is certainly both, meaning that the mental and spiritual makeup of John as a prophet is due to the work of the Holy Spirit in him. The title echoes Numbers 27:16 (NASB), "The LORD, the God of the spirits of all flesh" (also Num 16:22). In an echo of Revelation 1:1–2 the sovereign God revealed this book when "he sent his angel to show his slaves" these visions. This continues the emphasis on showing the visions to John (4:1; 17:1; 21:9–10; 22:1), thereby unveiling the future via divine revelation. The "slaves" in 22:6 are the believers in general who are the true recipients of this book.

The content of the prophecy is "the things that must soon take place" (as in 1:1, 19; 4:1). The nearness of these final events in history is one of the central themes of this epilogue (22:6, 7, 12, 20). While "soon" could refer to speed ("quickly, swiftly"), in all of these passages it stresses the imminence of the end. Jesus did envision a period of time before the end (Mark 13:7), and Paul also emphasized the nearness of Christ's return (Rom 13:11; 1 Cor 7:29–31; 1 Thess 4:15; 5:2), as did others (Heb 10:25; Jas 5:8; 1 Pet 4:7). The issue of the "delay of the **Parousia**" is answered in 2 Peter 3:8–9: to God, the period between the two advents is short and can be designated "soon." The church in every age is to await Christ's "soon" return, and the actual timing is up to him.

In Revelation 22:7 Christ speaks directly for the second time (with 16:15), proving that the "soon" refers to his **Parousia**. The prophecy inherent in "I am coming soon" summarizes a series of promises in 2:16; 3:11; 22:12, 20, and this is the culminating event of human history. It is followed by the sixth of the seven beatitudes (1:3; 14:13; 16:15; 19:9; 20:6; 22:14). In the others *makarios* connotes "God blesses," while here and in 22:14 it means "Christ blesses," stressing once more the unity of Father and Son in the book. As in 1:3; 16:15 the blessing is reserved for "the one who keeps the words of the prophecy," reiterating the central command of the book demanding faithful obedience to God's commands (1:3; 2:26; 12:17; 14:12; 16:15) as the core of the perseverance of the saints.[1] The Christian must be ready at all

1. See "Perseverance of the Saints" under "Theology of the Book" in the introduction.

times for Christ's return, and that readiness consists of right ethical and spiritual living.

THE ANGEL GIVES JOHN THREE COMMANDS (22:8–11)

There are three sayings of the angel here, moving from the centrality of worshiping God (22:9) to the nearness of the end (22:10) to the command to continue what they are doing until the end (22:11).

Worship Only God (22:8–9)

John begins this section by announcing that he is the official recipient of these prophetic visions, the "one who had heard and seen them." This is virtually a legal statement, similar to 1:1, that God had chosen him to be the official channel of these visions to the churches. But for the second time (after 19:10) he makes the mistake of worshiping the messenger (the angel) rather than the God who sent him. In both places, John—overwhelmed at the depth of the revelatory experience—fell at the feet of the angel and started to worship him, inadvertently committing idolatry. The angel rebukes him and tells him clearly not to do so. Once more the reason is spelled out: "I am a fellow slave [*sundoulos*] with you." There is no hierarchical relationship between angels and God's people; both stand together as equals and serve God in a priestly capacity (7:15; 22:3).

Three groups stand with the angels as servants of God: John, his "fellow prophets," and "all who keep the words of this scroll." The "prophets" could be a group of leaders in the church who hold the office of prophet (Eph 4:11) or a general reference to all Christians as having a prophetic ministry to the world (both may well be meant). These latter two groups are the victorious Christians who have persevered (see above on 22:7).

Do Not Seal These Prophecies (22:10)

Since the saints must "keep the words of this scroll" (22:9), it is essential that John not seal up these words. The contents of this book are seen as prophetic revelations from God, meaning they uncover the previously hidden truths that are now opened for the church. So this is a time for unsealing the divine books and revealing them, reversing 10:4 where John was told to seal the message of the seven thunders. The **eschaton** has indeed arrived, and nothing is to be held back.

The reason for this is that "the time is near," meaning the imminent arrival of the **Parousia** (1:3; 22:6). In light of Christ's soon return, the readers must be told these prophecies so they can keep the commands and heed the warnings. In short, this continues the emphasis on ethical responsibility in light of apocalyptic reality. The only viable response is to "worship God" (22:9) and live faithfully for the Lamb (22:11).

Choose Evil or Righteousness (22:11)

This passage spells out the ethical alternatives hinted at in 22:10, alluding to Daniel 12:9–10, "Many will be purified, many spotless and refined, but the wicked will continue to be wicked." The world will continue to consist of the wicked and the righteous. Yet the angel seems to command the evil to remain evil. Perhaps this orders the wicked to think carefully about what they are doing, or perhaps it is saying that the period is so brief that no one will have the time to change their behavior. Probably a combination of these is best. The unsaved are being warned to think very carefully about the lifestyle they have chosen in light of the imminent return of Christ. Throughout the book there is an emphasis that those who have ears to hear had better listen carefully (the seven letters as well as 13:9), building on Isaiah 6:9–10 and Ezekiel 3:27.

Still, the angel says, "Let the one who does wrong continue to do wrong; let the vile person continue to be vile." The terms "wrong/wicked" and "vile/filthy" are apt summaries of the evil deeds of 21:8 and 22:15. The moral defilement of the world will not go away until Christ comes with the rod of iron and destroys evil in this world. John and the other Christian leaders can do little to stem the tide of evil. Their task is not to act as moral policemen but to proclaim the prophecies (22:10) and leave the rest to God and the Lamb. In addition, they must encourage the righteous and the holy to continue in their good deeds and faithful living for Christ. They are to be light shining in darkness and expose the evil deeds of darkness (John 3:19–20).

CHRIST PRONOUNCES SEVEN SAYINGS (22:12–19)

There are seven sayings of Jesus here, and the central point is the necessity of right living in light of the near return of Christ. The parables that conclude the Olivet Discourse in Matthew 24–25 (the wicked servant, the 10 virgins, the talents) all note the journey of Christ away from his followers, his sudden and unexpected return, and the fact that his followers were held accountable for the way they were living their lives when he returned. That is the message here as well.

Coming Soon with His Reward (22:12)

This begins with a verbatim quote from 22:7, "Behold, I am coming soon," a major emphasis of this epilogue (22:7, 10, 12, 20). It provides the basis for the warnings of 22:11, 14–15. Since Christ is coming soon, we must be ready at all times, as in the Olivet Discourse noted above. There is promise as well as warning, for Christ states, "My reward is with me," alluding to Isaiah 40:10, "The Sovereign Lord comes with power … his reward is with him." There the message was the deliverance of God's people from the exile, and that was to be their reward. Here it is **eschatological** and refers to deliverance from eternal torment and God's recompense for a life lived faithfully for God, as in Revelation 11:18. God and the Lamb will vindicate and reward their followers for all they have sacrificed.

Almost certainly this is meant to include the sinners, since "reward" means "payment for work done," and so can refer to punishment as well as reward. This is seen in the added comment that God will "repay each person according to what they have done," a near verbatim quote from Proverbs 24:12. So this includes both sides of 22:11, punishment for those who do wrong and reward for those who do right. This sums up the doctrine of judgment according to works, which appears quite frequently in the Old Testament (Job 34:11; Psa 28:4; 62:12; Jer 17:10; Ezek 18:20), New Testament (Matt 16:27; Rom 2:6; 14:12; 2 Cor 5:10; 11:15; 1 Pet 1:17), and Revelation itself (2:23; 11:18; 14:13; 18:6; 20:12–13).[2] The emphasis on ethical responsibility and its consequences needs to become more central in modern preaching.

THE IDENTITY OF THE ONE COMING (22:13)

This is the final "Alpha and Omega" saying (1:8, 17; 2:8; 21:6), and it fittingly is the most complete, adding, "the First and the Last, the Beginning and the End." All three titles stress the sovereignty of God and Christ over history. They began human history in Genesis, they end it here, and this proves that they have been in control of every moment in between, guiding human history to its God-intended denouement at the **eschaton**. The triune Godhead, here especially Christ, are lords over their creation. These are the perfect titles to bring together Christ coming as Judge in 22:12 with the warnings to believer and unbeliever in 22:14–15. Christ is sovereign over all things and therefore the One who has authority over the destiny of every person.

BLESSING AND WARNING TO THE SAVED AND THE UNSAVED (22:14–15)

This is the final of the seven beatitudes (1:3; 14:13; 16:15; 19:9; 20:6; 22:7), and the one unifying theme is the necessity of remaining true to the Lord in order to participate in the resurrection to eternal life. This final beatitude reiterates 7:14, where the victorious saints stand before the throne as those who have "washed their robes and made them white in the blood of the Lamb." The image of washing in both places speaks of spiritual revival, ridding one's life of the accumulated filth of this world

2. See discussion of grace and works at 20:12.

and living in purity before God. Sardis ("soiled their clothes," 3:4) and Laodicea (purchase "white clothes," 3:14) failed in this. Throughout the book white garments symbolize both purity and the victorious Christian (6:11; 7:9, 13–14; 16:15).

Christ gives those who wash their robes a new "authority" (NIV "right"), and this term is used often in the book to depict the power of the saints over the nations (2:26) or of demonic forces over their followers (9:3, 10, 19). Here it symbolizes the new access of God's people to the tree of life, an image taken from the new Eden of 22:1–5 to mean eternal life. Adam and Eve after they had sinned were expelled from the garden lest they eat of that fruit and gain eternal life as sinners. Now that the blood of Christ has cleansed the saints from sin, they regain that "right" or "power" to live eternally. The picture in chapters 21–22 is one of total peace and security, an eternal city devoid of danger and discomfort, constantly open to its citizens.

In contrast to the blessings awaiting the redeemed, punishment and torment await the wicked (22:15). The righteous enter the gates into the city, while sinners are outside the city. This does not mean they get to live in the suburbs. The image parallels Jesus dying "outside the camp" in Hebrews 13:12–13, signifying the Old Testament curse for the blasphemer who was cut off from the covenant community (Lev 24:14, 23). It symbolizes exclusion and shame. They are "dogs," unclean animals and an epithet for fools (Prov 26:11) or those unworthy of God's truths (Matt 7:6). These are the ones who reject Christ and live lives of immorality. What follows in 22:15b is a list of five sins found in the vice list of 21:8 (sorcery, immorality, murder, idolatry, liars). The last refers especially to the false teachers spreading their lies and teaching accommodation with Rome.[3]

---

3. See commentary on 2:2, 6.

Jesus Sends Revelation to the Churches (22:16a)

This provides another parallel to 1:1–2, as Jesus "sends [his] angel," that is, authenticates his royal herald, to deliver his decree to the churches. In 1:1 it is God who sends the angel; here Jesus does so, another emphasis on the deity of Christ. The purpose of the message is "to testify," also a major theme in the epilogue (with 22:18, 20), linked with "the testimony of Jesus" in 1:2. In both places the visions are identified as Jesus' "testimony," his official witness sent from the heavenly court to his troubled churches on earth. One question regarding this verse is the antecedent of "you": whether this is sent to the seven churches to deliver to the other churches, or whether the recipient is the circle of prophets mentioned in 22:9. In light of the emphasis on prophets in the book and on the prophecies given to the church (22:6–7, 9–10, 16, 18–19), the latter is the more likely option. These prophets likely aided John in leading the churches and helping them understand the prophecies of this book.

Further Identity of Jesus (22:16b)

The Gospel of John is well known for its seven "I am" sayings of Jesus. Revelation has four: 1:8 ("Alpha and Omega"), 1:17 ("the First and the Last"), 2:23 ("I am he"), and this one. As in John, "I am" becomes a title of Jesus and designates him as Yahweh of Exodus 3:14; Isaiah 41:4; 44:6; 48:12.[4] Two further titles are added to anchor the reality of who he is. First, he is "the root and offspring of David," reiterating 5:5 and alluding to Isaiah 11:1, 10 where it is a military metaphor centering on the Warrior Messiah, the descendant of David who would deliver God's people. As David's offspring Jesus fulfilled all the Davidic messianic hopes as the Messiah. Second, he is "the bright Morning Star," recalling Revelation 2:28 and stemming from Numbers 24:17, "A star will come out of Jacob," seen as a messianic prophecy in Judaism. This too highlighted Jesus as the Warrior Messiah,

---

4. See the commentary on 1:17.

and together the two titles stress his glory and power over the enemies of God and his people.

A Cry to the Readers to "Come" (22:17)

This is a difficult verse; in light of the "I am coming soon" of 22:7, 12, it would seem this is a cry for the **Parousia**, for Jesus to "come." However, all the sayings of 22:2–19 stem from Jesus, and it is difficult to conceive that Jesus is asking himself to return. More likely, it is an invitation to the readers to come to Jesus and continues the mission emphasis of the book.[5]

The invitation first stems from "the Spirit and the bride." Some say this is not the Holy Spirit but Spirit-inspired prophets, but this is not an either-or; the Spirit is empowering the prophetic message (see 19:10). The bride is the church, but especially the end-time church entering the new Jerusalem (21:9–10), stressing its victory and joy as it enters eternity. The "one who hears" is the current church on earth as it bears the invitation of the Spirit and bride to the unbelieving nations. So both the final church and the current church bear witness to the thirsty among the nations who are searching and longing for answers. This points back to 21:6 and to Isaiah 55:1, "Come, all you who are thirsty, come to the waters." So unbelievers are called to repentance, and Christians are called to a deeper walk with Christ.

Warning Against Adding to or Subtracting from the Book (22:18–19)

"I warn" is actually "I testify," and here it has a strong legal connotation, producing a courtroom atmosphere in which the false teachers are on trial for committing the sin of falsehood (2:2; 3:9; 14:5; 16:13; 19:20; 22:15), that is, twisting the meaning of these visions. The purpose of this is to stress further the authenticity of these prophecies and to make certain that the false teachers do not tamper with them. This is based on Deuteronomy

5. See "Theology of the Book" in the introduction.

4:2 ("Do not add to what I command you, and do not subtract from it"; also Deut 12:32), which says that the Torah must be accepted as God intended it and obeyed in its entirety (the context stresses the Balaam incident). As in Deuteronomy, Christ is warning the false teachers that they dare not distort the God-intended meaning by adding their own teaching to it or by removing the truths in it.

These verses have often been misused to denigrate any theology different from the one we prefer—for example, other views of the millennium or other interpretive lenses.[6] A false teacher is not anyone from another theological perspective but someone who restructures the Christian faith and introduces heresy—views that counter the cardinal doctrines and destroy the nucleus of the Christian faith, like the Nicolaitans of John's day. We are all responsible to God to make certain we interpret this book in accordance with the message God revealed to John. It matters how we understand it.

Note the warnings themselves. They reverse the beatitudes of 22:7, 14 and impose a covenant curse (Deut 29:20) upon those who twist these prophecies to their own end. Those who add false material will have the plagues of the book added to them; that is, they will be treated as unbelievers and suffer the punishments to be inflicted on the wicked. Those who take away the truths of these prophecies will have God remove their share in the tree of life; that is, they will suffer the "second death" (2:11; 20:6), namely the loss of eternal life and eternity in the lake of fire. The first deals with earthly judgments; the second with eternal judgment. Many debate whether this amounts to apostasy from the Christian faith, and along with 20:8 that is certainly the case. Revelation is like Hebrews (6:4–6; 10:26–31), 2 Peter (2:20–22), or 1 John (5:16), each of which has a strong sense of warning. This is valid within a Reformed (it could not happen to the elect but could happen to other church members) as

6. See "Methods of Interpretation" in the introduction.

well as an Arminian (it could happen to anyone in the church) framework. All Christians must decide for themselves, but the danger is real either way. The readers are warned that deliberately distorting God's truths and denying cardinal doctrines is tantamount to apostasy.

JOHN PLEAS FOR CHRIST'S RETURN (22:20)

Jesus is once again, as in 1:5; 3:14; 22:16, "the one who testifies," namely the source of these prophecies and visions. This is the concluding promise of the imminent **Parousia** (with 22:7, 10, 12) and begins with "yes" (Greek *nai*), which as in 1:7 is used to authenticate the saying and provide the divine imprimatur to it. "Indeed," Christ is saying, the event the entire Bible anticipates will happen soon. The Lord's Prayer centers on this—"Your kingdom come" (Matt 6:10)—and this "living hope" (1 Pet 1:3) anchors everything the believer says and does.

The natural response of the church follows. The divine imprimatur leads into the church's "Amen," as the people of God add their affirmation to Christ's. It is possible that this has a eucharistic flavor, with Jesus' "presence/coming" in the Eucharist a foretaste of his final coming. However, there is no actual eucharistic language here, and "Come, Lord Jesus" is more likely a consuming desire for his return. It may well be a translation of "Marana tha" (Aramaic for "Our Lord, come") in 1 Corinthians 16:22 (and in the early church document the Didache 10:6), one of the oldest creedal prayers in existence.

JOHN CONCLUDES WITH A BENEDICTION (22:21)

Nearly all of Paul's letters (with Romans the exception) conclude with some form of "Grace be with you." So, as mentioned in the introduction, Revelation is not only an apocalypse and a prophecy but an epistle as well.[7] The purpose of "the grace of

7. See "What Kind of Book Is Revelation?" in the introduction.

the Lord Jesus" is the same as in Paul, a prayer for divine favor to fall on the readers. John wants the "Lord Jesus" (taken from 22:20) to shine upon them with sovereign power so they can indeed be overcomers and ready for the Lord's return.

John ends his letter/apocalypse by asking that Christ's grace be imparted to "all" (NIV has "God's people"), certainly meant of all his readers, not only the believers but also any unsaved who read this book. In keeping with the purposes of the book, John wants the grace of the Lord Jesus to strengthen the saints, bring the weak Christians back to Christ, and draw the unsaved to Christ's salvation. The grace of the triune Godhead is available to all who are open to the truths of the book—saints and sinners alike. "Amen!"

The epilogue of 22:6–21 serves as an appropriate conclusion to the whole book, summing up the key emphases—the sovereignty of God, the return of Christ, the necessity of conversion for unbelievers and of faithful perseverance for believers. God inspired this book to encourage beleaguered Christians, telling them that in reality their suffering was temporary and their final victory was certain. We need this message desperately in our time as well, for evil still seems to be in control. We need assurance that it is not and that in fact its days are numbered. From this book, we can know beyond any shadow of doubt that the answer to this world's ills is the same today as it was in John's day—"even so, Lord, quickly come."

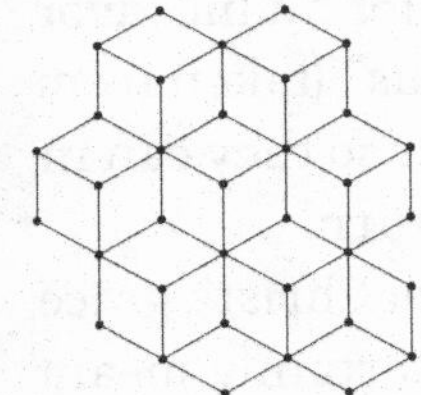

GLOSSARY

chiasm: A stylistic device used throughout Scripture that presents two sets of ideas in parallel to each other, with the order reversed in the second pair. Chiasms generally are used to emphasize the element or elements in the middle of the pattern.

eschatology (*n.*), **eschatological** (*adj.*)**:** The study of the last things or the end times.

eschaton: Greek for "end" or "last," referring to the return of Christ and the end of history.

Hellenistic: Relating to the spread of Greek culture after Alexander the Great (356–323 BC).

inclusio: A framing device in which the same word or phrase occurs at the beginning and end of a section of text.

lex talionis Latin for "law of retaliation." This is the principle, found throughout Revelation, that those who have done some wrong will be punished in a similar degree and kind.

Parousia: Greek for "presence" or "arrival," referring to the visible second coming of Christ.

prolepsis (*n.*), **proleptic** (*adj.*)**:** The presentation of a future act as if it has already been accomplished.

Septuagint: An ancient Greek translation of the Old Testament that was used extensively in the early church.

theophany: A visible manifestation of God, often involving natural phenomena such as lightning or earthquakes.

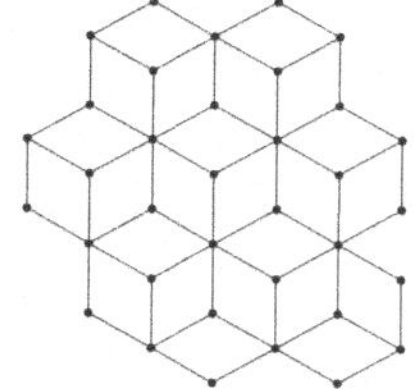

BIBLIOGRAPHY

Aune, David E. *Revelation*. Word Biblical Commentary. 3 vols.; Dallas: Word, 1997, 1998.

Bauckham, Richard. *The Theology of the Book of Revelation*. Cambridge: University Press, 1993.

Beale, Greg K. *The Book of Revelation*. New International Greek Testament Commentary. Grand Rapids: Eerdmans, 1998.

Beasley-Murray, George R. *The Book of Revelation*. New Century Biblical Commentary. London: Marshall, Morgan and Scott, 1974.

Hemer, Colin J. *The Letters to the Seven Churches of Asia in Their Local Setting*. Journal for the Study of the New Testament Supplement Series 11. Sheffield: JSOT Press, 1986.

Hendricksen, William. *More Than Conquerors: An Interpretation of the Book of Revelation*. Grand Rapids: Baker, 1967.

Koester, Craig R. *Revelation*. Anchor Bible Commentary. New Haven: Yale University Press, 2014.

Keener, Craig. *NIV Application Commentary: Revelation*. Grand Rapids: Zondervan, 1999.

Ladd, George. *A Commentary on the Revelation of John*. Grand Rapids: Eerdmans, 1972.

Michaels, J. Ramsey. *Revelation*. The IVP New Testament Commentary Series. Downers Grove, IL: InterVarsity Press, 1997.

Morris, Leon. *The Revelation of St. John*. Tyndale New Testament Commentaries. Grand Rapids: Eerdmans, 1987.

Mounce, Robert. *The Book of Revelation*. New International Commentary on the New Testament. Grand Rapids: Zondervan, 1998.

Osborne, Grant R. *Revelation*. Baker Exegetical Commentary on the New Testament. Grand Rapids: Baker, 2002.

Smalley, Stephen S. *The Revelation to John*. Downers Grove, IL: InterVarsity Press, 2005.

Thomas, Robert. *Revelation: An Exegetical Commentary*. Chicago: Moody, 1992, 1995.

Wall, Robert W. *Revelation*. New International Biblical Commentary. Peabody, MA: Hendrickson, 1991.

Walvoord, John. *The Revelation of Jesus Christ*. Chicago: Moody, 1966.

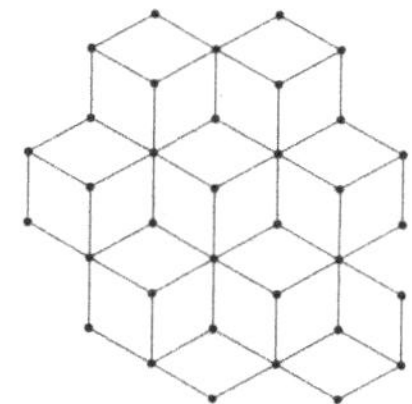

SUBJECT AND AUTHOR INDEX

A

Abaddon, 165
abyss, 159–60, 165, 172, 189, 322–25
accuser, Satan as, 211–12
Adam, 52–53, 357–60
adoption, of the victors, 80, 341–43, 358
adultery, spiritual, 278–80, 292–96
Ahab, 61, 64
allusion, John's use of, 11–12
Almighty One, 104–06, 267
Alpha and Omega, 31, 40, 70, 342, 367
altar, heavenly, 128, 166, 250
amen, 30, 90, 119, 143, 372–73
America, and Babylon, 305
angel
- and the abyss, 159–60, 165, 172
- announcing judgment, 243–45, 291–93
- commands of, 364–66
- and the dragon, 323–24
- and the eternal gospel, 241–43
- and the great prostitute, 281–87
- as guide, 345–46
- as measuring the new Jerusalem, 348–49
- mighty, 110, 174–78, 301–03
- in the sun, 317
- of the waters, 265

angels
- choir of, 116–17
- of destruction, 166–68
- fallen, 206–07
- and the harvest, 249–51
- and the heavenly council, 88, 100
- as priests, 150–52, 166
- and the saints, 138–39, 312, 360
- and the seven bowls, 258–61
- of the seven churches, 41–43, 84, 90
- and the seven trumpets, 150–52

animals
- as apocalyptic symbols, 222–23
- in the new creation, 336n3

annihilation, 336

antichrist
and the beast from the earth, 231
and the beast from the sea, 221–26, 229–30, 233–36
as the eighth king, 284–86
and the scarlet beast, 282–83
and the white horseman, 123–24
Antipas, 55, 90
apocalyptic literature, 2–7, 41–42, 98
apokalypsis, 20
Apollo, 60, 165
Apollos, 46
Apollyon, 165
apostasy, final, 186
apostles, 302, 347–50
false, 48
Aquila, 46
archangels, 110
Michael as, 209
seven, 150–52
ark of the covenant, 58–59, 200
Armageddon, 112, 269–72, 287, 320, 330
army
heavenly, 209
of the locust-scorpions, 162–64
messianic, 140–41, 313–18
Roman, 168–69
Artemis, 46, 83–85
ascension
of Christ, 207–08
of the two witnesses, 192–93
Asia, 19, 23–24, 32, 69–70, 82
persecution in, 8–10
Asiarchs, 8
Augustine, interpretation by, 102, 321
author, of Revelation, 6–7
authority
of the beast from the earth, 231
of the beast from the sea, 223, 227, 268
of Christ and the church, 66–67
of the locust-scorpions, 161–63
and the sealed scroll, 108–09
of the two witnesses, 185

B

Babylon
fall of, 243–44, 291–09
and the great prostitute, 277–80, 290
vs. the new Jerusalem, 339
and Rome, 154, 241, 274
and Satan's fall, 209
Balaam, 56–57, 67
Balak, 56
banquet, messianic, 59, 310, 317–20
beast
from the earth, 230–36, 270
scarlet, 279–80, 282–87
from the sea, 188–90, 219–36, 270, 318–19
beatitudes, 22–23, 247, 271, 311–12, 328, 363–64, 367–68
benediction, 372–73
bitterness, of the Word, 178–79
black, symbolism of, 125–26
blasphemy
by the beast from the sea, 225–26
by the earth-dwellers, 267–68, 275–76
blessing
on Christ, 117
See also beatitudes

blindness, spiritual, 92–93
blood
and Christ's robe, 315
of the Lamb, 27, 115, 144, 213, 228, 310, 367–68
of the saints, 266, 281
and the seven bowls, 259
and water, 153–54, 188, 264–65
and the winepress, 251
boils, plague of, 263–64
book, the
adding or subtracting to, 370–72
authentication of, 362–64
book of life, 88, 227–28, 283, 333–35, 355
bowls
of incense, 114
seven, 120–22, 131, 136, 175–76, 253, 258–76
bread of life, 59
breastplates, of the locust-scorpions, 163–64
breath of life, 191, 232–33
bride of the Lamb, 278, 309–11, 370
new Jerusalem as, 339, 345, 349–51
bronze, symbolism of, 37–38

C

Caesar, 284–86
vs. Christ, 317
vs. God, 99–100, 105–06
See also cult, imperial
calling, 311
camp, of the saints, 330
carrion birds, and the messianic banquet, 317–20
cavalry, demonic, 168–70
celibacy, 239–40
censer, and prayer, 150–52
censers, seven bowls as, 259
census, 140–41
chariots, symbolism of, 123, 164
choir, heavenly, 195–96
Christ, 15, 123, 247–49, 339
attributes of, 25–29
vs. the beast from the earth, 230–31
vs. the beast from the sea, 223–24, 234
as Divine Warrior, 16, 313–20
at the door, 94–95
millennial reign of, 321–28
name of, 59, 235–36
redemption by, 144–45
and revelation, 20–22
vs. Satan, 210–11, 217–18
sayings of, 65, 366–72
vs. the scarlet beast, 282
self-identification of, 47, 54, 60, 64, 70, 75–76, 83–84, 90–91, 367–70
as a thief, 86, 271
vision of, 35–43
and the woman, 204, 207–08
church, 178
gathering of, 192–93, 250
and the new Jerusalem, 347–48
priestly work of, 27–28, 145, 328, 359
prophetic witness of, 181, 199, 370
as the woman, 207–08, 217–18
See also saints
churches, seven, 23–24, 33–36, 41–96
cities, seven, 23–24, 33–34

citizenship, in heaven, 88–89
  See also book of life
Clement of Alexandria,
    interpretation by, 5, 51
clothing, 34, 87–88, 92–93, 100,
    186, 298
  of angels, 259, 316
  of the saints, 129–30, 141–44,
    310–11, 367–68
cloud, symbolism of, 174, 192,
    249, 260
Colossae, 60, 89–91
Colossus of Rhodes, 175
commission
  of angels, 259–60
  of John, 32–33, 39–43, 173–81
complacency, spiritual, 10, 92–94
compromise, temptation to, 10, 62,
    82, 343
conquest, lust for, 123–25
contract, sealed scroll as, 109
councils, church, 48
courtroom, heavenly, 211–12, 245,
    295–96, 304
covenant, and the new Jerusalem,
    340, 343, 347, 358
cowards, 344
creation, 14, 110
  and Christ, 90–91
  and cosmic signs, 131–32
  destruction of, 332–33, 338
  God's dominion over, 175–81
  and judgment, 122, 272–76
  new, 79–81, 336–55
  theology of, 106–07
  and the woman, 216–17
  worship by, 117–19, 242–43
Creator, God as, 106–07, 177
creatures, four living, 102–05,
    114–16, 119, 143, 259, 308
Croesus, 83
cross, the, 27
  victory by, 110–15, 201, 213,
    228, 255
crown
  as a reward, 73–74, 79
  of the woman, 204
crowns
  of the beast from the sea, 220–21
  of Christ, 314
  of the dragon, 205–06
  elders', 105
  of the locust-scorpions, 163
cult, imperial, 9–10, 18, 106
  in Asia, 46, 53–55, 60, 69–70
  and beast worship, 219, 222–24,
    230–32, 239
curse
  as done away with, 358
  on false teachers, 371
Cyrus, and Sardis, 83

D

Dan, idolatry of, 141
Daniel, and the divine plan,
    175–77
darkness, symbolism of, 155–56,
    268–69
date, of Revelation, 7–8, 285
David, and Christ, 26, 111–12, 369
Day of Yahweh, 130, 133–34, 156,
    160, 242
dead, the, 198
death
  Christ's sovereignty over, 40–41
  and judgment, 127, 155, 167–68
  and the lake of fire, 334–36

second, 74, 328–29, 334–36, 371
spiritual, 84–85
deception, by Satan, 211, 216, 324–25, 329–31
defeat, of Satan, 209–12
dei, 180, 284
demons, and worship, 170–72
denial, of Christ, 76–77
depravity, human, 276, 329–32, 344
and Babylon, 292–93
and judgment, 122–25, 133–35, 170
despair, of the earth-dwellers, 162
Destroyer, 165
destroyers, 199
destruction
angels of, 166–68
of Babylon, 243–44, 291–09
of creation, 332–33, 338
of the great prostitute, 288
and wind, 137–39
diadēma, 206, 314
Dionysius of Alexandria, on Revelation authorship, 6
discipline, vs. judgment, 93–94
doctrine, 48, 52, 56
and false teaching, 61, 64–66
Domitian, 126, 163
and the imperial cult, 9, 46, 106, 165, 232–33
and Revelation date, 7–8, 32, 285
door, symbolism of, 76, 79, 94, 98
doxologies, 118–19
dragon, 144, 202–18, 270
and the abyss, 159, 322–25
and the beasts, 219–20
defeat of, 318–19
See also Satan
drought, 187–88
dwelling, of God, 340, 352

E

eagle, 157–58, 215
earth-dwellers
and beast worship, 227–28, 232–33, 283
fear of, 132–35, 191
as rejecting God, 267–69
vs. saints, 136–37, 213–14
and Satan, 324–25
suffering of, 165–68, 172, 262
woe on, 158–59, 162
earthquake, 131–32, 192–93, 273–74
in Asia, 74, 83, 89, 92
eclipse, 155
Eden, and the new creation, 53, 336n3, 338–39, 356–61
edothē, 183, 223, 232, 267, 311
Egypt, 190
plagues of, 149, 152–55, 160, 253–54, 258, 264, 275
elders, twenty-four, 100–01, 105–07, 110, 114–16, 119, 143–47, 196–99, 308
Elijah
and the beast from the earth, 231–32
as a witness, 186–88, 192
emperors, of Rome, 284–86
endurance. *See* perseverance
Ephesus, 33, 44n1, 145–56, 60–61, 67–68, 89, 92
and the imperial cult, 9, 232
and magic, 171, 304, 344
epi, 180
equestrian class, 304
eschaton, 23, 29, 66, 86
timing of, 177–78, 193–94, 273

eternality, of God, 31, 39–40, 104–05, 176–77
eternity, 105
Eucharist, and Christ's coming, 372
Euphrates, 269–70, 278
Eusebius, interpretation by, 6, 32
evangelism, 16–17
Eve, 52–53, 211, 357–60
evil, 157
  eradication of, 334–36
  vs. righteousness, 365–66
excommunication, 75–76
eyes
  of Christ, 37, 64, 113, 314
  of the four living creatures, 103
Ezekiel, and John, 178–81

F

face
  of Christ, 39
  of God, 134, 359
faces, demonic, 163
faith, 61, 246
faithfulness, of Christ, 26
fall, of Satan, 209–10, 214
famine, 125–26
Father, and the Son, 67
fear, of the earth-dwellers, 132–35, 191–94
fear of God, 256–58, 309
feet, bronze, 37–38
fellowship
  of his suffering, 71, 189, 229, 247, 266, 281
  table, 94–95
fire
  demonic, 169, 232
  from heaven, 187, 328–31
  as judgment, 151–53, 267–68
  lake of, 244–45, 319, 328–31, 335–36, 343–44
first and the last, the, 40, 70, 367
firstborn, Christ as, 26
firstfruits, the 144,000 as, 240
flood, of the dragon, 216–17
food, and Babylon, 299–03
forehead, mark on, 139, 233–34
foundations, and the new Jerusalem, 347–50
frogs, spirits of, 270
fruit, of life, 358
future, the, God's sovereignty over, 20–21, 24–25, 197
futurist interpretation, 4–6

G

Gabriel, 25n4, 150, 174
garden, heaven as, 360–61
gates, of the new Jerusalem, 346–48, 353–54
gegonen, 273
gematria, 234–36
genre, of Revelation, 2–3
Gentiles, court of, 184
glory
  of an angel, 291–92
  of Christ, 28–29, 116–17
  of the earthly kings, 353–54
glory, of God, 99, 204
  and the new Jerusalem, 146, 346, 351–52, 360
  in worship, 105–07, 143, 193–94, 256–58
Gnosticism, 51
God, 2, 73, 98–99, 257
  and Christ, 39

and his people, 137–41, 216, 340–41, 359
and martyrs, 128–30, 133, 149–50
and revelation, 20–22
vs. the scarlet beast, 282–83
as speaking, 30–31
worship of, 103–07, 142–43
Gog and Magog, 133, 270–72, 288, 317, 329–31
gold, and the new Jerusalem, 348–51, 357
gospel, 178
eternal, 17, 30, 76, 113, 158, 194, 241–43, 252, 257
Gospel of John, vs. Revelation, 7, 15, 20, 31, 67, 113, 204, 231, 369
Gospels, and the four living creatures, 102
grace, 24, 372–73
grain, 125–26
harvest of, 248–50
grapes, harvest of, 248–52
grass, 153
green, symbolism of, 127
guilds, pagan, 9, 51, 57–59, 60–62, 234, 303

H

Hades, 127, 165, 334–36
keys of, 40–41
hail, as judgment, 152–53, 275
hair, white, 37
hallelujah, 307–09
harps, 114, 238–39, 255
harvest, of the earth, 248–52
heads
of the beast from the sea, 220–21
of the dragon, 205–06
of the scarlet beast, 284–86
healing
of the beast from the sea, 223–24
for the nations, 358
hearing, the Word, 22–23
heaven, vision of, 97–98. *See also* temple, heavenly
heavens, shaking of, 130–35
Hellenistic culture, 74, 80, 83, 89
heresy, 48, 56, 372–72
Hierapolis, 89–91
hills, seven, 284
historicist interpretation, 5, 44
history
God's sovereignty over, 24–25, 197, 266, 342, 367
and Revelation, 4–5, 8–10
holiness
of Christ, 75
of God, 104, 107, 257
and the new Jerusalem, 354–55
of the saints, 328
horn, little, 185, 189, 221, 225
horns
of the beast from the earth, 230–31
of the beast from the sea, 220–21
of the dragon, 205–06
of the Lamb, 113
of the scarlet beast, 286–87
horsemen, four, 122–27
horses, symbolism of, 162–64, 168–69, 313, 316
human beings, vs. demons, 163–64
hymn
of the angels, 116–17
doxological, 265–67

of the elders, 105–07, 145–47, 196–99
of the four living creatures, 104
of the heavenly choir, 195–96, 211–14
of the multitude, 306–09
of the 144,000, 238–39
of the saints, 142–43, 254–58

I

I Am, 24, 31, 40, 369
idealist interpretation, 5–6
idol, of the beast, 232–33
idolatry, 170–72, 243, 344, 364. *See also* cult, imperial
Ignatius, and the Ephesians, 50–51
imitatio Christi, 213, 240
imminence
of Christ's return, 23, 79, 363–67, 370–73
of the eschaton, 20–21, 242, 273, 313
immorality, 63, 56–57, 344
of Rome, 243–44, 295
incense, 114, 150–52, 299
interludes, 136, 173, 182, 189, 202–03, 237
interpretation, of Revelation, 1–6, 44–45, 120–22, 262–63, 282–87, 350
and the millennium, 321–22, 326–27, 330–31
Irenaeus, on Revelation, 6, 51
Israel, the woman as, 204
ius gladii, 38, 54, 125

J

Jerusalem, 190, 251, 330
new, 80–81, 337–39, 344–55
jewels, symbolism of, 99, 349–51
Jews, 4
in Asia, 70–72, 75–77, 83, 89
as believers, 137, 140
Jezebel, 61–65, 278
John the apostle, 31–33, 97–98, 144, 281–82, 364
as author, 6–7, 44
commissioning of, 3, 39–41, 173–81
concluding words of, 372–73
Joshua (high priest), 187
Judge, Christ as, 314–16
judgment, 7, 64, 371
on Babylon, 294–96, 301–04
on the beast's followers, 244–45, 263
by Christ, 38–39, 54, 314–16, 319–20, 366–67
final, 198, 322, 325, 332–36
and the grape harvest, 250–52
as imminent, 57–58
protection from, 78
and repentance, 29–30, 193–94, 241–43
by the saints, 326
seven bowls as, 253–54, 260–63, 272–76
and the seven churches, 50, 63, 85–88, 92–94
seven seals as, 120–22, 125–26
seven trumpets as, 149–50, 157, 194–95
by works, 248, 334
justice
of God, 256–61, 265–67, 274–76, 294–96, 301–02, 322
for martyrs, 128–33, 149–50
Justin Martyr, on Revelation authorship, 6

K

kairos, 198
key
  of the abyss, 159–60, 323
  of David, 75–76
keys, of death and Hades, 40–41
king, demonic, 165
kingdom of God, 32, 178, 195–96
King of kings, Christ as, 26, 317
kings, of Rome, 284–86
kings of the earth, 180, 269–72, 318
  and Babylon, 296–97
  and the great prostitute, 278–79, 286–89
  and the new Jerusalem, 353–54

L

lake of fire, 244–45, 319, 328–31, 335–36, 343–44
Lamb, 15, 27
  and the book of life, 227–28, 283, 355
  as opening seals, 122–23, 148
  and the saints, 142–43, 237–41
  as shepherd, 146–47
  in the throne room, 108–19, 352
  victory of, 255, 287
  wrath of, 134
laments, over Babylon, 296–01
lampstands
  seven, 35–36, 43, 47, 50, 101
  two, 186–87
language, of Revelation, 6–7, 21
language of equivalents, 4
Laodicea, 34, 44n1, 60, 82, 89–96
  and clothing, 37, 271, 289, 368
  and wealth, 10, 71
latreuō, 145, 359
letter, Revelation as, 3, 19–20, 372–73
letters, to the churches, 44–96
Leviathan, 205, 210, 216, 220, 323
lex talionis, 248, 335
  and Babylon, 199, 293–94, 302
  and martyrs, 128–29, 162, 266
  and the two witnesses, 187, 191, 319
liars, judgment on, 241, 344, 354–55
life
  breath of, 191, 232–33
  eternal, 40, 53, 70, 73–74, 328, 357–58
  spiritual, 84–85
  and water, 342–43, 356–57
  and the Word of God, 179
light, of God, 352–53, 360
Lion, 111–12
locusts, 160–64
locust-scorpions, 158–65, 168–69
Lord's day, 33
love, 49–52, 61
  of Christ, 27–28
Lycus River, 60
Lydia (convert from Thyatira), 60
Lydia, kingdom of, 83, 88

M

magic, 171, 304, 344
maleness, significance of, 207
manna, symbolism of, 58–59
Marana tha, 372
mark
  of the beast, 139, 233–38, 244
  of God, 137–41, 238
martyrdom
  as victory, 226–27, 246–47, 255

as witness, 17, 213
martyria, 17, 213
martyrs, 140, 147
blood of, 201, 247, 266–67
justice for, 167, 319–22
prayers of, 121, 127–30
as reigning, 326
two witnesses as, 188–91
martys, 55
Mary, and the woman, 204
meal, with Christ, 94–95
measurement, of the new Jerusalem, 348–49
Megiddo, 272
merchants, and Babylon, 297–04
messengers, angels as, 42
Messiah
Christ as, 27–28, 75, 111–12, 314–18, 369
and the kingdom, 196, 238
and the nations, 66–67
metals, precious, 298
Michael, 25n4, 150, 174
vs. Satan, 209–10, 214, 225, 324
midair, significance of, 158, 241
military, and the beast from the sea, 219–21
millennium, 321–28
mission, 16–17, 113
money, and false teachers, 62–63
moon, 204, 352
and cosmic signs, 131–32, 155–56
Moses, as a witness, 186–88
"mother of," 280–81
motto, of revelation, 29–31
mountain
on fire, 153–54
high, 345–46
mouth, 169, 216, 270
of Christ, 38–39, 58, 91, 96, 187–89, 315–19, 330
multitude, of the saints, 141–47, 306–13
myriad, 116
mystery, apocalyptic, 41, 177–78, 280–82
myths, dragon, 203–05

N

nakedness, spiritual, 92–93, 271, 288–89
name
of the beast, 222, 234–36
and the book of life, 88
of Christ, 236, 314–15
of God, 226
of the great prostitute, 280
new, 59, 80–81, 238, 314–15, 359
narrative, revelation as, 3
nations
and beast worship, 227–28
and Christ, 316–18
and the church, 66–67
fear of, 133
God's sovereignty over, 197–98, 256–57
prophecy to, 178–80
redemption of, 29–30, 115–16, 358
and Satan, 324–25, 329–31
See also earth-dwellers
neokoros, 9
Nero
and the beast's number, 235
and Revelation date, 7–8
Nero redivivus, 8, 224, 284–86
"newspaper approach," 4
Nicolaitans
and idolatry, 225, 232

in the seven churches, 47-48, 51-52, 55-58, 76-77
warnings concerning, 141, 241, 344, 354, 371
number
of the beast, 234-36
of Christ, 236
of kings, 284-86
of martyrs, 130
of years, 324

O

oath, of the angel, 176-78
obedience, and perseverance, 246, 363-65
oceans, as blood, 153-54
offspring, of the woman, 217
oil, 125-26
Old Testament, and Revelation, 11-12
Olivet Discourse, 23n2, 123, 131, 235, 274, 366
olive trees, two, 186-87
omniscience, of Christ, 64
144,000, 137, 140-41, 237-41
orthopraxy, and orthodoxy, 65-66
ouai, 158

P

Papias, on the "elder John," 6
papyrus, 109
paradise, 53, 337, 356
Parousia, 21, 313, 363-67, 370-73
and the final victory, 306, 309
and the two witnesses, 192-93
Parthians, cavalry of, 124, 164, 167-68
patience, of God, 21
Patmos, 19, 31-32
Paul, and Ephesus, 46-47
peace, 24, 125
pearls, significance of, 298, 351
peirazō, 73
perfumes, 299
Pergamum, 9, 45-46, 53-61, 67-68, 92, 234
and roads, 34, 74, 89
persecution, 32, 147, 201, 246-47
by the beast from the sea, 226-27, 234-36
by the prostitute/Babylon, 281, 290, 305
and the readers, 8-10, 229
in the seven churches, 54-55, 70-72, 77-78
of the woman, 215-18
perseverance, 17
blessing on, 363-64
call for, 229-30, 245-48, 343-44
and the seven churches, 48-49, 61, 73, 76-81
pestilence, 127
Philadelphia, 45, 70-71, 74-83
persecution of, 92, 137, 187, 234
and roads, 34, 89
pillars, symbolism of, 79-80
plagues
on Babylon, 295-96
of Egypt, 149, 152-55, 160, 253-54, 258, 264, 275
plan of God, 109-10, 174-76, 228, 342
poieō, 231-33
Polycarp, in Smyrna, 70-72
pottery, shattering of, 67
poverty, 71, 234
spiritual, 92-93
power
of Christ, 116-17

of God, 104–06, 197, 267
lust for, 295–96
prayers
of the martyrs, 121, 127–30, 149–52
of the saints, 114, 166, 274
preaching, of Revelation, 1
presence
of Christ, 39, 72–73
of God, 39, 145–46, 200, 226, 340, 352, 359–60
present, the, 24–25, 197
preterist interpretation, 5–6, 227
pride, 92, 295
priests
angels as, 150–52, 166
elders as, 100–01
saints as, 27–28, 115–16, 145, 328, 359
two witnesses as, 187
Priscilla, 46
prophecy
Revelation as, 3
of the two witnesses, 185–86
prophet, false, 230–36, 318–19. *See also* beast: from the earth
prophet, John as, 3, 178–81
prophets, 3, 199, 302, 364, 369
prostitute, great, 277–90, 307
prostration, before an angel, 312
protection
of the saints, 77–78, 137–41, 161, 183–84, 346–47
of the woman, 207–08, 215–17
punishment, eternal, 335–36
purity, 354–55, 367–68

R

Rahab (dragon), 205, 210, 215
ransom, by the Lamb, 115
rapture, secret, 30, 48, 56, 78, 306, 313
readers, words to, 22–23, 228–30, 370, 373
reading, public, 22
rebellion, of Satan, 206–07
red, symbolism of, 124–25, 205
redemption, by the Lamb, 108–19, 240–41
rejection
of Christ, 332
of God, 169–70, 267–69, 275–76
rejoicing, over Babylon's destruction, 301–02
remembering, 49–51, 86
repentance, 11–12, 50–51, 86, 242–43
and the earth-dwellers, 169–70, 193–94
and judgment, 29–30, 122
rest, for the martyrs, 247–48
resurrection
of Christ, 70
and the final judgment, 334–35
and the millennium, 326–27
of the two witnesses, 191–93
revelation, 20–22, 41, 364–65, 369
reward
victor's, 52–53, 73–74, 79–81, 87–89, 95–96, 145, 198–99, 343–44
for works, 64, 248, 334, 366–67
right hand, 38
righteousness
vs. evil 365–66
of God, 257–58, 265–66
river, of life, 356–57
roads, Roman, 33–34, 46, 74, 89

roar, of God, 175
robe. *See* clothing
rod
iron, 66–67, 207, 316
measuring, 348
Rome, 9, 190
and Babylon, 154, 241–44, 274, 292–01, 304
and the beast from the sea, 221–22, 236, 269–70, 268
and the great prostitute, 277–81, 288–90
and the scarlet beast, 284–86
Root of David, 111–12, 369
ruler, Christ as, 90–91

S

sailors, and Babylon, 300–01
saints, 136–47, 198–99, 229–30
and Babylon, 301–02, 305
and the beast from the sea, 226–27
blessings on, 367–68
judgment of, 333–34
measuring of, 183–84
in the messianic army, 287, 316–18
in the new Jerusalem, 339–41, 354–55
as reigning, 95–96 115–16, 326–28, 360
victory of, 210–13, 217–18, 254–58
salvation
praise for, 26–29, 142–45, 255–56
as victory, 212, 307
Sardis, 10, 34, 71, 74, 82–89, 99, 271, 368
sash, golden, 37
satan, 211–12, 331
Satan
and the abyss, 159, 322–25
and the antichrist, 139, 282
deception by, 211, 216, 324–25, 329–31
defeat of, 209–12
and false teachers, 48–50, 65
and the final war, 328–32
futility of, 14–16, 40–41, 161
and idolatry, 171
and the locust-scorpions, 161, 165
as a serpent, 169, 211, 323
and suffering, 73, 78, 281
synagogue of, 50, 72, 75–77
throne of, 54–55, 99
See also dragon
sayings, of Christ, 366–72
scales, symbolism of, 125
scorpions, 161–62
Scripture, revelation as, 22
scroll
little, 173–79
sealed, 108–19, 174
sea
crystal, 101–02, 254–55
symbolism of, 220, 334–35, 338
as turning to blood, 264
seal, of God, 137–41, 248
seals
seven, 120–35, 148–49, 364–65
of the thunder message, 175–76
seraphim, and the four living creatures, 102–03
serpent, Satan as, 169, 211, 323
sevenfold Spirit, 15, 25, 84, 101, 113
shaking, of the heavens, 130–35
Shekinah glory, 146, 174, 249, 260, 340, 345–56, 352, 359–60

shepherd, Christ as, 29–30, 146–47
shipping, and Babylon, 300–01
Sibyl Sambathe, 62
sign
  the dragon as, 205–06
  the woman as, 203–04
signs
  cosmic, 131–32, 200–01
  false, 231–32
silence, in heaven, 148–49
sin, 16, 27, 51, 115
  and the new creation, 338–42
Sinai, 101, 123, 131, 152, 160, 345–46
sinners
  defeat of, 317–19
  judgment on, 334–36, 343–44, 368
  resurrection of, 327
  See also earth-dwellers
skēnē, 226
slander, in Smyrna, 71–72
slaves
  angels as, 312, 360, 364
  saints as, 20, 139, 198–99, 308–09, 359
  trade of, 299
smoke, 169
  of Babylon, 297, 307–08
  symbolism of, 160, 245
  in the temple, 260
Smyrna, 9, 34, 44n1, 69–74, 81–82, 187, 234
snakes, and Satan, 169, 211, 323
Sodom, and the great city, 190
song, new, 100, 114–15, 238–39
song of Moses, 212, 216, 253–56
son of man, 29, 35–36, 249
soon, 20–21, 57–58, 195, 363. *See also* imminence
sovereignty, of Christ, 26, 43, 70, 95–96, 317, 367
sovereignty, of God, 2, 10, 14, 105–07, 180–81, 309–10
  over demonic forces, 161, 167–70, 188–89, 225–30, 232, 236, 289
  and history, 24–25, 31, 176–77, 196–98, 342
  in judgment, 122, 256, 332–33
sovereignty, of Satan, 206, 223
spices, 299
Spirit, 15, 187, 247
  and prophecy, 312–13, 362–63, 370
  and the seal of God, 138–41
  sevenfold, 15, 25, 84, 101, 113
  and the seven letters, 52, 58, 89
  and visions, 33, 98, 279
star, morning, 67, 369
stars
  falling, 101, 132, 154–55, 159
  symbolism of, 38, 41–43, 47, 84, 204–07
stephanos, 73, 163, 206, 249, 314
sting, of the locust-scorpions, 162–64
stone
  as thrown down, 302–03
  white, 59
storm, 131
  as a theophany, 152, 175, 200, 272–75
street, in the new Jerusalem, 351, 357
structure, of Revelation, 12–14, 45–46, 111, 136, 182, 202–03
suddenness, of judgment, 297, 300
Suetonius, on Domitian, 8

suffering
- of Christ and the saints, 71, 130, 189–90, 229, 247, 266, 281
- of the earth-dwellers, 161–62, 165–68, 172, 214, 288, 307–08, 368
- and the new creation, 146, 341, 355
- in Smyrna, 71–74
- of the two witnesses, 189–91

sulfur, 169, 244–45
sun, 204, 317, 352
- and cosmic signs, 131–32, 155–56
- scorching by, 267–68

supper, wedding, 310–12, 320
sweetness, of the Word, 178–79
sword, of Christ's mouth, 38–39, 54, 58, 187–89, 315–19, 330
symbolism, in Revelation, 3–5, 21
synagogue of Satan, 50, 72, 75–77
syncretism, 51, 55–57, 64–65

T

tabernacle, and the new Jerusalem, 340, 352
Tacitus, on Domitian, 8
tails, of the locust-scorpions, 163–64
tav, significance of, 139, 234
teachers, false, 46–49, 55–58, 61–64, 241, 354–55, 371
teeth, of the locust-scorpions, 163, 169
temple, heavenly, 102, 128, 145–46, 150–52, 260, 263
- measuring of, 183–85
- new Jerusalem as, 79–81, 339, 344–45, 348, 351–52, 360
- opening of, 200, 258, 313

temples, in the seven cities, 9, 32, 46, 53, 69–70, 85
temptation, vs. testing, 73
Tertullian, 6, 186
- on martyrs, 201, 247

testing, vs. temptation, 73
thanksgiving, 105, 143, 197
theology, of Revelation, 14–18
theophany, 39, 152, 173, 200, 272–73
thief, Christ's return as, 86, 271
three-and-a-half years, 175–77, 185–88, 192, 208
throne
- of the beast of the sea, 268
- of Christ, 95–96
- of God, 98–99, 105, 200, 332–33, 357

throne room
- saints in, 142–45
- vision of, 97–119

thrones
- of the saints, 326
- of the twenty-four elders, 196

Thyatira, 34, 38, 45–46, 53, 60–68, 79, 82, 92, 234
time, eschatological, 198
titles
- of Christ, 40, 70, 75–76, 90, 111–12, 367–70
- of God, 30–31

tolerance, and false teaching, 55–58
torture. *See* suffering
transcendence, of God, 2, 10
tree of life, 53, 357–58
trials, 48–49, 77–78
tribes, twelve, 140–41, 347–50

tribulation, great, 77–78, 120–21, 144, 159, 185, 192
Trinity, 17–19, 23–29, 34
trinity, false, 219–21, 231, 236, 270–71, 286, 289, 318
Trisagion, 104
true, Christ as, 75, 90, 313
trumpets, seven, 120–22, 131, 136, 148–72

V

vice lists, 171, 343–44, 354
victory
  of Christ, 40–41
  of the church, 52, 59, 66–67, 73–74, 79–80, 87–89
  by the cross, 110–15, 201, 213, 228, 255
  final, 287, 306–20
  of the martyrs, 129–30
  of the readers, 229–30
  of the saints, 142–45, 281
  over Satan, 210–13, 217–18
  of the two witnesses, 190
vigilance, spiritual, 85–87, 271
virginity
  spiritual, 310–11
  symbolism of, 239–40
visions, in Revelation, 2–3, 22, 32–33
voice
  of Christ, 33, 38
  of God, 273, 341–43
  from heaven, 175, 246, 293
  from the temple, 263
  from the throne, 273, 308–09, 340–41
volcanoes, 153–54

W

walls, of the new Jerusalem, 346–47
war
  civil, 124–25, 287–90
  cosmic, 16, 27–28, 57–58
  of the dragon, 206–11, 215–19
  final, 240, 251–52, 269–72, 287, 313–20, 328–32
  great, 219–36
warning
  by Christ, 49–51, 57–58, 64, 271, 370–72
  to the readers, 228–30
Warrior, Divine, 14–16
  Christ as, 36–38, 60, 67, 77, 313–20
watchmen, and Sardis, 83–85
water
  judgment on, 153–55, 188, 264–65
  and Laodicea, 89–91
  of life, 342–43, 356–57
waters, and the great prostitute, 278, 287–88
wealth
  of Babylon/Rome, 280, 297–01, 304
  of Christ, 117
  and the seven churches, 10, 74, 82–85, 89–96
wedding, of the Lamb, 309–11, 345
white, symbolism of, 37, 123–24, 313, 332
  and clothing, 87, 92–93, 100, 129–30, 310–11, 367–68
wilderness, significance of, 279
winds, of destruction, 137–39
wine, 125–26
  of adultery, 279–81, 292–93

of God's wrath, 243–44, 251, 280, 294–95
winepress, symbolism of, 250–51, 316
wings
of the four living creatures, 103
of the locust-scorpions, 163–64
of the woman, 215–16
wisdom
Christ as, 117
and interpretation, 235, 284
witness, 54–55, 185–86
Christ as, 26, 90, 369
of the Pergamum church, 54–55
victory by, 213, 217, 281
witnesses, two, 185–94, 201, 231–32
woes
over Babylon, 297, 300
and the seven trumpets, 157–59, 166, 194–95, 198
woman, symbolism of, 203–04, 207–08, 215–18
wood, expensive, 298–00
wool, 87, 93
Word of God, 179, 315
works
of the churches, 47, 51, 60–61, 84–86
of the saints, 248, 311, 334
Wormwood, 155, 167
worship, 17–18, 364
of the beast, 190–91, 219, 224–33, 244–45
of demons, 170–71
heavenly, 103–07
and judgment, 150–52, 242–43
of the Lamb, 114–19
by the multitude, 306–13
in the new Jerusalem, 354, 359
by the saints, 256–58, 142–43
worshipers, measuring of, 183–84
worthiness
of God, 266–67
of the Lamb, 110–11, 114–18
wrath, of God, 133–34, 197–98, 294, 316
and the seven bowls, 254, 259–63
and wine, 243–44, 251–52
wrath, of Satan, 214–20

Y

Yahweh, 24–25, 31
Christ as, 35–40, 75, 315, 369

Z

zeal, 94
Zerubbabel, 187
Zion, 238, 346
zodiac, and the twelve jewels, 4, 350

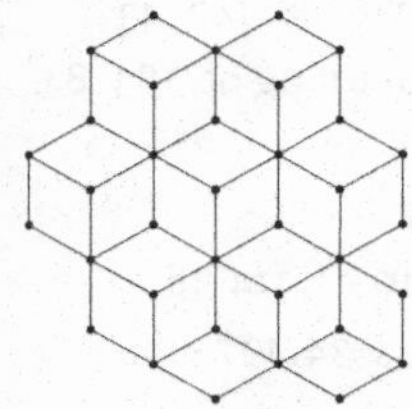

INDEX OF SCRIPTURE AND OTHER ANCIENT LITERATURE

Old Testament

Genesis

1:2 155
1:7 .... 102, 254
2–3 358
2:7 191
2:9 357
2:10 356
2:15 356
2:17 356
3:1 211
3:1–7 169
3:15 205
3:22 358
3:22–24 357
3:24 102
6:1–4 210
9:5–6 302
9:13–17 99
11:4 294
12:3 347
15:5 142
15:18 269
17:7 343
19:24 .... 74, 319
19:28 .... 160, 169
19:30 133
28:12 339
29:35 .... 72n2
32:12 142
35:23–26 141
37:1–9 204
40:19 190
48:15 146
49:8 111
49:9 111
49:9–10 111
49:10 111

Exodus

3:14 .... 31, 40, 369
3:14–15 24
4:17 231
6:8 176
7–10 149
7:9–10 231
7:14–21 .... 4, 153
7:20–21 .... *188*
8:10 225
8:19 193
8:22–23 .... 161, 264
9:4 .... 161, 264
9:6 .... 161, 264
9:9–11 264
9:13–15 275
9:13–26 200–01
9:13–35 152
9:18 153
10:1–2 231
10:13 138
10:14 160
10:21 268
10:21–23 155
10:21–29 268
10:23 .... 161, 268
12:5 207
13 .... 234n11
14:19 260
14:21 .... 127, 138

14:21–22 269
14:24 260
15 255
15:1 256
15:3 16
15:11 257
15:12 216
15:16 191
15:23 155
16:4 58
16:10 174
16:32 .... 208, 216
16:32–34 58
19–20 345
19:4 215
19:5 138
19:5–6 .... 27, 145
19:6 .... 27, 115, 328
19:6–9 200–01
19:10 144
19:14 144
19:16 .... 101, 200–01
19:16–18 .... 131, 273
19:18 160
20:7 226
22:4 294
22:7 294
22:9 294
24:6 263
24:8 263
24:15–16 260
24:15–17 346
25:8 146
25:29 114
25:31–40 36
27:2 166–68
27:3 .... 151, 259
28 350
28:14–20 350
29:1 241
29:18 151
29:45 .... 146, 340
30:18 263
32:10–11 215
32:32–33 88
33:7–11 330
33:20 359
34:29 39
36:23 77
37:16 114
37:25 166–68
38:3 259
39 350
39:10–13 350
40:34 352
40:34–35 260
40:35 260

Leviticus

1:3 207
1:9 151
4:3 241
4:7 263
4:18 263
4:23 207
6:2 174
11:40–43 354
11:44–45 354
16:2 259
16:23 259
17:10 134
21:9 289
22:19 207
23:9–14 240
23:40–43 142
24:14 368
24:23 368
26:11–12 340
26:21 258

Numbers

1 140
2:1–34 330
6:25 360
6:25–26 134
14:21 176
16:6–7 151
16:22 362
16:32 216
18:12 240
18:17 151
22–24 56
24:2 33
24:17 .... 67, 369
25:1–3 56
26 140
27:16 362
31:16 56
33:5–49 185

Deuteronomy

1:7–8 269
1:31 208
4:2 370–71
4:28 170
6 .... 234n11
6:4 234
6:8 234
7:6 138
7:25–26 354
8:3 208
10:17 287
12:32 371
13:1–4 231
14:3 354
18:4 240
19:16–19 302
23:9–10 240
28:38–42 160
28:47–48 146
29:18 155
29:20 .... 88, 371
31:6 139
32 255–56
32:4 .... 256, 265
32:16–17 170
33:2 116–17

34:1–4 345

Joshua

1:5 139
3:13–17 269
5:13–15 316
5:14 .... 39n3
7:6 301
10:7–14 156
10:11 .... 153, 275
10:16 133
11:4 329

Judges

1:19 164
4–5 272
5:4–5 131
7 272
8:19 176
9:54 162
18 141

1 Samuel

4:12 301
12:14 242
13:3 150
13:5 329
13:6 133
17:43–47 190
20:3 176
21:5 240
22:1 133
31 272
31:4 162
31:5 162

2 Samuel

5:10 31
6:2 200–01
7:14 343
11:8–11 240
17:23 162
22:9 160
22:28 295

1 Kings

1:34 150
1:39 150
5:17 347
6:20 348
6:20–22 349
7:21 79
7:23–26 .... 102, 254
7:49 36
7:50 151
8:10–12 .... 260, 346
8:11 260
10:19–20 111
10:26 164
12 141
12:11 161
12:14 161
16 62
16:18 162
17–18 188
17:1 185
18:1 185
18:12 33
18:19 62
18:36–39 232
19:3–9 .... 208, 216
19:4–6 279
19:18 193
21 62
22:19 .... 100, 196

2 Kings

1 187
1:10 331
1:10–14 232
1:12 331
2:11 192
6:17 316
11:14 80
19:18 170
19:21 240
23 272
23:3 80

1 Chronicles

16:24 242
16:31 .... 256, 309
19:7 164
24:4–5 100

2 Chronicles

3:15–17 79
4:8 259
5:12 150
6:23 248
12:6 265
21:12–15 45
35 272

Nehemiah

8:10–12 191
9:33 265

Esther

9:18–22 191

Job

1:6–12 211–12
2:1–6 211
2:1–13 264
2:12 301
3:8 205
7:12 205
7:15 162
9:13 205
12:22 155
15:8 .... 100, 196
25:3 116–17
26:6 165
26:12 205
28:9 153
34:11 .... 334, 367
38:22–23 153
39:19–25 163
41:1 205
41:19–20 169

Psalms

2 ... 66
2:1 ... 197
2:2 ... 197
2:4–5 ... 197
2:8–9 ... 66
2:9 ... 26, 207, 287, 316
3:8 ... 142
4:6 ... 134
5:5 ... 51
7:11 ... 265, 314
9:4 ... 265
9:5 ... 88, 355
9:8 ... 265
11:4 ... 128
11:6 ... 169
12 ... 128
13:1 ... 134
18:4 ... 216
18:8 ... 160
18:13 ... 200–01
19:1–2 ... 106
19:10 ... 179
22:23 ... 242
22:28 ... 256
23 ... 146
23:2 ... 146
23:5 ... 208
28:4 ... 334, 367
29 ... 175–77
31:7 ... 309
32:6 ... 216
33:2 ... 239
33:3 ... 114
33:9 ... 106
34:11 ... 242
35 ... 128
40:3 ... 114
45:7 ... 51
46:1–3 ... 72
47:8 ... 256
50:6 ... 314
51:7 ... 144
52 ... 128
57–59 ... 128
57:8 ... 239
62:12 ... 64, 248, 367
63:9 ... 160
64:4 ... 357
67:4 ... 265
68:4 ... 203–08
68:8 ... 131
68:17 ... 116–17
69:2 ... 216
69:28 ... 88, 355
71:19 ... 225
71:20 ... 160
72:8–14 ... 321
73:13–14 ... 254
74:13 ... 205
74:13–14 ... 205, 210
78:23 ... 98
78:44 ... 265
78:47 ... 153
79:3 ... 266
79:10 ... 129
79:12 ... 266
80:1 ... 146, 200–01
83:14 ... 153
84:11 ... 39
86:9 ... 257
89:27 ... 26, 100, 196
90:4 ... 324
95:7–11 ... 279
96:1 ... 114
96:11 ... 213, 302
96:13 ... 314
98:1 ... 114
99:1 ... 200–01
102:26 ... 333
103:16 ... 138
103:20–21 ... 316
103:20–22 ... 117
104:2 ... 204
104:26 ... 205
105:8–11 ... 294
105:38 ... 191
106 ... 307
106:17 ... 217
106:37 ... 170
106:48 ... 308
109:14 ... 294
110:1 ... 38, 145
111 ... 307
111:3 ... 256
111:5–6 ... 294
111:9 ... 226
113–18 ... 307
115:4–7 ... 170
115:13 ... 199, 309
118:24 ... 309
118:27 ... 360
119:103 ... 179
135 ... 307
141:2 ... 114, 151
144:5 ... 160
144:9 ... 114
145:17 ... 257, 265
146–50 ... 307
149:1 ... 114

Proverbs

3:18 ... 53, 358
3:34 ... 295
5:4 ... 155
10:11 ... 154
11:30 ... 53, 358
13:14 ... 154
15:11 ... 165
16:11 ... 125
24:12 ... 64, 366
24:13–14 ... 179
26:11 ... 368
27:20 ... 165
30:27 ... 165

Song of Solomon
5:2 94

Isaiah
1:9–10 190
1:18 144
1:21 278
2:1–5 339
2:10 133
2:12 295
2:12–18 275
2:17 295
2:19 133
2:21 133
4:3 ..... 88, 355
5:8–9 158
5:16 226
6 259
6:1 128
6:1–4 ..... 99, 346
6:2 103
6:3 ..... 102, 104
6:3–4 260
6:9–10 365
8:21 146
9:5 153
11:1 ..... 111, 369
11:2 ..... 15n4, 25
11:3 242
11:4 ..... 38, 112, 265, 314, 316
11:6–9 ..... 321, 331
11:10 ..... 111–12, 369
11:15–16 269
13:9–13 ..... 130, 273
13:10 39
13:21 292
13:21–22 292
14:2 77
14:12 67
14:12–14 ..... 159, 272
14:12–15 209
17:5 248
17:8 170
20:1–4 ..... 93, 271
21:1–10 279
21:9 ..... 243, 292
22:12 186
22:20–22 75
23:8 304
23:15–17 278
23:17 279
24–27 2
24:8 303
24:18–23 131
24:19–13 130
24:21–22 324
24:23 ..... 204, 238
25:6 310
25:8 146
25:18 341
26:18 204
26:19 198
30:3 169
30:8 33
30:19 341
30:26 204
30:30 200–01
30:33 245
31:4 ..... 111, 318
34:4 ..... 130, 132
34:9 245
34:9–10 ..... 245, 307
34:10 245
34:11–14 292
34:14 292
35:6–9 357–58
35:10 341
37:22 240
40:2 294
40:3 279
40:6–7 138
40:10 366
40:28 106
40:31 215
41:1–5 346
41:4 ..... 40, 369
41:7 225
41:17 71
41:18 155
42:6 353
42:10 114
42:12 242
42:13–16 16
43:2 216
43:3 77
43:4 77
44:6 ..... 40, 342, 369
44:21 50
44:23 213
44:27 269
45:2 275
46:5 225
46:8–9 50
47:9 295
48:12 ..... 40, 342, 369
49:2 ..... 38–39, 316
49:6 353
49:10 146
49:13 ..... 213, 302
49:18 310
49:23 77
49:26 ..... 266, 281
50:1 281
51:4 353
51:6 333
51:9 205
51:9–10 ..... 210, 215
51:17 293
51:21–23 71
52:1 339
52:11 293
53:7 113
54:5 310
54:5–6 339
54:11 ..... 71, 339

54:11–12 349
54:11–13 351
55:1 343, 370
55:5 353
57:3 57
57:8 57
58:11 155
59:17–20 318
59:20 339
60 353
60:1 353
60:3 352–53
60:5 352
60:11 352–53
60:14 77
60:19 39, 352, 360
61:6 27
61:10 310–11, 339
62:2 80, 314
62:6 347
63:1–5 318
63:1–6 316
63:3 251, 315
65:15 315
65:16 90
65:16–17 90
65:17 341–42, 338
66:6 263
66:7 207
66:12 338
66:24 198, 336

Jeremiah

2:13 154, 357
3:1–3 278
4:8 186
4:24 153
5:14 31
9:15 155
10:2–16 257
10:6 257
10:6–7 257
10:7 256
10:25 263
14:10 294
15:2 229
15:16 179
16:18 294
17:10 64, 248, 334, 367
17:18 294
23:14 190
23:15 155
25:10 303–04
25:15–18 293
25:30 248
29:1–23 45
31:32 310
31:33 340
32:18 266
36:28 33
38:23 265
46:10 281
46:23 160
49:36 138
50:8 293
50:19 146
50:29 294
50:39 292
50:44 111
51:7 244, 279–80
51:9 294
51:13 278
51:14 160
51:25 154, 199
51:34 205
51:36 138, 279
51:37 292
51:38 302
51:45 293
51:63–64 303
52:11 293

Ezekiel

1–2 2
1 97, 102, 259
1:1 313
1:5 102
1:5–6 102
1:7 37
1:10–11 102
1:12–13 102
1:13 101
1:18 103
1:19–21 102
1:22 102, 254
1:24 38
1:26–28 99
1:28 39n3, 174
2:2 279
2:3 179
2:8–3:3 178–81
2:9–10 109, 174
2:10 179
3:1–3 174, 178–81
3:2–3 179
3:4–7 179
3:12 33, 279
3:14 33, 179
3:27 365
8:3 279
9:4 234
9:4–6 139
10 102
10:2–3 174
10:2–4 260
10:2–7 151
10:4 174
10:12 103
10:20 102
11:1 279
14 127
16:3 93
16:8–14 310
16:46–49 190

18:3 ... 33
18:20 ... 334, 367
20:5 ... 176
20:15 ... 176
20:41 ... 226, 293
21:32 ... 153
23 ... 278
23:10 ... 93
23:29 ... 271
25:18–20 ... 102
23:25–29 ... 288
26:13 ... 303
27 ... 296
27:12–24 ... 298
27:12–25 ... 293
27:27 ... 297
27:29 ... 300
27:33 ... 296
27:35 ... 297
27:36 ... 297
28:13 ... 351
29:3 ... 205
32:2 ... 205
32:6–8 ... 130, 273
32:7 ... 39
32:7–8 ... 333
33:27 ... 64
34:20–24 ... 146
36:35 ... 339
37–39 ... 2
37:1 ... 33, 279
37:10 ... 191
37:27 ... 339–40
37:32 ... 301
38–39 ... 270–72, 318, 329
38 ... 329
38:2–6 ... 133
38:19–20 ... 193
38:20 ... 153
38:22 ... 74, 153, 169, 200–01, 245, 331
39 ... 329
39:6 ... 331
39:17–20 ... 317
39:18–19 ... 281
40–48 ... 80, 183, 329, 345, 348, 352
40–42 ... 184
40:1–2 ... 346
40:3 ... 183
40:5 ... 183
40:5–9 ... 348
41:5 ... 348
41:13 ... 348
42:15–20 ... 348
42:16–17 ... 348
43:2 ... 38, 138, 292, 346
43:2–5 ... 346
43:4 ... 138
43:5 ... 279
45:2 ... 348
47:1–12 ... 357
47:12 ... 53, 358
48:30–35 ... 347
48:35 ... 80

Daniel

1 ... 97
1:4 ... 284
1:12–14 ... 73
1:17 ... 284
2:28–29 ... 21, 41
2:37 ... 287
2:47 ... 287
3:1–6 ... 232
3:6 ... 233
3:11 ... 233
3:15 ... 233
4:33 ... 297
4:34 ... 194
4:37 ... 194
5 ... 297
7 ... 29, 221, 289
7:3 ... 189, 220
7:4–7 ... 223
7:4–8 ... 205, 221
7:6 ... 223, 225
7:7 ... 221
7:7–8 ... 286
7:7–12 ... 189
7:8 ... 225
7:9 ... 37
7:9–10 ... 228
7:9–11 ... 319, 336
7:9–12 ... 245
7:10 ... 116–17, 334
7:11 ... 225, 283
7:13 ... 29, 36, 192, 249
7:14 ... 29, 227
7:15 ... 282
7:15–16 ... 144
7:17 ... 230
7:17–18 ... 283
7:18 ... 360
7:20 ... 221, 225
7:20–25 ... 286
7:21 ... 189, 226
7:22 ... 326
7:23 ... 283
7:23–25 ... 221
7:24 ... 221
7:25 ... 185, 208, 216, 225
7:26 ... 283
8 ... 206
8:3 ... 230
8:9–14 ... 185
8:10 ... 206
8:17–18 ... 39n3
9:22 ... 284
9:27 ... 216
10 ... 289
10:1 ... 314
10:5 ... 37

10:5–6 ... 36
10:6 ... 37, 60, 314
10:10–18 ... 39n3, 40
10:13 ... 209
10:21 ... 209
11:31 ... 221
11:33 ... 284
12 ... 289
12:1 ... 88, 144, 209, 228, 274, 355
12:1–2 ... 333–34
12:1–3 ... 318
12:2 ... 74, 198
12:3 ... 67
12:4 ... 175–76
12:5–9 ... 177
12:5–10 ... 177
12:7 ... 176–77, 185, 208, 216
12:9–10 ... 365
12:10 ... 235
12:11 ... 185, 221
12:11–12 ... 175

Hosea

1–14 ... 278
2:2–7 ... 281
2:2–13 ... 57
2:16–20 ... 310
6:11 ... 248
11:10 ... 175
12:2 ... 64
13:15 ... 138

Joel

1–2 ... 160
1:2–2:11 ... 160
1:6 ... 163
1:6–7 ... 162
1:8 ... 186
2 ... 163
2:2 ... 156
2:4–5 ... 162
2:5 ... 164
2:10 ... 39, 131, 160
2:11 ... 134, 271
2:28 ... 33
2:30 ... 160
2:30–31 ... 130, 153, 273
2:31 ... 132
2:32 ... 238
3:2 ... 251, 271
3:9–16 ... 318
3:12 ... 249, 251
3:13 ... 248, 250
3:18 ... 155

Amos

3:7 ... 178
3:8 ... 175
5:2 ... 240
6:1–2 ... 158
6:8 ... 51
8:10 ... 186

Micah

4:1–2 ... 346
4:1–8 ... 238
6:5 ... 50

Nahum

3:4 ... 279

Habakkuk

2:9–10 ... 158
2:20 ... 128

Zephaniah

1:14–16 ... 134
1:15 ... 156
2:14–15 ... 292
3:8 ... 198

Zechariah

1:7–11 ... 123
2:1–5 ... 183
2:10 ... 146
2:11 ... 340
3:1–2 ... 212
4:1–2 ... 144
4:2 ... 15n4, 25, 36
4:2–6 ... 186
4:4 ... 186
4:6 ... 25
4:10 ... 15n4, 25, 36, 186
4:14 ... 187
6:1–8 ... 123
6:5 ... 138
8:3 ... 146
8:17 ... 51
12–14 ... 271
12:1–9 ... 29
12:2 ... 293
12:3 ... 185
12:3–9 ... 318
12:9–14 ... 272
12:10 ... 11, 29
13:1 ... 29
14:1–14 ... 29
14:2–9 ... 318
14:4 ... 193
14:4–5 ... 251
14:5 ... 316
14:5–17 ... 321, 331
14:8 ... 357
14:11 ... 358

Malachi

3:2 ... 134
3:17 ... 138
4:1 ... 134
4:5 ... 134

New Testament

Matthew

1:3 ... 141
2 ... 354
2:6 ... 141
2:11 ... 299
2:16 ... 207
3:12 ... 250
3:16 ... 98
4:1 ... 279
5:3–12 ... 22
5:5 ... 66
5:11–12 ... 198
5:12 ... 309
5:20 ... 354
5:22–30 ... 319
6:1–18 ... 198
6:5 ... 216
6:9 ... 226, 302
6:10 ... 372
6:13 ... 211
7:6 ... 368
7:15 ... 230
7:21 ... 354
7:23 ... 55
8:11 ... 310
8:12 ... 156, 268
8:27 ... 224
8:29 ... 331
9:18 ... 327
9:37–38 ... 250
10:26 ... 20
10:28 ... 72, 227, 319
10:32 ... 88
11:15 ... 52, 228
12:43 ... 292
13:24–30 ... 248, 306
13:36–43 ... 250
13:47–50 ... 250
14:27 ... 39n3, 40
15:31 ... 281
16:18 ... 183
16:18–19 ... 75
16:27 ... 64, 214, 248, 334, 367
17:2 ... 39, 174
18:9 ... 319
18:23 ... 354
19:12 ... 239
19:28 ... 66, 95, 326
21:9 ... 117
22:13 ... 156, 268
23:15 ... 319
24–25 ... 366
24:10–12 ... 190
24:11 ... 270
24:15 ... 228, 235
24:21 ... 229
24:22 ... 175
24:24 ... 211, 216, 270
24:30 ... 29
24:31 ... 33, 150
24:41 ... 303
24:42–25:30 ... 23n2, 86
24:42 ... 85
24:43 ... 86, 271
25:1–13 ... 312
25:13 ... 85
25:30 ... 156, 268
25:31–46 ... 306
25:35 ... 271
26:64 ... 38
27:26 ... 164
28:3 ... 100

Mark

1:1–15 ... 19
1:10 ... 132, 313
1:18 ... 240
1:35 ... 279
1:45 ... 279
2:19–20 ... 310
3:6 ... 207
3:14 ... 27
3:15 ... 28, 40, 204, 210
3:27 ... 40, 167, 211, 323–25
3:28–29 ... 234
3:28–30 ... 301
3:29 ... 302, 318
4:9 ... 228
4:23 ... 52, 228
4:29 ... 249
5:1–20 ... 162
5:4 ... 323–25
5:20 ... 224, 281
6:7 ... 28, 40, 204, 210
8:34 ... 17, 213, 240, 247
9:3 ... 37
9:14–29 ... 162
9:42 ... 302
10:6 ... 79
11:23 ... 153
12:19–31 ... 49
13 ... 123, 144n3
13:6 ... 270
13:7 ... 363
13:7–8 ... 125
13:8 ... 78
13:14 ... 235, 284
13:19 ... 144, 274
13:22 ... 270
13:24–27 ... 131, 306
13:26 ... 29
13:35 ... 85
13:37 ... 85
14:62 ... 29, 192
15:38 ... 258

Luke

1:13 ... 39n3, 40
1:17 ... 186

1:30 .... 39n3, 40
3:17 250
4:16–30 22
8:8 .... 52, 228
10:19 161
10:20 88
12:9 245
14:11 295
14:15 310
16:9–13 334
16:13 10
17:30 .... 20, 318
18:7–8 129
21:27–36 318
22:30 310

John

1:1–18 .... 19, 315
1:3 90
1:14 359
1:18 359
1:51 .... 98, 313, 339
2:9 142
3:5–9 186
3:16 214
3:18–21 155
3:19–20 .... 191, 366
4:10–14 357
4:10–15 343
4:34–38 250
4:42 22
5:20 20
5:22 7
5:25–30 231
5:29 327
5:30 7
6:35 .... 40, 59, 343
7:16–18 .... 20, 231
7:30 207
7:37–39 .... 343, 357
7:44–48 207
8:12 40
8:26 20
8:28 20
8:31–47 72
8:38 .... 20, 23
8:44 .... 72, 211, 216
8:58–59 207
9 93
9:18 169
9:39 .... 7, 93
10:3 147
10:7 40
10:11 .... 40, 147
10:14 147
10:30 15
10:32 20
11:25 .... 40, 327
12:13 142
12:31 211
12:47 23
14:6 40
14:10 20
14:23–24 23
14:26 113
14:30 211
15:1 40
15:6 250–51
15:26 113
16:7 113
17:15 78
19:30 .... 273, 342
19:37 29
20:12 100

Acts

1:7 192
1:9–10 29
2:17 33
2:17–21 132
2:36 27
4:24 79
6:1–7 295
6:5 51
7:56 .... 98, 313
10:11 .... 98, 313
14:22 32
15:28–29 65
16:12–15 60
18:18–25 46
19 46
19:8–9 46
19:10 46
19:19 171
20:29 48
20:29–31 46
20:32 343
21:9 62
26:18 211

Romans

1:1 20
1:16 72
1:24 232
1:26 232
1:29–31 .... 171, 344
2:6 367
2:28–29 77
3:25 144
4:17 107
8:9 84
8:14–17 .... 139, 343
8:15 80
8:17 .... 28, 343
8:18–22 .... 243, 333, 338
8:22–23 341
8:23 240
8:33 212
9:23 146
12:19 129
13:11 363
14:9 327
14:12 .... 64, 248, 334, 367
15:6 242

15:9 242
15:15 50
16:20 205

1 Corinthians

1:7 20, 214
1:24 117
1:30 117
3:16–17 183
5:9–11 171
6:2–3 66, 95, 326
7:1 240
7:29–31 363
7:32 240
8:4 170
8:4–8 62
10:13 73
10:18–22 62
10:20 170
11:5 62
11:28 64n12
11:30 64
12:28 62
13:1–2 50
13:13 61
14:6 20
14:29 63
14:32 63
15 193
15:20 70, 240
15:20–23 26
15:26 328, 335
15:51–52 250, 306, 327
15:52 33, 150
15:54–55 328
15:55 164
16:9 76
16:22 372

2 Corinthians

1:22 138
2:12 76
2:14 87
3:12–18 211
3:17–18 146
4:4 203, 206, 210–11, 225, 280, 282, 325
5:10 248, 334, 367
5:11 242
6:14 293
6:16 183
6:17 293
10:4 229
10:7 64
11:2 240, 310
11:15 64, 367
11:25 71n1
12:1–2 313
12:1–4 98
12:4 176
12:9 146

Galatians

1:12 20
3:29 140, 343
4:4 167
4:7 343
4:26 80, 339
5:19–21 171
6:16 140

Ephesians

1:4 271
1:7 144
1:7–8 71
1:13–14 138
1:14 343
1:20 145
2:2 210
2:6 145
2:6–7 359
2:8–9 248, 334
2:14 340
2:14–18 49
2:20 347
3:3 20
3:5 20
3:6 343
3:9 106
4:11 62, 199, 302, 364
4:14 47n3
4:25–32 171, 344
4:30 138
5:25–27 310

Philippians

1:1 20
1:19 84
2:9 81, 315
2:10–11 118
2:11 193
2:12 242
3:3 140
3:10 71, 119, 189, 214, 229, 247, 266
3:20 10, 32, 80, 184, 359
4:3 88
4:5 23n2

Colossians

1:15 26
1:15–16 90
1:16 106
1:24 119, 130
2:3 117
2:15 87

1 Thessalonians

1:3 47
2:1–13 222
4 193
4:13–18 250, 306, 327
4:15 363
4:16 33, 150
4:17 29, 192

5:1–3 318
5:1–11 306
5:2 363
5:2–4 .... 86, 271

2 Thessalonians

2:1–10 306
2:1–12 221
2:3 .... 190, 231, 270
2:8 318
2:9 231
2:9–10 216

1 Timothy

1:15 311
3:1 311
3:7 325
4:9 311
5:3–16 295
6:9–10 82
6:16 .... 99, 352
6:17 82

2 Timothy

2:11 312
2:15 334
4:8 265

Titus

1:1 20
3:7 343
3:8 312

Hebrews

1:2 .... 79, 90
1:9 51
4:1–11 248
6:4–6 .... 234, 236, 301, 344, 371
8:10 340
9:4 .... 58, 200–01
10:25 .... 23n2, 363
10:31 72
11 .... 266, 341
11:3 107
11:10 341
11:16 341
12:1–3 59
12:14 359
12:19 33
12:22 .... 80, 107, 339
12:23 88
13:3 72
13:6 72
13:7 334
13:12 251
13:12–13 368
13:17 334
13:20 147

James

1:1 20
1:12–14 49
1:17 352
1:27 295
3:14–16 344
4:13–17 304
5:2–5 300
5:8 .... 23n2, 363
5:19–20 344

1 Peter

1:1 .... 10, 32, 184, 214
1:1–2 23
1:3 372
1:4 343
1:6 73
1:6–7 49
1:7 93
1:17 .... 10, 32, 64, 184, 214, 242, 248, 334, 367
1:22 68
2:9 .... 20, 138, 140, 360
2:11 .... 10, 32, 184, 214
2:12 .... 71, 242
2:15 71
2:23 .... 71, 229
3:14–15 72
3:16 71
4:3 344
4:4 .... 71, 84
4:7 .... 23n2, 363
4:12–14 72
4:13–14 184
4:14 71
4:15 344
5:6 295
5:8 .... 163, 211
5:13 .... 154, 241, 280

2 Peter

2:1 270
2:4 .... 160, 211, 292, 323–25
2:9 .... 78n5
2:20–22 371
3 338
3:7 .... 107, 122, 132, 213, 333
3:8–9 .... 21, 363
3:10 .... 86, 107, 122, 132, 213, 271, 333
3:10–13 306
3:13 338
5:8 325

1 John

1:8–10 65
2:9–10 49
2:18 .... 189, 221–22, 231, 236, 270, 283
3:9 65
4:1 63
4:1–3 .... 47n4
4:3 .... 221–22, 270
4:16–21 49
5:16 .... 234, 301, 344, 371
12:13 117

Jude

6...160, 211, 292, 323–25

Revelation

1–5 ... 111
1–3 ... 97
1 ... 41, 44, 47, 98
1:1 ... 6, 57, 79, 98, 278, 308, 359, 363–64, 369
1:1–2 ... 19–22, 33, 362, 369
1:1–11 ... 19–34
1:2 ... 32, 128, 213, 217, 312, 315, 326, 369
1:3 ... 3, 19, 22–23, 52, 247, 271, 311, 328, 363, 365, 367
1:4 ... 2, 5n4, 24–25, 31, 40n4, 41, 52, 84, 104, 113, 197, 266, 282
1:4–5 ... 3, 15, 19, 23
1:4–6 ... 23–29, 34
1:4–15 ... 60
1:5 ... 17, 23, 25, 90, 110, 129, 144, 180, 185, 213, 230, 246, 310, 313, 315, 362, 372
1:5–6 ... 23, 25–29, 111, 115, 118
1:6 ... 23, 29–30, 115, 118–19, 143, 145, 187, 196, 199, 212, 328, 341, 350, 359
1:7 ... 11, 30, 119, 143, 192, 247, 249, 258n2, 352, 358, 372
1:7–8 ... 19, 29–31, 34
1:8 ... 2–3, 24, 30–31, 40, 70, 98, 104, 106, 197, 256, 266, 282, 309, 342, 367, 369
1:9 ... 17, 22, 26, 61, 128, 186, 213, 217, 246, 312, 315, 326
1:9–11 ... 19, 31–34
1:10 ... 20n1, 36, 98, 247, 279
1:11 ... 22, 24n3, 39, 41, 180, 246, 311, 342
1:12 ... 43
1:12–13 ... 98
1:12–16 ... 35–36, 39
1:12–20 ... 35–43
1:13–3:22 ... 35
1:13 ... 37, 47, 249, 259
1:13–16 ... 35, 174
1:14 ... 37, 64, 314, 332
1:14–16 ... 313
1:15 ... 37–38, 174, 309
1:16 ... 36, 38–39, 43, 47, 54n7, 174, 187, 206, 267, 316–17
1:17 ... 3, 31, 40, 70, 342, 367, 369
1:17–18 ... 35, 39
1:17–20 ... 39–43
1:18 ... 127, 282, 323–25, 327, 334
1:19 ... 21–22, 33, 39, 98, 180, 246, 342, 363
1:20 ... 38–39, 41, 84, 177, 206, 280
2–3 ... 3, 8, 25, 33, 41, 198, 311
2 ... 111
2:1 ... 36, 47, 206
2:1–7 ... 44–53
2:2 ... 10, 47, 51, 61, 152, 230, 232, 241, 246, 344, 354, 370
2:2–3 ... 47–49
2:3 ... 47, 61, 230, 232, 246
2:4 ... 49–50
2:4–5 ... 61
2:5 ... 49, 57, 79, 86
2:5–6 ... 49–52
2:6 ... 10, 47, 141, 152, 199, 224
2:7 ... 23, 26, 52–53, 358
2:8 ... 40, 70, 327, 342, 367
2:8–11 ... 69–74
2:9 ... 10, 50, 70–71, 77, 234
2:10 ... 10, 72–74, 79, 90, 163, 229–30, 246, 310
2:10–11 ... 328
2:11 ... 23, 26, 74, 371
2:12 ... 54, 58, 316
2:12–17 ... 53–59
2:12–29 ... 44–46
2:13 ... 54–55, 90, 230, 246
2:14 ... 10, 51, 56, 152, 344
2:14–15 ... 51, 55–57, 216, 224, 232
2:15 ... 47, 56, 141, 199
2:16 ... 21, 57–58, 63n11, 79, 195, 314, 316, 363
2:17 ... 23, 58–59, 81, 238, 314–15
2:18 ... 37–38, 60, 64, 314
2:18–29 ... 60–68

2:19......60–61, 230, 246
2:20......10, 51, 152, 278, 308, 344
2:20–23.................. 51, 61–64, 216
2:20–25.................224
2:21............ 57, 63, 275
2:22 .... 216, 269
2:22–23............ 63, 65
2:23 ....40, 64, 248, 309, 367, 369
2:24–25...................65
2:25 .... 66, 79
2:26 ....27, 66, 76, 185, 314, 363, 368
2:26–27..... 96, 287, 316, 318, 322, 326
2:26–29............ 65–66
2:27 .... 26, 66–67, 207, 240
2:28 ....67, 369
2:28–29.....................11
2:29 23
3............................ 111
3:1................. 15n4, 25, 83–85, 206
3:1–6.................82–89
3:2 .... 48, 271
3:2–3................. 85–87
3:3 ....23, 76, 79, 86
3:4 .... 85, 87, 368
3:4–5................ 93, 129
3:4–6 87–89
3:5 ....87, 227, 334, 355
3:6 ....23, 84, 89
3:7 ....75–76, 129, 313, 323–25, 328, 362
3:7–13 74–81
3:8 ....76–77, 234
3:8–9 76
3:9 .... 50, 75, 77, 241, 344, 354, 370
3:9–11..................77–79
3:10 ....77, 79, 113, 121, 137, 139, 161, 214, 230, 246, 264
3:11 ....21, 25, 73, 79, 163, 195, 363
3:12......... 315, 326, 341, 351, 359,
3:12–13......... 23, 79–81
3:14........ 17, 26, 90–91, 106, 119, 129, 185, 213, 242, 246, 313, 362, 368, 372
3:14–22 89–96
3:15–16..................... 91
3:17–18.............. 92–93
3:18........... 37, 271, 289
3:19–20............. 93–95
3:20........... 94–95, 354
3:21......27, 322, 326, 357
3:21–22 .... 23, 95–96
3:22 96
4–22 41
4–5 .... 103, 107, 118
4...................13, 96–97, 99–100, 103, 105, 108, 116–17, 134, 143
4:1 ....21, 98, 180, 192, 200–01, 278, 313, 363
4:1–11:19..................195
4:1–11...............97–107
4:2....... 25, 33, 105, 108, 124, 247, 279, 332
4:2–3 .... 98–99, 105
4:3...... 99, 101, 124, 174, 298, 346, 349
4:3–6 349
4:4........ 73, 93, 100–01, 105, 129, 163, 196n6, 245, 249, 326, 332
4:5 .... 15n4, 25, 113, 200–01, 272
4:5–6 .... 101–02, 123
4:6................. 254, 349
4:6–7 259
4:6–8 ....102–03, 122
4:6–9 102
4:7 .... 158, 163, 223n6, 242
4:8................ 2, 24, 97, 104–06, 115, 119, 158, 197, 236, 245, 249, 257, 265–66, 282, 309, 328
4:8–10...................308
4:8–11 .... 103–07, 114, 118
4:9.......40, 99, 106, 118, 124, 143, 196–97, 354
4:9–11 .... 105–07, 357
4:10 .....40, 99, 105, 124, 143, 196, 308
4:10–11........97, 101, 196
4:11 ....18, 87, 105–06, 108, 110, 117, 143, 242, 266, 353–54
5–6 .... 138, 174
5.......... 13, 96–97, 100, 104, 108, 119, 134, 173–74, 342
5:1............. 99, 108–10, 113, 174
5:1–14...............108–19
5:2 .... 33, 115, 174, 302
5:2–5.................110–12
5:3 .... 110, 118
5:4 110
5:5 .... 110–12, 117, 134, 255, 369
5:5–6........... 27, 111, 134
5:5–7.......................147

5:6 .... 15, 25, 27, 102, 108, 110, 113, 116–17, 128, 134, 144, 205, 208, 213, 221n2, 228, 230, 287, 313, 333
5:6–7 .... 113–14, 259
5:6–10 111–16
5:7 .... 99, 113, 117
5:7–8 178–81
5:8 ..... 100–01, 143, 150, 255, 259, 308
5:8–9 .... 102, 239
5:8–10 114–16
5:8–12 118
5:9 .... 16, 18, 27, 30, 87, 114–15, 134, 144, 180, 213, 227, 239–40, 258n2, 288, 310, 315, 348
5:9–10 .... 12n3, 358
5:9–12 118
5:9–13 357
5:10 .... 27–28, 115, 145, 187, 199, 212, 326, 328, 341, 350, 359
5:11 .... 100, 143, 168, 308
5:11–12 116–17
5:12 .... 27, 87, 108, 110, 116–18, 143, 266, 353
5:12–13 .... 143, 354
5:13 .... 28, 97, 99, 117, 119, 196, 242
5:13–14 117–19
5:14 .... 143, 247, 308
6–20 107
6–16 ...... 97–98, 111, 136, 202, 276
6:1–11:19 202
6 .... 137, 142, 195n5, 264
6:1 .... 164n3, 167n5
6:1–2 ...... 123–24, 269n1
6:1–8 .... 122–27, 161, 259
6:1–17 .... 16n5, 120–35, 262
6:2 ..... 122–24, 223, 255, 267, 311, 313
6:3 282
6:3–4 .... 124–25, 288
6:4 ..... 122–24, 139, 205, 223, 267, 282, 311
6:5–6 125–26
6:7–8 127
6:8 .... 40, 122–24, 127, 168–69, 193, 223, 267, 296, 311, 334
6:9 .... 17, 22, 26, 166–68, 186, 189–90, 213, 217, 250, 266–67, 305, 315, 326, 344
6:9–11 .... 114, 121, 127–30, 149–50, 161–62, 187, 196, 247, 250, 259, 266, 302, 307, 322
6:10 .... 30, 176, 214, 265, 315–16, 328
6:10–11 289
6:11 .... 93, 129–30, 137n1, 140, 142, 167, 196, 204, 230, 248, 319, 326, 332, 368
6:12 .... 39, 186n2, 193
6:12–14 .... 101, 131–32, 152, 200–01, 239, 272–73
6:12–17 130–35
6:13 154
6:14 .... 274, 333
6:15 .... 133, 180, 233
6:15–17 ..... 12n3, 131–35, 260, 266
6:16 ..... 99, 113, 133, 142, 287, 313–14, 357
6:16–17 .... 15, 254
6:17 .... 134, 271, 287
7 .... 136–47, 152, 220, 238
7:1 .... 167, 265
7:1–3 137–39
7:1–8 ..... 121, 137–41, 161
7:1–17 .... 13, 173
7:2 .... 33, 78, 122, 223
7:2–3 .... 138, 184
7:3 .... 78, 81, 167, 203, 234, 238, 280, 308, 359
7:3–4 .... 173, 199, 238, 264, 309
7:4 .... 280, 349
7:4–8 140–42
7:9 .... 16, 30, 115, 140, 145, 147, 180, 227, 288, 307, 332–33, 348, 358, 368
7:9–12 .... 142–43, 195
7:9–14 145
7:9–17 .... 129, 137, 140–47, 237, 254, 357
7:10 ..... 99, 142–43, 212, 307, 357
7:11 .... 102, 143, 259
7:11–17 308
7:12 .... 28, 116–19, 143, 196–97, 247, 307, 354
7:13 144
7:13–14 .... 93, 100–01, 368
7:13–17 .... 144–47, 196
7:14 .... 27, 78, 95, 120, 145, 159, 185, 188,

192, 208, 213, 229, 236, 247, 287, 310, 315, 367
7:15......28, 99, 145, 245, 249, 328, 339, 359, 364
7:15–17.............. 26, 145
7:16................. 146, 267
7:17...........146, 341, 343
7:27 360
8:1–11:19................. 182
8:1 .... 148–49, 195, 260, 272, 286, 324
8:1–6...................... 149
8:1–12 148–56
8:2..... 122, 150, 152, 223
8:2–5 ....149, 152, 161, 250, 253, 274, 307
8:2–6 149–52
8:3..................122, 128, 150–51, 250
8:3–4 .... 101, 114, 151, 166–68
8:3–5.............. 121, 129, 166–68, 259
8:4.... 150, 189, 245, 308
8:5............101, 128, 131, 151–52, 166–68, 193, 200–01, 250, 273
8:6–12........121, 157, 242
8:7........152–53, 161, 275
8:7–9 138
8:7–11..................... 139
8:7–12 152–56
8:8................. 188, 225
8:8–9 .... 153–54, 264
8:10 ....101, 225
8:10–11..............154–55
8:11 ....167, 297
8:12....... 39, 131, 155–56, 160, 267–68
8:13–9:21...........157–72
8:13......137, 157–58, 166, 194, 214, 241
8:18–22 131
9.............. 158, 169, 214, 232, 269, 288
9:1 .... 57, 122, 159–60, 165, 323–25
9:1–6...................... 166
9:1–11 .... 158–65, 189, 214
9:1–19 122
9:2.............39, 160, 189
9:2–6 160–62
9:3...........122, 160, 185, 189, 368
9:4....... 78, 121, 137, 153, 161, 173, 264
9:5......122, 161, 164, 191
9:5–6 167
9:7.........................249
9:7–10.............162–64, 166, 168
9:8......................... 163
9:9......................... 164
9:10 ....164, 185, 206, 368
9:11............ 159, 165–66
9:12................ 166, 194, 214, 297
9:12–21........165–72, 195
9:13–14................... 267
9:13–16.............166–68
9:13–19........... 214, 269
9:14 ....138, 166–68
9:14–15................... 138
9:15.................167, 242
9:16 167
9:17–18........... 169, 297
9:17–19.......166, 168–69
9:18 .... 92, 193, 254
9:19 ....169, 185, 206, 368
9:20..........113, 122, 168, 171, 242, 254, 269, 344
9:20–21......... 7, 16, 122, 149, 161, 166, 169–72, 180, 188, 275, 344
9:21.................. 171, 344
10–13 .... 177, 217
10 ....173–81, 342
10:1–11:14 13
10:1–11:13 .... 136, 173, 179, 182, 195
10:1–11:12 152
10:1.... 174, 249, 267, 317
10:1–2 .... 110, 302
10:1–4 ....174–76, 178–81
10:1–11 .... 173, 175
10:2 178–81
10:3 175
10:4 ....175, 178–81, 246, 293, 365
10:5.................... 178–81
10:5–7 176–78
10:6 ....40, 106, 130, 174, 177, 196, 242
10:7 .... 177, 199, 254, 257, 280, 289
10:8 .... 177–81, 246, 293, 303
10:8–10 173
10:8–11...... 174, 179, 184
10:9 179
10:9–10...........179, 196
10:10.............. 179, 303
10:11 ....3n1, 26, 115, 180, 227, 288
10:26–31.................371
11–13 208
11.............. 182–01, 221
11:1..... 183–84, 208, 226

11:1–2.........173, 182–85, 199, 200–01, 303, 309, 348
11:1–13.....................175
11:2.....177, 182, 184–86, 208, 216, 225, 286, 339
11:3..... 90, 177, 185, 187, 208, 216, 225, 286
11:3–6........180, 185–88, 192n4, 229
11:3–10................... 128
11:3–12 199
11:3–13.............173, 182
11:4................. 106, 186
11:5 ....232, 302
11:5–6......... 187–88, 231
11:7 ...... 52, 58, 160, 186, 189, 192, 206n3, 220, 226, 255, 283
11:7–10...........173, 182, 188–91, 319
11:7–13 188–94
11:8......... 106, 190, 193, 238, 251, 260, 274, 297, 330, 339, 351
11:9................. 115, 190
11:10 ....191, 199
11:11 .... 192, 232, 247
11:11–12 ....173, 191–93, 196
11:11–13...................250
11:12................246, 249
11:13..... 12n3, 16–17, 30, 122, 131, 191–94, 258, 358
11:14..... 21, 166, 194–95, 214, 297
11:14–19...... 182, 194–01
11:15.... 40, 116, 178, 182, 195–96, 313, 357
11:15–19...........177, 272
11:16........254, 308, 326
11:16–18............196–99
11:17........... 2, 116, 266, 282, 309
11:18......... 12n3, 30, 64, 134, 165, 194, 198, 254, 302, 308–09, 359, 366–67
11:19........101, 128, 131, 1 52, 193, 200–01, 249, 258, 273, 275, 313, 339
12–22.....................180
12–14.........97, 202, 237
12–13..... 8, 237, 253, 337
12 .... 144, 217, 252
12:1–16:21........ 195, 202
12:1–14:21................. 13
12:1–14:20 136
12:1–14:11................ 245
12:1 .... 163, 203, 253, 267, 317
12:1–2........ 203–04, 217
12:1–6 203–08
12:1–17 ....202–18, 237
12:2........................204
12:3...........15, 125, 203, 205–06, 221, 231, 314
12:3–9 270
12:4..........206–09, 211, 214–15, 219
12:5............. 26, 67, 99, 215, 217
12:5–6 207–08
12:5–7 159
12:6................ 177, 185, 207–09, 215–16, 225, 279, 286
12:7..........174, 189, 225
12:7–9 ......202, 206–07, 209–12, 214–16, 219, 220, 250
12:7–12.............208–14
12:8..................210, 217
12:9.......54, 62, 113, 169, 203, 211–12, 231, 307, 319, 323–25, 329, 331n2, 355
12:10 .... 30, 142, 196, 211–12, 214, 307, 323–25
12:10–12 ......209, 211–14
12:11.......... 8, 26–27, 52, 141, 144, 184, 186, 210–12, 214, 225–26, 230, 240, 247, 255, 281, 287, 315, 355
12:11–12..................202
12:12 ....41, 130, 163, 206, 210–11, 213, 215, 226n7, 268, 283, 297, 302, 331, 334
12:13 215
12:13–17......... 203, 209, 215–18, 220
12:13–18 270
12:14 ....158, 169, 177, 185, 208, 215, 225, 279, 286
12:14–16 215–17
12:15..........169, 216, 237
12:15–16...................217
12:16 ....215–16, 242
12:17 ....17, 23–24, 26, 128, 189, 204, 213, 215, 217–20, 246, 287, 312, 326, 363
12:17–18 ....220, 238
12:18–13:18 219–36
12:18–13:10 ....237, 279n1

12:18–13:4......... 220–25
12:18–13:2......... 220–23
13..............29, 154, 159, 189, 221, 224, 231, 238, 244, 252
13:1 ....160, 189, 203, 205–06, 214, 220, 230–31, 267, 279, 283, 314, 334
13:1–2..................... 255
13:1–10 .... 219, 270
13:2....202, 219, 222–23, 225, 268, 291
13:3.... 113, 203, 223–24, 270n2, 282–84
13:3–4 .... 224–25, 231
13:3–6 173
13:4.......... 30, 202, 224, 280, 301
13:4–15 ....282, 344
13:5...........122, 177, 185, 208, 216, 223, 227, 286, 291
13:5–6 .... 225–26, 231
13:5–8 ....161, 189, 225–28, 232
13:6........................267
13:7.......... 8, 52, 58, 115, 122, 141, 144, 184, 189, 210, 226–27, 247, 255, 281, 287, 343
13:7–8 .... 30, 227–28
13:8......27, 88, 110, 202, 271, 280, 283, 334, 355
13:9....................... 365
13:9–10 ......228–30, 237
13:10 .... 8, 10, 229, 246, 310
13:11.....189, 214, 230–31
13:11–12 ....23n2
13:11–18....190, 219, 221, 230–37, 270
13:12 ....202, 223, 231, 282
13:12–15.................. 318
13:12–16 231
13:13.......................203
13:13–14...... 224, 231–32
13:14 .... 62, 122, 223, 232, 255, 282, 324, 327, 354
13:14–15.....202, 232–33, 280, 292
13:15......... 122, 232, 247
13:16 .... 139, 161, 199, 203, 238, 301
13:16–17............ 233–34
13:16–18 238
13:17–18...... 234–36, 255
13:18 ....246, 284
14 .... 237–53, 255
14:1 ..... 81, 238, 349, 359
14:1–5................ 237–41
14:2.....114, 123, 255, 293
14:2–3 .... 238–39, 309
14:3......... 100, 239–40, 259, 293, 308
14:4..................310, 357
14:4–5 239–40
14:5.......... 344, 355, 370
14:6 ....115, 158, 241
14:6–7 ....7, 12n3, 17, 30, 76, 113, 122, 194, 241–43, 257, 268, 344, 358
14:6–13....... 237, 241–49
14:7.........106, 224, 243, 257–58, 341
14:8 ...... 30, 57, 243–44, 248, 274, 279, 292, 293n1, 296, 302, 307, 344
14:8–11 .... 12n3
14:9 .... 244, 255
14:9–11 244–45
14:10 ....30, 134, 244, 250, 254, 260, 279, 293, 302, 315–16
14:10–11.......... 162, 244, 248, 274, 336
14:11......... 151, 247, 263, 297, 307
14:12 ....23, 128, 217, 246, 310, 363
14:12–13.............245–48
14:13 ....22, 33, 106, 246, 271, 309, 311–12, 328, 342, 363, 367
14:14 .... 73, 163, 249, 313, 332
14:14–16 .... 192, 248–50, 333
14:14–20............248–52
14:15.......... 242, 249–50
14:15–16 250
14:15–17..................339
14:17 128
14:17–20................248, 250–52, 333
14:18 . 128, 223, 250, 265
14:19 .... 250, 260
14:19–20 .... 250, 316
14:20.........237, 251, 348
15–16...................... 254
15...................... 253–61
15:1 .... 253–54, 258, 261, 264
15:1–8..................... 253
15:2 ....114, 244
15:2–4 .... 239, 253–58
15:3 .... 255–56, 258, 265, 267

15:4........16–17, 30, 191, 194, 224, 242, 256, 258, 265, 358
15:5.................128, 313
15:5–6..............258–59
15:5–8...........249, 253, 258–61, 263
15:6..................37, 258
15:7......40, 253–54, 259
15:7–8..............259–61
15:8........245, 260, 308
16............144, 262–76
16:1...............249, 254, 260, 263
16:1–2...................273
16:1–4...................266
16:1–9.............263–68
16:2......121, 133, 262–64
16:2–4...................139
16:2–9............121, 242
16:3........................264
16:3–4............188, 273
16:4..................264–65
16:5.............2, 24, 256, 265, 282
16:5–6.............161, 307
16:5–7............121, 129, 265–67, 274, 302
16:6.....8, 137, 199, 205, 247, 266–67, 302, 315–16, 326
16:7........106, 128, 256, 265, 267, 307, 313
16:8..........39, 223, 273
16:8–9.............267–68
16:8–11..................344
16:9.........7, 16–17, 113, 122, 149, 176, 194, 242, 275
16:10.............156, 268
16:10–11..........268–69
16:10–21..........268–76
16:11.......7, 16, 113, 122, 149, 176, 242, 268, 275
16:12.............138, 167, 269, 286–87
16:12–13................353
16:12–16..........269–72
16:13........165, 187–90, 202, 219, 222, 230, 344, 354, 370
16:13–14..........269–72
16:13–16................318
16:14...........26, 58, 113, 165, 180, 189, 207, 224, 256, 270, 286–87, 318, 330
16:14–16................330
16:15........3, 22–23, 86, 247, 269, 271, 328, 363, 367–68
16:16.............112, 207, 269–70, 272, 286–87, 303
16:17......249, 263, 268, 273, 342
16:17–21...........272–76
16:18–19................273
16:18–21................101, 131, 200–01
16:19.......134, 137, 190, 254, 260, 274, 289, 294, 297, 316, 339
16:20..............132, 333
16:20–21...............274
16:21.........................16
17–18..........13, 117, 276
17.............277–91, 307, 310, 355
17:1–20:15..............322
17:1–19:5........277, 306, 309, 345
17:1...............282, 284, 288–89, 363
17:1–2..............278–79
17:1–3....................345
17:1–6....................282
17:2......26, 57, 165, 278, 280, 296, 307, 344, 353
17:3.....33, 247, 282, 345
17:3–6..............279–81
17:4......57, 279–81, 296, 298, 300, 311, 344, 351
17:4–5............344, 354
17:5..........177, 282, 292
17:6.......26, 30, 90, 186, 205, 247, 275, 281, 315–16
17:6–7....................282
17:6–14.............281–87
17:7........................177
17:8..........88, 160, 189, 227–28, 271, 282–84, 291, 334, 355
17:9–11............284–86
17:9–14..............4, 280
17:10......................284
17:10–11..........165, 180
17:11......................282
17:12......................270
17:12–13.................223
17:12–14.................133, 221, 286–87
17:13........196, 271, 286
17:14.......58, 66–67, 88, 96, 106, 113, 212, 230, 246, 255–56, 287, 311–14, 316–17
17:15.........115, 278, 284
17:15–18...........287–90

17:16 ....282, 288, 296, 303
17:16–17...................159
17:17.................. 22, 315
17:18 .... 26, 190, 271, 282, 288–89, 297, 339, 353
18 .... 199, 222, 243, 277, 290–05
18:1 223
18:1–3................ 291–93
18:1–8 291
18:2......... 279, 300, 304
18:2–3 274
18:3........26, 30, 57, 278, 292, 296, 304, 307, 344, 353
18:4 .... 293, 305, 308
18:4–8........191, 293–96
18:5.......................294
18:6 ....30, 64, 248, 274, 302, 309, 367
18:6–8............. 294–96
18:7............... 296, 304
18:7–8...................295
18:8 295–96
18:9 ....26, 57, 278, 307–08, 344, 353
18:9–10 296–97
18:9–19 .... 291, 296–01, 324
18:10........191, 242, 274, 286, 296, 300
18:10–21.........190, 289
18:11–13.................293
18:11–17.....297–00, 304
18:12 .... 279, 311
18:12–13 298
18:14.....................303
18:15 191
18:16........274, 279, 300
18:17 ....242, 286
18:17–19 300–01
18:18........274, 297, 308
18:19 .... 242, 274, 286, 300–01
18:20 ....199, 301–03, 305–06, 326
18:20–24..........301–05
18:20–34 291
18:21 ....110, 225, 274
18:21–24.......... 302–05
18:22–23 .... 300, 303
18:23........133, 324, 344
18:23–24 304
18:24....... 199, 205, 247, 266, 315–16, 326
19 ....306–20, 330
19–22........197, 273, 276
19–20....................... 13
19:1.......... 142, 212, 309
19:1–2 307
19:1–3..............306–08
19:1–5........301, 306–09
19:1–10...........309, 338
19:2......... 199, 256, 265, 267, 296, 307, 315–16, 359
19:3......33, 151, 245, 307
19:3–4.....................251
19:4 ....99, 119, 143, 224, 259, 308
19:5......... 194, 199, 242, 260, 308–09, 359
19:6–20:15............. 319
19:6 .... 116, 123
19:6–10 ....59, 306, 309–13
19:6–21 309
19:7............... 194, 242, 309–11, 345
19:7–8..... 240, 304, 339
19:8 ....259, 316
19:9 ...... 22, 33, 246–47, 278, 310, 328, 362–63, 367
19:9–10 ....22, 311
19:10.......26, 39n3, 199, 217, 224, 247, 312, 326, 360, 364, 370
19:11–21:8.............. 338
19:11.........123, 246, 313, 316–17, 332, 362
19:11–12...................195
19:11–13...................313
19:11–16..........238, 306, 315, 313–17
19:11–21..........303, 322, 330, 332
19:12 ......37, 59, 81, 203, 206, 317
19:13 317
19:14 ...... 66–67, 88, 93, 95–96, 240, 256, 259, 287, 311–12
19:14–16 313–14
19:15 .... 39, 67, 134, 187, 207, 251, 287, 315–16, 318
19:16 .... 256, 287, 314, 317
19:17 ..... 39, 157–58, 225
19:17–18 ....127, 189, 251, 292, 306, 317, 319
19:18 ....26, 133, 199, 233
19:19 .... 26, 189, 271, 318, 342
19:19–20 .... 207, 287, 303
19:19–21 .... 287, 297, 306, 318–20, 327, 330

19:20 .... 62, 154, 160, 165, 169, 245, 318, 336, 344, 354, 370
19:20–21 .... 319, 331
19:21 ....39, 157, 292, 319, 325, 353
19:22.......................313
20–21..................... 193
20..................... 321–36
20:1 159
20:1–3..............322–25
20:1–6...................238
20:1–10 322–32
20:2..........54, 169, 211, 323–25
20:3..........62, 211, 307, 324, 329, 355
20:4........22, 26–27, 66, 96, 116, 128, 186, 196, 212–13, 217, 247, 263, 315, 326–28, 333–34, 360
20:4–6 ...... 322, 326–28
20:5...........327, 333–35
20:6........22, 26–28, 74, 116, 187, 196, 247, 327–28, 335, 350, 357, 359, 363, 367, 371
20:7.......................270
20:7–8 325
20:7–10................ 322, 325, 328–32,
20:8.....62, 171, 189, 211, 271, 329–30, 371
20:9.............. 232, 326, 330, 339
20:10 .... 62, 154, 160, 162, 165, 169, 211, 214, 322, 331, 336
20:11 .... 99, 122, 274, 332–33
20:11–14 187
20:11–15 ....30, 198, 268, 274, 322, 325, 332–36
20:12...............88, 199, 227, 248, 309, 333–35, 355, 367n2
20:12–13.......... 333, 367
20:13..........40, 64, 127, 333–34
20:13–15 ....303, 307, 331, 334–36, 343
20:14.......... 40, 74, 127, 160, 165, 169, 245, 335
20:14–15..........154, 319
20:15....... 160, 227, 245, 333–35, 355
21–22 368
21 .... 226, 337–55
21:1–22:5 .... 53, 322, 343, 360
21:1 ..... 14, 107, 122, 213, 276, 333–34, 338
21:1–2..............338–39, 345, 352
21:1–6 238
21:1–8 337–44
21:2........ 190, 240, 304, 310, 339, 345–46
21:2–4 80
21:3.........200–01, 226, 340–41, 343, 347, 352
21:3–4 340–41
21:4....... 74, 341–42, 358
21:5....22, 30, 33, 59, 99, 246, 311, 313, 362
21:5–6 341–43
21:6......31, 98, 273, 342, 367, 370
21:7 347
21:7–8 343–44
21:8.............57, 74, 241, 328, 343–44, 354–55, 365, 368
21:9–22:5............... 338
21:9........278, 304, 310, 348, 351n1, 356, 362
21:9–10 ....344–46, 363, 370
21:9–27 .....200–01, 337, 344–55, 360
21:10 .... 33, 190, 247, 278–79, 345
21:11.......... 99, 344, 346
21:11–21............ 346–51
21:12 346
21:12–14 .... 140, 344
21:13 .... 347, 351
21:14 ....302, 347, 349
21:15.......................348
21:15–17..................344
21:16 348
21:17 348–49
21:17–18 346
21:18 .... 99, 346, 348, 351
21:18–21 .... 99, 344, 349
21:19–20 ....298, 346, 349
21:21 ....348–49, 351, 357
21:22–27......344, 351–55
21:23 ....118, 267, 351, 353, 360
21:24......... 16, 180, 194, 340, 351–53, 358
21:25 .... 351, 360
21:26..........16, 30, 194, 340, 351, 353, 358
21:27 .... 88, 227, 241, 344, 349, 351, 354–55
22:1.......... 208, 351, 363
22:1–2 356–57

22:1–5 .... 338, 356–61, 368
22:2 .... 53, 351, 357
22:2–3.........26, 357–58
22:2–19 370
22:3 .... 308, 328, 364
22:3–4...................359
22:4 .... 234, 359
22:5 ......27, 96, 106, 116, 212, 267, 328, 360–61
22:6 ....3, 21, 106, 199, 246, 278, 308, 311, 313, 359, 362–63, 365
22:6–7....... 362–64, 369
22:6–9 22
22:6–21 362–73
22:7 .... 3, 22–23, 195, 214, 247, 362–64, 366–67, 370–72
22:8 ....6, 31, 39n3, 278, 362
22:8–9 364
22:8–11...... 362, 364–66
22:9 ....3, 23, 199, 224, 302, 360, 364–65, 369
22:9–10.................369
22:10..... 3, 23, 278, 362, 364–66, 372
22:11 364–66
22:12......... 64, 195, 198, 214, 248, 309, 362–63, 366–67, 370, 372
22:12–19.... 362, 366–72
22:13 .... 31, 70, 98, 342, 367
22:14..........22, 26, 247, 354, 363, 371
22:14–15.....251, 366–68
22:15....57, 171, 198, 241, 344, 365, 368, 370
22:16.......... 40, 67, 362, 369–70, 372
22:17................ 26, 247, 313, 370
22:18................. 3, 369
22:18–19............3, 362, 369–72
22:19...................3, 328
22:20 .106, 119, 195, 214, 247, 362–63, 366, 369, 372–73
22:20–21 ....143n2
22:21.......... 3, 106, 119, 372–73

Deuterocanonical Works

Tobit
13:7–8 ....351n2

Wisdom
2:24 210

Sirach
47:22 .... 112n1

2 Maccabees
2:4–7 59

Old Testament Pseudepigrapha

Apocalypse of Elijah
3:5–13................ 222n3

Apocalypse of Moses
16 169

Apocalypse of Zephaniah
6:11–15 .... 312n1

Ascension of Isaiah
4:1–13.................... 222
7:21–22 .... 312n1

2 Baruch
4:3–7..................... 356
6:7–10.....................59
6:7–8 ....351n2
11:1........................280
22 .... 98n1
29:8 310
40:1–2.....................251
44:12..................... 338
51:11 104

3 Baruch
9:6–8 169
9:7 210

1 Enoch
1–36 .... 98n1
1:3..........................251
1:6–7..................... 275
6:1–7:6 .... 210n5
10:4–6...................160
14:10–11.................. 98
14:19–23................ 245

14:22–23............116–17
17:6........................156
18:8 346
18:9–16 160
20.......................25n4
20:2–8 150
20:5 209
21:6........................324
24:1–25:3...........284n2
24:1–3 346
39:12...................... 104
40:7 ....212n7
45:4–5.................... 338
46:1 .... 36n1
47:1–4 ....130n31
56:55–57:3 167
62:14...................... 310
63:6 156
72:1........................ 338
83:3–4.................... 338
86:3 ....159n1
88:1–3 ....159n1
90:24–27............... 319
90:9–12.................. 113

2 Enoch

7:1...........................156
10:2 319
29:4–5.........159n1, 210

4 Ezra

2:38 310
4:35–37 .... 130n31
6:23 150
7:28 324
12:32 .... 112n1
15:35–36 251
15:42 275

Jubilees

1:29........................ 338
4:26 338
5:1.................... 210n5
11:4 170
17:15–18:13..........212n7
23:27–28 324

Life of Adam and Eve

13:1–2.................... 210

Odes of Solomon

22:5 ....205n2

Psalms of Solomon

2:25–26..................222
17:23–25............ 66n13

Sibylline Oracles

2:196–09............... 319
3:63–74 .... 222n3
5:158–59.................154

Testament of Dan

5:10–13.................. 210

Testament of Isaac

6:22 310
8:6......................... 310

Testament of Levi

5:5–6......................209
5:6 ....212n7
18:10–11 356

Dead Sea Scrolls

4QpIsa............. 351n2

4QTestimonia

22–24................ 222n3

Mishnah

Sukkoth

5:5 150

Apostolic Fathers

Didache

10:6 372

Ignatius

To the Ephesians

1:1........................ 51n6
9:1 .... 51n6

Other Ancient Writings

Eusebius
Ecclesiastical History
3.5 .... 208n4

Josephus
Jewish Wars
5.13.6 .... 126n2

Philo
On Rewards and Punishment
12:70.................... 74n3

Pliny the Younger
Epistles
10.96................. 233n10